Navigating Psychology

PSYC 4: California State University, Sacramento

Tara L. Kuther | Robert D. Morgan

CENGAGE
Learning

Australia • Brazil • Japan • Korea • Mexico • Singapore • Spain • United Kingdom • United States

CENGAGE
Learning™

Navigating Psychology
**PSYC 4: California State University,
Sacramento**

The Psychology Major's Handbook, Third Edition
Tara L. Kuther

© 2012, 2006 Wadsworth, Cengage Learning. All rights reserved.

Careers in Psychology: Opportunities in a Changing World, Third Edition
Tara L. Kuther and Robert D. Morgan

© 2010 Wadsworth, Cengage Learning. All rights reserved.

Executive Editors:
 Maureen Staudt
 Michael Stranz

Senior Project Development Manager:
 Linda deStefano

Marketing Specialist:
 Courtney Sheldon

Senior Production/Manufacturing Manager:
 Donna M. Brown

PreMedia Manager:
 Joel Brennecke

Sr. Rights Acquisition Account Manager:
 Todd Osborne

Cover Image:
 Getty Images*

*Unless otherwise noted, all cover images used by Custom
Solutions, a part of Cengage Learning, have been supplied
courtesy of Getty Images with the exception of the Earthview
cover image, which has been supplied by the National
Aeronautics and Space Administration (NASA).

For product information and technology assistance, contact us at
Cengage Learning Customer & Sales Support, 1-800-354-9706
For permission to use material from this text or product,
submit all requests online at **cengage.com/permissions**
Further permissions questions can be emailed to
permissionrequest@cengage.com

This book contains select works from existing Cengage Learning resources and
was produced by Cengage Learning Custom Solutions for collegiate use. As such,
those adopting and/or contributing to this work are responsible for editorial
content accuracy, continuity and completeness.

Compilation © 2011 Cengage Learning
ISBN-13: 978-1-111-97370-4

ISBN-10: 1-111-97370-9

Cengage Learning
5191 Natorp Boulevard
Mason, Ohio 45040
USA
Cengage Learning is a leading provider of customized learning solutions with
office locations around the globe, including Singapore, the United Kingdom,
Australia, Mexico, Brazil, and Japan. Locate your local office at:
international.cengage.com/region.

Cengage Learning products are represented in Canada by Nelson Education, Ltd.
For your lifelong learning solutions, visit **www.cengage.com/custom.**
Visit our corporate website at **www.cengage.com.**

Printed in the United States of America

Custom Table of Contents

Contents

Chapter 1

What Is Psychology?   *1*

Chapter 2

Choosing a Major: Is Psychology for You?   16

Chapter 3

Take an Active Role in Your Education   45

Chapter 4

Study Tips: Tools for Academic Success   71

Chapter 5

Writing a Literature Review   98

Chapter 6

Writing an Empirical Paper   123

Chapter 7

What Can I Do with a Bachelor's Degree in Psychology? *144*

Chapter 8

Finding a Job with Your Bachelor's Degree   *161*

Chapter 9

What Can I Do with a Graduate Degree in Psychology?   *177*

Chapter 10

Applying to Graduate School in Psychology   **193**

Preface

Psychology is consistently among the most popular college majors, with about 90,000 baccalaureate degrees awarded each year. Despite this, many students are unaware of the psychology major's versatility and the wide range of skills that psychology majors develop. *The Psychology Major's Handbook* fills the gap by providing an overview of the major, including the combination of liberal arts and scientific skills that psychology majors acquire, as well as career options at the undergraduate and graduate level. Perhaps more important, *The Psychology Major's Handbook* provides practical information to help students make informed decisions about whether to pursue psychology as a major and career. Chapters discuss how to succeed in college, develop an active learning style, hone study skills, and become more self-aware. New college students often are surprised by the autonomy required of students. Perhaps the biggest difference between high school and college is that college requires students to take an active role in their education. *The Psychology Major's Handbook* is intended to help students recognize their role in steering their own education. No book can replace the guidance of a faculty advisor, but *The Psychology Major's Handbook* is a helpful resource for students who seek general assistance and it may serve as a springboard for student–advisor discussions as well.

The third edition of *The Psychology Major's Handbook* includes additional quizzes, exercises, and checklists to help readers employ the techniques described in this book and take an active role in their professional development. Each chapter includes at least two exercises and three prompts for journal writing, in-class assignments, or take-home essays. Other specific changes include adding the following discussions: ethics (Chapter 1), what students learn in college and what an education in psychology adds (Chapter 2), how to become active outside of the classroom through applied activities and participation in organizations (Chapter 3), and the value of considering careers by skills rather than simply by setting (Chapter 7). In addition, each chapter was reorganized and streamlined.

This book is organized to accompany students on their journey from Introductory Psychology through the college years. Chapter 1 introduces students to the scope of psychology, including subspecialties, the wide range of places where psychologists work, and academic degrees. Chapter 2 addresses the challenge of choosing a college major by becoming self-aware through journal writing and self-assessment exercises. Readers are encouraged to consider their skills, abilities, and interests when determining whether psychology is the right choice. Each subsequent chapter closes with journal exercises that encourage readers to learn about themselves and apply the chapter material to their own lives.

Chapters 3 through 6 are intended to accompany students through the college years, serving as a resource to review periodically. Chapter 3 examines the skills that are honed in college and helps students identify and take advantage of the resources at their schools so that they can get the most from their college years. Specifically, the chapter covers how to develop relationships with faculty and how to get research and field experience. The chapter also surveys the range of presentation and publication opportunities available to undergraduates in psychology. Chapter 4 emphasizes study skills as the key to success in college and provides detailed tips and strategies to improve time management, reading, note taking, studying, and test taking. Chapter 5 examines the psychology term paper or literature review: how to choose a topic, narrow it, locate information, understand the format of research articles, take notes, avoid plagiarism, write the first draft, and revise it. In Chapter 6, the empirical paper is demystified. Readers learn about the structure of the empirical paper, what to include in each section, and APA style; a template illustrating APA style is provided at the end of the chapter.

Chapters 7 through 10 offer specific information for psychology majors and students who are considering psychology as a major. Chapter 7 addresses the pervasive myth that there are no jobs available for psychology majors. Readers learn about the value of a liberal arts degree, what employers look for, how to acquire useful skills, and jobs for psychology majors in business, human resources, and social service fields. Learning about jobs is one thing; getting them is another. Chapter 8 provides advice on how to obtain a job after graduation: finding positions, completing applications, resumes, cover letters, and interviews.

Chapter 9 provides information about careers that require a graduate degree, takes a close look at the master's degree with specialties in psychology and related fields, and discusses the job outlook and salary prospects. Careers, employment settings, and salaries for doctoral degree-holders are presented, as well as the impact of managed care on psychologists. The final chapter, Chapter 10, provides advice for students who are interested in attending graduate school. Readers are encouraged to examine their reasons for applying to graduate school. Specific advice is provided on gathering program information, evaluating programs, preparing for the GRE, completing admissions essays, acquiring recommendation letters, and succeeding in interviews. Like earlier chapters, Chapter 10 presents exercises as a means for self-exploration and to help readers determine their priorities.

Acknowledgments

The Psychology Major's Handbook has benefited from the input of many. I am most appreciative of the constructive comments and helpful suggestions that I received from reviewers and colleagues: Jessica Irons — James Madison University; Leonard Mark — Miami University; Frank Vattano — Colorado State University; Peggy Skinner — South Plains College; and Holly Straub — University of South Dakota. Thanks to Vinny Prohaska and Erin McDonald for reviewing and commenting on drafts of the first edition. Drew Appelby has shared many class activities and ideas. All of these contributions have vastly improved this book. It is my pleasure to work with Tim Matray at Wadsworth/Cengage Learning on this third edition, and I thank Vicki Knight for her guidance on the first and second editions. Much of what appears in these pages has come from interaction with my students at Western Connecticut State University, whom I thank for sharing their experiences, questions, ideas, and enthusiasm. My parents, Philip and Irene Kuther, have provided unwavering support and guidance throughout my education and career. Finally, I thank Fred Martell for enriching my life in innumerable ways.

Dear Student,

Welcome to the world of psychology! *The Psychology Major's Handbook* is intended to accompany you on your journey through college. A comprehensive book such as this can sometimes be overwhelming, so here are some guideposts to help you find your way:

- If you're wondering, "What's psychology?" check out Chapter 1, which explains the scope of psychology, including the many subspecialties and the wide range of places where psychologists work.
- Not sure what to major in or whether psychology is for you? In Chapter 2, you'll learn about yourself through journal exercises and activities that help you to identify your skills, abilities, and interests.
- Ever wonder exactly what you're getting out of college? Feeling confused with the lack of guidance? Chapter 3 explains the hidden curriculum in college: how you can take control of your education by getting involved with faculty, research, and field experience.
- Does it seem as if you study and study and still don't get the grades you want? In Chapter 4 you'll learn about essential study skills, including time-management tips, suggestions on how to read more effectively, advice on note taking, study tips, and guidance for taking tests with ease.
- Have a big paper assignment and don't know where to start? Turn to Chapter 5 for tips on how to choose a paper topic, where to get ideas, and how to find information, take notes, write the paper, and revise it.
- Taking Experimental Psychology or a laboratory class and don't know how to write a lab report? Chapter 6 demystifies the empirical paper or research article. You'll learn about the special structure of empirical articles, what to include in each section, and APA style. A template appears at the end to help you conquer APA style.
- Want to major in psychology but have no clue what to do after graduation? Chapter 7 dispels the myth that psychology majors are unemployable. You'll learn about the value of a liberal arts degree, what employers look for, how to acquire useful skills, and jobs for psychology majors in business, human resources, and social service fields.
- Getting close to graduation and want to find a job? Turn to Chapter 8 and learn how to obtain a job after graduation. Everything you need to know is covered, including how to find positions, complete applications, prepare a resume, write cover letters, and ace interviews.
- Think you might want to continue your education but aren't sure of the choices? In Chapter 9 you'll learn about graduate degrees in psychology and the variety of careers for graduate degree-holders in psychology. You'll also have the opportunity to take a close look at the master's degree: reasons for obtaining one, your choices of fields, and the job

outlook and salary information for master's degree-holders. You'll take a similar look at the doctoral degree and the differences among PhD, PsyD, and EdD degrees. Chapter 9 also covers careers, employment settings, and salaries for doctoral degree-holders, and the impact of managed care on psychologists.

- So you think graduate school is for you? Chapter 10 tells you how to gather program information, evaluate programs, prepare for the GRE, complete admissions essays, acquire recommendation letters, and handle interviews.

WHAT IS PSYCHOLOGY?

CHAPTER OUTLINE

Close your eyes and envision a psychologist at work. What do you see? What is he or she doing? Does your image include any of the following?

- Conducting research with monkeys
- Monitoring a magnetic resonance imaging (MRI) machine to understand what parts of the brain are active when people view pictures of various items and situations
- Creating and administering a survey on employee perceptions of their work environments
- Developing and evaluating an intervention for families with a history of domestic violence
- Helping educators learn about how the mind works and how to teach most effectively
- Counseling a client who suffers from depression
- Teaching physicians how to understand the emotions that accompany illness and to communicate more effectively with patients
- Developing and implementing training programs for employees
- Helping police departments by providing information about criminal behavior, assisting officers in managing stress, or understanding the limitations of eyewitness testimony

All of these activities are conducted by psychologists. Are you surprised? Although psychologists are most often portrayed in the media as therapists in private practice settings, psychologists do much more than provide therapy. In this chapter we discuss the broad range of activities and responsibilities that fall under the umbrella of psychology.

PSYCHOLOGY'S BREADTH

A formal, though broad, definition of psychology is *the scientific study of behavior*. Behavior refers to anything an animal or a person does, feels, or thinks. Many students are surprised to learn that some psychologists work with animals. Psychologists often study animal physiology and behavior to extend what they learn to humans. They apply scientific methods of observation, data collection, analysis, and interpretation to learn more about what makes people and animals behave like they do. Psychologists generate hypotheses, or educated guesses about what might cause a particular behavior or phenomenon, and conduct careful research to test those hypotheses. Psychologists also work directly with people. Psychologists who practice apply the findings of research in their work with people.

Psychology examines the interactions among the brain, the environment, psychological functioning, and behavior. Topics of psychological study include social relationships, the brain and the chemicals that influence it, vision,

PSYCHOLOGY STUDENT TIP

Many students find the Introductory or General Psychology course challenging. There's a good reason for that: Introductory Psychology presents the entire field of psychology at a whirlwind and dizzying pace. As you learn, try to remember that each chapter of the book presents an entire subfield of psychology—an area in which psychologists specialize and spend their entire lives working. If you find a particular chapter interesting, note that your college offers at least one and often more than one course in that area. If you find a chapter (and thus subfield) uninteresting, the good part about the Introductory Psychology course is that you'll move on to a different chapter and different subfield in just a week or two.

human development, the causes of normative and atypical behavior, and much more. Psychologists conduct a variety of activities in many settings. You're probably most aware of psychologists as service providers, providing psychological therapy and treatment to clients. However, less than one-half of new psychologists work in service provider roles (Wicherski, Michalski, & Kohout, 2009). What do the rest do? Some psychologists are employed as professors at universities, community colleges, and high schools. Others work as researchers in university, hospital, corporate, and government settings. Psychologists work as administrators, managing hospitals, mental health clinics, nonprofit organizations, government agencies, businesses, schools, and more. Most psychologists perform in more than one of these roles. For example, a psychologist who works as a college professor might also have a private practice or conduct research with a social service agency.

A wide range of topics fall under the umbrella of psychology, and each topic is its own specialized field of study. The following sections present the most common specialties within psychology. In each of these areas, some psychologists spend most of their time conducting research to expand the knowledge base, some practice or apply research findings to help people and communities, and some do both, as scientist-practitioners. In addition, over one-third of psychologists teach and conduct research at colleges and universities.

Clinical Psychology

Clinical psychologists study, diagnose, and treat persons who experience emotional, behavioral, and psychological problems or disorders. Researchers in this area study questions like how to best treat a particular diagnosis (e.g., which therapy works best?). The problems may range from normative difficulties like helping someone deal with grief or a crisis to more serious and chronic disorders like schizophrenia or mood disorders. The practitioner role of a clinical psychologist is commonly depicted on television.

Clinical psychologists work in universities as professors and researchers. They also work in health care settings including hospitals, mental health centers, and private practice. Some clinical psychologists specialize in particular populations, such as children or older adults. Others specialize in particular problems, such as depression or anxiety. Some psychologists are generalists and treat people of all ages and with all types of problems.

Counseling Psychology

Counseling psychologists engage in many of the same activities as clinical psychologists but focus their activities on normative functioning rather than psychological disorders. Counseling psychologists conduct research on how to help people manage everyday life issues and transitions, such as divorce, remarriage, career changes, and transitions to and from college. Practicing counseling psychologists help people adjust to life changes, and provide vocational assessment and career guidance. Counseling psychologists are found in many of the same places as clinical psychologists. Many counseling psychologists work in academic settings as professors and researchers. Others work in community settings such as mental health clinics, halfway houses, college counseling centers, criminal justice settings, and social service agencies.

Developmental Psychology

Developmental psychologists study human development across the life span. In academic settings, developmental psychologists teach and conduct research on the emotional, intellectual, and physical development of children, adolescents, and adults. Research topics include a diverse array of issues such as whether most adults experience a midlife crisis, how babies learn to crawl, or what factors influence adolescent drug use.

Developmental psychologists also work in applied settings, such as pediatric hospitals, geriatric centers, and nonprofit organizations. They work as consultants for parenting magazines, toy companies, and children's television programs. Some developmental psychologists, known as *applied developmental psychologists*, engage in practice activities, such as conducting developmental assessments of children to ensure that they are timely in meeting developmental milestones. Developmental psychologists work with people in all phases of life. For example, a developmental psychologist might provide advice on how to design a nursing home that meets the needs of older adults or might develop and evaluate intervention programs like Head Start, a prominent child development and educational enrichment program for young children and their families that has existed since the mid 1960s.

Educational Psychology

Educational psychologists study how people learn and apply that knowledge to educational settings. They develop methods and materials to increase the efficiency and effectiveness of educational programs and curricula designed for people of all ages. Educational psychologists work in academic settings and conduct research on learning and instruction. Some study how people learn to read, or complete math problems. Others train teachers and develop methods of instruction to enhance the educational setting.

Experimental Psychology

Experimental psychologists conduct research and teach on a wide variety of topics including learning, sensation, perception, human performance, motivation, memory, language, thinking, and communication. Many experimental psychologists study and specialize in specific aspects of human cognition: how we take in, store, retrieve, and apply knowledge. Other experimental psychologists study animals to apply what they learn to humans, or simply because animal behavior is interesting. Most experimental psychologists are employed in academic settings, teaching and conducting research. Others work as researchers for businesses, corporations, and the government.

Forensic Psychology

Forensic psychologists study legal issues from a psychological perspective. They conduct research on topics such as the reliability of eyewitness testimony, juror selection, and how to interview eyewitnesses without contaminating their testimony. Forensic psychologists provide expert testimony on cases in criminal, civil, and family courts. They may evaluate prisoners, assist in making parole decisions, and assess defendants to determine whether they are competent to provide testimony. Forensic psychologists work not only with lawyers and judges but also with police departments to select, train, and evaluate police officers.

Health Psychology

Health psychologists study how psychological, biological, and social factors influence health and illness. They conduct research on health-related topics, such as whether relaxation techniques and social support can help people overcome illness more quickly, or how to change people's attitudes about smoking. Health psychologists design, assess, and modify programs to promote health and wellness (e.g., stress management, smoking cessation, weight loss). They work in academic and research settings such as universities and medical schools, as well as in applied settings such as hospitals and clinics.

Human Factors Psychology

Human factors or engineering psychologists study how people interact with machines, environments, and products. They conduct research on how people understand and use machines to increase people's safety, efficiency, and productivity. Human factors psychologists might work on designing a computer monitor to prevent user fatigue and eyestrain, or they might arrange the instruments on a car's dashboard to enhance access and safety. Human factors psychologists design, evaluate, and modify military equipment, airplanes, computer terminals, and consumer products. Most human factors psychologists work in industry and government; some work in academic settings.

Industrial-Organizational Psychology

Industrial and organizational psychologists apply psychological principles to the workplace. They are concerned with the relation between people and work. Industrial and organizational psychologists often work for companies, corporations, and the government, studying how to recruit, select, train, and evaluate employees. They conduct applied research on questions like what personality factors make a good employee, how to improve worker productivity, and characteristics of effective leaders. Industrial and organizational psychologists develop programs to improve employee morale and make the workplace more efficient and pleasant. Others teach and conduct research as members of academic departments in psychology and business.

Neuropsychology

Neuropsychologists examine the relation between the brain and behavior. How do neurotransmitters influence our behavior? What part of the brain is responsible for motivation, language, or emotion? Neuropsychologists conduct research to answer questions about how the brain influences our emotions and behavior. They teach and conduct research in academic settings, as well as train neuropsychologists, medical doctors, and clinical psychologists. Some neuropsychologists assess and treat persons with brain injuries within neurology, neurosurgery, psychiatric, and pediatric units of hospitals, and in clinics.

Quantitative Psychology and Psychometrics

Quantitative psychologists study and develop new methods and techniques for acquiring, analyzing, and applying information. A psychometrician may create or revise psychological tests, intelligence tests, and aptitude tests. Quantitative psychologists help other researchers in designing, conducting, and interpreting experiments. Quantitative psychologists and psychometricians primarily work in research and academic settings.

Social Psychology

Social psychologists study how people interact with each other and how they are influenced by the social environment. They conduct research on personality theories, attitude formation and change, persuasion and conformity, and how people relate to one another, including attraction, prejudice, group dynamics, teamwork, and aggression. Social psychologists work in academic settings as teachers and researchers, but they also work for corporations and advertising agencies, conducting marketing research and studying how consumers view products.

School Psychology

School psychologists work to foster the intellectual, emotional, educational, and social development of children. They apply psychological principles to the school environment. School psychologists conduct research on educational topics such as how the classroom climate influences student learning, or how to promote appropriate behavior in the classroom. They work in schools to assess and counsel students, work with parents and teachers, and develop behavioral interventions.

Clearly, psychology is diverse and entails much more than conducting therapy with patients relaxing on leather sofas. Instead, the field of psychology offers a variety of careers in direct service, academics, government, and business. Not all psychologists conduct therapy or even study people. What all of the subfields of psychology have in common, however, is a concern with understanding the causes of behavior.

EXERCISE 1.1
Psychology in the Media

Locate a magazine article or Web site describing psychology research findings.

1. Provide a brief summary of the findings.
2. Explain what subfield of psychology the research represents.
3. Identify one potential ethical issue related to the research topic.
4. Reconsider the findings described in the article. What further questions do you have? What questions should be addressed next? If you were the researcher whose work was mentioned in article, what would you try to learn next?

ACADEMIC DEGREES

Students major in psychology because they are interested in understanding human behavior and often gravitate towards a particular psychological subspecialty. One of the most important things that psychology majors must understand is that the bachelor's degree in psychology does not prepare graduates to be psychologists. Psychologists undergo many years of training after obtaining their bachelor's degrees. A career in each of the subfields of psychology requires a graduate degree. What is a graduate degree? Let's begin by considering the bachelor's degree.

The bachelor's degree, a bachelor of arts (BA) or bachelor of science (BS) degree, typically is the culmination of four years of undergraduate study. Whether a student earns a BA or BS often depends on the university they attend; psychology students are awarded BA degrees in some universities and BS degrees in others. Most students who earn bachelor's degrees enter the work world after graduation. Some enter graduate school to earn a master's degree or doctorate degree.

The master's degree is a graduate degree that typically requires two years of study. A far greater number of students pursue master's degrees than doctoral degrees in psychology. Can master's trained individuals provide effective therapy? Studies have shown that there are no convincing differences in therapeutic outcomes as a function of the practitioner's level of training (Christensen & Jacobson, 1994; Seligman, 1995). There are many different types of master's degrees, most commonly the MA (master of arts) and MS (master of science). Master's degree programs last from one to three years, depending on the program. Requirements for service-oriented fields such as clinical, counseling, and school psychology usually include practical experience in an applied setting.

What can you do with a master's degree? Depending on the program and curriculum, a master's degree enables graduates to: (a) teach psychology in high school (other certification may be needed); (b) become more competitive for jobs in government and industry; (c) obtain certification as a counselor or marriage and family therapist and practice counseling; (d) obtain certification to practice school psychology (depending on state); and (e) practice industrial/organizational psychology in business settings.

A doctoral degree is an advanced graduate degree. A doctoral degree provides a greater range of flexibility and autonomy than the master's degree, but it usually requires five to seven years of graduate work to complete. In clinical or counseling psychology, the requirement for the doctoral degree generally includes a year or more of internship or supervised experience. A doctoral degree requires a great commitment of time.

Why do students seek doctoral degrees? Generally students pursue doctoral degrees for any of the following reasons: (a) to teach college, (b) to conduct research in a university or private organization in industry or business, (c) to practice clinical psychology without supervision, or (d) to engage in a variety of consulting roles affording autonomy. There are several types of graduate degrees in psychology.

The PhD refers to the doctor of philosophy. Like the master's degree, the PhD is awarded in many fields. It is a research degree that culminates in a dissertation based on original research. The PsyD refers to the doctor of psychology. It is offered only in clinical and counseling psychology and is considered a professional degree, much like a JD (doctor of jurisprudence, a lawyer's degree). The doctor of education (EdD), a third doctoral option for psychology students, is less common than the PhD and PsyD. The EdD is offered in departments of education, rather than psychology.

In short, there are many levels of education in psychology and many educational paths that will prepare you to work with people. Not all psychology majors will become psychologists. In fact, the vast majority will not. Then why major in psychology if you will not become a psychologist? Psychology is a solid liberal arts major that teaches students how to think. In Chapter 2 we take a close look at the skills imparted by a liberal arts degree such as psychology. So why choose psychology? Because it is interesting. A background in psychology will change how you see your world. As you learn more about psychology you will become able to see the world through a psychology lens, offering a unique perspective and understanding of people. Just because you're not a psychologist doesn't mean that you can't learn psychological principles and apply them in your day to day life. A psychological perspective can shape much of what you do. For example, the ethical guidelines that psychologists follow can inform your behavior. Let's consider the information about ethical issues and responsibilities of psychologists.

ETHICS AND PSYCHOLOGY

Psychologists affect people directly and indirectly through their work as researchers, teachers, writers, and therapists. Psychologists have a responsibility to act professionally and both protect and promote the welfare of others. Therefore, psychologists' attention to ethics, or principled conduct, is paramount. The following section examines some of the ethical issues that psychologists face.

Ethical Dilemmas Experienced by Psychologists

Psychologists in all subfields confront ethical challenges each day. For example, psychologists who provide therapy must balance challenging their client to confront issues plaguing them with the need to protect the client from self harm. Establishing professional boundaries with clients is another challenge that practicing psychologists face; for example, is it ever appropriate to hug a client?

Psychologists in each of the subfields experience ethical issues that are unique to their field. For example, forensic psychologists might assess a defendant to determine his or her capacity to stand trial. In this situation, who is the client? To whom is the forensic psychologist responsible (the court, the defendant, the prosecuting attorney)? Consider the industrial-organizational psychologist working in a business setting who must advise employers in making decisions about whom to lay off. Should the psychologist consider the individual's performance alone or also consider his or her personal life? Should the employee's marital and family status influence the decision?

Psychologists who conduct research manage another set of ethical issues. How do psychologists balance the benefits of research against the possible harm that can occur to participants—the mental, emotional, and physical risks of research participation? One critical way in which participants' rights are protected is the federal requirement that researchers seek informed consent from participants before conducting a study. Informed consent is a participant's informed, rational, and voluntary agreement to participate. By informed, it must be made with knowledge of the risks and benefits of participation. Researchers are obligated to explain the scope of the research and whether the potential for harm exists. By rational, it must be made by a person capable of making a reasoned decision. Parents provide parental permission for their minor children to participate because we assume that minors are not able to meet the rational criteria of informed consent. Finally, it must be voluntary, meaning that it must be made freely and without coercion.

Researchers' responsibilities continue after the research is completed. Scientists' work ultimately can impact society. In reporting results, a psychologist should be mindful of the social and political implications of his or her work (Society for Research in Child Development, 1996). Researchers must consider how their findings will be portrayed in the media and must work to correct misinterpretations. Researchers must attempt to foresee the inferences that people may draw about their findings and prepare to correct misinterpretations.

Ethics and You

How do psychologists navigate the ethical issues that may arise in their work? The American Psychological Association, a professional organization of psychologists, has published an *Ethics Code* (2002) that articulates psychologists' responsibilities and ethical obligations. The basis for the *Ethics Code* is the following five General Principles. Although intended for psychologists, the

General Principles outline a model of behavior that is applicable to all. What are the principles, and how might they apply to you?

Beneficence and Nonmaleficence   Psychologists work to help others, benefit them, and not harm them. In addition, psychologists attempt to be aware of their own mental and physical health and how their health influences others. Psychology students can apply this principle to their own lives by seeking to help others—friends, family, and the community—with whom they come in contact and to do no harm. Our own functioning—physical and mental—influences our interactions with others. An awareness of this can help us to make decisions and act in ways that help and do not hurt others.

Fidelity and Responsibility   Psychologists are aware of their professional and scientific responsibilities to people, communities, and society at large. They uphold ethical standards, take responsibility for their actions, and are concerned about their colleagues' behavior. Applying this principle as a student entails choosing a set of ethical principles by which to live. Become aware of your responsibilities to others—family, friends, pets, and more—and work to behave in accord with your principles. Finally, be aware of others' behavior and show concern when friends, for example, show inappropriate behavior.

Integrity   Psychologists are accurate and honest in their work as scientists, teachers, and practitioners. Psychologists do not lie, cheat, or steal, and they keep promises. Psychology students show integrity in much the same way as psychologists. They are honest in their work as students, but also in their everyday nonacademic life.

EXERCISE 1.2
Can You Identify Academic Dishonesty?

Circle the instances that exemplify academic dishonesty and inappropriate academic behavior.

1. Copying a sentence from an article, noting the author but not enclosing the material in quotation marks.
2. Listing facts, statistics, or other information without citing the source.
3. Reviewing another student's paper to learn about writing style and how to organize your paper on a different topic.
4. Copying a graph from an article and listing the source and page number.
5. Listing information and citing a reference that was not the source of the material.

6. Citing articles and books that were not read.
7. Being unsure of the source of a particular piece of information, so listing a likely source.
8. Changing the data in your study, by mathematically doubling the number of participants, for example, to improve your research findings.
9. Copying from another student's test.
10. Reading another student's paper and rephrasing his or her responses in your own paper.
11. Writing important points on your desk to use during an exam.
12. Working with other students to complete a take-home exam despite the professor's instructions to work independently.
13. Copying a sentence from an article, enclosing the copied material in quotation marks and listing the author.
14. Submitting a paper that you wrote for one class as an assignment in a different class.
15. Writing a paper for someone else.
16. Writing a paper by explaining ideas found in many articles and books and citing each.
17. Explaining an idea or theory from a book in your own words, without listing the source.
18. Participating in an online class discussion as someone else.
19. Cutting and pasting information from a Web site into your paper or discussion post in an online class.
20. Copying your tests from a particular instructor and class to share with friends who currently are enrolled in that class.

Answer: All *but* the following items are examples of academic dishonesty: 3, 4, 13, 16

Justice   Psychologists work to ensure that people they come into contact with are treated with fairness and justice, permitting them equal quality in services. Psychologists are aware of their own biases, competencies, and limitations and work to ensure that all people they come into contact with are treated fairly and equitably. Students treat others fairly. They are aware of their own perspectives and biases and how those might influence their interactions with others.

Respect for People's Rights and Dignity   Psychologists recognize and respect the inherent worth of all people and their rights to privacy and self determination. They are aware of the role of individual differences, such as culture, ethnicity, gender, age, sexual orientation, and more, and consider them in their work with individuals. Psychologists attempt to be aware of their own biases, eliminate biases in their work, and do not condone biases in the work of others. Psychology students who respect the dignity and value of others and work to eliminate biases in their thought and behavior will grow into model citizens who can positively influence others around them.

EXERCISE 1.3
Internet Scavenger Hunt

Use the Internet to answer each of the following questions about specialties in psychology. Provide the search terms used, the Web site, and your response.

1. In what states can psychologists prescribe medication?
2. How is forensic psychology different from psychology and the law?
3. What is a specialist degree in school psychology? Why earn one?
4. During World War II, psychologists used their skills in new ways to help the war effort. In what ways did psychologists contribute? What field of psychology developed from these contributions?
5. What is Principle A of the American Psychological Association Ethics Code?
6. What subfield(s) is (are) concerned with a biopsychosocial model? What is a biopsychosocial model?
7. When was the PsyD born?
8. Discuss two subfields of experimental psychology.
9. Identify three ways in which psychologists can contribute to businesses and corporations.
10. What is *Eye on Psi Chi*? What did it replace?

OVERVIEW OF *THE PSYCHOLOGY MAJOR'S HANDBOOK*

Now that you have had an introduction to the field of psychology, let's talk about what you can expect from this book. Your first step in choosing a major and preparing for a career is to get to know yourself. Chapter 2 will introduce you to new ways of understanding yourself. A major theme of this book is that *you* play a major role in determining your success in college and beyond. Chapter 3 will show you how to take an active role in your education and shape your own future. Regardless of your major, you'll need to learn how to study and how to write papers. Chapters 4, 5, and 6 will introduce you to time management and study tips as well as specific information about how to write college papers—and specifically, psychology papers.

The remaining chapters of this book encourage you to look ahead and consider your future. What can you do with a bachelor's degree in psychology, and how do you look for a job after graduation? Chapters 7 and 8 address these questions. In Chapter 9 you'll learn what careers are available with a graduate degree in psychology, and Chapter 10 provides an overview of how to apply to graduate school. The college years offer opportunities and challenges. The *Psychology Major's Handbook* will help you navigate these years and keep the big picture—your future—in mind.

SUGGESTED READINGS

Kuther, T. L., & Morgan, R. D. (2010). *Careers in psychology: Opportunities in a changing world.* Belmont, CA: Wadsworth.

Ruscio, J. (2005). *Clear thinking with psychology: Separating sense from nonsense.* Belmont, CA: Wadsworth.

Smith, R. A. (2002). *Challenging your preconceptions: Thinking critically about psychology.* Belmont, CA: Wadsworth.

Stanovich, K. E. (2009). *How to think straight about psychology.* New York: Allyn & Bacon.

INTERNET RESOURCES

About Psychology

http://psychology.about.com

Posts articles about all areas of psychology and the most up-to-date psychology links on the net.

Psychology: Scientific Problem Solvers . . . Careers for the Twenty-First Century

http://www.apa.org/careers/resources/guides/careers.pdf

This online brochure, from the American Psychological Association, provides an excellent overview of the diverse fields within psychology, complete with interviews from established professionals in each field.

Psych Web

http://www.psywww.com/index.html

This Web site is a portal to psychology-related material for students and professors. You'll find links to pages on careers in psychology, psychological classics on the Web, and a plethora of Web sites devoted to psychology.

Classics in the History of Psychology

http://psychclassics.yorku.ca/

One this Web site you'll find the full text of classic books in psychology, from Sigmund Freud to B. F. Skinner and more.

Psi Chi: The International Honor Society in Psychology

http://www.psichi.org

The Psi Chi Web site offers a variety of resources for psychology students, including full-text access to all of the articles published in *Eye on Psi Chi*, the organization's quarterly newsletter. Articles cover areas in psychology, career preparation, personal growth, and more.

CHOOSING A MAJOR: IS PSYCHOLOGY FOR YOU?

CHAPTER OUTLINE

EXERCISE 2.4: VALUES   **INTERNET RESOURCES**

CHOOSING PSYCHOLOGY   **JOURNAL EXERCISES**

SUGGESTED READINGS

One of the most difficult decisions that students face is choosing a college major. How do you decide what to do with your life? Selecting a major can be daunting if you believe that your undergraduate major determines your career; fortunately, this is not true. Choosing a major is not the same as choosing a life-long career, yet this myth persists. For example, many people assume that students who major in the arts, humanities, or social sciences (e.g., psychology) are either not qualified for any jobs or qualified only for careers in those specific areas. However, students who earn undergraduate degrees in these fields find jobs in business, research, human resources, teaching, the military, and a variety of other occupations (see Chapter 7 for more information about careers with a bachelor's degree in psychology). Your major will not limit you to only one career choice.

Within ten years after graduation, most people work in careers that are not directly connected to their undergraduate majors. In addition, new types of jobs are emerging each year, and most of us have no way of knowing what those jobs will be or what type of education will be needed in order to qualify for them. For example, fifteen years ago, most people had never heard of a Web designer (someone who creates Web pages and designs Internet sites). It's likely that other careers will evolve over the coming years. Consequently, career counselors recommend that college students focus on developing general transferable skills—including writing, speaking, computer literacy, problem solving, and team building—that employers want and that graduates will need in order to adjust to a rapidly changing world. Choose a major that reflects *your* interests and abilities, and provides you with opportunities to develop and hone skills that are useful for a variety of careers. The exercises in this chapter will help you to learn more about yourself; assess your interests, skills, and abilities; and determine which major is right for you.

WHAT DO YOU LEARN IN COLLEGE?

The liberal arts constitute a range of subjects including the humanities (such as history, literature, and philosophy), social sciences (such as psychology and sociology), and natural sciences (such as biology and physics). A liberal arts degree is designed to impart broad general knowledge and intellectual skills and expose students to a world of ideas, people, cultures, and history. The liberal arts teach students how to consider multiple perspectives, examine ideas, explore possibilities, and challenge their own and others' assumptions. Let's take a closer look at what you may learn though a liberal arts education.

What a Liberal Arts Degree Imparts

No matter your major, you will learn from two sets of curricula during your college years. You will learn the specific content of your major, the material that's printed in the course catalogue, including specific facts, concepts, and theories that college courses are designed to impart. However, you will learn much more than the content of your courses. College also entails a covert curriculum, a subtle set of skills of which students often are not aware, such as how to acquire information, think, and learn—skills that are more important than any set of facts you might learn (Appleby, 2001). Liberal arts majors have the opportunity to develop the following competencies that will prepare them for their careers after graduation.

Communication Skills   The ability to communicate in a clear, organized, and persuasive way is a skill that is useful to all careers and can be applied throughout life. All of your college courses provide opportunities to develop and strengthen your oral and written communication skills, but some courses, such as in English composition, public speaking, and writing, offer specialized practice. Many students approach writing and communications courses as simply requirements to complete. Instead, these courses are an important foundation for communication skills—the capacity to get a message out to the world and be heard. Savvy students take additional courses in writing or public speaking because no matter the career, the ability to be understood in a clear and persuasive way is invaluable throughout life. Remember that each course you take—communications or otherwise—contributes something unique to your education. No course is "a waste" or simply something to endure.

Reading Skills   The ability to read complex material quickly, understand it, extract the relevant material, and use the information to solve problems are skills that students hone in college and will use in their careers (Appleby, 2001). For example, employees in business, management, and advertising must keep abreast of the literature in their field by reading books, magazines, and trade publications to help them to perform their jobs more efficiently. Savvy students quickly recognize that they must adapt their reading to the content at hand and take a different approach when reading scientific articles as compared with reading fiction. Students who recognize the covert curriculum, the lifelong skills that they will develop in college, approach assignments as opportunities to learn and sharpen their reading comprehension skills, as well as adapt their reading styles to the material to be read.

Listening and Note-Taking Skills   The ability to take accurate notes and identify the arguments and important points that emerge from discussion are just as important to success after graduation as they are in college. Successful employees and graduate students have the ability to listen carefully and attentively and to understand and follow instructions. Lectures and class discussions offer valuable opportunities to develop active listening and note-taking skills that stretch beyond the content of the course.

Computer Literacy   Technology is an inevitable part of the workplace. All liberal arts majors have opportunities to learn basic computer skills, such as word processing and spreadsheet programs, as well as how to use databases and the Internet to find information.

Critical Thinking and Problem-Solving Skills   The most important skill that a college education imparts is the ability to think. Certainly, you're able to think well before you enter college, but the quality of thinking improves radically over the college years with practice analyzing complex problems, thinking critically, and constructing arguments that are supported by evidence. Critical thinking refers to the ability to gather, comprehend, analyze, evaluate, and apply information to solve problems. These thinking skills are essential to making wise decisions throughout life.

Self-Management Skills   College is often the first time that students are independent and responsible for their own behavior. At first it is very difficult. Students may be late for class, forget about assignments, or neglect to do their laundry. It is often mistakes that encourage learning. Successful students don't dwell on mistakes, but rather, learn from them. With time, students become more independent, responsible for their actions and well-being, and more organized—all skills that prepare them for today's demanding work environments. College students face multiple demands: classes, projects, outside activities, meetings with professors, athletic practices and games, socializing with friends, part-time work, and volunteer work, for example. Part of the unwritten curriculum of college is learning to become more punctual, reliable, mature, and respectful—skills critical to a happy, healthy, and productive adulthood (Appleby, 2001). The stresses that most college students encounter—managing multiple commitments—aid them in developing skills in managing their emotions and behavior, essential self-management skills.

A liberal arts education provides the tools for students to learn how to think independently and critically, develop mature and reasoned decision making, solve complex problems, effectively communicate their ideas with others, and exercise self control (Bare, 1988). Become engaged with your education and you'll develop thinking, analysis, and self-management abilities that last a lifetime. This is true no matter your major. If you put in the time and hard work, you will receive a broad and fulfilling education regardless of your major, whether it's in the humanities, social sciences, or natural sciences. Why choose a psychology major, then? What does a psychology major impart?

Why Major in Psychology?

The psychology major is a general liberal arts degree that prepares graduates for "lifelong learning, thinking, and action" (McGovern, Furumoto, Halpern, Kimble, & McKeachie, 1991, p. 600). Like other liberal arts majors, psychology students gain knowledge and skills that generalize to the world outside the classroom; however, the emphasis on learning and applying principles of psychology to understand human behavior makes the degree unique (McGovern et al., 1991; Dunn et al., 2007; Halpern, 2009).

Knowledge of Human Behavior   Undergraduate education in psychology is intended to expose students to the major facts, theories, and issues in the discipline. Understanding human behavior entails learning about physiology, perception, cognition, emotion, development, and more. Consequently, psychology majors construct a broad knowledge base that serves as the conceptual framework for lifelong learning about human behavior as well as the capacity to apply their understanding in everyday situations.

Information Acquisition and Synthesis Skills   The knowledge base of psychology is constantly expanding. Successful psychology students learn how to gather and synthesize information. Psychology students learn how to use a range of sources including the library, computerized databases, and the Internet to gather information about an area of interest. More important, psychology students learn how to weigh and integrate information into a coherent and persuasive argument. In addition, successful psychology students apply their advanced understanding of cognition and memory to enhance their processing and recall of information.

Research Methods and Statistical Skills   Psychology students learn how to apply the scientific method to address questions about human behavior. They learn how to identify a problem, devise a hypothesis, choose and carry out scientific methods to gather information about the problem, conduct statistical analyses to evaluate a hypothesis, and interpret data summaries to devise a conclusion. In other words, psychology students become able to pose and answer questions about human behavior and experience.

Critical Thinking and Problem-Solving Skills   Exposure to the diverse perspectives within psychology trains students to think flexibly and to accept some ambiguity. Introductory psychology students often ask for the "right" answer; they soon learn that answers often aren't black or white, but many shades of grey. Psychology students acquire skills in thinking critically about complex problems. They learn to weigh multiple sources of information, determine the degree of support for each position, and make a reasoned decision about which position has more merit and how a problem is best solved.

Reading, Writing, and Speaking Skills   Psychology students develop reading, writing, and presentation skills for effective oral and written communication. They learn how to think critically about what they read, as well as comprehend and present arguments from a psychological standpoint. Moreover, their understanding of human behavior aids students in constructing arguments that are easily comprehended by others. Information derived from psychology regarding cognition, memory, listening, persuasion, and communication enhances psychology majors' ability to communicate orally and in writing.

Interpersonal and Intrapersonal Skills   Psychology students develop the ability to communicate their ideas and use their knowledge of human behavior to devise persuasive arguments. Successful students are able to lead, collaborate with others, and work effectively in groups. Psychology students are primed to be effective communicators because they are trained to be sensitive to issues of culture, race, class, and ethnicity. Students of psychology also develop intrapersonal awareness, or self-knowledge. They are able to monitor and manage their own behavior, which is critical in succeeding in academic and interpersonal tasks.

Computer Literacy   Psychology students develop familiarity with computers and understand how to use common statistical, word processing, and spreadsheet programs. The capacity to use statistical software to analyze data makes psychology majors stand out from other liberal arts majors. They also understand how to learn new software and computer programs, and they have basic knowledge for using and accessing e-mail as well as browsing the Internet.

Adaptability   Psychology students quickly learn that the perfect experiment is an unattainable goal toward which all researchers strive. Students learn how to design the best research studies possible, given limited resources. The capacity to evaluate and adapt to changing circumstances is highly valued in today's often volatile economy and workplace.

An undergraduate education in psychology will provide you with the opportunity to develop these as well as many other skills. The combination of liberal education and training in human behavior makes the psychology degree very special. Education in statistical, thinking, research, writing, and interpersonal skills embodies the psychology major, supports the goals of a liberal arts education, and will help you to develop into a well rounded and well educated person who has skills applicable to a broad range of careers (Kierniesky, 1992).

The psychology major satisfies the objectives of a liberal arts education, which include developing critical, independent, and analytical thinking, leadership skills, communication skills, an understanding of how to learn, the ability to take multiple perspectives on an issue, and an understanding of human diversity (Winter, McClelland, & Stewart, 1981). Training in research design and statistical analysis, as well as human behavior, is what makes the psychology major unique among liberal arts degrees.

CHOOSING A MAJOR

As you begin the process of selecting a major, remember that there is no bad choice. Every college major provides opportunities to develop a unique blend of skills and competencies. Majors differ in the specific set of competencies emphasized. The emphasis on scientific reasoning and problem solving, coupled with a focus on understanding how people think and behave, is what makes psychology unique among majors. Carefully consider your options, your skill set, and your interests when selecting a college major. At the end of this process you may find that psychology is the major for you—or you may make another choice. Listen to yourself and make the decision that is right for you, but also recognize that many students change their major some time during their college years. Don't let this choice paralyze you. It is not set in stone. Follow these steps to ensure that you're true to yourself in choosing the college major that is right for you—and one that you'll stick with throughout your college years.

Become Informed

The first step in making any decision is to become informed of your options. What majors does your college offer? Some majors, including psychology, English, and economics, are available at all colleges and universities. Other majors, such as engineering, can be found only at some institutions. What options does your college offer? Flip through your college handbook and look at each department and each major. Take a moment to review each program, even if you think it isn't interesting or right for you. Sometimes we have preconceived biases and incorrect information about a discipline or major. For each major, ask yourself the following questions and note your responses in writing so that you can easily revisit your work and compare majors later.

- What is this field? What does it study?
- Do I have any experience in this area?
- Have I taken a class in this area?

- If so, what was it like? (Remember that a professor can color your view of a discipline. For example, a professor who you find unappealing may make a subject that you'd otherwise find interesting seem boring. Try to determine how much of your opinion is influenced by the subject matter and how much by the professor.)
- What classes can I expect to take as a major?

It is likely that you will not find answers to all of these questions in your college handbook. Examine the department Web site to find information about the program, faculty (including their research interests and involvement with students), and opportunities for graduates. Most department Web pages will provide answers for many of these questions. After completing this task, list all of the majors that sound interesting to you, without making judgments. Then, for each major, gather information from a variety of sources.

Speak with Current Students   Ask other students how they chose their major, why they think it's a good choice, and what they think about the content, professors, and opportunities after graduation. What are the required courses like? Every major has its most challenging set of courses—what are those courses? Why are they considered challenging? What about the professors? Do students have out-of-class interactions with faculty? What kind? What out-of-class experiences are available? Is there a student club?

Speak with Recent Graduates   Ask recent graduates about their experiences in college and afterwards. Ask them some or all of the questions you asked current students. Also ask about their experiences after graduating.

- What was the job search like?
- What kinds of jobs did they seek?
- How were they received by potential employers?
- Where were they hired?
- How well does their job match their expectations?
- What are the positive and negative features of their work?
- What role, if any, did their major play in their job search and career?
- If they could do it again, what major would they choose? Why?

If you don't know any recent graduates, visit the department and/or your college's career center. Most college career centers maintain databases of recent graduates; you can contact a few graduates to learn more about their work and career experiences.

Speak with a Career Professional   Visit your college's career center to seek advice. Tell the career counselor what you've learned about yourself in completing the exercises in this chapter, and he or she can help you narrow your choice of majors. It is likely that your career counselor will present you with additional surveys and tasks to help you decide on a major and career.

Speak with Professors   Don't forget to talk with professors to learn more about potential majors. Visit the office hours of a professor in whose class you are enrolled, or one who seems approachable or works in a field of interest to you. Talk with him or her. Ask questions about the undergraduate major and what kinds of jobs recent graduates have obtained. Ask informed questions. For example, know a little bit about the major, basic course requirements, and, if possible, what courses the professor teaches. You might explain that you're thinking about becoming a major in their field and would like to know more about it.

- What do graduates do?
- Are there formal opportunities to work with faculty, such as research courses with small enrollments?
- Do many students interact with faculty outside of the classroom, for example, assisting with research?
- Do students tend to participate in clubs and outside activities, such as group trips to conferences?
- Do students engage in applied activities like internships?
- How did the professor choose his or her major?
- What are the important attributes for a successful student?
- Any advice on choosing a major?
- Advice for students in the department?

There are multiple sources of information about any given major. Approach the task as if you were solving a puzzle. Each source and person provides a unique bit of information and perspective. Sources may disagree about particular qualities or characteristics of a major. Compile all of the information and weigh it based on the person's perspective (student, graduate, or faculty, for example), perceived accuracy (Does the information seem accurate? What is the source's perspective?), and perceived similarity (How similar are your and the source's views?).

Once you have gathered information and decided on several majors that may be a good fit for you, it's time to shift your attention inward and learn about yourself.

Know Yourself: Write

You may have noticed that keeping notes—writing—is a useful tool for organizing what you know about majors. Writing is also useful for learning and organizing what you know about yourself. Always good advice, understanding yourself is critical to choosing a major that will satisfy your intellectual curiosity and fulfill your career goals. One of the best ways to learn about yourself and record what you learn is by writing. Consider keeping a journal, a record of self-reflective writing. A journal is a collection of your creative activity and can take many forms: a notebook, computer file, iPhone or other smartphone file, or even a personal for-your-eyes-only blog. Your journal is a private learning space where you can reflect upon yourself, your experiences, goals, dreams, and anxieties—learn more about who you are.

Why Write?   Writing is a way to explore your thoughts about yourself and the world around you. Sometimes we're not aware of our thoughts and feelings until we capture them with the written word. Expressing your ideas and feelings in words forces you to focus your thoughts, identify your opinions and values, and clarify your sense of identity.

Write for therapy   After a long day or a difficult experience, write to reflect. Writing offers a private opportunity to let out feelings of frustration, anger, or anxiety. Write about your deepest thoughts, but also everyday mundane matters, to help you figure out what you think or feel about a situation and to release stress. Don't censor yourself; your journal will never say, "I told you so." You'll find that you're better able to concentrate after you've cleared your head by writing.

Write to get organized   Perhaps the easiest way to begin keeping a journal is to use it as a place to record lists of immediate tasks to be accomplished. With regular use, writing becomes a habit and can grow beyond making lists to include self-reflection, planning, and goal setting. You can write about your goals and document the steps needed to achieve them, as well as your progress. In this way, a journal can help to organize your daily life.

Write to solve problems   Writing is an effective tool for problem solving because writing is thinking. The next time you find yourself confronted with a problem or a big decision, try writing about it. Explain the problem in words: What do you know about it? Discuss your feelings about the problem and analyze it. Writing may lead you to brainstorm potential solutions. Then your writing might shift towards analyzing each solution. Expressing ideas in written form requires a different thought process from thinking. We think in new ways when we write. This allows us to conceptualize problems differently and come to solutions more quickly.

Write to enhance communication   The more often you write, the more your writing will improve. Writing strengthens communication skills because it lets you practice identifying and expressing ideas, which is one of your major goals as a college student.

Write to unleash your creativity   Writing offers a creative outlet, a place to generate stories, essays, and poetry. If you're having a tough time thinking up ideas for class papers or essays, your journal is the place to turn. Through writing, we become more creative. There are a variety of techniques and exercises that can help you to find your center of creativity and inspire new ways of thinking and expressing yourself. Check out the exercises in this chapter and throughout this book. Also take note of the Web resources at the end of this chapter for places to turn to learn how to record your ideas.

Write to record your experience   A journal provides a record of your life. Days, weeks, and months pass all too quickly. Memory is fallible. A journal helps you to remember events, experiences, feelings, and intentions. It offers a place to record accomplishments, hopes, and dreams as well as to retain details that you would probably otherwise forget. From a therapeutic perspective, looking back over old journals allows the opportunity to reflect on patterns of experience, interaction, and emotion, providing insight into yourself and your perspective on life. How have you changed and grown? You can gain insight about yourself by reviewing your journal.

How to Begin Writing   If you're ready to start your own journal, simply begin. Your journal can take many forms. Some students prefer to keep their journal as a word processing file on their laptop. Others write in a bound composition book or simply keep a folder of loose papers. You might keep your journal on your PDA or smartphone or even create a blog, a private web log using an Internet service such as typepad.com (http://www.typepad.com), blogger.com (http://www.blogger.com), or a similar site. The cardinal rule of journal writing is to remember that your journal is for your eyes only. Don't let spelling, handwriting, and grammar be major concerns. Get your feelings and experiences down in writing, any way that you can. No one else will review or grade it.

Just write   Many students are puzzled: What to write about? There are no rules when it comes to journals. You can write about anything that comes to mind, like poetry, story ideas, and reflections, as well as more everyday items such as lists of accomplishments and tasks to be completed. Even everyday frustrations can be topics for your writing. Take time to observe your life. If you're having difficulty, try writing about the trouble that you're experiencing starting the journal. Write your thoughts as they come, even if you're writing that you don't know what to write. Try writing about events that are happening to you or around you, from a third-person perspective. For example, begin writing with the phrase, "It was a time when . . .," and then describe the event in detail, using as many of your senses as possible. What were the sounds, smells, sights, and feelings that were present? Pretend that you're an outside observer and use pronouns like *he* and *she*. This exercise can help you to put things into perspective; it is especially effective when writing about life changes (like the transition to college), relationships (like that argument with your boyfriend or girlfriend), and events that you found upsetting (like finding out that you didn't do so well on that test). Throughout this book, you'll find plenty of topics and ideas to write about in your journal, which will help you learn more about yourself and make plans for your future.

Write for brief periods, often The goal of keeping a journal is to catch your thoughts. The more often you write in your journal, the more you'll learn about yourself. Take your journal with you. If you have fifteen minutes between classes, write in your journal. You might even write about what you've learned in your prior class and how it relates to your experience. Try writing at bedtime or right after waking up. It doesn't take much time. You'll be surprised at how much you can write in just a few minutes. The key is to keep from censoring yourself. Allow yourself to be thoughtful and write what's on your mind. Explore your thoughts about a specific topic or about life in general. Try to get into the habit of writing each day, even if it is just a short entry. Also try to write some longer entries because they will give you the opportunity to flesh out your thoughts and make insights about yourself.

Reading is optional It doesn't matter if you read your journal. Some people return to their journals often, as chronicles of their lives. However, many people rarely read their journals but instead use writing to process their thoughts. Remember that the information is always there should you choose to read it, but you don't have to read it.

Set no expectations Your journal does not have to be filled with descriptions of monumental experiences. Journal entries don't have to be well written or scholarly. Don't let these myths rob you of the chance to benefit from journal writing.

Give journal writing a shot, in whatever format works for you—handwritten or electronic. Writing will help you to explore who you are and discover who you hope to become. Through writing and reflecting, the mundane can become profound. Take a chance and explore yourself through writing.

Learn About Yourself Through Self-Assessment

Understanding yourself is critical to choosing a major that intrigues you. Journal writing is an important start, but choosing a major requires a more thorough self-assessment. It sounds technical, but self-assessment is the process by which you examine your skills, abilities, motivations, interests, values, experience, and accomplishments. In other words, it's how you learn about yourself. Through self-assessment you'll build a firm foundation of knowledge about yourself. You can then use this knowledge to make sound decisions about your major. The following exercises will help you to better understand yourself, but remember that self-awareness will not be achieved instantaneously. It takes hard work, soul-searching, and time.

Assess Your Personality and Attitudinal Traits   Who are you? What personality characteristics best describe you? Understanding your unique personality will help you to choose a major that is right for you. After you graduate, knowledge about your personality traits will help you to find a position or career that meshes with your characteristics and is rewarding and fulfilling. Exercise 2.1 will help you to get a better understanding of your personality, which is essential to choosing a major that you'll be happy with. Consider writing in your journal about what you learn about yourself after completing Exercise 2.1.

EXERCISE 2.1
Assess Your Personality Traits

Check off those traits that describe you. Include additional traits if needed. Take your time to think about each one, and be honest with yourself. Then complete the questions that follow.

❑ Academic	❑ Extroverted	❑ Practical
❑ Active	❑ Fair-minded	❑ Private
❑ Accurate	❑ Farsighted	❑ Productive
❑ Adaptable	❑ Feeling	❑ Progressive
❑ Adept	❑ Firm	❑ Protective
❑ Adventurous	❑ Flexible	❑ Prudent
❑ Affectionate	❑ Forceful	❑ Punctual
❑ Aggressive	❑ Formal	❑ Quick
❑ Alert	❑ Frank	❑ Quiet
❑ Ambitious	❑ Frugal	❑ Rational
❑ Analytical	❑ Future-oriented	❑ Realistic
❑ Appreciative	❑ Generous	❑ Receptive
❑ Articulate	❑ Gentle	❑ Reflective
❑ Artistic	❑ Good natured	❑ Relaxed
❑ Assertive	❑ Gregarious	❑ Reliable
❑ Astute	❑ Hardy	❑ Reserved
❑ Athletic	❑ Helpful	❑ Resourceful
❑ Attentive	❑ Honest	❑ Responsible
❑ Balanced	❑ Hopeful	❑ Reverent
❑ Brave	❑ Humorous	❑ Risk-taker
❑ Broad-minded	❑ Idealistic	❑ Sedentary

- ❏ Businesslike
- ❏ Calm
- ❏ Candid
- ❏ Capable
- ❏ Caring
- ❏ Cautious
- ❏ Charitable
- ❏ Cheerful
- ❏ Clean
- ❏ Clear
- ❏ Competent
- ❏ Competitive
- ❏ Congenial
- ❏ Conscientious
- ❏ Conservative
- ❏ Considerate
- ❏ Consistent
- ❏ Conventional
- ❏ Cooperative
- ❏ Courageous
- ❏ Creative
- ❏ Critical
- ❏ Curious
- ❏ Daring
- ❏ Decisive
- ❏ Deliberate
- ❏ Delicate
- ❏ Democratic
- ❏ Dependable
- ❏ Detail-oriented
- ❏ Diligent
- ❏ Discreet
- ❏ Distinctive
- ❏ Dominant
- ❏ Dynamic
- ❏ Eager
- ❏ Easygoing
- ❏ Effective
- ❏ Efficient
- ❏ Eloquent
- ❏ Emotional
- ❏ Empathetic

- ❏ Imaginative
- ❏ Impersonal
- ❏ Independent
- ❏ Individualistic
- ❏ Industrious
- ❏ Informal
- ❏ Initiator
- ❏ Innovative
- ❏ Intellectual
- ❏ Intelligent
- ❏ Introverted
- ❏ Intuitive
- ❏ Inventive
- ❏ Jovial
- ❏ Judicious
- ❏ Just
- ❏ Kind
- ❏ Liberal
- ❏ Likable
- ❏ Literary
- ❏ Logical
- ❏ Loyal
- ❏ Mature
- ❏ Methodical
- ❏ Meticulous
- ❏ Mistrustful
- ❏ Modest
- ❏ Motivated
- ❏ Nurturing
- ❏ Objective
- ❏ Observant
- ❏ Open-minded
- ❏ Opportunistic
- ❏ Optimistic
- ❏ Orderly
- ❏ Organized
- ❏ Original
- ❏ Outgoing
- ❏ Patient
- ❏ Peaceable
- ❏ Perceptive
- ❏ Persistent

- ❏ Self-confident
- ❏ Self-controlled
- ❏ Self-disciplined
- ❏ Self-starter
- ❏ Sensible
- ❏ Sensitive
- ❏ Serious
- ❏ Sincere
- ❏ Sociable
- ❏ Sophisticated
- ❏ Stable
- ❏ Strong
- ❏ Strong-minded
- ❏ Structured
- ❏ Subjective
- ❏ Successful
- ❏ Tactful
- ❏ Talented
- ❏ Tenacious
- ❏ Thorough
- ❏ Thoughtful
- ❏ Tolerant
- ❏ Trusting
- ❏ Trustworthy
- ❏ Truthful
- ❏ Understanding
- ❏ Unexcitable
- ❏ Uninhibited
- ❏ Verbal
- ❏ Versatile
- ❏ Vigorous
- ❏ Warm
- ❏ Wholesome
- ❏ Wise

Reflection

Examine the list of personality descriptors that you have checked off. Carefully consider each. How well does each adjective describe you? Choose 3–5 adjectives that you find most important.

1. Why do these words describe you? Provide examples from your experience that illustrate how each word describes you.
2. Think back to your childhood dreams. Do you remember talking to friends and family about what you wanted to "be" when you "grew up"? Write about your memories. What careers did you select as a child? Why?
3. Do you still have the same career-related dreams? How have your views changed?
4. Consider your personality traits listed in question 1. How do these traits compare with those needed for the career of your childhood dreams? How do they fit with your revised, adult view?

A more precise way to use what you know about yourself to help you choose a major is to identify your Holland personality style. Your personality determines the work environment that you'll find most appealing. Holland (1959) proposed that people's personalities and their matching work environments can be loosely categorized into six groups. Which of the following personality types suits you best? After completing Exercise 2.2 you may find that your personality is a combination of several types.

EXERCISE 2.2

Identify Your Holland Personality Type (Holland, 1959)

Realistic	Investigative
❑ I am mechanically inclined.	❑ I like learning, observing, problem solving, and working with information.
❑ I am athletically inclined.	
❑ I like working outside with tools, plants, or animals.	❑ I like solving abstract, vague problems.
❑ I like creating things with my hands.	❑ I am curious.
❑ I am practical.	❑ I am logical.
❑ I like to see direct results of my work.	❑ I am reserved.
	❑ I am introspective.
	❑ I am independent.
❑ I am a nature lover.	❑ I am observant.
❑ I am systematic.	❑ I am interested in understanding the physical world.

Realistic

❏ I am persistent.

❏ I am calm and reserved.

❏ I am independent.

❏ I dislike vagueness and ambiguity.

Investigative

❏ I like working alone or in small groups.

❏ I like to be original and creative in solving problems.

❏ I enjoy intellectual challenges.

Artistic

❏ I am imaginative and creative.

❏ I like to express myself by designing and producing.

❏ I prefer unstructured activities.

❏ I am spontaneous.

❏ I am idealistic.

❏ I am unique.

❏ I am independent.

❏ I am expressive.

❏ I am unconventional.

❏ I am compassionate.

❏ I am bold.

❏ I prefer to work alone.

Social

❏ I am compassionate.

❏ I like helping and training others.

❏ I am patient.

❏ I am dependable.

❏ I am supportive.

❏ I am understanding.

❏ I am perceptive.

❏ I am generous.

❏ I am idealistic.

❏ I am cheerful, well liked.

❏ I am people-oriented and friendly.

❏ I am concerned with the welfare of others.

❏ I am good at expressing myself and getting along well with others.

Enterprising

❏ I like to work with people.

❏ I like persuading people.

❏ I like managing situations.

❏ I like achieving organizational or economic goals.

❏ I am a leader.

❏ I am talkative.

❏ I am extroverted.

❏ I am optimistic.

❏ I am spontaneous and daring.

❏ I am assertive.

Conventional

❏ I am good with numbers.

❏ I like to work with data and carry out tasks in detail.

❏ I am persistent.

❏ I am practical.

❏ I am conforming.

❏ I am precise.

❏ I am conscientious.

❏ I am meticulous.

❏ I am adept.

❏ I am practical.

Enterprising	Conventional
❏ I am energetic.	❏ I am frugal.
❏ I am good at communicating.	❏ I am stable and dependable.
❏ I am good at selling and persuading.	❏ I am well controlled.
❏ I prefer tasks that require quick action.	❏ I prefer tasks that are structured.
	❏ I prefer to know what's expected.
	❏ I prefer a well defined chain of command.

Count your checkmarks to determine which Holland descriptions match your personality characteristics. Most students find that two or more descriptions of personality characteristics fit them.

After considering Holland's personality descriptions, you probably have a good idea of your interests. For a more formal assessment, consider taking the Self-Directed Search (Holland, 1994), a self-report questionnaire that assesses your personality type according to Holland's theory. Check with the career development office at your university to learn more about it; there's even an online version, which you can take for a fee at http://www.self-directed-search.com. Understanding your personality type may make it easier to choose a major because some majors are better suited to particular personalities than are others. Table 2.1 lists college majors, organized by Holland personality type. Remember that this is simply a guide to careers. Not all possible careers are listed, and the categories are much more fluid than they appear.

Notice that many college majors appear within more than one category. Use this exercise as a general guide; however, recognize that the characteristics for success in various college majors often overlap to some degree.

Assess Your Skills, Interests, and Values   In addition to understanding your personality, your choice of major should reflect your skills and abilities. What are your skills? What activities do you do best? If you're unsure, try writing an experiential diary to get a better grip on your skills. An experiential diary lists all the jobs, leadership positions, and extracurricular activities that you've engaged in, and then lists all the tasks comprising each of these activities and jobs (DeGalan & Lambert, 1995). Once you've created a master list, write down all of the skills required to perform the tasks on your list. For example, if the task was answering the phone, it probably entailed the following skills: communication skills (the effective use of language), problem solving, and the ability to direct inquiries. Also identify specific skills that you've

TABLE 2.1 HOLLAND PERSONALITY TYPES AND COLLEGE MAJORS

Realistic	Investigative	Artistic
Agriculture/Forestry	Animal Science	Advertising
Criminal Justice	Anthropology	Art History
Engineering	Astronomy	Art Education
Health and Physical Education	Biochemistry	Architecture
Plant and Soil Sciences	Biological Sciences	Communications
Architecture	Chemistry	English
Recreation and Tourism Management	Computer Science	Foreign Language
Environmental Studies	Engineering	Graphic Design
Geology	Geography	History
Medical Technology	Geology	Interior Design
Exercise Science	Mathematics	Journalism
Sports Management	Medical Technology	Music
Engineering	Medicine	Music Education
	Nursing	Speech/Drama
	Nutrition	
	Pharmacy	
	Philosophy	
	Physical Therapy	
	Physics	
	Psychology	
	Sociology	
	Statistics	

Social	Enterprising	Conventional
Audiology	Advertising	Accounting
Counseling	Broadcasting	Business
Criminal Justice	Communications	Computer Science
Elementary Education	Economics	Economics
History	Finance	Finance
Human Development	Industrial Relations	Mathematics
Library Sciences	Journalism	Statistics
Occupational Therapy	Law	
Nursing	Management	
Nutrition	Marketing	

(Continued)

TABLE 2.1	HOLLAND PERSONALITY TYPES AND COLLEGE MAJORS (CONTINUED)	
Social	**Enterprising**	**Conventional**
Philosophy	Political Science	
Political Science	Public Administration	
Physical Education	Speech	
Psychology		
Religious Studies		
Sociology		
Social Work		
Special Education		
Urban Planning		

Source: Adapted from Lock, 1988; University of Tennessee, n.d.

learned, like the ability to use computer programming languages or speak a foreign language. Even with an experiential diary, it is sometimes difficult to list and remember all of your skills and abilities. Exercise 2.3 will help you to better understand your skills.

EXERCISE 2.3
Assess Your Skills

Check all of the skills that apply to you, then complete the activity that follows.

- ❑ Acting or performing
- ❑ Administering
- ❑ Advising
- ❑ Analyzing Data
- ❑ Applying
- ❑ Arranging social functions
- ❑ Budgeting
- ❑ Calculating
- ❑ Checking for accuracy
- ❑ Coaching
- ❑ Collecting money
- ❑ Communicating
- ❑ Compiling statistics
- ❑ Conceptualizing
- ❑ Controlling

- ❑ Coordinating events
- ❑ Counseling
- ❑ Creating new ideas
- ❑ Decision making
- ❑ Designing
- ❑ Dispensing information
- ❑ Dramatizing ideas or problems
- ❑ Editing
- ❑ Entertaining people
- ❑ Evaluating
- ❑ Expressing feelings
- ❑ Finding information
- ❑ Fund raising
- ❑ Generalizing
- ❑ Goal setting

❑ Handling complaints
❑ Identifying problems
❑ Illustrating
❑ Implementing
❑ Improving
❑ Initiating with strangers
❑ Innovating
❑ Interpreting
❑ Interviewing
❑ Investigating problems
❑ Judging
❑ Leading
❑ Listening to others
❑ Managing
❑ Measuring
❑ Mediating
❑ Motivating
❑ Navigating
❑ Negotiating
❑ Observing
❑ Organizing
❑ Painting
❑ Persuading
❑ Photographing
❑ Planning
❑ Problem solving

❑ Programming
❑ Promoting
❑ Proofreading
❑ Questioning
❑ Reading
❑ Reasoning
❑ Recording
❑ Record keeping
❑ Recruiting
❑ Researching
❑ Scheduling
❑ Selling
❑ Singing
❑ Sketching
❑ Speaking
❑ Supervising
❑ Synthesizing information
❑ Teaching or training
❑ Team building
❑ Thinking logically
❑ Tolerating ambiguity
❑ Translating
❑ Troubleshooting
❑ Visualizing
❑ Writing

Reflection

1. What skills did you check?
2. Can you think of examples of how each skill has developed or how you've used it to achieve a goal?
3. Based on your consideration, choose the top 3–5 skills and explain your choices. These skills are your strengths.
4. Now look at all of the skills that you checked, including those for which you found it difficult to think of supporting examples.
   a. Do any of these skills need further development?
   b. Which of these skills do you prefer using? Why?
   c. Which are you interested in using in the future? Why?
   d. Which skills do you dislike? Why?
5. Are there any skills that you don't currently have, but would like to develop? Explain.

By now you realize that you already have an array of skills. Are you interested in using and pursing those skills? We tend to like and be interested in things that we are good at. Is that true for you? You may not have skills in a particular area, but if you find it interesting, you can seek the education and training to develop the necessary skills. Don't let your current competence levels dictate your choices. If you are willing to work, you can make great strides and meet many career goals.

The question that you must answer is: What interests you? The happiest and most successful students choose majors that they find engaging. Many students decide on a major before considering their interests and values. They take courses for a semester or two and then realize that they've chosen a major in which they have minimal interest. Identifying your interests early in your college career can save you from changing majors and wasting time. What appeals to you?

An effective way of assessing your interests is to write about your personal history.

1. In your journal, on scrap paper, or on a word processor, write about all of the times that you can think of when you have encountered a problem (regardless of its size) and have taken action to solve that problem. In other words, write about all of your accomplishments.

2. List as many as you can. Don't stop when it becomes difficult, but probe further. If you're stumped, try free writing about your achievements. Free writing entails writing whatever comes to mind, without censoring or editing it. Keep the ideas flowing, or even write about the difficulty you're experiencing in coming up with ideas. Eventually you'll produce a number of interesting items to reflect on.

3. The accomplishments that you list need not be monumental. Accomplishments can be small, and they don't have to be recognized by other people. Write about the achievements that are personally relevant to you and that you are proud of.

4. Next examine your accomplishments carefully. Which have brought you the most satisfaction? Which do you value most highly? Why?

This exercise helps you to identify your strengths and is a fantastic self-esteem builder because it illustrates your accomplishments—the things that make you special. By understanding which achievements you cherish, you'll have a better idea of your interests and values, which is essential to choosing a major or career.

While choosing a major does not tie you to a particular career, it is useful to consider what career you aspire to in order to choose a major and seek the educational experiences that will prepare you for it. What do you want out of life? How do you define success? Would you rather live in a city or in a rural area? Is personal time and flexibility important to you? Would you like a family (and if so, large or small)? Is financial success important? Values are the things that are important to you, that you see as desirable in life. Spend time thinking through your priorities. Journal writing can help you to understand and clarify your values. Consider the following collection of values, categorized by theme.

EXERCISE 2.4
Values

Service	Adventure	Leadership
❑ Active in community	❑ Excitement	❑ Influence people and opinions
❑ Help others	❑ Risk taking	❑ Supervise others
❑ Help society and the world	❑ Travel	❑ Power authority and control
❑ Work with and help people in meaningful way	❑ Drama	❑ Make decisions
	❑ Exciting tasks	❑ Direct work of others
	❑ Good health	❑ Leadership
		❑ Coordinate people, data, and stuff
		❑ Hiring and firing responsibility

Creativity	Relationships	Financial Reward
❑ Aesthetic appreciation	❑ Organization affiliation	❑ High earnings
❑ Artistic creativity	❑ Work friendships	❑ Commission-based work
❑ Creative expression	❑ Family	❑ Material possessions
❑ Develop and express new ideas	❑ Work with others—teamwork	❑ Very high salary
❑ No routine	❑ Public contact	❑ Extra pay for extra work
❑ Work on own or as creative team	❑ Friendly work atmosphere	❑ Long hours
❑ Flexible working conditions	❑ Work with people you like	❑ Changing work responsibilities
❑ Recognition	❑ Spirituality	❑ Diversity of tasks
❑ Status	❑ Personal fulfillment	❑ New projects

Prestige	Meaning and Purpose	Variety
❑ Respect / stature	❑ Work related to ideals	❑ Varied tasks
❑ Professional position	❑ Make a difference	❑ Meet new people
❑ Responsibility	❑ Express inner self in work	❑ Range of settings and situations
❑ Responsibility and pay are related to education and experience	❑ Integrate belief system into work	

Security	Independence	Physical Activity
❑ Stability	❑ Time freedom	❑ Outdoor work
❑ Predictability	❑ Autonomy	❑ Physical challenge
❑ Low pressure	❑ Set own pace and working conditions, flexible hours	❑ Physical fitness
❑ Job assurance		❑ No desk job
❑ Guaranteed annual salary in secure, stable company	❑ Choose team or work alone	
❑ Retirement benefits		
❑ Live in familiar location		

Intellectual Challenge	Productivity	Advancement
❑ Address challenging problems	❑ Competent and proficient	❑ Promotions
❑ Pursue/obtain knowledge	❑ Fast paced work	❑ Work under pressure
❑ Constant updating of information and ability to deal with new ideas	❑ Efficient work habits	❑ Competition
❑ Work with creative and intellectually stimulating people	❑ Hard work is rewarded	❑ Limited only by energy and initiative
❑ Acknowledged expert	❑ Quality and productivity rewarded by rapid advancement	
❑ Research and development		

1. What values did you check? Do your selected values cluster into a few areas?
2. How have these values influenced your choices and behaviors? Consider your extracurricular activities and interests.
3. How might these values inform your career choices?

Source: Adapted from Anderson, 2006

Put It Together   Now that you're aware of your personality traits, skills, interests, and values, compile this information to get a comprehensive view of yourself. Review the lists and descriptions of majors in your college handbook. Do any seem to fit your set of traits, skills, and interests? Some majors and careers will match many of the personal traits and skills that you possess, and others will not match your self-description (DeGalan & Lambert, 1995). In your journal, list all of the majors that sound interesting and seem to fit. Examine the course entailed in each. Study your college handbook and the department Web site to find information about the programs and opportunities for majors after graduation.

Once you have narrowed down your choice of majors to two (or even three), compare them with regard to the following:

1. Your level of interest
2. Curriculum (What kinds of classes are you required to take?)
3. Your skills and abilities (Is the major too easy or too challenging for you?)
4. Professors
5. Motivation to study the subject
6. Kinds of jobs that graduates hold (Is it likely that the major will prepare you for the kind of career you desire?)

In short, consider the pros and cons of each major.

Finally, once you have chosen a possible major, again reflect on your choice. Free write about the following questions to be sure that you've made the right choice for you.

1. Do I enjoy this subject?
2. Can I perform well in this subject?
3. Do I tend to seek out other students and faculty in this department for discussions and other informal interactions?
4. How will this major prepare me for graduate study or employment?

CHOOSING PSYCHOLOGY

If you choose to major in psychology, you will develop and expand your knowledge of human behavior. You'll become increasingly able to discriminate relevant from trivial information. You'll learn how to find and pull together (or

TABLE 2.2	REMINDERS FOR CHOOSING A MAJOR

❏ Assess your personality and attitudinal traits

❏ Assess your skills and abilities

❏ Assess your values and life goals

❏ Research majors

❏ Explore courses

❏ Talk with other students and recent graduates

❏ Visit the career center

❏ Talk with professors

❏ Compare alternatives

❏ Reflect on your choice

❏ Remember that your major is not your career

synthesize, in "professor-speak") information from a variety of sources. You'll learn about psychological theories, concepts, and terms that will help you to understand and influence the world around you. If you study and take college seriously, you'll develop advanced critical thinking, communication, and interpersonal skills, which are valuable to all careers, regardless of whether they are directly related to psychology.

What, specifically, can you expect as a psychology major? As a psychology major you can expect to complete a range of courses required by the university, often referred to as General Education requirements because they're intended to provide you with a broad education covering many subjects that are essential to a well rounded and capable thinker. Whereas the General Education curriculum provides breadth of knowledge, your major is intended to provide depth of knowledge in a specific area. As a psychology major you can expect to learn about human behavior and the methods that psychologists use to study human behavior. Specific requirements may vary by university; however, you can expect to complete the following:

Introductory Psychology/General Psychology   Your first course in psychology will provide a whirlwind tour of the field and its dizzying array of subfields. Some students find Introductory Psychology challenging, overwhelming, or even boring because it is often a fast paced experience intended to provide an overview of the entire field—all of the subdisciplines mentioned in Chapter 1—within a single semester. Every chapter in the textbook and every week in the course introduces a new subfield, and it is likely that the

Psychology Department at your college offers at least one course in each of those fields. Some students are put off by the fast pace—once they become interested in a topic, it's time to move on to the next chapter and the next sub-field. Perhaps the most helpful way to consider the Introductory Psychology class is as a primer to the field and a way to learn more about what areas you may want to pursue in the future.

Methodology and Statistics   It is the methodology courses that will teach you how psychologists learn about human behavior—the methods we use to make discoveries. Schools vary in their methodology and statistics require-ment. Students learn the research methods that psychologists use to ask and answer questions about human behavior. They also learn statistics and the methods psychologists use to compile and draw conclusions from the informa-tion they collect. Finally, students gain experience in designing and carrying out research studies that give them practice in asking and answering questions about human behavior.

Breadth Courses   Just as the college General Education curriculum is designed to provide students with a broad knowledge base for a well rounded education, the Psychology breadth requirement imparts psychology majors with a well rounded education in human behavior. The particular sets of courses vary across schools, but all will require you to enroll in courses in the Developmental, Cognitive, Biological, and Social/Personality subfields. Others may include required courses in Clinical or Applied areas. Common courses offered by Psychology departments are listed in Table 2.3.

Elective Courses   You can expect to take several elective courses in your major—courses that are not required but are your choice. These courses are opportunities to explore your interests or gain knowledge and skills that you think will be helpful in the future.

Capstone Course   The capstone course is intended to be the pinnacle of your education in psychology. It is an advanced course that is intended to help you tie it all together—bring together your knowledge about how to study psychology, how to ask questions, devise methods of addressing questions, and draw conclusions. You might conduct an independent research study or write a lengthy review paper or senior thesis. Talk to your professors to learn more about the capstone requirement and get advice so that you can plan ahead and take the courses that you believe will best prepare you for this experience.

Is psychology right for you? Only you can answer that question. Psychology offers many opportunities, but other majors offer different sets of

TABLE 2.3   COMMON PSYCHOLOGY COURSES

Applied Psychology	History, Methods, and Statistics
Family Psychology	Research Methods
Health Psychology	Experimental Psychology
Industrial Psychology	Psychological Statistics
Organizational Psychology	History of Psychology
Psychology and Law	**Learning and Cognitive Psychology**
Sports Psychology	Psychology of Learning
Consumer Psychology	Psychology of Creativity
Biological and Neuropsychology	Educational Psychology
Physiological Psychology	Behavior Modification
Sensation and Perception	Cognitive Psychology
Psychopharmacology	Cognitive Neuroscience
Clinical Psychology	**Personality, Social Processes, and Measurement**
Clinical Psychology	Group Dynamics
Abnormal Psychology	Social Psychology
School Psychology	Psychology of Motivation
Developmental Psychology	Psychology of Personality
Adolescent Psychology	Psychological and Educational Testing
Adulthood and Aging	Psychology of Adjustment
Life-Span Development	Psychology of Gender
Developmental Psychopathology	Psychology of Women
Child Psychology	Cross-Cultural Psychology

The above courses may be grouped in several ways, depending on department. Some psychology courses are required for majors at nearly all schools, while others are electives found at only a handful of schools.

opportunities. You are the only expert in choosing your major. No one else can do it for you, and no test provides all of the answers. While parents, friends, professors, and counselors might offer assistance and advice, ultimately this is your decision. Your major will not lock you into one career path—there are many roads, and a psychology major can be the first step toward a variety of careers.

SUGGESTED READINGS

Andrews, L. L. (2006). *How to choose a college major.* New York: McGraw Hill.

Johnston, S. M. (2005). *The career adventure: Your guide to personal assessment, career exploration, and decision making.* Upper Saddle River, NJ: Prentice Hall.

Kuther, T. L., & Morgan, R. D. (2010). *Careers in Psychology: Opportunities in a changing world.* Belmont, CA: Wadsworth.

Lock, R. D. (2005). *Taking charge of your career direction: Career planning guide.* Belmont, CA: Wadsworth.

Lore, N. (2008). *Now what? The young person's guide to choosing the perfect career.* New York: Fireside.

INTERNET RESOURCES

Career Assessment

http://www.quintcareers.com/career_assessment.html

This is an excellent and comprehensive site with articles, tools, and other resources for assessing your career interests.

Self-Directed Search

http://www.self-directed-search.com

Available for a fee, this self-report questionnaire assesses your personality type, according to Holland's theory.

About Web Logs

http://weblogs.about.com/

As we discussed, your journal can take the form of a web log. This Web site provides articles, tips, prompts, and resources for beginning and experienced web log writers.

Career Key

http://www.careerkey.org/english/

The Career Key is a free Web site with assessments to help you with career choices, career changes, and career planning, job search, and choosing a college major or training program.

JOURNAL EXERCISES

My Questions

This exercise helps you to identify unanswered questions and gives you prompts for future journal entries. Use your journal to formulate and record questions that you wonder about. What questions do you have about your schoolwork, personal life, values, or current events and items that you've read about in newspapers, magazines, or books? As a college student, what do you need to know? Don't worry about the answers yet; just let your questions flow and create a list of questions to which you seek answers. Later on, weeks, months, or even years from now, when you're looking for something new to write about, look over your list. If any of the questions strike you as compelling, begin formulating an answer in your journal.

Journal Reflection

Once you've amassed several weeks' or months' worth of journal entries, you might use your journal to reflect on how you're changing. Read over earlier journal entries. How have you changed? Do you have different ideas about the journal entry? Do you have new interpretations of events? Do you disagree with an earlier entry? Try to understand how you think and track how your thinking is changing. Can you draw conclusions about yourself from what you've written?

Life's Pleasures

What makes you happy? Record your favorite things and activities. What are you grateful for? This isn't just a corny exercise. Writing about the good things in your life is a form of celebration that makes you a happier person. Stop and feel the moment. Find something beautiful in your immediate surroundings. Record all of your senses. What does it look like? Listen to it. Can you smell it? What does it feel like?

Why College?

Why did you decide to attend college? What did you hope to gain? What have you learned since beginning college? Do you still have the same reasons for attending?

TAKE AN ACTIVE ROLE IN YOUR EDUCATION

CHAPTER OUTLINE

One of the biggest differences between high school and college is that college requires you to take an active role in your education. Whether you take anything of substance away from your college years—whether you learn anything—is up to you. Your own interest, motivation, and hard work will make or break your college years. Students often are surprised by this new level of autonomy and they often are unsure of how to take control of their education. This chapter will help you to take advantage of the resources in your department, college, and field so that you can get the most from your college years.

GET AN ADVISOR AND MENTOR

Many students don't take advantage of their school's most valuable resource: the faculty. Sure, they attend class, take notes, and learn the content of their discipline, but learning occurs in many places beyond the classroom. When students take an active role in their education, they soon realize that there is much to learn from professors, learning that can extend beyond mere content knowledge. Perhaps one of the most important pieces of advice in this book is to get to know your professors. Establish relationships with faculty.

Faculty help your professional development in more ways than lecturing, overseeing class discussions, and bestowing grades. Professors can also help you to enrich your college years through a variety of learning experiences outside the classroom. For example, professors can involve students in their research, providing opportunities to assist them in making new discoveries and generating new knowledge. Faculty aid students' professional development in other ways too, such as by introducing students to others who can help them to meet their goals (e.g., a professor in a graduate department to which you might apply). Professors also can help their students obtain special opportunities such as internships, summer positions, and teaching assistantships. Finally, job and graduate applications often require several letters of recommendation from faculty. Recommendation letters discuss more than just grades; they discuss students' abilities and aptitudes from academic, motivational, and personal perspectives. Of course, persuasive recommendation letters should not be your only reason for developing relationships with faculty members, but helpful letters are an important motivator and reward.

If you would like to develop out-of-classroom professional relationships with faculty, note that professors want to work with students who are bright, motivated, committed, and enthusiastic. Your behavior both in and out of class can attract or deter a professor from developing a professional relationship with you. Do you display behaviors that faculty appreciate? Take Quiz 3.1 to assess your knowledge about appropriate in-class and out-of-class behavior.

Also examine Checklist 3.1 for a list of behaviors that professors clearly do not want to see in class. Some of the items may appear humorous, but (believe it or not) they are regularly seen in class.

Quiz 3.1
Do You Display Appropriate In- and Out-of-Class Behavior?

Circle Yes or No for the following items. Be honest!

1. Yes No I attend presentations and activities sponsored by the department, such as Psi Chi or the psychology club.
2. Yes No During class, I often send e-mail or text.
3. Yes No I smile and say hello when I see professors.
4. Yes No I take more than one make-up exam.
5. Yes No I stop by during professors' office hours to discuss something from class that sparked an interest or to seek assistance with class material.
6. Yes No I let my phone ring during class.
7. Yes No I help other students by sharing lecture notes and forming study groups.
8. Yes No I often leave class early without apparent reason.
9. Yes No I sit towards the front of class.
10. Yes No I often hand in assignments late.
11. Yes No I rarely miss class.
12. Yes No When the professor asks, "Are there any questions?" I often ask "Is this going to be on the test?"
13. Yes No When my professor gives a particularly interesting lecture, I often offer a compliment and ask additional questions afterward.
14. Yes No After each exam I often nitpick over test questions, trying to get additional points.
15. Yes No I turn off my cell phone or turn the sound off and don't answer it in class.
16. Yes No I often read other books or newspapers in class.
17. Yes No I prepare before class.
18. Yes No I often leave class at break.
19. Yes No After missing class or arriving late, I often e-mail my professor with a request to e-mail the lecture or an explanation of what I missed.
20. Yes No I talk with my friends and catch up on gossip during class.
21. Yes No I participate in class, but try not to dominate class discussions (i.e., I let others speak too).
22. Yes No I often interrupt my professor's lecture with, "But you said. . ."
23. Yes No I try to show interest in the course and remain attentive during class.
24. Yes No I often arrive late to class.
25. Yes No I try to ask well-reasoned and well-formulated questions during class.

Scoring:
Add up the number of times you responded "yes" to odd items and "no" to even items. The higher your score, the greater number of appropriate behaviors you display and the more likely that professors view you favorably.

Reflection:
1. Given your score, how favorably are professors likely to view you? Why?
2. How might your in- and out-of-class behavior influence your ability to develop professional relationships with faculty?
3. How can you improve your in- and out-of-class behavior? Discuss at least three ways in which you can improve your behavior.

CHECKLIST 3.1

What Not to Do: Behaviors That Most Faculty Abhor

- ❑ Pass notes in class
- ❑ Chat in class
- ❑ Pack up books and notes before class is over
- ❑ Ask, "How many cuts are allowed?"
- ❑ Do homework in class
- ❑ Say, "I missed last class, did I miss anything important?"
- ❑ Near the end of class, close your books firmly and jingle you car keys to help remind your professor that time is just about up
- ❑ Attempt to make term papers look longer by adding blank pages after the front and back pages, using large fonts and huge margins
- ❑ Sit in the back of class when there are empty seats in the front
- ❑ Visit a professor's office for the first time at the end of the semester, after receiving a poor mark, to ask for extra credit
- ❑ Roll your eyes at the professor's lame jokes
- ❑ Be more interested in grades than learning
- ❑ Sleep in class
- ❑ Sneer when you don't agree
- ❑ Read a book in class
- ❑ Text during class
- ❑ Balance your checkbook in class
- ❑ After an hour-long presentation on a topic not included in the required reading, ask, "Is this going to be on the test?"
- ❑ Keep your phone at high volume and let it ring during class
- ❑ Get up and leave during the middle of class
- ❑ Repeatedly interrupt your professor
- ❑ Take more than one make-up exam
- ❑ Hand in assignments late without explanation
- ❑ Miss classes repeatedly
- ❑ Arrive late to class repeatedly
- ❑ After missing class or arriving late, ask the professor to go over what you missed
- ❑ Repeatedly dominate office time with personal needs and problems
- ❑ Nitpick over test questions after each exam

Source: Adapted from Keith-Spiegel & Wiederman, 2000.

Your Academic Advisor

When students select a major, they are assigned an academic advisor. An academic advisor is a faculty member whose role is to help you select courses and other learning opportunities to provide you with a well-rounded education and prepare you for your chosen career. Your advisor may assist you with academic advising, which focuses on issues such as course scheduling and availability, meeting prerequisites, fostering academic success, and graduation requirements. He or she may also assist you with career advising, which emphasizes your short- and long-term career goals and will occur during multiple discussions over your years in college. The advisor–student relationship is a two-way street; you should come prepared to discuss your interests, needs, and goals. Your advisor may have as many as sixty other students to advise, so use your scheduled time with him or her wisely. Help your advisor to help you by following the tips in Checklist 3.2.

CHECKLIST 3.2
Advising Checklist

❑ Know who your advisor is
  Advisor name: _____
  Location: _____
  Phone number: _____
  E-mail: _____
  Office hours: _____
❑ Schedule an appointment at least one week prior to your registration date.
❑ Study the university handbook to determine what courses are required of your major.
❑ Write down questions as they arise.
❑ List the courses that you have taken. Most departments have a worksheet for majors to complete that lists all general education and major requirements. Complete this sheet and keep an up-to-date copy filed away someplace safe.
❑ Examine the registration booklet to choose potential courses.
❑ Prepare a tentative schedule with several course alternatives.
❑ Be prepared to explain how the courses you have selected fulfill the curricular requirements of your major.
❑ Consider your ultimate career goals and write down any questions that you have about your plans for after graduation.
❑ Actively discuss your career goals with your advisor and seek advice as to how to plan to meet them.

Your academic advisor likely is quite busy, but he or she has time for you. Consult with your advisor when you are having academic difficulties, or considering adding or dropping a course, changing your major, withdrawing from school, or transferring to another college. Stop by during office hours to seek information on class registration, but if your questions are of a serious nature, such as whether to change your major, schedule an appointment so that you have the time to openly discuss your concerns. Your advisor has your best interests in mind and will provide you with the advice that you need to make sound decisions. When making big decisions such as whether to change your major, drop out of school, or go to graduate school, your advisor may suggest that you seek additional input and feedback from other sources such as other faculty, family, friends, and the counseling center. Your academic advisor is an important source of feedback and advice; take advantage of this resource. But always remember that your academic and career decisions are your own. Seek advice and assistance in order to make informed decisions, but accept ultimate responsibility for the decisions that you make.

Seek a Mentor

Seek to develop a special relationship with a faculty mentor. A mentor is a person with expertise who takes a special interest in you; he or she may be a college professor; advisor; or job, research, or practicum supervisor. Mentors provide their protégés with opportunities to learn, be advised, and obtain moral support (Keith-Spiegel & Wiederman, 2000). Seek a faculty mentor, and you'll have opportunities for intellectual engagement that will enhance your college career. Note that mentors are more than academic advisors; your academic advisor may or may not also become your mentor. A mentor facilitates your undergraduate accomplishments, provides intellectual and emotional support, and helps you on the path toward your career.

How Do You Find a Mentor?   Students who are motivated and visible in their departments and who seek to get involved in faculty research will usually find it easier to meet professors who are interested in developing professional working relationships. Seek opportunities and approach professors. It may seem scary and require initiative, but the rewards are immense. Tell professors that you're looking to become involved in research. Explain that you hope to work closely with someone on their research and ask questions about their work. Demonstrate honest intellectual curiosity and motivation. If you are perceived well, word will get around that you're an excellent student looking for research experience. Remember that classroom behavior is an important indicator of a student's maturity and motivation that influences professors' views of students.

If you do well in your courses and present yourself as competent, motivated, wanting to get involved, and committed, you may even be approached by a faculty member who wants to mentor you. Students with excellent literature searching, critical analysis, and writing abilities are helpful assistants. Students with expertise and interest in research and statistical analysis are often especially appealing to faculty because they require less instruction—and therefore can become deeply immersed in research at a faster pace.

As you look for a mentor, remember that the most popular professors may have more students coming to them than they can mentor. Working closely with a student in a mentoring relationship entails a great deal of time, attention, and intellectual focus; faculty can mentor only so many students at once. Some faculty may not be able to take on additional students. Remember that popularity—whether a particular professor is liked by the majority of students—should not be your main criterion for selecting a mentor. Look to faculty who are actively involved in research and whose interests parallel yours as closely as possible. Visit during office hours to ask a question or two about graduate school or your career interests; get a feel for the professor's approachability. If he or she seems interested in discussing these questions, express your desire to gain some experience in research. In the vast majority of cases, there is no pay involved for assisting professors with their research. Instead, you'll get a free learning experience that will improve your skills and abilities as well as make you more appealing to graduate schools and employers. Sometimes you may earn course credit for your work. Finally, volunteer to work closely with a professor only if you have the time to commit. Remember that falling behind or dropping out will reflect negatively on you—more so than if you hadn't become involved at all.

What to Look for in a Mentor   The role of a mentor is to provide guidance so that students are aware of resources and opportunities and understand their options. Successful mentoring relationships are not an accident. Mentoring relationships are most successful when students make careful and conscientious efforts to find mentors who possess certain characteristics and who complement their needs. A successful mentoring relationship requires chemistry, the ability to work together.

In order to find a helpful mentor, be aware of your needs and career goals. Where are you now, in terms of skills? Who do you want to become? How must you grow and what skills and experiences must you obtain to do so? A well chosen mentor can help you to find the answers to those questions, while a poorly chosen mentor might leave you hanging, frustrating you with more questions than answers. Some desirable characteristics to look for in mentors are listed in Checklist 3.3. No one person will have all of these characteristics; you must decide which are most important to you and find someone who approximates them.

CHECKLIST 3.3
Choosing an Effective Mentor

Check off the characteristics that match the attributes of faculty members you are considering as mentors.

Effective mentors are interpersonally skilled. They are:
- ☐ Responsive, warm, and encouraging
- ☐ Empathetic and nonjudgmental
- ☐ Helpful in promoting students' positive self-concepts
- ☐ Promoting and sponsoring in that they help to open doors to careers and graduate school opportunities by telling others of the positive aspects of their protégés
- ☐ A source of emotional support
- ☐ Challenging and demanding, motivating students to attempt new tasks that stretch their abilities
- ☐ Unwilling to accept less than optimal performance

Effective mentors have positive personal attributes. They are:
- ☐ Mature and wise
- ☐ Providers of accurate and useful advice
- ☐ Friendly and optimistic in that they appear to enjoy mentoring
- ☐ Positive in their life outlook
- ☐ Admired and respected in that they possess characteristics that students aspire to attain
- ☐ Held in high regard by peers
- ☐ Trustworthy and dependable
- ☐ Ethical and have high moral standards
- ☐ Willing to provide assistance even under difficult circumstances

Effective mentors have attained professional competency. They are:
- ☐ Qualified and competent; they are experienced
- ☐ Willing to provide advice
- ☐ Knowledgeable and informative (with up-to-date information)
- ☐ Able to communicate well
- ☐ Actively involved in professional or academic organizations
- ☐ Involved in research
- ☐ Interested in life-long learning

Source: Adapted from Appleby, 1999.

As you consider potential mentors, ask yourself the following questions, or respond to them in your journal:

- Is the professor in a position to share his or her time and advice?
- Does he or she have a reputation for producing high-quality and timely research?

- Is the professor interested in mentoring you?
- Are you comfortable with the professor's demeanor and personality? Does it fit your academic style and needs?
- From your perspective, does the professor exhibit the ability to communicate openly and clearly?

Choose a mentor who you admire, with whom you can communicate, and whose interpersonal skills and interactional patterns work well with your own.

GET RESEARCH EXPERIENCE

Taking an active role in your education entails looking for opportunities to learn and develop useful skills. Engaging in research promotes a host of abilities and skills that employers and graduate programs seek. Make yourself more competitive by seeking opportunities to assist professors in their research and perhaps even carry out your own research studies under the guidance of a faculty mentor. A research assistantship is an opportunity for undergraduate students to assist a faculty member in his or her program of research. Assisting a faculty member in research is an exciting opportunity to do the research rather than just read about it.

Why Become a Research Assistant?

Research generates new knowledge. When we engage in research, we make new discoveries and learn new things. Sure you read about psychology research, but carrying it out is an altogether different animal that will help you learn more than you have in any class. It's an opportunity to be on the cutting edge of psychology. Aside from the thrill of generating new knowledge, assisting a professor with research provides many other valuable opportunities, such as (Grover 2006; Landrum & Davis, 2010):

- Gaining skills and knowledge that aren't easily attained in the classroom working one-on-one with a faculty member
- Exposure to methodological techniques that will be helpful in completing your senior thesis or, perhaps, graduate work
- Practicing written and oral communication skills by learning how to express research findings and preparing papers for submission to, and presenting at, professional conferences and journals
- Developing a mentoring relationship with a faculty member
- Obtaining experiences that will enhance your applications to employers and graduate programs
- Acquiring outstanding letters of recommendation, as faculty who work closely with you can write more detailed letters that fully demonstrate your capacities and strengths

Engaging in research is a worthwhile experience for all students because it provides opportunities to learn how to think, organize information, and solve problems, as well as demonstrates commitment to a project—all skills coveted by employers and graduate admissions committees (Sleigh & Ritzer, 2007). In fact, graduate school admissions committees rate research experience as a "very important" factor in the admissions process and more important than GPA (Keith-Spiegel & Wiederman, 2000; Mayne, et al., 1994; Walfish & Turner, 2006).

What Does a Research Assistant Do?

What will be expected of you as a research assistant? We cannot predict the specific tasks that you will be assigned, as a research assistant's tasks will vary by faculty member, project, and area of psychology. Some might be involved in data collection by administering surveys, or maintaining and operating lab equipment. Others might code and enter data, make photocopies, or write literature reviews. The following are some general tasks that research assistants perform (Landrum & Davis, 2010).

- Collect data by administering surveys, interviews, or running research protocols.
- Score, code, and enter data into a spreadsheet or statistical analysis program.
- Conduct library research including literature searches using databases (e.g., PsycINFO, Social Sciences Citation Index, PsycARTICLES), making copies of articles, and ordering unavailable articles and books through interlibrary loan.
- Assist the faculty member to develop new research ideas.
- Use computer skills such as word processing, spreadsheet, scheduling, and statistical analysis programs.
- Assist in preparing submissions for local or regional conferences and, if accepted, work on poster or oral presentations for professional conferences.
- Assist faculty in preparing a manuscript to submit the results of collaborative research to a scientific journal.

Frequently students who work with faculty members as research assistants develop their own ideas for research projects that stem from the faculty's work. For example, one of my students worked with me on several related projects and developed her own hypothesis to extend my work by adding additional variables. She carried out her project under my supervision as her senior thesis, presented it at a regional psychology conference, and together, we published it in a scholarly journal. Research assistantships provide substantial educational and professional development opportunities.

How Do You Become a Research Assistant?

First and foremost, you should perform well in class, and be motivated and visible in your department. Let faculty know that you're interested in getting involved in research, but do not send out a mass e-mail or a form e-mail notifying them of your availability. Instead, approach professors during their office hours and ask for leads on who might be looking for research assistants. Before you approach a professor you would like to work with, learn about his or her work. Read some of the professor's articles, especially the most recent ones. When you find a professor who is looking for an assistant, carefully and honestly describe what you can offer (computer skills, Internet skills, statistical skills) and the number of hours per week you're available. Let the faculty member know that you're willing to work hard (be honest). Ask thoughtful questions, such as those in Table 3.1. Ask questions about the professor's expectations and how you will be evaluated. Professors are often vague in describing their expectations for students during the research assistantship as well as for the products of the collaboration (such as a paper) (Landrum, 2008). Ask. The specific expectations will likely vary from project to project and from student to student, but a student might expect to be evaluated on at least some of the abilities listed in Table 3.2.

It may be tempting to consider turning the professor down because the hours don't fit your schedule or the research isn't interesting enough, but the opportunity to work as a research assistant is a coveted prize that will enhance your academic and professional development in many ways. Don't be hasty in turning down such an important opportunity. You may not work on a project that you find fascinating, but you will obtain excellent experience. Also, research projects often become more interesting once you're immersed in them. Your academic interests most likely will change as you gain more experience and education.

TABLE 3.1	QUESTIONS TO ASK ABOUT A RESEARCH ASSISTANTSHIP

❑ Are the work hours set or is there some flexibility? Might I expect to sometimes work overtime and other times finish early?

❑ What will I do? What are specific kinds of examples?

❑ Will I be evaluated? How?

❑ Will I be asked to submit a paper or other project at the end of this experience?

❑ How long will the project last?

❑ How long is the commitment (full semester, part semester)?

TABLE 3.2   SAMPLE FACULTY EXPECTATIONS FOR RESEARCH ASSISTANTS

Research Methods and Data Analysis
❑ Generate research questions
❑ Determine ways to measure phenomena
❑ Create surveys
❑ Collect data
❑ Enter data into statistical software
❑ Use statistical software to analyze data

Communication Skills
❑ Conduct literature searches
❑ Manuscript preparation
❑ Prepare submission to conferences
❑ Present at conferences
❑ Preparation of tables, graphs

Interpersonal Skills
❑ Leadership
❑ Teamwork
❑ Communication skills
❑ Listening skills
❑ Relationship with faculty member

Self Management
❑ Time management
❑ Meet deadlines
❑ Ethical behavior

Source: Adapted from Landrum, 2008.

Why Do Professors Seek Student Research Assistants?

You're now aware that there are many benefits of getting involved in research. Did you know that there are benefits for faculty too? They get a hard-working student to do some labor-intensive parts of research. Faculty, especially those at undergraduate institutions without graduate programs, often depend on undergraduates to further their research programs (Landrum & Davis, 2010). Many faculty members have ideas for studies that they don't have time to conduct. Motivated students can help them to carry out these studies. If you develop a relationship with a faculty member, you might be able to help him or her conduct a project that may otherwise remain shelved for lack of time.

Involving undergraduates in research also offers the opportunity for faculty to develop a relationship with a student and witness his or her professional growth, which can be quite rewarding. There are other benefits for faculty who involve undergraduates in their research (Davis, 1995). They:

- Remain current by conducting reviews of the current literature in a particular research area
- Keep analytic skills active through the design and completion of research
- Maintain and expand professional networks through attending conventions to present research completed with students
- Bring research into the classroom and enhance teaching effectiveness through active involvement in research

Student–professor research relationships offer benefits to all involved; however, the commitment to become a research assistant is a big one. You will be given responsibility to ensure that aspects of the project get done. The faculty member will count on you to be responsible and complete your assignments correctly. This includes asking questions and seeking assistance if you don't understand the task. Your performance as a research assistant can give a professor many good things to write in a letter of recommendation, including specific examples of your skills, competencies, and personal characteristics. If you complete tasks competently, you might be asked to take on more responsibility, and you will learn more as well as earn a reputation as an excellent student and potential future colleague (and thereby earn excellent letters of recommendation). However, there is a positive payoff from conducting research with faculty only if you consistently perform competent work. If you don't take the commitment seriously, are unreliable, or make repeated mistakes, your relationship with the professor will suffer (as will your standing in the eyes of other faculty because professors often share information about their experiences with students). If you decide to work with a faculty member on his or her research, treat it as a primary responsibility.

EXERCISE 3.1

Seek Out-of-Class Opportunities

Many students want to get involved in research and other psychology-related extracurricular activities. Some opportunities are highly visible, such as participating in the psychology club. Others are much more subtle. Scout out the opportunities available to you in the Psychology Department.

1. Is there a psychology-related student club?
2. Is there a Psi Chi chapter? What are the requirements to join?
3. How many faculty members are in the department? What are their specialties (such as developmental, cognitive, clinical, etc.)?

4. Does the department schedule outside and in-house speakers regularly? Are any scheduled for this semester?

5. Are there any department activities scheduled for this semester?

6. Locate the department Web page. What information is provided about course scheduling? Research opportunities? Grad school prep? Internship and practica opportunities? Tutoring?

7. Do any professors have Web pages? Visit each Web page. Does the professor explain his or her research? Are publications listed? Write a two-sentence summary of his or her area of expertise and research. In what ways is it interesting? Is there anything unappealing? Why?

8. Are there formal classes designed to provide one-on-one interaction with a professor? For example, a guided readings course in which a student and professor jointly choose a collection of readings about a topic or an independent research study in which a student completes a project under the guidance of a faculty member. If so, what are the prerequisites and requirements to enroll? Do all faculty participate? If not, identify faculty who supervise students in one-on-one coursework.

GET APPLIED EXPERIENCE

Taking an active role in your education entails seeking opportunities for personal and professional development. As you consider your own academic and professional development, attempt to gain experiences that will round out your competencies. Research experience is an important contribution to your academic development, but applied experiences, such as working as a teaching assistant or completing field experiences such as internships or practica also build important competencies.

Get Teaching Experience

Although less common than research assistants, teaching assistants have opportunities to learn a variety of skills. Many professors, myself included, observe that teaching a topic helps students to develop a new, more complex understanding of that topic. Explaining material to another person helps you identify gaps in your own knowledge—and prompts learning.

What do undergraduate teaching assistants do? They work with a faculty for one semester, offering assistance with a specific course. They may help an instructor plan discussion questions or in-class group assignments, run discussion or laboratory sessions, or serve as class assistants. More specifically, a teaching assistant might do any of the following, depending on the instructor and institution:

- Attend lectures
- Conduct review sessions for exams

- Facilitate discussions
- Prepare lectures as needed
- Request or acquire necessary equipment
- Hold regular office hours
- Tutor students
- Manage and respond to course-related e-mail
- Update course Web pages
- Participate in electronic bulletin boards and discussion lists
- Grade assignments
- Proctor exams
- Maintain course attendance records
- Attend instructor/TA meetings
- Act as liaison/mediator between student and professor

Not every department and college offers teaching assistantships. Some departments have formal programs with application procedures that entail completing forms, submitting a statement of intent, and soliciting recommendation letters. Others have no formal program, but students informally assist faculty as volunteers. Still others offer teaching assistant opportunities as an independent study course in which a student earns course credit for working as a teaching assistant and completing an academic project, such as a paper examining his or her experiences. Ask your professors if teaching assistant opportunities exist. Ask even if no one you know has worked as a teaching assistant. Sometimes opportunities exist, but they are largely unadvertised. Ask and you may be pleasantly surprised. At any rate, asking never hurts and will only make you appear motivated and eager to learn and gain experience.

Get Field Experience

Field experiences in the form of internships or practica involve students in relevant academic experiences and provide a useful service to agencies and communities (Jessen, 1988). Examples of field placements include being an intern at a social service agency (where you might observe or assist in intake of clients, psychological testing, report writing, and behavior modification) and working in a human services department of a company or business (where you might observe and learn to administer structured interviews, write performance appraisals, and coordinate special projects or programs). As an intern, you have a chance to get an idea of what it is like to work in a particular setting. For example, you might sit in on a group therapy or parent training session or help personnel plan sessions and analyze the outcomes of sessions. You may learn new skills and hone others—and come to recognize that you have skills to contribute to practical settings.

Why Seek Field Experience?   There are many benefits to participating in field experience. If you hope to become a mental health professional and provide services to others, it is important to seek practice opportunities as an undergraduate in order to clarify your interests (Walter, 2007). It is not uncommon for a student to believe that clinical or counseling psychology is for them until they gain some experience and realize that they don't like working with people. Therefore, one of the most important reasons for seeking field experience is to become more certain of your career choice. Working in the field helps you to identify not only what work-related outcomes you value (e.g., pay, autonomy, responsibility) but also what interests and abilities you need to be satisfied in that work (Taylor, 1988; LoCicero & Hancock, 2000). It is a job tryout. You'll learn about a particular job environment, duties, and support. You'll learn about typical clientele you might work with and what you can expect in terms of resources. If you choose to apply to graduate school, field experiences will suit you well. Admissions committees and directors of applied subfields of psychology, such as clinical, counseling, or school psychology, look favorably on field experience because it is a good indicator of a student's interest, motivation, and competence in applied settings.

Other benefits of field experience include the opportunity to apply what is learned in class in a real-world setting, acquire knowledge and new skills, and learn about the practice of psychology (Jessen, 1988; LoCicero & Hancock, 2000). Depending on the placement, you may learn more about psychological problems, ways of helping, agency functioning, professional relationships, interviewing techniques, psychological testing, report writing, consultation, behavior modification, and group therapy. Field experience gives you a chance to develop useful skills that may be hard to practice and develop in class, and it helps you to integrate what you've learned. Personal benefits include developing responsibility, maturity, and confidence (LoCicero & Hancock, 2000).

Aside from educational and personal benefits, field experience offers professional benefits. These include gaining a realistic understanding of work environments, developing professional contacts, and enhancing your resume (Landrum, et al., 2000; Jessen, 1988). Interns get formal and informal job sources and contacts, are evaluated positively by recruiters, earn higher salaries in the workplace, and report greater satisfaction in jobs (Taylor, 1988). Students who work as interns are more likely to be satisfied with their jobs after graduation. They also remain in their jobs longer than the students who do not obtain field experience. Students who obtain field experience are able to consider the match between their academic preparation and work requirements (e.g., students are often poorly equipped for the stresses of work, including the realities of politics, difficult clients, and the conflict between theory and application) while they're still in school. Doing so gives students time to learn more and to resolve the conflicts early. Therefore it may not be surprising that after graduation, students who obtain field experience often have a smoother, easier transition to work, without the "reality shock" that other graduates often experience (Taylor, 1988).

How Do You Get Field Experience? The organization of field experiences varies by institution and department. Many departments have a faculty member who serves as a campus coordinator for field experience and internship programs. He or she makes sure that internship sites are appropriate, develops a working relationship with them, and evaluates student performance. Other departments may not have one coordinator; in some cases different faculty are responsible for each internship site, depending on their relationship with the site. Some colleges have an office that specializes in placing students in internships. Sometimes these offices and opportunities are referred to as co-operative education.

Your department may require that you obtain an internship through the co-operative education office. Sometimes a department may require a student to find his or her own practicum site. If you are in this position, begin at least two to three months early, as locating a site, making contact and meeting with the director, obtaining a faculty supervisor, and getting permission to proceed requires time. Look up the social service agencies in your area, such as women's centers, shelters, and not-for-profit agencies that help individuals and families. E-mail the director and explain that you are a student and looking to volunteer and perhaps get course credit for your work. Attach a resume. Alternatively you might call and ask if they'd like more information. Anticipate meeting and interviewing with the agency staff. Be prepared to have a faculty speak with the agency, vouching for you and taking responsibility of providing academic supervision. Field experience is a challenging experience that will test your knowledge and help you learn much about yourself.

GET INVOLVED IN THE FIELD

Research, teaching, and field work offer important educational opportunities, but there are many other ways to learn and advance your competencies. Disseminating the results of research—formally telling others about what you have found—requires another set of competencies and offers many benefits. Another way of becoming active in the field is to become active in a local or national psychology organization, as described in the following sections.

Disseminate Research

If you conduct research with a faculty member and the results of the research project turn out favorably, the next step in the project is to disseminate the results and tell the scholarly community about your findings. Most commonly, research results are disseminated through presentations at professional conferences or articles in scholarly journals. Most students obtain their first experiences with research dissemination through presentations at local or regional professional conferences. Most professional organizations for psychologists host annual or biennial meetings where psychologists meet, present current research findings, and network. Presenting research results at a conference is a wonderful learning opportunity that is an impressive addition to a resume or graduate school application.

Typically, conference presentations take two forms—papers and posters. A paper is a 12- to 15-minute presentation made to an audience in which you describe your research concisely, with the aid of handouts, overheads, or slides. Checklist 3.4 offers suggestions for paper presentations. Posters are more common formats for student presentations. A poster presents your research concisely on a 3-by-5- or 4-by-6-foot freestanding bulletin board. All posters are displayed in a large room for a period of time (usually 1½ to 2 hours), and the audience wanders through, browsing posters of interest. A poster presentation offers opportunities for lots of one-on-one interaction, as audience members stop at posters of interest to them and ask questions about the project. Designing an effective poster isn't easy; Checklist 3.5 offers some advice on how to create an informative poster.

CHECKLIST 3.4
Checklist for Preparing Effective Paper Presentations

Preparation: Before Your Talk
- ❏ Carefully plan your talk. Recognize that you can make a limited number of points in your 12- to 15-minute time frame.
- ❏ Be aware of your audience's attention and comprehension limits; don't overwhelm them.
- ❏ Consider the "big picture." What are the main ideas and findings of your project?
- ❏ Minimize the extraneous details.
- ❏ First, write out your presentation. Then look over your write-up and decide whether there are any details to be eliminated.
- ❏ Using the write-up that you've prepared, create a detailed outline to guide your talk.
- ❏ Remember that your goal is to tell a coherent story about your data. State the point of your research, what you found, and why it matters.
- ❏ Practice giving your talk in front of a mirror, or videotape your practice sessions.
- ❏ Practice giving your talk to an audience, and accept their constructive feedback.

- ❏ Prepare overheads, slides, or handouts to enhance the informational value of your presentation.
- ❏ Be sure to include identification information on your handouts—your name, the conference source reference, and whether the paper may be quoted.
- ❏ Try to visit the room that you will be speaking in beforehand to familiarize yourself with its layout.

During Your Talk
- ❏ Do not read your talk; use your outline as a guide.
- ❏ Speak loudly and clearly.
- ❏ Look out at the audience.
- ❏ Understand that there will be distractions, such as people getting up and leaving or reading—don't take it personally.
- ❏ Try to be enthusiastic and focused; look away from distracting stimuli.
- ❏ End on time, and be prepared for questions if time permits.
- ❏ Bring copies of your paper and a sign-up sheet in case you run out of copies.

Source: Adapted from Karlin, 2000.

CHECKLIST 3.5
Tips for Preparing Effective Poster Presentations

- ❏ Consider the "big picture." What are the main ideas and findings of your project?
- ❏ Remember that your goal is to tell a coherent story about your data in very limited space.
- ❏ Your poster should reveal the point of your research, what you found, and why it matters.
- ❏ Present only what is necessary to tell your story—only essential details.
- ❏ Remember that you are there to answer readers' questions. Your goal is to engage the reader and have a conversation about the study.
- ❏ The components of your poster should be clearly visible from three feet away.
- ❏ Include the title, authors, affiliation, and an abstract of the research.
- ❏ Use a large font (at least 18 point and preferably 24 point).
- ❏ Pictures, tables, and figures are helpful.
- ❏ If possible, use color in your figures and pictures.
- ❏ Bring thumbtacks and tape.
- ❏ Bring at least fifty copies of a handout to provide additional information about the study and contact information.
- ❏ Be sure to include identification information on your handouts: your name, the conference source reference, and whether the paper may be quoted.

- ❏ Be on time. Often poster sessions are scheduled back to back, so it is important that you end on time and take your poster down because someone else will be waiting.
- ❏ Never take your poster down early.
- ❏ Have your name badge prominently displayed, and be ready to answer questions.

Source: Adapted from Karlin, 2000.

If the research that you are conducting with a faculty member turns out especially favorably, you might prepare the results for submission to a scholarly journal. While professional journals in psychology abound, there are a handful of journals that specialize in publishing the work of undergraduates. The most prestigious of the undergraduate journals is the *Psi Chi Journal of Undergraduate Research,* which is sponsored by Psi Chi and published quarterly. Submissions to the *Psi Chi Journal of Undergraduate Research* are reviewed by three psychology professionals. Other undergraduate journals and criteria appear in Table 3.3.

If you decide to submit to a journal, recognize that it will take a great deal of time and effort. The time it takes to prepare a paper for submission is always longer than anticipated. Once the paper is submitted, there will be a long wait (typically several months) to hear from the publisher. Even if a paper is accepted, it is usually under the condition that further revisions be made. It is important to understand that not every paper submitted to a journal is published. The standards for publication are much higher than those for getting an A in a course. Journal editors expect articles to make a contribution to the literature, and "nonsignificant results are typically not a big contribution in their eyes" (Powell, 2000, p. 28). Despite these cautions, the rewards of publishing are great. Publishing in a scholarly journal is a major achievement that employers and graduate schools look upon favorably.

However, not every student has research experiences that lend themselves to submitting to scholarly journals. Fortunately there are respectable non-refereed outlets for students to demonstrate initiative and writing skills. Newsletters published by psychology departments, student organizations, and other groups on campus offer opportunities to write about topics related to psychology. Professional organizations such as the American Psychological Association (APA), the American Psychological Society (APS), and regional psychological associations (such as Eastern Psychological Association (EPA), New England Psychological Association (NEPA), and Western Psychological Association (WPA) have student publications or member publications that are open to student writers. Finally, Psi Chi and Psi Beta offer opportunities for students to contribute to their newsletter magazines. Although these publications are not peer reviewed, and the articles are not empirical, they

TABLE
3.3 UNDERGRADUATE PSYCHOLOGY JOURNALS

Journal Title	Publication Schedule	Description/Requirements	Contact Info
Canadian Undergraduate Journal of Cognitive Science	Two issues per year: Fall and Spring	Online journal that showcases "quality research by other undergraduate students, improving the contact and exchange of ideas between students and cognitive scientists alike, and illustrating the interdisciplinary work that is the hallmark of the field."	http://www.sfu.ca/cognitive-science/journal/
Journal of Psychological Inquiry	Annual	Primary author must be an undergraduate student from (a) institutions sponsoring the Great Plains Students in Psychology Convention and the *Journal of Psychological Inquiry* or (b) whose manuscript has been accepted for or presented at the meeting of the Great Plains Students in Psychology Convention, the Association for Psychological and Educational Research in Kansas, or the Nebraska Psychological Society. Publishes empirical and theoretical papers.	http://puffin.creighton.edu/psy/journal/JPIhome.html
Journal of Psychology and Behavioral Sciences	One issue per year	Authors may be undergraduate students. Submission deadline is February 1. Publishes empirical and theoretical papers.	http://view.fdu.edu/default.aspx?id=784
Journal of Young Investigators	Monthly	Online journal publishes original scientific research in all disciplines.	http://www.jyi.org/about/
Modern Psychological Studies	Two issues per year, in September and March	Primary author must be an undergraduate student. Submissions deadlines April and October. Publishes empirical papers but will consider theoretical papers.	http://www.utc.edu/StudentOrgs/ModernPsychologicalStudies/

(Continued)

TABLE
3.3

UNDERGRADUATE PSYCHOLOGY JOURNALS (CONTINUED)

Journal Title	Publication Schedule	Description/Requirements	Contact Info
Psi Chi Journal of Undergraduate Research	Published quarterly	Print journal. First author must be an undergraduate Psi Chi student. Submissions accepted on an ongoing basis. Publishes only empirical research.	http://www.psichi.org/pubs/journal/submissions.aspx
Undergraduate Research Journal for the Human Sciences	Annual	The primary author of a submitted paper must be an undergraduate student. "Papers may represent a full range of research design, including experiments, surveys, case studies, and documentary research."	http://www.kon.org/CFP/cfp_urjhs.html
University of California Los Angeles Undergraduate Psychology Journal	Two issues per year: Fall and Spring	"We are looking for research that draws upon the varied areas of psychology and related fields. Research should emphasize possible behavioral, psychological, cognitive, neurological, physiological, social, developmental, and/or emotional mechanisms behind psychological functioning." See Web site for submission requirements.	http://www.studentgroups.ucla.edu/upj/
Yale Review of Undergraduate Research in Psychology	Annual	Online journal "showcases the best and most original research in psychology conducted by undergraduates from around the world."	http://www.yale.edu/yrurp/

Source: Adapted from Jalbert, 1998.

demonstrate initiative, writing ability, and interest in psychology—all valued by employers and graduate admissions committees.

Participate in Professional Organizations

One of the simplest, most effective, yet underappreciated ways of forming an identity as a lifelong student of psychology is to get involved in professional organizations, on and off campus. Likely the most visible resource for psychology students on your campus is Psi Chi, the International Honor Society in Psychology, a psychology organization designed for students. Founded in 1929, its purpose is to encourage, stimulate, and maintain excellence in scholarship and to advance psychology as a science. Students enrolled at institutions that have a chapter must meet minimum qualifications and apply for membership to Psi Chi. Students at community colleges are eligible to apply to Psi Beta, the sister organization of Psi Chi.

Get involved in your institution's chapter of Psi Chi, and you'll have the opportunity to get to know other psychology students, develop leadership skills, and get involved in departmental activities. Psi Chi also offers opportunities for students at the regional and national level. Psi Chi sponsors sessions at most regional and national conferences that promote the research and scholarly achievements of undergraduate psychology students. In other words, Psi Chi sponsors opportunities for students to present their research. Psi Chi offers programming relevant to psychology students at these conferences, such as presentations on careers in psychology and how to apply to graduate school. Another important benefit of membership in Psi Chi is the quarterly magazine, *Eye on Psi Chi*. Each issue includes articles on psychology as well as practical advice on how to pursue a career in psychology. The *Psi Chi Journal of Undergraduate Research* is also published by Psi Chi; it's a national, peer-reviewed scholarly journal that is dedicated to research conducted by undergraduate students. Because there are so many benefits to becoming a member of Psi Chi, if your institution does not have a chapter, discuss with a faculty member the possibility of starting a chapter.

Another opportunity to get involved in psychology and promote a campus culture oriented towards psychology is to get involved with (or start) a psychology club. Most psychology clubs are open to anyone with an interest in psychology, regardless of major. Many students who do not meet the academic criteria to join Psi Chi get involved in a school's psychology club. Frequently the psychology club and Psi Chi work together to organize psychology-related activities for students.

When considering ways of getting involved in psychology-related activities, don't forget to pay attention to what's happening in your department. Departments often invite guest speakers to campus or faculty members give presentations on their research interests. Attend these activities to support the department's efforts and to demonstrate your interest and commitment to learning more about psychology.

Finally, two professional organizations for psychologists offer resources that are helpful to students: APA and APS. Both offer advice on entering the field of psychology, and APA offers a student affiliate membership that permits you to join for a reduced fee and obtain discounts on psychology journals and books. APA and APS sponsor annual conferences in which thousands of psychologist researchers and practitioners gather to learn about the latest research, attend workshops, and network. Attend either of these conferences, or any of the conferences sponsored by regional psychological associations, for an amazing learning opportunity.

There are a variety of ways to take an active role in your education, but all involve stepping back and recognizing the covert—unstated—college curriculum (Appleby, 2001); you can learn much more in college than just theories and facts. Taking an active role in your education means that you must seek out opportunities to learn and enhance your skills. It means that you must develop relationships with faculty and do more than just attend class. Though taking an active role in your education takes effort—it's much easier to sit back and just attend class—the benefits are immense.

EXERCISE 3.2

Academic and Professional Organizations

Several professional organizations offer opportunities for students to learn about the field of psychology and make contacts with other students and professionals.

1. Visit the Psi Chi Web site (http://psichi.org). What is the purpose of the organization? Under the publications link, what is *Eye on Psi Chi*? Browse the collection of articles organized by category. Read three articles from three different categories (such as career preparation, fields of psychology, or promotion of research). Write a one- to two-sentence summary of each article.

2. Visit the American Psychological Association Web site (http://apa.org). Locate the Students page. Identify two helpful resources. What are they? How are they helpful? Can students join APA? What are the benefits? How much does it cost?

3. Visit the Association for Psychological Science Web site (http://psychologicalscience.org). Locate the Students page. Can students join APS? What are the benefits? How much does it cost? Identify two ways of getting involved in APS.

Suggested Readings

Beins, B., & Beins, A. (2008). *Effective writing in psychology: Papers, posters, and presentations.* Hoboken, NJ: Wiley.

Landrum, R. E., & Davis S. F. (2010). *The psychology major: Career options and strategies for success.* Upper Saddle River, NJ: Prentice Hall.

Nist-Olejnik, S., & Holschuh, J. P. (2007). *College rules! How to study, survive, and succeed in college.* Berkeley, CA: Ten Speed Press.

Santrock, J. W., & Halonen, J. S. (2007). *Your guide to college success: Strategies for achieving your goals.* Belmont, CA: Wadsworth.

Silvia, P. J., Delaney, P. F., & Marcovitch, S. (2009). *What psychology majors could (and should) be doing: An informal guide to research experience and professional skills.* Washington, DC: APA.

Van Blerkom, D. L., & Mulcahy-Ernt, P. I. (2005). *College reading and study strategies.* Belmont, CA: Wadsworth.

Watson, D. (2001). *Learning skills for college and life.* Belmont, CA: Wadsworth.

Internet Resources

Academic Skills Center

http://www.dartmouth.edu/~acskills/success/

At this Web site, you'll find everything you need to succeed in college. There are links to study tips and other information to get you motivated.

APS Observer Student Notebook

http://www.psychologicalscience.org/apssc/news.cfm

Monthly column written for graduate students in psychology, but valuable to undergraduate students as well.

Psi Chi

http://www.psichi.org

International Honor Society in Psychology Web page. Review the *Eye on Psi Chi* articles for help with all aspects of student development (research, field experiences, graduate school, and more).

Becoming an Active Learner

http://www.lafayettehigh.org/Course%20Guide/becoming_an_active_learner.htm

Describes the benefits of active learning and presents concrete strategies for changing your learning style and becoming a more engaged learner.

JOURNAL EXERCISES

My Advisor

Who is your advisor? Write down the contact information for your advisor. Now reflect on your meetings with him or her. Did you set up an appointment or just visit during office hours? What kind of advice has he or she given you? Do you feel comfortable interacting with your advisor? Identify questions to ask during your next meeting.

Relationships with Faculty

Explore your feelings about interacting with faculty. How often do you interact with professors? List the professors you interact with. Explore the context of your discussions. For example, is it after class or in the professor's office? Are your discussions focused on the course material or do you talk about other things, like life and career goals? What, if anything, is holding you back from interacting with professors? Explore your feelings. How can you overcome these obstacles?

Find a Mentor

This exercise helps you to gather information about faculty and use it to make decisions. First, write down the name of each faculty member in the department. After you have listed everyone, begin gathering information on their research activities. Look at department bulletin boards, explore the department and faculty Web sites, and use databases to find information about each faculty member's research interests and activities. Take a few minutes to speak with the faculty member about his or her research. In your journal, write your overall impressions: What type of work do they do? Do you find it interesting? Why or why not? How comfortable do you feel speaking with this faculty member? If you're uncomfortable, try to identify why. Complete this process for each faculty member, and you'll begin to get ideas about which faculty you're more inclined to work with.

My College Career

An important part of taking an active role in your education is planning your course work. Look through your college handbook, and write down the requirements for your major. What courses are required? Are any other experiences required? Now list all the courses that you have taken. Make a list of all the courses that you need to take. In what ways have you been active in shaping your education to match your goals? What steps can you take to be more active?

STUDY TIPS: TOOLS FOR ACADEMIC SUCCESS

CHAPTER OUTLINE

Have you ever spent hours studying for a test, only to get a mediocre grade? Meanwhile, your friend says he or she only studied for an hour and got an A. What's the deal? Consider this scenario:

> Tom gets home from his part-time job and fixes himself a snack. It's been a long day. It's almost 6 p.m., and he knows that he has to start studying for tomorrow's test. It's been a rough semester, and he's gone to all of his classes but doesn't have a lot written in his notebooks. Tom finds that his mind wanders in class and it's difficult to understand the point of the professors' lectures. He usually doesn't read before each class because it's hard to keep up with five classes while working over twenty hours a week. Tom decides to complete the reading tonight, hoping that he'll remember some of it for tomorrow's test. He brings his snack to the kitchen table and clears a space among the breakfast dishes piled on the table. He tries to read while eating his snack. He begins reading but finds it difficult to concentrate. "Those dishes!" Tom exclaims, "That's why I can't focus." He takes a break to wash them. Twenty minutes later, after washing the dishes and clearing off the counters and stove, Tom sits down to read. Thirty minutes into his reading, his roommate comes home and begins a long story about his horrendous day. Nearly an hour later, Tom realizes that his studying isn't working, but he's hungry, so he and his roommate order a pizza. He vows to study after dinner. "This will be an all-nighter," he thinks to himself.

Sound familiar? Tom has good intentions and is motivated to study, but he's developed poor study habits, such as cramming. He's having trouble keeping up with his classes and is simply studying in the wrong place at the wrong time. Tom's predicament is common, but don't fall prey to this damaging cycle.

An important theme of this chapter is somewhat counterintuitive: Spending lots of time studying will not guarantee you good grades. Instead, it's the *quality* of your studying that counts. It doesn't do you much good to spend countless hours poring over your books if you don't retain anything. Work hard, but also work smart. This chapter describes simple techniques to help you manage your time, get organized, and improve your study habits so that you don't find yourself in Tom's shoes. Improving your study habits will take time and effort, but the work that you put in now will help you save time later. Learn to make the most constructive use of your time, and you will accomplish more in less time. With effort and consistent practice, you'll find that you can study more efficiently and be more productive—in less time.

ARE YOU PREPARED TO SUCCEED?

Before you can improve your study skills you must take a hard look at yourself. Knowing yourself—your habits, skills, preferences, and needs—is critical to devising study strategies that work for you. In this chapter we discuss general strategies, but you will need to tailor these ideas and strategies to fit your own needs and capacities. There is no right way to study; do what works for you, which means you must be self-aware.

Evaluate Your Skills

How do your study skills rate? If you're like most students, they can use improvement. Complete the study skills assessment in Exercise 4.1 to learn more about your study needs.

EXERCISE 4.1
Study Skills Assessment

Use the following scale to respond to the study skills assessment below. Be honest!

1 = none of the time
2 = some of the time
3 = most of the time
4 = all of the time

How often do you:

_____ 1. Manage your time to meet school and job responsibilities, as well as relax
_____ 2. Set and monitor academic and personal goals
_____ 3. Read your textbooks before class
_____ 4. Understand how you learn
_____ 5. Maintain attention during classes
_____ 6. Use active listening strategies to get the most out of classes
_____ 7. Take effective notes that are useful for later studying
_____ 8. Study early and often for exams rather than cramming
_____ 9. Use a variety of strategies for recalling information
_____ 10. Test yourself to determine whether you understand the material
_____ 11. Have a well defined study space
_____ 12. Differentiate between essential and nonessential information in lectures
_____ 13. Differentiate between essential and nonessential information in readings
_____ 14. Take notes on readings
_____ 15. Vary your learning and study strategies according to the material at hand

Scoring:
Add the points for each item. Higher scores indicate more effective use of study skills.

Reflect:
1. Consider your score. Identify the areas in which you can improve.
2. Identify one area of strength. How can you take advantage of this study skill?
3. Identify one area of weakness. How can you improve your skills in this area?

For a more detailed analysis of your skills and capacities, turn your attention inward and learn more about yourself by free writing—write whatever is on your mind without censoring or editing it. Later read what you've written and consider what you have learned about yourself. To explore your study skills, preferences, and interests, free write about any or all of the following questions:

1. Think back to a course in which you excelled. Describe the circumstances surrounding the course. What kinds of assignments were required? Why do you think you did well?
2. How do you learn best? Consider subject areas, course format, types of assignments, and personal factors.
3. Under what conditions can you best concentrate? For example, do you require absolute silence to concentrate, or do you need some background noise?
4. What are your academic strengths and weaknesses? Consider each of these areas: listening, speaking in class, memory, taking notes, and taking tests.
5. Describe your study environment. Where, when, and how do you study?
6. Do you know where your notes from last week are? How about last semester? Do you feel organized? Where can you improve?
7. Do you know what assignments are due next week? Are any major term papers due for any of your classes? Have you begun working on them? Why or why not?
8. Do you have a calendar or planner? How often do you use it?
9. Have you forgotten an appointment or assignment recently?
10. Do you feel overwhelmed with work? List all of the tasks of which you must keep track.

Carefully consider your answers and you may glean clues about where to focus your efforts to improve your studying. No one can do this part for you. You'll need to develop your own formula for academic success based on your understanding of yourself. Once you understand how to focus your attention and concentration, you'll increase your academic efficiency and get more work done in less time.

Understand Your Use of Time

At one time or another, most of us complain about feeling overwhelmed—like there is not enough time in the day to get it all done. Although you can't add more hours to the day, you often have more free time than you realize. How do you find those free hours and allocate them as you choose? Use time management strategies. The term time management sometimes turns students off because it sounds complex and formal. It isn't. Time management simply refers to planning your time—figuring out what you need to do, how much time you have, and how you will spend your time.

Why Plan Your Time?   Some students and faculty fear that planning their time by using time management strategies will rob them of flexibility or creativity (Fry, 1991). This is a myth. The philosophy behind time management is that by controlling or planning part of your time you are able to be more flexible with the rest of your time. There are concrete benefits to planning your time. Create a schedule to plan your time and you will:

Know when and where to begin   When faced with multiple tasks and deadlines it's easy to feel overwhelmed and not know where to begin—and therefore not begin. One of the primary benefits of creating a schedule is that you won't waste time deciding what to do. You will have already planned how to spend your time and so your task becomes implementing that plan. Don't underestimate the value of knowing exactly what you need to do and how you will spend your time. Removing the thought and planning can free your energy to actually complete what's on your list and spend your time productively.

Be less likely to avoid distasteful tasks   It's human nature: we spend time on activities that we like and that we are good at. Many students put other tasks first and find that they've run out of time to study subjects that they dislike. A schedule prevents this type of forgetfulness.

Free your mind and reduce anxiety   Recording your to-dos—tasks that you need to complete—relieves them from your mind. Once you've written an item down, there's no need to worry about forgetting it, so you're free to focus on other things. Seeing everything that you have to do on paper, with time allotted for each item, can help to alleviate anxiety and pressure because you have a concrete plan to get it all done.

Behave in line with your priorities   What is important to you? Where does college fit in your life? How important is each of the classes that you are taking to your academic standing and future plans? How many assignments does each of your courses entail? What is the relative weight or value of each assignment? It's easy to spend lots of time doing busy work that is not worth much of your final grade while not allocating enough time to study for a test or prepare a major paper. A schedule forces you to list all the tasks that must be done and prioritize them to ensure that the most important tasks are completed—even if that means that you don't get everything done.

Think about what you're learning   By scheduling regular periods to work, you will have regular periods to think about what you are learning rather than just simply prepare for looming deadlines. Without the pressure of cramming for an exam, you have time to think about what you're studying. When you have the chance to think about a subject and how it fits with your experience and perspective, learning can become more interesting and enjoyable—and you retain the information.

Not overlook fun   We need balanced lives to stay healthy. As the semester progresses and you get busier, it's easy to forget to take care of your personal needs or, in turn, to avoid your academic duties because it seems that you can't do it all. It's important to have fun. You need to engage in physical and social recreation so that you maintain a balanced and less chaotic life. A schedule also can help you to enjoy leisure without feeling guilty that you're not studying. If you schedule time to do your work, you know that it will get done. Then you can enjoy "play time" without worrying or thinking about studying.

Learn how to study smarter, not harder   By getting organized and in control of your time and tasks, you'll find that you can concentrate more effectively and get more done in less time. Breaking a project or semester's worth of reading into small, manageable, and regular blocks means that you will complete it at a more relaxed pace than many other students. You will also learn more. It's easier to stay motivated when you make steady progress and can see the results of your work. A schedule also helps you stay aware of deadlines and keep the big picture in focus, allowing you to plan ahead so that busy weeks are in control and papers are done ahead of time.

How Do You Use Your Time?   Before you can begin studying, you must gain control over your time: "Be the master of it instead of its slave" (Pauk & Fiore, 2000, p. 2). Most students could use some help in managing their time. The first step toward gaining control over time is to understand how you use it. Take the time management quiz in Quiz 4.1 and see how you rate.

Quiz 4.1
Time Management Quiz

Respond Yes or No to each item.
1. Do you use a weekly/daily calendar, a PDA, or a calendar on your PC?
2. Do you ever feel that you can't control your time?

3. Do you find yourself doing your coursework at the last minute?
4. At this very moment, do you know what your priorities are?
5. Do you ever struggle to begin unpleasant tasks?
6. Is your workspace neat and tidy?
7. Do you have a to-do list for today?
8. Do you often find yourself daydreaming when you should be working?
9. Do you feel like your friends are better organized than you?
10. Do you tend to hand in coursework and papers late?
11. Are you easily distracted?
12. Do you put off things that require big blocks of time?
13. Do you have a to-do list for this week?
14. Do you know what time of day you work best?
15. Do you check e-mail more than four times a day?
16. Do you often feel overwhelmed with work?
17. Do you know how long it takes for you to write a twenty-page paper for a course?
18. Do you ever attend class/seminars/workshops unprepared or wishing that you had done the reading?
19. Do you find yourself surfing the Web when you should be working?
20. Do you have a wall chart showing the important deadlines for the semester and year?
21. Do you prioritize your tasks and activities?
22. Do you set aside time for relaxation and socializing?
23. Do you put off things that are unpleasant?
24. Are you usually in a panic to complete course, research, and lab assignments? Do you often lose important papers or articles?
25. Do you often forget to complete important tasks?
26. Do you feel in control of your time?
27. Have you ever gone on a cleaning frenzy (i.e., cleaning your room or home) instead of working?
28. Do friends often just drop by your office or home, interrupting your work time?
29. Do you write down what you need to get done?
30. Do you know any useful time management techniques that you are not using right now?

Scoring:

Give yourself one point for each Yes response for items 2, 3, 5, 8, 9, 10, 11, 12, 15, 16, 18, 19, 23, 24, 25, 27, and 28; and one point for each No response for items 1, 4, 6, 7, 13, 14, 17, 20, 21, 22, 26, 29, and 30. The higher your score, the more help you need in managing your time.

Reflection:

1. Consider your score. Consider each check mark. Why did you check it?
2. Given your response to the first item, what aspects of time management are challenging for you?
3. How can you improve your time management skills? Discuss three strategies for improving your time management skills.

There is more time available in the day than you realize. Take a look at your own use of time. For a few days or a week, keep track of how you spend the hours of your days. Each day record your activities for each hour of the day. You may find it difficult to remember to record your activity. Do the best you can. You might even set an alarm for every thirty minutes or so to remind you to stop and record your activities. Be honest. We may not like to admit the amount of time that we spend on Facebook or playing video games, but it is important to construct an accurate picture of your time use so that you can identify areas to change (and those to keep). After a few days or a week, analyze your patterns of time use. Are you using your time most efficiently? Where can you cut back? Are you spending enough time to complete your studying? Does your time use reflect your priorities? You might be surprised at where all the time goes. That 10-minute coffee break might really be closer to 40 minutes! You may find that there's lots of lost time—time that you can find and use if you manage it better. Once you understand your time-use patterns, create a plan to use some of that "lost" time. In other words, create a schedule so that you can use the time that you usually waste.

Plan Your Time

Many of us let too much time slip through our fingers because we aren't taught how to manage it. Some take a "natural" approach to time management, taking things as they come without a schedule or plan (Fry, 1991). Juggling school, a job, extracurricular activities, and a social life is difficult and nearly impossible to manage successfully without a plan. I often hear students say that if they just tried harder they'd be able to do it all. They resign themselves to all-nighters and walk around campus like zombies. This approach, trying to do everything without acquiring the skills to manage your time, will lead to burnout. Life may seem busy now, but it doesn't suddenly get easier after graduation. In fact, demands on time often increase with career and family responsibilities. How do you take control of your time? Follow these principles.

List Your Activities   If you've decided that you're ready to get a handle on your time, the first thing you must do is to write down all the demands on your time. Now, evaluate your list. Are you committing yourself to too many activities? Are you trying to do too much? You might love music, but can you juggle jazz band, a guitar trio, and an off-campus rock band? Can you write for the school paper and maintain several blogs and Web pages at once? Recognize that sometimes you can't do it all. Decide what is important and what isn't. Difficult as it might be, you must remove activities that aren't meaningful to you in order to devote time to those that are. Don't eliminate all *fun* activities, but prioritize them and make choices about what's important to you and what will help you meet your goals. Make conscious choices about how to spend your time so that you have more control over your days and your life, rather than running late on everything and constantly feeling harried and behind.

Now that you've listed all of your activities, you might realize that you are quite busy—and perhaps overextended. A schedule will help you to feel more in control. Where do you begin? Decide how you will record your schedule. Browse the office supply store, and you'll find a myriad of calendars and time management tools. You might use a notebook, calendar, smartphone, or other method. Whatever format you choose, make sure that it works for you, is easy to use, and is always present so that you will be motivated to use it.

Create a Schedule   As early as possible in the semester, preferably before school begins, create a schedule. Create a plan for the whole semester, so you can see all that needs to be done. As you receive each syllabus, write in all class assignments for the semester. This will permit you to consider your entire semester at once and will help keep you from spending too much time on a low-priority class that has regular assignments while falling behind in an important class with a major term paper. Write in all of your classes and regular commitments (e.g., part-time job). Include appointments, extracurricular activities, and other personal commitments. Enter time to study.

Examine each assignment and record reminders to yourself beforehand, making personal due dates for portions of each assignment. For example, suppose you have a major term paper due at the end of the semester. During the second week of class, schedule time to search for topics. In later weeks, set aside time to go to the library, read articles, compose an outline, and write a first draft. If each step for each assignment is recorded in your schedule, you'll be more likely to stay on track and finish assignments on time (or early).

Use To-Do Lists   Each week, create a to-do list of tasks that must be accomplished. Rank their priority so that if you don't have time for everything, you can at least finish the most important tasks. Look at your schedule and decide when you will work on each task. Each evening, plan your next day by listing what needs to be done and when you'll do it. List the subjects you plan to study; your errands, appointments, and activities; and the time allotted for each. Schedule enough time for each task, including time to warm up and finish. Don't overdo it, but plan for rest breaks and fun. Use your schedule each day. The advantage of a daily schedule is that it forces you to break large tasks into small bites of time, making them seem easier and more manageable.

It's important to make a to-do list each night so that you have a plan for the morning and so that you unclutter your mind. It requires only five to ten minutes but is especially valuable. The act of thinking through your day puts together a sort of psychological clock that helps to prepare you for the day. Make the day's to-do list and schedule easily accessible by writing it on a 3-by-5 card so that it's handy and fits in your pocket.

Tailor Your System   The time management system that is best for you will be one that is tailor made to you. Make it work for you by altering and modifying it as needed. Give your time management system a trial run and time to work. It's hard at first, but once you get the hang of it, you'll find that you don't have to think about it. And it gets easier. Don't be surprised at the initial effort that is required. It takes practice, but it is worth it. Below are some more tips for making the most of your time (Pauk & Fiore, 2000).

- Plan blocks of time, preferably hour or half-hour blocks. Even twenty minutes can be productive.
- Schedule the most difficult tasks during daylight hours, when people tend to be most alert and awake.
- Avoid too much detail in your schedule. You don't want to spend too much time writing it, and you should also leave some flexibility. Allow time for play; leave room for last-minute problems.
- Allow time for sleep. You need at least eight hours of sleep each night (this is supported by psychological research). Without sleep you are less likely to remember material, which means that you're less likely to learn.
- Schedule down time, exercise time, and social time. The only way to ensure that all of your needs are met consistently is to plan ahead. Care for yourself by setting aside time just for you.
- Start big projects early. Most people tend to underestimate the time needed to complete a hefty project. To avoid finding out that you can't write a ten-page paper the night before it's due, start early—even if it seems ridiculously early. For example, begin considering topics for your ten-page term paper during the second week of the semester so that you have enough time to get the needed articles and books, read and comprehend them, and write the paper without feeling pressured.
- Use "lost" time to think. Each day we lose time as we go about the tasks of our day, such as walking from one place to another, waiting in line, and traveling. For example, while walking from class, try to think of the main points of the lecture and how they apply to what you know. While exercising on the elliptical machine, brainstorm topics or titles for papers or think about how to organize papers.
- Carry pocket work (reading, an article, flash cards) that you can do while waiting in lines, at the bus stop, sitting, and so on. Ten minutes here, fifteen there, it all adds up. In addition, cognitive psychology and memory research has shown that we can recall more information if we study in short periods rather than long ones, so you just might learn more.
- Know your sleep pattern and work with it. We all have a natural rhythm of times in which we are alert and awake and times in which we are less alert. Arrange your study times around your natural rhythm. Study when you're alert and sleep when you're sleepy.

Be Consistent   The cardinal rule of time management is that you must write everything down—all of your plans. It's difficult to make detailed plans far in advance if you don't have a record of your activities and commitments. Keep a record of all your assignments and obligations in one place, including class times, study times, project due dates, assignments, appointments, and social events. Consistently write everything down so that you don't forget anything—and more importantly, so that you're free to think without worrying that you've forgotten something. Always carry your schedule and to-do list so that you can bring order to your life and have peace of mind. Make no mistake about it, this will take some time and practice; but creating a schedule produces important returns. You'll feel like you have extra time. You'll feel more in control.

Create a Study Environment

Improving your skills in time management means that you will set aside consistent periods for reading, writing, and studying. Setting aside time is a big part of learning how to be a master student. Another part, however, is creating a place conducive to your work. It is one thing to set aside time, but you need to ensure that you will be productive during that time. As a psychology student you are likely aware of how our environment influences us. Take advantage of that knowledge and create a study environment that will support your work—and encourage your work.

Become aware of your current study environment. Paying attention to where and when you study might seem overly conscientious, but it is simple advice that can help you to study more efficiently. Create a place just for study. Why? We're conditioned by our environment to behave in certain ways. The more we behave a certain way in a given environment, the stronger the tendency gets. This is a powerful principle of psychology that you can use to your advantage. Create a habit for yourself. Designate an area just for studying.

Choose a quiet place with adequate light. Make your study area pleasant and motivating. Avoid distractions; don't set up a study area in a high-traffic place (like the kitchen). If you are prone to distraction and procrastination, be sure to set up your study area away from the television or anything else that might distract you (e.g., a big window). Create a barrier between you and the world. If possible, shut the door or at least create an invisible barrier by facing the wall.

Your study area should be convenient—a place that's easy to use, so you'll use it often. Don't underestimate the importance of a sturdy, comfortable chair. You'll spend a great deal of time in this chair, so you want to be comfortable (though not so comfortable that you fall asleep). An uncomfortable chair might make studying even less appealing and dampen any motivation that you muster up. Some students need light background noise to study—though be careful that it's not distracting. Before you decide that you "need" background noise like the television or radio, try spending some time without any noise to see how it feels. If it's tough, then try studying with a little background noise as a comparison. Depending on your schedule, you might consider studying in more than one place (e.g., at home and at school). Find other places, like a corner of the library, where you can study regularly. Is your study space conducive to learning? Quiz 4.2 will help you to evaluate your study area and determine if it is conducive to work.

Quiz 4.2
Study Environment Quiz

Check off items that you find are true for your study environment.
- ❏ Your desk is free of clutter, with space to spread out books and papers.
- ❏ Lighting is good.
- ❏ Desk is in a quiet area.
- ❏ There is no television nearby.
- ❏ The chair is sturdy and comfortable.
- ❏ Pencils, pens, paper, sharpener, and eraser are handy.
- ❏ Tape, scissors, stapler, calculator, and a wastebasket are handy.
- ❏ Desk is in a low-traffic area.
- ❏ Desk faces wall.
- ❏ Your calendar and schedule are handy.
- ❏ Your to-do lists are handy.
- ❏ Books, binders, and files are handy.
- ❏ Telephone answering machine is on, and the phone's ringer is off.
- ❏ Area is clutter free.
- ❏ E-mail announcement is turned off.
- ❏ There are few distractions.
- ❏ There are few things here that have nothing to do with school work.
- ❏ I work well and feel that my studying is effective here.

Scoring:
Count your check marks. The higher your score is to 18, the better your study environment.

Reflection:
1. How does your study space rate? Reflect on your score.
2. In what ways might the quality of your workspace influence your learning and academic achievement?
3. In what ways can you improve your study space to make it a place more conducive for working? Identify three strategies for improving your workspace.

We've discussed the importance of creating a habit of studying by monitoring the study place and atmosphere, but you should also pay attention to the time of day. Create a routine time to study—ideally when you're at your best, when you're awake and alert. Try to study at the same time each day. When you set a concrete period of time aside for studying each day, your mind gets used to the pattern. It becomes easier to work during that time. If you stick to a routine study time and place, psychological research suggests that you'll spend less time warming up and more time studying effectively.

Be Organized

Studying is easier if you're organized. Have you ever sat down to study only to realize that you needed materials from another room? Not having your materials together is a time trap because you'll need to spend extra time gathering them and risk getting sidetracked and wasting time. Save time by keeping all your study materials in one place, near your desk.

Do you have a filing system? If you wanted to look at your notes from last month or last year, do you know where to look? One of the best ways to get organized is simple: Use a three-ring binder for your schoolwork. Keep lecture notes and handouts from each class together, marked by a tab. Use one large binder for all of your classes, separating each class with tabbed dividers. You can also add a section for other necessities such as calendars, weekly schedules, lists, and phone numbers. All that you have to carry around is a single binder—not five notebooks, folders, and many scraps of paper. You're also less prone to losing handouts if they're in your binder.

If your binder is full or gets too bulky, empty the contents into file folders marked for each class. Keep a small file holder near your desk to hold the semester's work, or consider using a filing cabinet to keep all of your college work. This, of course, isn't the only way to get organized. There are many ways to organize your study space and materials. The important thing is always to have everything handy when you study.

Organization is especially important if you plan to study in more than one place (e.g., at home and school). Each morning, be sure to look over your schedule and determine what you'll need for the day. It might be easier to pack your book bag the night before, to avoid wasting time during the hectic morning and possibly forgetting something important.

Some students might choose to schedule the morning and afternoon, but keep evenings free, for example. Your time management system can be as flexible as you choose. The best time management systems are simple guides (Fry, 1991).

READING: TIPS FOR IMPROVING COMPREHENSION AND EFFICIENCY

Have you ever read a chapter yet were unable to remember much about it? Many students have difficulty retaining what they read. Reading a scholarly book is very different from reading novels or magazines for pleasure, yet students often attempt to read textbooks and other scholarly books as if they were novels. Reading a scholarly book requires a different set of strategies.

Preview the Text

Before beginning a scholarly book, preview it. It's easy to get lost in the prose within and later find that you cannot explain the author's perspective and supporting points. Savvy readers learn about the author's purpose and thesis *before* they read the book. It is counterintuitive but true: To get the most out of a book in the least amount of time possible, know what you're getting into and what you're looking for before you begin.

What is the book about? Read the back cover and book jacket. More importantly, read the preface. Most students skip the preface; however, the preface contains essential information for understanding the book's thesis. The preface usually provides information about the author's objective, the organizational plan of the book, how the book is different from others on the market, and the author's background and qualifications (Pauk & Fiore, 2000). Once you know the author's objective or goal, it's easier to see relationships among the facts presented. The organizational plan is like a road map explaining where the author will take you. Reading the author's view of what the book contributes to the field and learning about his or her background and qualifications gives you more insight into his or her perspective, perhaps making it easier to comprehend the ideas that appear in the book.

In addition to (or sometimes in place of) a preface, most books begin with an introduction section or chapter. Read the introduction because it is a window into the book. It provides an overview to a text, making it easier to digest information in the subsequent chapters. The introduction usually is packed with facts and ideas so as to lay the foundation for the book (Pauk & Fiore, 2000).

Use the SQ3R Method

Particularly suited to reading dense college textbooks, the SQ3R method (Robinson, 1970) is designed to help students read faster and retain more. The name stands for the steps in reading: survey, question, read, recite, review. Let's examine each step of this technique.

Survey   Before reading a book chapter, quickly survey it to get an initial impression of its contents. Glance through the topic headings to get an overview of the chapter. Skim the sections, and read the summary paragraphs to get an idea of where the chapter is going. Your survey should take only a few minutes, but it will highlight the main ideas of the chapter and provide an initial orientation that will help you to organize the material as you read it. Surveying a chapter gives you background knowledge to link with other material that you are learning and what you already know. Pauk and Fiore (2000) warn, "If you skip this step, you will lose time, not save time. If you burrow directly into one paragraph after another, you'll be unearthing one compartmentalized fact after another, but you won't see how the facts relate to each other" (p. 71). Instead, you'll develop tunnel vision and won't be able to see the big picture. Surveying holds other benefits, such as warming up or limbering the mind, and eases you into studying (Pauk & Fiore, 2000).

Question   Look at the first heading in the chapter. Turn it into a question. Your task in reading the following section is to gather information and answer that question. Posing questions will help you remember information that you already know and arouse curiosity about the reading assignment, which will increase your comprehension. This step requires conscious effort but is worth it because active reading is the best way to retain written material. For example, if the heading is "Prevalence of Substance Use and Abuse in Adolescence," you might ask, "How many adolescents use illegal drugs?" If the heading is "Multiple Personality Disorder," you might ask, "What are the characteristics of multiple personality disorder?" Asking questions focuses your concentration. Take an active role in your reading. Don't read passively: Interrogate the author.

Read   Read to answer the questions you pose. Actively search for answers. If you finish the section and haven't answered the question, reread it. Read reflectively. Consider what the author is trying to say, and think about how you can use that information.

Recite   Now that you've read enough to answer your question, look away and try to recite the answer to your question. Use your own words and examples. If you can do this, it means that you understand the material. If you can't, glance over the section again. Once you've said each answer, write it down. You might also reconsider your initial question, fine-tune it, write it in the margin of the text, and underline the key words that provide an answer (Pauk & Fiore, 2000).

Review   Once you have read the entire chapter, test your memory by asking yourself the questions that you've identified. Review your notes and get a bird's-eye view of the chapter. Consider how it fits with what you know from the course, experience, and other classes. What is the significance of the material? What are the implications or applications of this material? What questions are you left with?

Whether or not you decide to employ the SQ3R method, you should always preview the material to be read. Skim the table of contents, preface, headings, and conclusions. In addition to previewing the text, stop and think about the instructor's purpose in making the assignment. What does your professor want you to get out of this reading? How does this assignment contribute to the course content? Identify your purpose for reading: What can you gain from this reading assignment? The most obvious response might be, "an understanding of the course material," but other responses might include, "a possible topic for my paper," or simply, "learn something new and interesting."

More Tips on Reading

By now you understand that reading for comprehension often requires more than one pass. It usually takes two, three, or even more readings to grasp difficult concepts. Rereading takes time and may seem inefficient; however, thoroughly understanding what you have read and integrating it with your existing knowledge will save you time in the long run, when it is time to study for a test. It is easy to remember material that you understand, so you will spend less time studying. Here are some additional pointers:

- Keep a dictionary nearby to look up unfamiliar words. If you don't understand a word, stop and look it up in the dictionary. After looking up an unknown word, consider its meaning in the sentence.
- Pace yourself. Note that difficult readings will require more than one pass. Permit yourself the time to read such assignments over more than one session.
- Read the chapter before attending the lecture so that you're familiar with the material beforehand. Note unanswered questions or particularly difficult material, and seek answers during the lecture.
- If you underline text, do so minimally and stay focused on the important details. Avoid the temptation to highlight every line. Heavy highlighting is a procrastination technique because usually you're marking what you should learn instead of focusing on learning it.
- Instead of underlining or highlighting, take the briefest of notes while reading by adding brackets in margins or underlining minimally. Note pages where you might want to take formal notes. After reading, take more extensive notes. Write the main points, in your own words.

As you finish each section, or even each paragraph when reading dense material, take a moment to write down what you've learned. Be sure to use your own words and not those of the author (to lift the author's words is plagiarism, as we will see in Chapter 5). Your notes will be a valuable resource when it comes time to study. However, don't write down concepts that you don't understand. Reread the section until you understand the concept, or explain as much of it as you can and indicate your questions so that you can ask your instructor for assistance. When reading and note taking are complete, reread all of your notes, think about what you've read, and add more notes based on your reflections (Kahn, 1992).

GETTING THE MOST OUT OF LECTURES: NOTE-TAKING TIPS

If you expect to learn and retain information from lectures, you must take notes. Without notes, even professors find it difficult to remember the main points of lectures. Your class notes are an important study resource, a sort of handwritten textbook that may contain information that is not available anywhere else. When you take notes, you listen more actively and are more involved in the subject, promoting learning and memory, and reducing boredom. Note taking is a lifelong skill; most careers require at least some note taking (how else can you remember what happened in that staff meeting, for example). How can you improve your note-taking skills?

Come Prepared

Listening to a lecture, participating in class, and learning is easier if you are prepared. Professors assign reading prior to class to ensure that students have the background knowledge needed to help them learn the day's material. Another way to become aware of main ideas and major points is to preview the material before coming to class. Read before class so that the lecture material isn't completely new. Reading beforehand will also help you to see how closely the instructor follows the textbook. The main benefit of previewing the lecture material is that you're on the same wavelength as the instructor and can participate in discussions as well as answer questions. You'll be able to recognize and organize the main ideas and terms more easily (Kahn, 1992).

Be Selective

Don't write everything the instructor says; just record the main points. Identifying the main points requires active listening. Beginning note takers often make the mistake of trying to write every word and become frustrated when they find that it's impossible. Instead, take notes in your own words. Listen actively, that is, think about what you are hearing, evaluate it, determine your understanding, and make connections with what you already know. Your notes should include not only what the speaker said but also a critical response to what was said (clearly marked as *your* response to differentiate it from the professor's; Kahn, 1992).

Determine the Main Points

"Easier said than done," you're probably thinking. How do you determine the main points? The instructor usually provides clues to what is important. One clue is repetition; material the instructor repeats is more important. Notes written on the board or presented in PowerPoint slides offer other clues. Remember that when you copy notes from the board or follow along with the PowerPoint slides, you will need to write more than the phrase or words indicated. Also write an explanation. The instructor's tone of voice might signify important information. Finally, instructors often highlight essential information by using specific phrases. Table 4.1 lists signal phrases that instructors might use to draw attention to critical information.

Understand the Mechanics of Note Taking

Take class notes using a telegraphic style that includes only the essential elements and leaves out unnecessary words. Forget grammar; grammatical sentences require more time than you have while taking notes. Instead, record

TABLE 4.1   SIGNAL WORDS AND PHRASES

Listen For	Type of Phrase
To illustrate, for example, for instance	Examples to make a point more clear
Before, after, formerly, subsequently, prior, meanwhile, first, second, last	Time words to note the time relationships among ides or enumerate them
Furthermore, in addition, moreover, also	Additional information to add to a list
Therefore, as a result, if...then, accordingly, thus, so	Suggests cause and effect
On the other hand, in contrast, conversely, pros and cons	Contrast words to discuss both sides of a controversy
More importantly, above all, remember	Emphasize important information
In other words, in the vernacular, it simply means, that is, briefly, in essence	Repeats the information presented in a simpler form

a streamlined version of the instructor's lecture. Here are some other note-taking tips:

- Create your own abbreviations for common words used in class (just be sure to record what each abbreviation stands for). For example, as a student of developmental psychology, many of my lecture notes referred to "dev" instead of development and "Ψ" for psychology.
- If you have poor handwriting, do not write in script. Most students should print their notes to ensure that they are legible. Many students plan to type their notes after class (and often do not get to it), but unless a student's handwriting is indecipherable, simply typing up notes is a waste of time. The typing itself takes too much concentration, robbing your learning and distracting you from comprehending and recalling the material. Instead, typing your notes in order to organize and integrate them with prior lectures and readings is useful *if* you remember to focus on compiling information and creating links among sources of information rather than simply typing it.
- Consider using a loose-leaf binder for your notes so that you can rearrange the pages as needed, add handouts from class, and remove pages neatly. Write notes on only one side of each loose-leaf page, so that you can see all the information at once.
- As you take notes, indent your paragraphs deeply to help you note the organization of the lecture (like an informal outline) and to provide room for later notes and comments.
- If you find note taking particularly difficult in a class, leave extra blank space at the end of each section or paragraph so that you can add more later after asking a question or reading the text.
- Note specific examples the instructor uses.
- Listen actively during class discussions. The instructor will comment on important points and draw conclusions from the discussion. Record these.
- Review your notes soon after class, making corrections or adding information as needed. Identify follow-up questions to ask your professor.

One bad habit that many students fall prey to is relying too heavily on a professor's PowerPoint slides. Many professors use software such as PowerPoint to create overheads and visual presentations to accompany their lectures. It is tempting to simply copy the information on the overhead slides, but professors require you to know much more than is on the slides. Likewise, many professors make PowerPoint slides available for students to download. Some students print the slides as a substitute for taking notes in class. This is not a good idea because professors explain much more than is on their slides. Use the slides as an outline of the professor's lecture and add information to support each bullet point. Consider what the bullet point is saying. Listen to the professor's explanation. Practice active listening and listen for information.

Try to pull out the main point. What information supports or refutes this point? How does it relate to theory?

Note taking is important not simply for recording information but for learning. Explaining ideas in your own words will ensure that you understand, recall, and apply it later to achieve your goals as a college student. The act of writing helps you retain material.

What If You Miss Class?

Regardless of how good a student you are, how detail-oriented, hard working, or diligent, you can be certain that you will miss a class at some point in your academic career. What do you do after missing class? Do you just show up at the next class and start fresh? What about material that you've missed? How do you get the notes and find out what happened?

First, be aware of class attendance, late work, and make-up policies. This information is listed in your course syllabus. Some professors do not accept late work or offer make-up exams, regardless of the reason. Others offer opportunities to make up for lost work, but have very strict policies about when they will accept make-up work. Read the syllabus to ensure that you don't miss any opportunities.

Try to e-mail your professor before missing class. Understand that most faculty do not consider family vacations, flying home early for break, or work obligations appropriate reasons for missing class. If you're ill or have an emergency, try to send an e-mail to inform the professor that you cannot attend class and, if you wish, provide an excuse. Be professional—offer a concise explanation without going into personal details. If you cannot e-mail before class, do so afterwards. If possible, hand in assignments beforehand by e-mail (and offer to hand in a hard copy when you're back on campus, but an e-mailed assignment shows that it's completed on time).

Upon returning to class, never ask if you "missed anything important." Most professors feel that class time itself is important. This is a surefire way to make a professor's eyes roll (maybe inwardly, at least!). Also do not ask the professor to "go over what you missed." The professor lectured and discussed the material in class and likely will not do it for you now. Instead, demonstrate that you care and are willing to try by reading the course material and hand-outs, and then asking questions about specific material that you don't understand. This is a more productive use of your (and the professor's) time. It also demonstrates initiative.

Finally, turn to your classmates for information about what happened in class and ask whether they will share their notes. Be sure to read more than one student's notes because different students have different perspectives and might miss some points. By reading notes from several students, you're more likely to get a complete picture of what happened in class.

Test-Taking Tips

We've discussed habits of studying, reading, and note taking that should keep you immersed in the subject matter of your courses. A test is on the horizon; how do you prepare?

Prepare Ahead of Time

Well ahead of the test, conduct an overview of all work that needs to be done. Make a list of tasks, and allocate time to complete them. If you're behind on your reading, approach the unread material with a plan. What do you need to get from the readings? Decide how much time you have to catch up. Preview the reading, deciding which parts are most important to focus on and which can be omitted. Use the reading techniques described earlier in this chapter.

Create Study Sheets   As you conduct your overview, list all the major topics covered in the course. Create a series of study sheets that summarize important information for each major topic. The study sheet should list relevant factual information, vocabulary, and theories relating to the topic. Note similarities and differences among the ideas, facts, theories, and other observations presented in the course.

Anticipate Test Questions   Ask yourself, "If I were making up this test, given what we've focused on in class and the readings, I would probably ask my students . . . ," and then answer the questions. How do you anticipate questions? Think about how the various course topics relate to one another. Are there any repeated themes? Examine your notes and readings to determine how the course content supports the major themes of the course (you can often find these in the syllabus, first few lectures, and first chapter of the text). Note that in class, instructors often use cues to communicate content that is important and that may appear on a test. What kinds of cues do you look for?

- Repetition
- Repeated use of examples
- Changes in the tone of the voice
- Pauses when speaking to permit students to take notes
- Writes on the board or emphasizes a point on an overhead
- Stops pacing and makes eye contact with the class

You have more power than you think when it comes to test taking. The trick is to determine the importance of material as it is presented in class and in reading assignments.

Rehearse   Practice the activities that encompass the test. If you will be solving problems, then solve problems while you study. If you will be conjugating French verbs, then write (and say) them. If you will be writing essays, then anticipate potential questions and write out answers. Rehearsal will make you more comfortable with the test-taking situation, reduce anxiety, and improve your performance.

Use Your Memory   How do you ensure that you'll remember what you study? Become personally invested in the material. Care about and be interested in what you're studying. In other words, find something interesting about the material. Identify how it is relevant to your life. How does it fit with what you already know? Associate what you want to learn with something that you already know, and intend to remember it. Tell yourself, "I will remember this because . . ." (Kahn, 1992).

Review and recite the information to be remembered by recalling it often. Use short 15- to 20-minute review sessions, spaced out over several days (Kahn, 1992). In addition, try to recite the information at odd moments (say them in the shower or while walking to your car). By verbalizing the material you'll get an idea of how well you know it and where your weaknesses lie.

Use cumulative review. Contrary to popular belief, long study periods (e.g., four to six hours) aren't effective. The best way to retain knowledge and prepare for exams is to squeeze in short review periods throughout your day. Distributing four 30-minute sessions throughout the day is less fatiguing and more effective than a single two-hour session (Pauk & Fiore, 2000). Why? The more often that you encounter material, the more likely you are to remember it. By distributing your learning sessions over the semester, you'll find that you learn more and don't need to cram.

An essential element to performing well on tests is preparation; however, preparation is not always enough to perform at your best. Test-taking skills also count. Students who excel understand *how* to take tests. They tailor their strategies to the type of test (e.g., multiple choice or essay) and know how to prepare themselves emotionally. Let's examine test taking in detail.

Preview Your Test: Read Everything

The first step after receiving any test is to read the directions carefully. This is true even if it is a multiple-choice test. For example, some instructors might require that you choose the *best* answer, while others might require you to mark *all* correct answers. If you are asked to choose the best answer and you mark more than one response, you'll lose credit. On the other hand, if you are asked to mark all correct answers, you may lose credit if you don't choose more than one answer. So read the directions carefully; if they are not clear, ask your instructor to explain them.

Once you have carefully read the directions, preview the entire test. Check to be sure that your test has no missing or duplicate pages. Read through the test and decide how to allocate your time. If your head is swimming with information that you're afraid you'll forget, jot it down quickly. The following sections present strategies for taking multiple-choice tests and essay tests, as well as for test preparation in general.

Multiple-Choice Tests

When answering a multiple-choice test, begin each item by reading the question. Then read all of the options. Don't rush, but take your time to read the question and each option completely. If the question is difficult, cross out any options that don't fit. In other words, eliminate distracters. If you can eliminate all of the distracters, you'll have the correct answer. How do you identify distracters? Combine the question and each option into a complete statement. If the resulting statement is false, you've found a distracter. Stick with the subject matter of the course. If an option includes terms that seem out of place or that you don't recognize, it's probably a distracter (Pauk & Fiore, 2000). Other tips include:

- If one of the options is "all of the above," all that you need to do is determine whether two of the other options are correct. If so, then "all of the above" is your answer.
- Multiple-choice tests often include options that look alike; two options might be identical except for one or two words. It's logical to assume that one of the pair is correct (Pauk & Fiore, 2000).
- Note that correct answers are often longer and more inclusive than distracters.
- Tests often give away relevant information for one question in another question.
- After you have selected your answer, read the entire statement to be sure that it makes sense.
- Don't waste time on difficult questions. Eliminate as many distracters as possible. If you still don't know the answer, guess, mark the question, and return to it later.
- Don't leave any items blank.
- Sometimes questions are simple. Don't read into questions. Don't make the question more complex than it is intended to be.
- Because your first choice is usually correct, change your answers only if you are certain of the correction.

Essay Tests

Your first step in taking an essay test is to read all of the questions thoroughly. Jot down any ideas and examples that come to you so they don't clutter your mind. Consider the difficulty of each question, and answer them in a strategic order. Complete the easy questions first to reduce anxiety and facilitate clear thinking. After completing the easy questions, move on to those with the highest point value. The last questions you answer should be the most difficult, take the greatest amount of writing, or have the least point value.

As you consider each essay question, determine what is being asked. What do you know that is related to the question? Take a moment and organize your essay. Jot some notes or an outline of points that you want to make. Once you have a list of points or a basic structure, start writing. Don't meander, but get right to the point. Use your first paragraph to provide an overview of your essay. Be sure to state your main point within the first paragraph. Use the rest of your essay to discuss your points in more detail. Back up each point with specific information, examples, or quotations from the class readings and notes. Leave space at the end of each paragraph to allow you to add further information, if needed, as you proofread. Write on every other line and on just one side of the page, not only to allow space for adding information but also to make the answers easier for your instructor to read.

Budget your time for each essay question. When you reach the end of your allotted time for a given question, list your remaining points, leave extra space, and move on to the next item. Partially answering all questions (especially by listing all of the points that you want to make) is better than fully answering only a few questions and skipping others. You won't earn credit for the questions that you skip. After you've completed the rest of the test, return to items that are incomplete.

Once you're done with the test, proofread your answers. Modify them for clarity, adding details, if needed, to make your answer complete. Check for spelling, grammar, and punctuation errors. Remember that students tend to lose points on essay tests because they fail to answer the question asked, don't provide examples or evidence to support their statements, don't write enough, are disorganized, or don't follow directions. Finally, avoid the "kitchen sink" method of answering essays—writing all that you know about a subject, hoping that the answer is somewhere in your essay (Landrum & Davis, 2010).

General Suggestions for Test Taking

Test-taking skills are important, but they may not be enough to perform at your best. Take care of your physical and emotional needs too. Get a good night's sleep. Set your alarm a little bit early, and take the time to have breakfast. Arrive early for your test, allowing time to acclimate yourself, relax, and prepare. Bring all the materials you will need for the test, including pencils and pens, a calculator, and a watch. Having all the materials necessary and arriving early will help you focus on the task at hand. Choose a seat that is well lit, located where you can't see many other students (and can't be easily distracted).

Don't let yourself become anxious. Try not to talk to other students before a test because their anxiety can be highly contagious. If you feel anxious, take some slow, deep breaths to relax, and use positive self-talk to raise your confidence. Research shows that students who are anxious tend to engage in negative self-talk (e.g., "Everyone in this class is smarter than I am," "I always screw up on tests," and "If I don't do well on this exam, I'll flunk the course"). Negative self-talk just brings you down and increases your stress level. When you find yourself engaging in negative self-talk, catch it and stop. Try to encourage yourself as you would a friend. Repeat positive statements to yourself in place of the negative. Remind yourself that you are well prepared for the test, and believe that you are going to do well.

If you feel the tension rising, try using progressive relaxation techniques to help reduce your muscle tension. Breathe in deeply and flex your toes. Release and breathe out. Do the same for your calves, then your thighs, buttocks, stomach, chest, arms, shoulders, and neck. Repeatedly tense and release your major muscle groups; it takes only a moment and produces big results. You'll feel more relaxed and able to concentrate.

Learn from Returned Tests

Think that your learning is over once the test is? Not! There's a lot you can learn from returned tests, so don't fall into the trap of checking your grade without reviewing the test. When you get a test back, you should examine it carefully and consider your errors. Why was the correct answer correct? Identify why you missed a question. Did you read it correctly? What do you need to learn to fill in these gaps in your knowledge?

Get clues for the next test. Look for the origin of each question (text, lectures, labs, supplementary readings, discussions). Check the level of detail and skill of the test. Were most of the questions about vocabulary, or did they ask for precise details and facts? Were the questions about main ideas, principles, applications, or all of these?

Decide which strategies worked and which didn't. Were you prepared for the test? Did you run out of time? How might you have better allocated your time? Identify those strategies that didn't work well and replace them. Use your tests to review when studying for final exams. Did you have any problems with anxiety or blocking during the test? Did you really know the answer to a question, but fail to read it carefully enough to recognize it?

Academic success requires work; it's an active process. Practice the tips in this chapter and refine them based on your needs. Not everyone studies in the same way. Be flexible in your study habits, and do what works for you. Above all, remember that a little work on getting organized, creating a schedule, and staying on top of your reading can save you from cramming later. Perhaps even better is knowing that you'll retain what you've learned well beyond the test, the course, and college.

SUGGESTED READINGS

Gardner, J. N., & Jewler, A. J. (2009). *Your college experience: Strategies for success.* New York: St. Martin's Press.

Hallberg, E., & Hallberg, K. (2004). *Making the dean's list.* Belmont, CA: Wadsworth.

Longman, D. G., & Atkinson, R. H. (2005). *CLASS: College learning and study skills.* Belmont, CA: Wadsworth.

Tyler, S. (2001). *Been there, should've done that: More tips for making the most of college.* Lansing, MI: Front Porch Press.

Van Blerkom, D. L. (2008). *College study skills: Becoming a strategic learner.* Belmont, CA: Wadsworth.

INTERNET RESOURCES

Study Tips

http://www.utexas.edu/student/utlc/learning_resources/

At this site, you'll find a collection of handouts addressing common problems like motivation, time management, reading tips, and more.

Interactive Study Tips

http://studytips.admsrv.ohio.edu/studytips/

Quizzes and interactive exercises on time management, memory, reading, notes, exam preparation, and more make this site an essential stop on your next trip online.

How to Study

http://www.howtostudy.org/resources.php

This site organizes a collection of links for all aspects of study skills.

Learning Strategies: Maximizing Your Academic Experience

http://www.dartmouth.edu/~acskills/success/index.html

The pages on this site provide a variety of suggestions and resources for maximizing your academic experience. View an online video, read about helpful strategies, or download a handout. In-depth tips for time management, reading, studying, and more.

JOURNAL EXERCISES

I'm at My Best When . . .

When are you at your best? When do you find it easiest to concentrate on difficult tasks? Are you a morning person—someone who accomplishes the most in the early morning? Do you work better at night? Why do you think you have these working patterns? What are the implications for scheduling classes and studying? How can you use this knowledge to help yourself?

Analyzing My Time

List all of the demands on your time. What are your responsibilities? What takes up your time (e.g., family, classes, research, meetings, social life, activities)? Are you doing too much? Identify places where you can cut back. What can you not do? Choose two places to cut back.

Ideal Day

Suppose that you managed your time well. What would an ideal day look like? Write about it—realistically. Deal with life as it is now, not as a fantasy. What would you do; how would you handle yourself in all situations? What two things would you do to bring yourself closer to that ideal? Suppose you suddenly had an extra two hours each day. How would you spend the time? Why?

Evaluating Time Management Strategies

After you've had a chance to try the time management strategies described in this chapter, free write about your experience. Which strategies worked well? How might you modify them to fit your style and needs?

WRITING A LITERATURE REVIEW

CHAPTER OUTLINE

It's the first day of class, and the professor has just handed out the course syllabus, which includes a 15- to 20-page paper on *a topic of your choice*. "Fifteen pages! How am I supposed to know what I want to write fifteen pages about before taking the class? How can I write a paper on anything without knowing a little about it first?" Sound familiar? Don't know where to begin? The typical ambiguous term paper assignment makes even the best students feel queasy. Don't stress. Take control of your academic destiny by beginning your paper immediately. It's tempting to put off challenging or work-intensive assignments, but waiting until the last minute to write your paper will only increase your stress and make writing even more difficult. This chapter will walk you through the steps in writing a literature review, from selecting a topic to proofreading the final draft.

WHAT IS A LITERATURE REVIEW?

The term paper assigned by most professors usually is more appropriately called a literature review because it is intended to present and critically evaluate the literature on a given topic. The purpose is to discuss current and/or historical research on a topic, organizing your presentation by theme, such as research objective, thesis, problem, or issue. Writing an effective review of the literature entails choosing a method to organize the studies that you will discuss in your paper (such as by thesis, methodology, or theoretical approach) and then identifying, synthesizing, and evaluating the published work relevant to your topic. Your paper should present literature in a way that tells a story about your topic, such as how theoretical perspectives on your topic have changed over the decades, supporting and leading readers to your main point. Another way of thinking about the literature review is that it answers a question. What's the question you'd like to answer? Pose your question and then synthesize an answer, using your research to support the answer. Ultimately your paper will give readers a detailed summary of the existing knowledge base regarding your topic as well as your informed evaluation of the literature.

At this point most students wonder, "Is my instructor a masochist? Why assign such a difficult project?" The answer is that writing is an integral part of learning psychology. It's an opportunity to learn about a topic of interest and acquire a host of skills, such as:

- Collecting information
- Reading and understanding scientific studies of psychology
- Evaluating an author's claims
- Integrating ideas from multiple sources to support your ideas

- Developing writing skills and vocabulary, enabling more effective communication
- Exploring new topics and subjects within psychology
- Thinking and writing like a psychologist

You'll use information seeking and critical thinking skills to complete your paper. Information seeking skills enable you to find useful research articles and other materials and to scan the literature efficiently. Critical thinking skills entail applying principles of analysis to identify appropriate research studies; evaluating the literature; and organizing your review in sections that identify themes, major issues, or trends. Your job in writing a literature review is not to list as many research articles as possible, but rather to present a comprehensive discussion about what has been published on your topic. A literature review should accomplish the following objectives:

- Discuss the major findings relating to your topic.
- Summarize what is and is not known about the topic.
- Evaluate the existing research, identifying controversy when it appears in the literature.
- Discuss further questions for research (e.g., identify gaps in the knowledge base: What questions remain? What direction should further research take?).

As you might imagine, constructing a quality literature review takes work and insight. The degree of difficulty entailed in writing your paper is directly influenced by the topic you choose.

SELECT A TOPIC

Choosing a topic is one of the most important tasks in writing a paper because "the paper can be no better than the topic" (Sternberg, 1993, p. 17). How can you choose a topic that is well researched and will sustain your (and your reader's) interest? Plan ahead, and pay attention to the tips discussed in the following sections.

To write a good paper, you must begin to think about it early—when you receive the assignment. Don't underestimate the amount of time that it will take for you to decide on a topic for your paper. Choosing a topic obviously requires thinking, but students are sometimes surprised to discover that it also requires reading. How are you to decide what to write about without knowing a little about the course and the topic first? How can you choose a topic when you don't know much about the literature? You cannot. Scan the literature and learn a little bit about each topic to inform your decision.

Sources of Ideas for Paper Topics

It may not feel like it, but, believe it or not, you're surrounded by ideas for papers. Paper topics might come from watching television, reading magazines and books, observing people, or observing yourself. Pay attention to the social world around you, observe people's behavior, and ask, "Why?" You'll never be at a loss for ideas. You may also find ideas by using the following resources, which are often overlooked.

Your Textbook   Leaf through your class textbook and carefully scan the table of contents, which lists all of the topics covered in the text. Once you find a topic that sounds interesting, turn to that section of the text and skim through it. Textbook chapters usually provide short overviews of topics that condense broad areas of theory and research into a few pages. If you're still interested after reading more, you've found a potential paper topic. You may have to read several sections of the text to get to this point, so it's important to start early in the semester and try not to get discouraged. Once you've found a topic of interest, use the material in your text as a starting point to expand the topic into a paper. Read the appropriate sections of your text, and take note of any references that look promising.

Encyclopedias and Dictionaries   The reference section of most libraries contains behavioral science dictionaries and encyclopedias, in which you'll find overviews of specific areas. Table 5.1 lists commonly available psychology reference books. These resources can often help you in selecting and narrowing a topic, but remember that they are only a starting point. Also realize that the more recently the book was published, the more useful it will be in guiding

---

TABLE 5.1   PSYCHOLOGY DICTIONARIES AND ENCYCLOPEDIAS

Colman, A. M. (2009). *A dictionary of psychology.* Cambridge, MA: Oxford University Press.

Fundukian, L. J. & Wilson, J. (2007). *The Gale encyclopedia of mental health.* New York: Gale.

Kazdin, A. E. (2000). *Encyclopedia of psychology.* Washington, DC: American Psychological Association.

Matsumo, D. (2009). *The Cambridge dictionary of psychology.* Cambridge, MA: Cambridge University Press.

Reber, A S. & Reber, E. S. (2009). *Penguin dictionary of psychology.* New York: Penguin.

Vandenbos, G. R. *The APA dictionary of psychology.* Washington, DC: APA.

Weiner, I. B. & Craighead, W. E. (2010). *The Corsini encyclopedia of psychology and behavioral science,* Vols. 1–4. New York: John Wiley & Sons, Inc.

your research. In most cases you will not cite the encyclopedia in your paper, but will use it to develop an initial understanding of the breadth and depth of the topic at hand.

Psychology Journals   For a paper in an Introductory Psychology course, look through general psychology journals that have articles spanning all of the fields within psychology. This will help you to get a feel for the wide range of psychological topics that you have to choose from. For example, *Current Directions in Psychological Science* publishes short, review-type articles (in a student-friendly writing style) that may spark some ideas. Also take a look at *American Psychologist* and *Psi Chi Journal of Undergraduate Research*. If you're writing a paper for a class in a particular subfield, such as Developmental Psychology, look through more specialized psychology journals to find recent articles and get ideas. For example, if you're searching for a topic for your Adolescent Psychology paper, leaf through recent issues of journals specializing in adolescent development (e.g., *Journal of Research on Adolescence, Journal of Adolescence, Journal of Adolescent Research, Adolescence*). Once you find an article that's interesting, read it carefully and examine the reference section to find related articles.

Professors   If your professor has provided a list of suggested topics, give them serious consideration. Recognize that your professor can be an important source of information and ideas. However, professors are more likely to offer you help if you've done some work first. Approach your professor for feedback, but understand that you should come with several ideas and ask for advice. Don't expect your professor to provide you with a topic for your paper.

Media   Television, magazines, and newspapers can offer ideas for papers. For example, each Tuesday, *The New York Times* newspaper includes a science section that usually has at least one article about psychology. These articles are a fantastic source of information and ideas. As you read or watch television, stop and consider the topic of the program or article. Ask why: Why does the problem occur? How can it be prevented? What do we know about it? Ideas are everywhere; finding them requires an enquiring mind.

The Internet   The World Wide Web offers an overwhelming array of resources for learning about psychology and coming up with ideas for research papers. Where do you start? Try these specialized psychology search engines and lists of resources.

- PsychWeb—http://www.psychwww.com/
- AmoebaWeb—http://www.vanguard.edu/faculty/ddegelman/amoebaweb/
- Encyclopedia of Psychology—http://www.psychology.org/

- American Psychological Association—http://www.apa.org
- American Psychological Society—http://www.psychologicalscience.org
- Psych Wurld Megapsych—http://www.tulsa.oklahoma.net/~jnichols/bookmarks.html

Browse these resources, and when you find something interesting, try searching for more material. Use synonyms for your topic to get the most information possible. Remember that you'll have to go beyond Web searches when it comes time to find resources for your paper. Most instructors require the use of articles from psychology journals as references for student papers. Internet links can provide a start but cannot serve as the basis of your paper, and many professors prohibit Internet articles as references for student papers.

Narrow Your Topic

By now you should have one or two topics in mind. Review the literature—research articles from psychology journals—for each topic to determine if it is appropriate for your paper assignment. Is the topic well researched? Is the topic narrow enough? Is the topic too narrow? You won't be able to determine the answers to these questions without searching and reading through some of the literature.

How do you locate additional readings to narrow your topic and get started? First, check your textbook to see if additional readings are listed. Frequently, the final page of each chapter lists additional resources that can serve as a useful starting point. You might also look up the references cited in parentheses throughout the text (you can find the full references for this text in the References section at the back of the book). The next step is to search for other sources of information. As you begin your search, remember that the Internet is a valuable tool for locating information, but it cannot replace a trip to the library. A literature review is a scholarly paper that integrates information from reputable sources—academic journals and scholarly texts—which are often not available through the Internet. In addition, most professors will require that you use only scholarly sources and none from the Internet.

Consult the Reference Librarian Your best source of information about the library resources and holdings is the reference librarian. Discuss your paper with him or her, and explain what you're looking for (that's why it's important to have selected a preliminary topic beforehand). Ask the librarian to suggest sources of information. He or she can help you to devise specific search strategies to help you find what you need more quickly and efficiently; however, you must approach him or her with one or more topics in mind. Do not expect the reference librarian to give you a paper topic.

Locate Psychological Research   The American Psychological Association publishes an important resource for locating journal articles: PsycINFO. PsycINFO is a Web database of abstracts from journal articles, book chapters, books, and dissertations published in psychology and the behavioral sciences. Each article entry includes bibliographic information (which helps you locate the article) and an abstract (which provides summary information to help you decide if the article is useful for your paper). PsycINFO is updated frequently and indexes articles from 1887 to the present, permitting a thorough search of the literature. Most institutions maintain a subscription to PsycINFO and some also have a subscription to PsycARTICLES, a service that provides full-text articles from journals published by the American Psychological Association from 1894 to the present.

PsycINFO and other reference databases make it easy to conduct a thorough literature search, saving you lots of time in your research, *if* you know how to use them effectively. Skill, flexibility, and creativity are required to get the most from computerized reference databases. Sometimes the search for a topic yields few results because the wrong search words are used.

How do you determine the appropriate search terms? The *Thesaurus of Psychological Index Terms*, published by the American Psychological Association and linked to PsycINFO, can help you select search terms as it lists all descriptors or index terms (called key terms) that are used for PsycINFO. Use the *Thesaurus* before beginning your search to brainstorm the most appropriate descriptors, and you'll save time and hassle. Also, after locating an article that is useful to your paper, look for the key terms under which the article is labeled. Use these key terms to find additional articles.

Additional features that make PsycINFO especially useful are the tools for refining searches; you can combine the results of several searches and limit the results of a search. Table 5.2 illustrates the steps in using an electronic database, including how to combine the results of several searches and how to limit the results of a search. Finally, note that if your institution does not subscribe to PsycINFO, you can access it online for free through the American Psychological Association Web site (http://www.apa.org). You'll have to obtain the articles through your school (or purchase them for a fee online), but this online resource permits you to do a great deal of research at home.

Determine If There Is Enough Research   Once you have an initial idea for a topic, you're not yet ready to begin writing your paper. Before committing yourself to a topic, be sure that there is adequate literature on it. Can you find articles that address your topic, or do you find too many? The most common mistake that students make in choosing a paper topic is to choose one that is too broad. A literature review, by its very nature,

TABLE 5.2 CONDUCTING A LITERATURE SEARCH WITH PSYCINFO

Before beginning your search, remember that you won't find everything in one pass. Instead, you'll need to refine your searching strategies and, depending on your topic, you may conduct several searches. For example, consider a paper on the influence of parents and peers on early adolescent drinking.

1. Run the Initial Search

To gather articles about alcohol use, I typed in "alcohol or drinking" as keywords and found that over 8,000 articles have "alcohol or drinking" in their title, abstract, or subject.

2. Narrow the Search

Because the paper is for a course in adolescence, I decided that I would limit my findings to only those that examine adolescence. This required a two-step process. First, I typed "adolescent or adolescents or adolescence or teen" as search terms and found nearly 15,000 results. Next I combined this search with my initial search (see step 1) to narrow down the number of articles to a little over 1,100. That's still too many references for my paper!

3. Combine with "And"

Because my paper will examine parental and peer influences on adolescent alcohol use, I limited my search to those articles that discuss parents or peers. I entered "parents" as a keyword and got 12,000 references. I then entered "peers" as a keyword and got over 2,800 results. The third step required combining the results of the two searches. I combined the searches by using "and" to get all the references that examine both parents and peers, and found nearly 600 references. Finally, I combined this search with my initial search on adolescent alcohol use (see step 1) and narrowed the results to 25, a manageable number.

4. Combine with "Or"

Alternatively, I might search for articles that examine parents *or* peers. If I combine the "parent" search with the "peer" search using "or," I get 14,000 articles. After combining this search with the initial search on adolescent alcohol use (see step 1), I get over 250 references that examine adolescent alcohol use and either parents or peers. If I limit the results to journal articles published within the past five years, I get 182 results.

provides comprehensive coverage of a topic. In order to provide comprehensive coverage, you'll need to choose a narrow topic (otherwise you're writing a book, not a class paper). Table 5.3 provides an example of how to narrow and broaden your topic when searching PsycINFO and other computerized databases.

Narrowing your topic means that you'll target your paper to a specific line of research or aspect of your topic. Unless you are already knowledgeable about the research area, you can't preselect a topic that is narrow enough. This is another reason why you shouldn't procrastinate because choosing an appropriately narrow topic requires reading and getting a handle on the literature. Once you have tentatively chosen a topic, scan the literature (using the techniques described earlier in this chapter) to determine how well researched it

TABLE 5.3   NARROWING AND BROADENING A TOPIC

1. Initial Topic: Violence

A search on PsycINFO revealed over 10,000 sources. This topic is way too broad.

2. Narrowed: Child Abuse, Spouse Abuse, School Violence, Community Violence, Dating Violence, Bullying

Even these topics are too broad for an assignment calling for a 10-page paper. For example, consider child abuse; it yielded nearly 10,000 sources on PsycINFO.

3. How to Narrow a Topic

Consider the problem more specifically. Ask who, what, when, where, how? For example, consider child abuse.

Who?	What population are you researching?
What?	Are you interested in causes of abuse? Prevention? Treatment programs?
When?	Historical ? Recent trends?
Where?	The entire world? United States? Urban? Suburban?
How?	How does the abuse take place? What form of abuse? Physical? Sexual? Emotional? Neglect?

4. Sample Narrowed Topic: Child Abuse

Who?	Infants
What?	Causes
When?	Recent
Where?	United States
What?	Physical abuse

After entering each of these terms into PsycINFO, I have 0 results.

5. Broaden the Topic

Broaden the topic by deleting some terms. When I delete "Infants, Recent, and United States," my search yields 56 results.

is and narrow your topic, if necessary. This is a good time to visit your professor or teaching assistant to get some feedback on your choice. Think you have a good understanding of how to use PsycINFO to locate articles as well as broaden and narrow searches? Try Exercise 5.1 to test your competence.

EXERCISE 5.1

Using PsycINFO

Choose an area of research in which you are interested (e.g., the effects of child abuse on development). Be specific in order to narrow the results of your PsycINFO search to yield a manageable number of articles. For example, instead of examining child abuse on development, use more narrow terms such as abuse in infancy; rather than development, use more narrow terms such as cognitive development, or memory development.

1. What is your research question?
2. Write the search terms that you will use.
3. Enter your search terms into PsycINFO. How many results did you get? Were your terms too narrow or too broad? Print out the first page of your results.
4. Try narrowing your topic. Write down the search terms used. How many results did you get? Print out the first page of your results.
5. Take a closer look at the results from the first page of your narrowed search. How do these results differ from those in your first search? Discuss any patterns that you notice in article titles.
6. Try broadening your topic. Write down the search terms used. How many results did you get? Print out the first page of your results.
7. Take a closer look at the results from the first page of your broadened search. How do these results differ from those in your narrowed search? Discuss any patterns that you notice in article titles.
8. Return to the results page of your narrowed topic search. Choose one article that is particularly interesting. Retrieve the first page of that article using your library's full-text and print resources. The reference librarian can assist you if you're experiencing difficulty. Print the first page of the article.

Choose an Appropriate Match to Your Abilities

Try not to choose a topic that is too easy or "safe" for you; try also to avoid choosing a topic that's too difficult (Sternberg, 1993). The purpose of writing your paper is to learn something about a subject. Choose a topic that you're relatively unfamiliar with, to maximize the learning opportunity. Choosing a safe topic (e.g., one you've already written papers on) deprives you of the opportunity and challenge of gaining competence in a new area.

The opposite is also true; try not to choose a topic that is too difficult. Scan the abstracts of articles in your topic to be sure that you can understand the purposes and the underlying concepts and ideas. Avoid topics that you can't adequately present and evaluate from the information presented in articles. In other words, be "certain that the topic you choose does not require an understanding of concepts that your background does not permit you to grasp" (Sternberg, 1993, p. 18).

Begin considering your paper early so that you have time to select a topic that will maintain your interest. Allow yourself the opportunity to consider several topics, and choose the one that appeals most to you. In other words, don't procrastinate. Too often, students wait until the last possible moment to select a topic. Then they choose hastily and end up with a topic they are only marginally interested in. Be nice to yourself by taking the time to find an interesting topic. Few scholarly tasks are worse than working on an uninteresting paper.

COLLECT AND READ YOUR RESEARCH MATERIAL

The primary sources that you will use in writing your paper will be published articles from psychological journals. Journal articles are the most important sources for current findings in psychology. Most professors prefer journal articles as sources over books because scholarly journals are published more frequently and have a more rigorous review and acceptance process than do books. As a psychology major, you will need to become familiar with journal articles—if you aren't already.

What Are Refereed Articles?

How are journal articles different from magazine articles? Magazines pay writers, whereas journals do not pay their authors. Magazine articles might be checked for accuracy, but they do not undergo peer review and are not scrutinized to the same extent as journal articles. Journal articles more extensively document the sources of ideas and evidence; magazines are rarely as extensively documented. Most importantly, journal articles in psychology are refereed, or published after a process of peer review, whereby several professionals review article submissions before an acceptance decision is made. When an author submits a manuscript to a journal, the editor sends copies of it out for review by the author's peers. This means that other psychologists are asked to read the article and determine whether it is suitable for publication. The peers who do the review are called referees. Sometimes peer-reviewed journals are referred to as refereed journals.

How do referees evaluate manuscripts? Although each reviewer may use slightly different criteria, manuscripts are reviewed based on scholarship. A scholarly manuscript offers an important contribution to the field of psychology and includes a comprehensive review of the literature, concise writing, appropriate methodology and statistical analyses, and an understanding of the audience (Landrum & Davis, 2010). Once the editor has received the reviews, a decision is made whether to reject the paper, accept it, or suggest that the author make some changes and resubmit. As you might imagine, this is a long and tedious process, but it ensures that the articles appearing in scholarly journals have scholarly merit.

Even those who are unfamiliar with journal articles quickly see that research articles have a specific format and layout. Understanding the layout will make articles more comprehensible. An empirical article consists of several sections: the abstract, introduction, method, results, discussion, and references. Each section has a specific purpose. The abstract (usually located underneath the article title and before the text of the article) briefly summarizes the study. The introduction is the first section of an article. It provides an overview of the research question, reviews the literature, and identifies the purpose of the study (the specific purpose and hypotheses are usually found at the very end of the introduction section). The method section explains how the research was conducted; it describes the participants, measures, instruments and equipment, and procedure. The results section presents statistical analyses that address the research questions. Here, the study findings are presented, with information displayed in graphs and tables. In the discussion section, the author examines the significance of the study's findings in light of prior research, discusses limitations of the study, and offers suggestions for further research. For more information about empirical articles, see Chapter 6.

How to Read Scholarly Articles

Thoroughly reading an article requires several passes. Your first pass should be an initial scan to determine whether the study is essential for your paper. Reading and taking notes is time consuming; therefore, you want to be sure that the article will suit your needs before you spend a great deal of time on it. During your initial scan of the article, determine the research question, specific hypotheses, findings, and interpretation. After you've scanned for this material, stop and consider whether the article fits with the purpose of your paper. Is it relevant? How does the article apply to your paper? How will you use it?

If you've decided that the article is relevant to your paper, your next task is to read for depth. What is the problem or issue addressed? Discern the theories tested and the methods used. Who were the participants, and how were they tested? How were the findings interpreted? Consider the following questions:

- Is the author's hypothesis ambiguous or clearly articulated?
- What is the author's research orientation and theoretical framework? What are the author's underlying assumptions? From what theoretical framework does the author address the problem? (You can find clues in the author's choice of citations and how often particular references are cited.)
- Could the problem have been approached more effectively from another perspective?
- Has the author evaluated the literature relevant to the issue? Were any areas of literature excluded from the author's review?

- Does the author take a balanced perspective and include articles that take contrary positions?
- Is the sample large and representative of the population the author wishes to address? How were participants selected?
- What measures were used? Are the instruments' psychometric properties presented? How valid are the instruments? Do you think the instruments measure the intended constructs?
- Were the data analyzed properly? What are the findings? Are the findings meaningful? Sometimes researchers find differences between variables that are statistically significant, but small; these differences may not be meaningful when applied.
- How are the findings interpreted? Do you agree with the interpretation?
- What are the strengths and weaknesses of the study? Every study has strengths and weaknesses.
- Do the findings have applied or policy implications?

As you read, remember that journal articles can lead you to other articles and sources for your research. When you find a current article that is especially useful, examine the references and you'll find other sources that are relevant to your paper. If you examine the reference list for each article that you cite in your paper, you'll find that a great deal of your research is complete. However, it is important not to rely on this as your only strategy for locating articles because you may end up with a distorted view of the literature. Some authors may not cite other seminal works because of differences of opinion and bias. If you obtain all of your sources from the references of other articles, you might miss some important pieces of research, and you will certainly miss out on new research.

How to Read Scholarly Books

When you consider books as sources for your paper, understand that the more recently a book was published, the more likely it is to contain current theory and methodology (Scott, Koch, Scott, & Garrison, 1999). Edited books, which contain chapters written by many different authors, are often good sources of information. Because each chapter is written by a different author, it usually presents a different view of your topic.

Before you spend a great deal of time searching for books, be familiar with your professor's recommended and required resources. Some professors advise their students not to use books as sources because they're too long for student papers. In addition, many books are not scholarly. Many popular self-help books, for example, are of questionable scientific value. Therefore, some professors discourage students from using books as sources because it can be difficult to evaluate their scholarly value.

If you decide to use books as source material for your paper, examine each one carefully. How do you determine the academic trustworthiness of a book?

- Examine the author's background. What are the author's academic credentials and experience?
- Examine the reference section because the number and type of references can indicate how well the book has been researched. How many of the references are the author's?
- How sound are its facts, methodologies, and findings?
- Does the book have an index? Scott et al. (1999) suggest that "in addition to making your search for relevant material easier, an index suggests a certain amount of professionalism on the part of the authors. Also, browsing through an index can give you a feel for the book's level of professionalism" (p. 109).
- Skim the introduction, preface, forward, or first chapter to find clues about the book's purpose, intended audience, and scholarly quality.

As your mass of journal articles and other research sources grows, you may feel a sense of unease and wonder how you will sift through the pages and pages of information. Reading the articles and synthesizing the ideas into a cohesive paper may seem like a daunting task, but break it down into smaller pieces and it will seem more manageable. If you've taken your time in choosing a topic and narrowed it down appropriately, you've already begun reading some of the literature, or at least scanned some of it, and you have a better sense of how to organize your paper than you think.

Define Your Purpose

Once you begin reading, it's easy to forget the purpose of your paper. Instead, you may find yourself describing every detail of each article. Stay focused. Before you begin reading and taking notes, clarify the purpose of your paper. Remain focused as you read and consider articles, and your paper will seem more manageable. Consider your thesis, problem, or research question. What is your angle? Are you considering issues of theory, methodology, or policy? What is the scope of the review? How have you limited the literature? For example, a student might limit the scope of a paper about conduct disorder to examining evaluations of behavioral interventions. Defining the scope of the review involves restating your narrow topic and setting rules for including or excluding articles. Write down your ideas about the purpose, angle, and scope of your paper. Write the purpose on a note card or sticky note and keep it near you. Refer to it often to remember and focus.

At first, concentrate on reading the abstracts for the articles that you've chosen. If you've defined your purpose well, you may find that after reading only the abstracts, you can eliminate some articles from consideration because they're not relevant to your paper. As you read, take occasional breaks to re-read your stated purpose. Consider whether what you've read is within the scope that you delineated for your paper. Perhaps your reading has suggested that you change your focus or narrow your paper. Realize that your ideas about your paper will change and become more refined with your reading. Be open to change, and take notes on how you might refocus your paper.

The most important tip about reading is to begin early. Notice a trend? Lots of time and effort will be spent before you begin to write, but ultimately you will write your paper more quickly. You'll need plenty of time to think about your paper, collect articles, and read them before any writing occurs. Reading for your paper is a process of information gathering and synthesis. As you read, you might encounter references that seem important. Return to the library to gather these new sources.

When do you stop reading and taking notes? One clue that you have done a thorough review is when you notice that article authors cite studies that you have already reviewed. But this doesn't mean that you're ready to write the paper. Understand your sources, take notes, and think carefully about their implications before beginning to write. Consider how the articles fit together and how you might organize your review.

RECORD YOUR RESEARCH: TAKE NOTES

As you read, summarize the main findings and methods of each study that you think are important enough to include in your paper. If you consistently take the time to write a brief summary of each article that you plan to include, your literature review will be largely done by the time you sit down to formally write. Summarize each article in a page or less. Don't write down everything. Avoid copying word for word from a source; doing so makes it too easy to commit plagiarism without realizing it (we'll talk more about plagiarism later). Instead, explain the concept in your own words. Note taking is a skill; it requires critical thinking and evaluation to record only the most essential features of a study (purpose, method, findings, and interpretation).

Take Notes

The method that you use to take notes is a personal choice. Some experts (e.g., Landrum & Davis, 2010; Sternberg, 1993) suggest using a note-card system. Use 5-by-7-inch cards, organized by topic. Use a separate card for each article. Write the APA style reference on the back of the card and your notes on the front (if you're not sure what an APA style reference is, see Chapter 6 for a discussion of APA style). Note cards allow you to physically organize information and sort it into topical categories that will help you to organize the outline of your paper. Note cards travel well and offer a handy way of arranging and rearranging information.

I prefer to take notes in my word processing program. If you take notes on a computer, clearly mark each reference and the notes associated with it, and print out a hard copy. You'll find that most of the notes that will become the prose of your first draft are already typed. You can then edit them, adding transitions, analysis, and interpretation (after making a "safe copy"). You can also cut and paste the material to organize it, making writing a lot easier. If you choose to take notes in a word processor, it is essential that you take care in summarizing the article in your own words.

Whatever method you choose, remember that good notes concisely and accurately summarize the main points of a source. Be precise in indicating paraphrases and direct quotes. It's also essential that you take the time to record the reference, using correct APA style. Take it from my own experience, hunting for an unrecorded reference is very frustrating! It can sometimes take hours to locate a source once you've begun writing whereas it takes only a few minutes to record the information properly while you're taking notes. Also, take special care to note any information that you quote or copy verbatim. Sometimes students forget that a sentence or two was copied from a source—and is not their own summary—and inadvertently commit plagiarism. Regardless of whether intended, plagiarism is a serious breech of academic honesty.

Avoid Plagiarism

Plagiarism means using another person's work (i.e., ideas, research, writing, Web sites, charts, data, or other original work) without giving credit and without clearly acknowledging its source. The rules of plagiarism apply to all sources, both published (books, magazines, newspapers, Web sites, and textbooks) and unpublished (class lectures, notes, handouts, speeches, and student papers). To avoid plagiarizing, writers must give credit any time they use information from a source. Citations giving the source of information must accompany: (1) discussions of another person's ideas, arguments, or theory; (2) facts that are not common knowledge; (3) direct quotations of a person's spoken or written words; and (4) paraphrases of another person's spoken or written words.

How can you avoid plagiarism? By using your own words to express the ideas of others, and then giving credit to the originators of those ideas. Try to convey the author's main idea without using his or her words or sentence structure. Always cite information and ideas that are learned through your research, no matter where you find them (even if it is on the Internet or in an encyclopedia). Common knowledge is not cited, but be careful of what you consider to be common knowledge. Examples of common knowledge are well-known dates and familiar sayings. Generally, information that could be found in a number of general sources (e.g., popular magazines) may not have to be cited. Whenever in doubt, cite. It is better to be safe and over cite your sources than to accidentally plagiarize.

Appropriate Use of Quotations   When you repeat an author's exact words, you must indicate that the material is a direct quote and give its source. APA style requires that you enclose the material in quotation marks and cite the author's last name, year, and the page number for the quote (American Psychological Association, 2010). Here is an example of a short quotation, given in text:

> Bornstein and Arterberry (1999) argued that "perception begins our experience and interpretation of the world, and is crucial to the growth of thought" (p. 231). This is … .

If the quotation contains forty or more words, it should be displayed as a freestanding block, with the quotation marks omitted:

Bornstein and Arterberry (1999) argued that

> Perception begins our experience and interpretation of the world, and is crucial to the growth of thought, to the regulation of emotions, to interaction in social relationships, and to progress in most aspects of our development. The input, translation, and encoding of sensory information in perception is requisite to reflection and action. (p. 231)

In summary, it is permissible to include a direct quote in your paper as long as it is appropriately documented. Enclose the material in quotation marks, and cite the authors, year of publication, and page numbers. Quoting a source without providing documentation is plagiarism. That said, check with your instructor, as some professors prefer that students not use direct quotations in their papers.

Now that you've reviewed the appropriate use of quotes, be aware that it's best not to use too many of them in your paper. A paper represents the synthesis and analysis of what you've read. When you use direct quotes too often, the resulting paper is just a string of other people's words and ideas, rather than your own analysis, interpretation, and expression of their ideas. Be careful not to quote because of laziness; it is much easier to use direct quotes than it is to paraphrase. Quote directly from a source only when you cannot capture the original ideas in your own words. Use quotes only when the author's language is distinctive and enhances your argument. In other words, record quotations only when "(1) the language of the original was especially important or vivid and therefore worth preserving, and (2) when you wanted to invoke the authority of your source" (Meyer, 1985, p. 78).

Appropriate Paraphrasing   Paraphrasing refers to restating an author's ideas or information in your own words. Even though you are using your own words, you must cite the source of your information. In APA style, appropriate citation of paraphrases includes the author's last name and year of publication; you are encouraged but not required to provide a page number. Note that you are required to provide the page number when quoting directly from a source. For example, a paraphrase of the text quoted earlier might read as follows:

> Perception is essential to cognitive, emotional, and social development because it determines how we interpret and react to the sensory world around us (Bornstein & Arterberry, 1999, p. 170).

As you can see, the paraphrase concisely restates the main idea of the passage, using different words and sentence structure.

How do you paraphrase? First, be sure that you understand the information you wish to paraphrase. Your goal is to restate the idea and convey the same meaning, so it is essential that you understand the original passage before trying to paraphrase it. Realize that you may have to edit your paraphrase several times. Write your paraphrase, then reread the original passage to check for accuracy and to be sure that you haven't borrowed language or structure. Revise your paraphrase as needed. Remember to use your own grammatical structure, restate the material in your own words, and cite the source. Pretend to explain the idea to a friend—then write what you say. Practice is important because appropriate paraphrasing is difficult. Paraphrasing allows you to summarize an author's main points concisely and in your own writing style, contributing to the "flow" of your paper. Test your ability to quote and paraphrase as well as learn about how your institution views plagiarism and its consequences by completing Exercise 5.2.

EXERCISE 5.2
Understanding and Avoiding Plagiarism

1. Identify an interesting passage from your textbook. Write a short paragraph about the topic, including the quotation, using appropriate APA style to indicate that it is a quotation and not your own words.
2. Now write a short paragraph that paraphrases instead of quotes the passage. Note that paraphrasing entails more than using a thesaurus to replace a few words. Appropriate paraphrasing requires conveying the ideas in an entirely new set of words and sentence structure from the original.
3. Reflect on the process of paraphrasing. Was it challenging? Why? How might you gain experience and become more comfortable with this new skill?

4. Identify reasons why students might plagiarize.
5. Look up your institution's definitions and policies about plagiarism. What are the consequences of plagiarism at your institution?

Frequently students commit plagiarism without realizing it, by incorrectly quoting and paraphrasing material. Remember that ignorance of the rules—or laziness—is no excuse for plagiarism. Many professors don't provide a "get out of jail free card." In other words, if you inadvertently plagiarize, you might find yourself with an F or a zero on an assignment and no way to make it up.

Avoid the Easy (Dishonest) Way Out

Writing papers is difficult. It is tempting to take shortcuts. Some of these shortcuts may seem harmless, but all are forms of academic dishonesty:

- Recycling an old paper used in a prior class
- Buying a paper online
- Downloading a paper online
- Cutting and pasting from Internet pages
- Using a service that writes papers for students
- Asking someone else to write a paper
- Using a sibling's, parent's, or friend's paper

Recognize that these are dishonest and unethical ways of completing paper assignments. You'll cheat yourself of the learning and skills that are developed by researching and writing papers. Professors also have ways of discovering the use of these techniques, so success with these devious methods is unlikely. Do you want to be marked as a dishonest, lazy student? A cheat? A liar? This is not an exaggeration. Plagiarism is a serious offense that marks offenders as unethical. For more information and resources to help you understand the scope of plagiarism as well as quizzes to determine if you really understand acceptable use of information and how to appropriately cite material, see the Web sites at the end of this chapter.

WRITE YOUR PAPER

Now that you've read your articles, taken notes, and spent time thinking about the articles, it is time to organize and write your paper. Where do you begin?

Prepare an Outline

Before you begin writing, prepare an outline. It's much easier to prepare an outline once you've read and taken notes, so save this step until you have a set of notes from your reading, have had time to think about the reading, and have made lists of the material that you think is important to include in your paper. Consider the theme, issue, or research question that you plan to explore in your paper. What have you learned so far? Outlining helps you to get a better understanding of your paper because it forces you to list your ideas and to arrange them logically. Perhaps most important, an outline is a concrete plan for your writing. It will not only help you to stay on track (i.e., keep you from introducing irrelevant topics) but also keep you from leaving important material out of your paper. You'll find that you can write your paper more quickly because you'll know exactly what to put in each section. An outline doesn't have to be fancy. Just jot down the points you want to make and then order them so that they make sense. It's easier to do this with a computer, using a word processing program to cut and paste your ideas as you wish.

Some students and professors dislike using outlines and think they are a waste of time. Typically, if you are experiencing difficulty structuring your outline, it means that your ideas are too vague and fuzzy. Read and think about your project, and organizational themes will emerge. Outlining is a valuable skill; but if you really can't write an outline, then just begin writing. Some authors prefer to write a rough draft of their paper, allowing thoughts and creativity to flow freely. Once you've written a rough draft, read through it and outline what you've written. The resulting outline will help you to see the structure of your argument. You can then reorder the outline as needed to make sense and present your argument skillfully.

All good literature reviews can be outlined easily. The first sentence of each paragraph should provide an overview of the paragraph. Therefore by examining the first sentence of each paragraph, one can compile an outline of the structure of the paper. Once you have done so, examine the structure. First, ask yourself whether each paragraph has a purpose. Then examine the ordering of paragraphs. What idea is expressed in each paragraph? Are the ideas ordered in a logical fashion? Reorder as needed.

Write

Students often worry about how to start writing, and then don't begin. A simple list of points to address helps prevent writer's block. Once you have an outline, your paper is organized, and you can work on filling in the outline. Don't worry about starting at the beginning. Don't get stuck on a first sentence or paragraph. Just start anywhere. Write with a word processing program on the computer, which allows you to cut and paste your writing into endless patterns. Take advantage of this technological capability and begin writing whatever part of your paper flows most naturally. You can arrange and rearrange your writing later.

Ultimately your paper will be organized into several sections. The first section of your paper, the introduction, establishes the research question and explains why it is worth examining. The last paragraph of the introduction section should outline the organization of the paper. In the body of the paper you will present evidence from research studies to support your points. Describe and evaluate each study, and make comparisons among the studies. Compare studies based on assumptions, theories tested, hypotheses, research designs, methods, findings, and interpretations. How do the studies support the theme of your paper? In the final section of the paper, draw conclusions, discuss implications, and suggest avenues for further research. Based on the studies reviewed and the comparisons and evaluations made, what conclusions do you draw? What research is left to be done? Recommend future studies. By now you should have a list of all the important ideas you hope to convey in your paper.

As you begin to write, remember that this is only your first draft. Not every word will stay, and not every word has to be perfect. Don't worry about errors. Just get the ideas out; you'll catch the errors later as you edit. Write anything that appears relevant, and think about where to put it and how to reorganize it later. Regularly save your work on the internal hard drive and a flash drive or other external storage so that your work is protected in the event of a computer catastrophe. Print a hard copy at the end of each writing session, and preferably more often (e.g., after completing two or three pages, or an hour's worth of work).

Begin working early, to give yourself time to write and rewrite. Time is essential to writing a comprehensive review of the literature; time to read, let ideas simmer, write, gain perspective on what you've written, and revise. As you write, you may find that some elements of your research are incomplete. Go back to the library and gather additional resources to fill in any gaps in your research or argument.

Revise

The most important part of writing is rewriting, so be prepared for lots of editing and rewrites. Many students neglect this part of the writing process and instead print out a paper and submit it right away. The best papers ferment over time. Once you have a draft, spend at least twenty-four hours away from it. Let it sit for a day or two, and you'll be able to approach it with fresh eyes. With time, you'll find it easier to separate yourself from your work and become more objective.

Before you begin the editing and revising process, make a "safe" copy of your paper in case you decide to undo some of your revisions. Read through your draft and note what needs to be done. Is the organization consistent with your outline? Are you happy with the outline, or should it be modified based on your paper? As you read, you might want to list gaps in the paper's organization that need to be filled, missing details to provide, and other tasks to complete, such as checking spelling and grammar or tracking down an errant reference. Recognize that you will revise the paper several times; don't feel the need to complete the final draft right away.

Read your paper aloud. Reorganize sections, edit them, or even delete them if you deem them unnecessary. Examine the order of sentences and paragraphs. Sometimes moving a sentence up in a paragraph (or even deleting it) makes a world of difference. As you revise your paper, consider whether you've left anything out. Can anything be deleted? Are there extraneous details or sections? Are the paragraphs and sections coherent and logical? Have you used transitions between paragraphs and sections so that the paper flows? Have you used a consistent style throughout? Have you used the proper guidelines, as stipulated by your instructor or APA style? (See Chapter 6 for more on APA style.)

Think you're done? Print out your final draft and proofread it aloud. Check for the placement of commas and your use of grammar. You might be surprised by the errors that you find. Take your final draft to the writing center at your college or university. You'll get an extra pair of eyes to read your work and some helpful feedback on how to improve your paper. Now make your corrections and print out your final draft.

Remember that good writing is the result of practice. The process gets easier with experience, but we all begin a paper with at least a little trepidation. Start early and take time to read and mull over your articles. Revise your paper several times, waiting a day or two between each draft, to gain distance. Use the literature review checklist in Checklist 5.1 as a guide to writing your literature review. Finally, don't procrastinate or let fear stop you from writing.

CHECKLIST 5.1
Literature Review Checklist

- ❑ Is the topic appropriate (e.g., is it a topic within the field of psychology)?
- ❑ Does the title of your paper describe the topic of your review?
- ❑ Does your review include an introduction section that defines the purpose of the review and its significance?
- ❑ Does the introduction section explain the organization of the literature review?
- ❑ Does your review include journal articles as sources?
- ❑ Does your review include the most current (and appropriate) articles as sources?
- ❑ Does your review discuss the major findings relating to your topic?
- ❑ Does your review evaluate existing research?
- ❑ Have you explained why particular studies and sets of findings are strong?

- ❑ Have you explained why particular studies and sets of findings are weak?
- ❑ Have you included enough detail about each study to help the reader determine the significance of each article?
- ❑ Have you described relationships between studies?
- ❑ Have gaps in the literature been noted and explained?
- ❑ Have any controversies in the field been described?
- ❑ Have you chosen a method of organizing the literature reviewed in your paper?
- ❑ Have you outlined your paper after writing it to examine its organization?
- ❑ Does your literature review answer an identifiable question?
- ❑ Does each study you reviewed correspond with a specific part of your topic outline?
- ❑ Have you deleted studies that do not relate to your purpose or argument?
- ❑ Does each part of your review flow logically from the preceding part?
- ❑ Do you use transitions between paragraphs to indicate the flow of major points in your outline?
- ❑ Does your review include a conclusion section?
- ❑ Does your review discuss further questions for research?
- ❑ Does your conclusion address the purpose identified in the introduction?
- ❑ Did you revise your manuscript several times?
- ❑ Did you spell check the manuscript?
- ❑ Are quotations used only when needed?
- ❑ Are quotations appropriately cited? Can any quotations be paraphrased?
- ❑ Are all paraphrases appropriately cited?
- ❑ Have you avoided the use of slang, abbreviations, and contractions?
- ❑ Have you used the past tense to refer to research studies?

SUGGESTED READINGS

Beins, B. & Beins, A. (2008). *Effective writing in psychology: Papers, posters, and presentations.* Hoboken, NJ: Wiley.

Lipson, C. (2008). *Doing honest work in college: How to prepare citations, avoid plagiarism, and achieve real academic success.* Chicago: University of Chicago Press.

Mitchell, H. L. & Jolley, J. M. (2009). *Writing for psychology.* Belmont, CA: Wadsworth.

Rosnow, R. L. & Rosnow, M. (2008). *Writing papers in psychology.* Belmont, CA: Wadsworth.

Scott, J. M., Koch, R. E., Scott, G. M., & Garrison, S. M. (1999). *The psychology student writer's manual.* Upper Saddle River, NJ: Prentice Hall.

INTERNET RESOURCES

A Guide to Writing in Psychology

http://psychology.gmu.edu/writing/

This Web site contains an excellent guide to all forms of writing in psychology. Essential reading!

Writing the Literature Review

http://www2.smumn.edu/deptpages/~tcwritingcenter/Forms_of_Writing/LitReview.htm

A collection of Web sites and resources.

Writing a Psychology Literature Review

http://depts.washington.edu/psywc/handouts/pdf/litrev.pdf

Excellent handout describes the steps in writing a literature review paper and provides helpful advice for student writers.

PsycINFO Guide

http://www.library.auckland.ac.nz/docs/helpsheets/psycinfoguide.pdf

Everything you need to know about using PsycINFO is in this handy guide. A must-read that will make finding relevant articles much easier.

Plagiarism Tutorial

http://www.lib.usm.edu/research/plag/plagiarismtutorial.php

Excellent site with several lessons and two quizzes to assess your understanding of plagiarism.

JOURNAL EXERCISES

How I Feel About Writing

How do you feel about writing? Imagine receiving a paper assignment in class. What are your initial thoughts and emotions? Would you like to change any of these reactions? Which ones? How would you prefer to react? What small steps can you take to make it easier to react in a more satisfactory way?

What I Like to Write

Which writing experiences do you find fun? Do you prefer free writing, or do you like writing papers, essays, or creative pieces? How are these different for you, and what do you prefer about each? What topics do you most prefer writing about? Why?

My Habits

What are your habits and typical ways of completing a writing assignment? Do you find that you procrastinate? How? Is there any way that you can prevent this? How can using some of the techniques described in this chapter make the writing task quicker and easier?

WRITING AN EMPIRICAL PAPER

CHAPTER OUTLINE

The ability to write empirical papers is a critical skill for success as a psychology major. Unlike many other majors, psychology students must learn how to report the results of empirical work, that is, research studies. Psychology is a science and, as a major, you must learn how to read and understand scientific literature, and contribute to the literature by writing empirical papers and lab reports. All colleges and universities require psychology majors to complete at least one or two courses in research methodology in which students must conduct research studies and write empirical papers to describe their research. Specifically, these papers discuss the question under study, the methods used to gather information about the question, and the findings and their implications. Understanding how to write an empirical paper is essential to your academic success. In this chapter we discuss the mechanics of the empirical paper. After a brief discussion of the *Publication Manual of the American Psychological Association* (2010), we will examine each section of an empirical paper. The chapter closes with a sample template for your empirical paper.

APA STYLE: THE *PUBLICATION MANUAL* OF THE *AMERICAN PSYCHOLOGICAL ASSOCIATION*

While reading journal articles, you've probably noticed the distinct style of scientific writing. Why is the style so structured? Consider the purpose of written reports: communication—to tell readers about your research and explain what you did and what you found. Excellent scientific communication provides readers with enough information to enable them to evaluate critically the procedures, judge the quality of the research, and replicate (or reproduce) the results. Scientific writing is filled with facts that are appropriately paraphrased and documented. Because publication space in scholarly journals is limited, authors attempt to provide complete information in as few words as possible. Each word is carefully chosen for its precision. Scientific writing promotes clear communication, but it is very different from other types of writing and often requires more practice to master.

In psychology, authors are expected to follow the standard format specified by the sixth edition of the *Publication Manual of the American Psychological Association* (2010). Although learning the format known as APA style is challenging, ultimately a standard style of scientific communication makes it easier for researchers to report findings and for readers to comprehend them. This chapter provides a brief overview of APA style and the structure of research reports. Remember that this presentation is brief and cannot replace the *Publication Manual*, which is nearly 300 pages long. If you have questions about specific issues, consult the *Publication Manual* and your professor.

STRUCTURE OF THE EMPIRICAL PAPER

As we've discussed, an empirical paper or research article is a highly structured, concise, professional way of communicating the results of a research study. It consists of several sections, each with a specific purpose. The *title page* communicates the title, the authors, and the authors' institutional affiliations. The *abstract* provides a brief summary of the study. The *introduction* is the first section of an article. It gives an overview of the research question, discusses the relevant literature, and identifies the purpose of the study. The *method* section explains how the research was conducted; it includes a description of the participants, measures, instruments and equipment, and procedure. The *results* section presents statistical analyses that address the research questions, with information displayed in graphs and tables. The *discussion* section explores the implications of the study's findings in light of prior research, limitations of the study, and suggestions for further research. Last but not least is the *reference* section, which provides accurate references for all material that was cited in the paper. Now let's examine each section of the empirical paper.

Title Page

Don't underestimate the importance of a title. The title gives readers a mini-introduction to your paper and helps them to decide if they want to read the abstract and paper. The title should offer a concise summary of the paper——the topic, variables, and theoretical issue under study——all in no more than twelve words. According to the *Publication Manual*, "a title should be fully explanatory when standing alone" (APA, 2010, p. 23). A good title is hard to write; plan to spend some time on it. It's often easier to write the title once the paper is complete.

- The paper title is written in uppercase and lowercase letters, positioned in the upper half of the first page, and centered between the right and left margin.
- Center the author's name, written in uppercase and lowercase letters, on the line below the title.
- The institutional affiliation appears in uppercase and lowercase letters, centered on the line below the author's.
- The running head is a short version of your title that appears at the top of the pages of a paper or published article. The running head is typed flush left (all uppercase) following "Running head:" on the first page, then appears on its own (without the "Running head" label) on all subsequent pages. The running head should not exceed fifty characters, including punctuation and spacing. Using most word processors, the running head

and page number can be inserted into a header, which then automatically appears on all pages.

- The page number appears in the top right-hand corner.
- Similar to the entire paper, the title page is double spaced, in 12-point font, with 1-inch margins.
- The title is not in bold type, italics, or underlined.
- For a sample title page, see the sample template at the end of this chapter.
- Note that you may decide to change your title as you complete your research study. Your title is not set in stone; revise it, if needed, to reflect the findings and the content of your paper.

Abstract

Like the title, the abstract gives readers a glimpse into your paper. The abstract provides a brief comprehensive overview of your study, including enough information for readers to decide if they want to read the article itself (that is, determine whether the article is likely to provide information to address their questions). Write the abstract after you've completed your paper and have a firm perspective of the findings and their importance. Describe the problem under investigation, presenting the major hypotheses, participants, materials, and procedure. Summarize the results and conclusions, indicating the implications or applications. A good abstract interests readers and convinces them that the study is worth reading. An abstract should be self-explanatory and range from 150 to 250 words. Adhering to the word count is very difficult, but well-written shorter abstracts are best. Most writers begin by composing a longer summary and slowly pare down unneeded words.

Introduction

The title of the paper appears on the first line of page 3, centered and typed in uppercase and lowercase letters. The introduction begins on line 2, flush with the left margin and indented. The introduction is your opportunity to introduce readers to your research question, what is known about the topic, why the topic is important, and how your study contributes to what is already known. Consider the introduction as three separate sections. The first section, a paragraph or two in length, introduces the problem: What is the topic under study, and how will it be approached? Why is it important? The second section of the introduction provides a review of relevant literature to explain what is known about the specific question under study (review Chapter 5 for suggestions on how to conduct a literature review). Be specific and present only research that is directly relevant to the research question.

What has prior research shown? What are limitations in prior research? How is your study an extension of prior research? The third section of the introduction states the purpose and rationale of the research study, and provides a brief overview of your study. Now, let's consider each part of the introduction in more depth.

Introductory Paragraphs   The introductory paragraphs lure readers into your paper. These paragraphs often are the most difficult to write, so consider saving them for later, after you've written the rest of the paper. Use the funnel approach to structure the introduction. Begin with a general statement (the wide opening of the funnel) and get more specific (narrow the funnel) with each sentence, until the final sentence introduces the purpose of your study. An additional introductory paragraph may explain why the research question addressed by your study is important. Your goal is to make readers see the point of your study and to convince them that your project tackles an important question or issue.

Review of the Relevant Literature   The next component of the introduction reviews the literature relevant to your study. It typically is several pages long, and cites theory and research that expand and support the rationale for your study. The literature searching and summarizing strategies discussed in Chapter 5 illustrate how to search the literature, take notes, and organize a literature review. Your goal is to inform readers of the published literature on your problem, demonstrate the importance of the question, and justify the rationale for your methods (Scott et al., 1999). As you review the literature, it is important to remain focused on your research topic. Discuss only research that is pertinent to your project. The review is selective and should "avoid nonessential details; instead emphasize pertinent findings, relevant methodological issues, and major conclusions" (American Psychological Association, 2010, p. 28). Refer readers to published reviews that examine more general issues, so that they can obtain additional information, if desired.

An effective review of the literature orients readers to what is known and answers several questions (Austin & Calderon, 1996; Landrum et al., 2010; Sternberg, 1993):

- What is the purpose of the study?
- What do we know about this area of research?
- How does the study relate to prior research? How does it draw upon and extend prior work? What is the nature of your contribution?
- Why is the study important or interesting?
- What rationale links the research questions and research design? How did you choose the research design, and how does the design address the question?

It is vital that you demonstrate the logical continuity between prior research, your research question, and your research design. Unquestionably, this is the most difficult part of writing the introduction. As you write, keep your purpose in mind: Your goal is to interest readers, explain why your study is relevant, and motivate them to continue (Sternberg, 1993). Finally, be very careful to appropriately cite the sources of information in your literature review. If you are unsure of the overall use of citations or how to appropriately quote or paraphrase sources, see the section on plagiarism in Chapter 5 and the *Publication Manual*.

Purpose and Rationale   The final component of the introduction section explains the purpose and rationale for your study. Explain your hypotheses (your specific predictions about the research results) and provide a brief overview of your study. How does your research design relate to the theoretical issue that you wish to address?

Method

The introduction answers the questions, "What?" and "Why?" The method section explains, "How." The purpose of the method section is to clearly explain how you conducted your study. The method section should provide enough pertinent details so that readers can replicate your research. Typically the method section contains several sections—participants; apparatus, materials, or measures; and procedure. Begin the method section, titled "Method," typed in boldfaced type, and on a new line, centered between the right and left margin.

Participants   On a separate line, flush with the left margin, list "Participants" in boldfaced type. On the next line, indented, begins the participants section, which answers the questions, "Who participated in the study?" "How many participated?" and "How were they selected?" In this section, describe the demographic characteristics of the participants. Explain any demographic details that might affect your study, including age, sex, ethnicity, geographic location, and number of participants assigned to each treatment group. Explain how participants were selected and how they were assigned to groups. What were the circumstances in which they participated, and were any inducements offered (e.g., extra credit)?

Apparatus, Materials, or Measures   Depending on your study, this section might be entitled apparatus, materials, or measures. Similar to the Participants section, this section begins on a new flush left line with the label "Apparatus," "Materials," or "Measures," listed in boldfaced type.

Indent the next line and describe the equipment or instruments used to conduct the study. If you used specialized equipment to conduct the research, describe it and explain how it was used. If the equipment is a manufactured item, include information on the manufacturer and the model number. If you developed an apparatus or any materials for your study, describe them in enough detail so that readers could reproduce them (including exact dimensions and physical properties of any apparatus that you construct). If standardized tests or measures were used, describe them, include their psychometric properties (e.g., reliability and validity), and explain how they were coded or scored. As you write this section, remember that your goal is to describe how you measured your variables and what methods you used to collect data.

Procedure   On a new line, flush left and in boldfaced type, the "Procedure" section describes the steps you took in conducting your research. Tell readers what was done, how, and in what order. Clearly describe what happened to participants from the time they walked into the lab until the time they left the lab—the beginning to the end of their experience. If you administered surveys to participants, describe the survey conditions and instructions provided. If your research was experimental, describe how participants were exposed to the independent variable; include a description of any instructions that participants received. Describe your methods and any control features of the design, such as counterbalancing or the use of control groups. Again, your goal is to provide sufficient detail so that a reader can replicate your study.

Results

The heading for the Results section appears centered between the right and left margin, with "Results" written in boldfaced type. On the following left-justified line, begin your results section. First, ask yourself, "What did I find? How can I say what I found in a careful, detailed way? Is what I am planning to say precise and to the point? Have I left out anything of importance?" (Rosnow & Rosnow, 2008, p. 58). Sternberg (1993) suggests that you report the most interesting results first, or those that are most relevant to the hypotheses tested. Save results that are less interesting and relevant for later in the results section. "You may wish to report first a general conclusion or interpretation, followed by some descriptive statistics that support your assertion, followed only at the end by the inferential statistics that buttress the conclusion" (Sternberg, 1993, p. 51). In other words, think about the importance of your findings and present them accordingly. Don't just give your readers a laundry list of findings. Instead, carefully consider how to present the results, including the order and style of presentation.

The results section provides answers to your research questions in the form of reports of descriptive and inferential statistics. Descriptive statistics summarize the data. Inferential statistics examine your hypotheses and test the likelihood that the results are not due to chance. As you report tests of statistical significance, the *Publication Manual* recommends that you include the name of the test, obtained value, degrees of freedom, significance level, and effect size. Note that these guidelines are intended for publication in scholarly journals. Your professor may modify these guidelines for your class by, for example, excluding effect size. Tables and figures are effective ways of concisely conveying a great deal of information. The *Publication Manual* recommends including tables to list means, medians, standard deviations, and confidence intervals. Any tables that you use must be self-explanatory (e.g., with titles and fully labeled) and should not repeat information that is presented in the text. Review the *Publication Manual* for detailed explanations of how to construct tables to represent your data. Note that tables and figures do not appear in the results section but rather at the very end of the paper, following the results section.

Discussion

The discussion section, labeled "Discussion" in boldfaced type centered on the page, describes the importance of your findings, places them in context, and discusses their implications. In other words, the discussion takes a big picture, bird's eye view perspective. As you structure the discussion section, ask yourself: What did I set out to learn, what was the purpose of the study, and what did I find? Also consider: "Were there any serendipitous findings of interest? How valid and generalizable are my findings? Are there larger implications of these findings? Is there an alternative way to interpret my results?" (Rosnow & Rosnow, 2008, p. 53).

Begin the discussion section by reminding readers of the purpose of your study. Then consider your data. Was there support for your hypotheses? Explain. If the data do not support your hypotheses, can you provide another interpretation? If so, clearly state that your interpretation is speculative and that further research is needed to confirm it. Now, discuss your findings within the context of prior research. How do your findings compare with those of other researchers? Does your work extend prior findings? If your findings do not replicate prior work or do not make sense given the literature you have reviewed, you might explore methodological differences or other factors that may account for the disparate findings. What are the theoretical and practical implications of your findings? As you write this section, remember that your goal is to connect your findings with prior research. Do not present new statistical analyses not included in the results section. Instead, the discussion section is a place for you to explain the value of your findings, and not the data itself.

The discussion section should also explore limitations or shortcomings of your study (every study has weaknesses). What factors might limit the extent to which you can generalize your results? Try to think of objections someone might make to the conclusions that you draw (whether the objections are correct or not), and either answer them or qualify your conclusions to take them into account. If you think that possible objections are weak, explain why. Help readers to understand exactly what can and cannot be concluded from your study. Finally, consider avenues for future research. Do not end your discussion section, and therefore article, with the sentence, "More research is needed." Be specific. What are the remaining unanswered research questions? Given what you have learned, what research is the next step? Provide specific questions and topics for further research.

EXERCISE 6.1

Test Your Understanding of Journal Articles

Using PsycINFO, locate an empirical journal article in an area of interest. Retrieve the article using your library's full-text and in-print resources. The reference librarian can offer assistance if you experience difficulty. Read the article and answer the following questions:

1. Write the article's citation in APA style.
2. Examine the abstract of the article. Based on the abstract, what do you expect to learn in this article?
3. What was the purpose of the study? Where did you find that information?
4. How was the study conducted? Describe the methodology. Where did you locate that information?
5. What were the findings of the study? Where did you look to learn about the findings?
6. What were the author's conclusions? How did the results of this study compare with prior research? Where did you look to learn about the findings?
7. Reflect back on the abstract. How well did it reflect the content of the article? Did you learn what you thought you would?

References

The reference section appears at the end of your paper, on a new page with "References" centered on the first line (no boldfaced type). The reference section lists all articles or books that you cited in your paper, including enough information so that an interested reader can locate them. If a work is listed in the reference section, it must be cited within the paper. List only the works that you used. The most common sources of reference material in student papers are journal articles, books, and perhaps material from reputable sources on the Internet. The *Publication Manual* lists slightly different formats for journal articles, books, and Internet sources, as well as slight differences depending on the number of authors. Table 6.1 illustrates how to cite journal articles, books, and Internet sources. Let's examine each type of citation.

List journal articles in the following way:

- List by the author's last name and first initial.
- The year of publication follows, in parentheses, followed by a period.
- The article title comes next. Don't capitalize each word of the title; only the first word of the article title is capitalized. If the article title contains a colon, the first word after the colon is capitalized as well. Follow the article title with a period.
- The title of the journal and volume number come next and are italicized. Capitalize each word of the journal title. Place a comma after the journal title and after the volume number. Note that only the number is used to indicate volume; don't use "V," "Volume," or "Vol.". Include the issue number in parentheses if the journal is paginated by issue.
- Last are the page numbers, followed by a period. Again, note that only the numbers themselves are used to indicate pages; don't use "page," "p," or "pg."
- Following the page number is the digital object identifier (DOI). References that are obtained online, such as through subscription services such as PsycINFO, are labeled with a DOI that is a unique string of numbers and letters that labels an article for database searches. The DOI usually appears on the first page of an article, near the copyright notice. Older articles may not list DOIs. If you include a DOI, it appears after the period following the page numbers as "doi:". List the numbers without a space after the colon. Check with your professor. Including the DOI is a recent addition to the *Publication Manual* and some instructors may not require their students to include them.
- The first journal article example in Table 6.1 illustrates an article by one author, the second example illustrates two authors, and the third illustrates three authors.

List books as follows:

- Books are listed by the author's last name and first initial.
- The year of publication follows, in parentheses, with a period.
- Next comes the book title, italicized. Like the journal article title, only the first word of the book title is capitalized. If the book title contains a colon, the first word after the colon is capitalized as well.
- Finally, list the place of publication, a colon, and the publisher.
- The first book example in Table 6.1 illustrates a book by one author, the second example illustrates two authors, and the third illustrates three authors.

TABLE 6.1   APA STYLE REFERENCES

Journal Articles

One Author:

Bem, D. J. (1995). Writing a review article for Psychological Bulletin. *Psychological Bulletin, 118*(2), 172–177. doi:10.1037/0033-2909.118.2.172

Two Authors:

Dearnley, C., & Matthew, B. (2007). Factors that contribute to undergraduate success. *Teaching in Higher Education, 12*(3), 377–391. doi: 10.1080/13562510701278740

Three Authors:

Cooley, E. L., Garcia, A. L., & Hughes, J. L. (2008). Undergraduate research in liberal arts colleges: Reflections on mutual benefits for faculty and students. *North American Journal of Psychology, 10*(3), 463–471.

Books

Note that only the first word of book titles, as well as the first word following a colon, are capitalized. All other words in book titles appear in lowercase letters.

One Author:

Palladino Schulthesiss, D. E. (2008). *Psychology as a major: Is it right for me and what can I do with my degree?* Washington, DC: APA.

Two Authors:

Landrum, R. E., & Davis, S. F. (2010). *The psychology major: Career options and strategies for success.* Upper Saddle River, NJ: Prentice Hall.

Three Authors:

Silvia, P. J., Delaney, P. F., & Marcovitch, S. (2009). *What psychology majors could (and should) be doing: An informal guide to research experience and professional skills.* Washington, DC: APA.

Chapters in Edited Books

One Author:

Handlesman, M. M. (2001). Learning to become ethical. In S. Walfish & B. Tolan (Eds.), *Succeeding in graduate school: The career guide for psychology students* (pp. 189–202). Mahwah, NJ: Erlbaum.

Two Authors:

Campbell, C., & Anderson, T. L. (2010). Mentoring in professional psychology. In M. B. Kenkel & R. L. Peterson (Eds.), *Competency-based training for professional psychology* (pp. 237–247). Washington, DC: APA.

Three Authors:

Wasik, B. H., Song, S., & Knotek, S. Preparing for careers in school psychology. In S. F. Davis, P. J. Giordano, & C. A. Licht (Eds.), *Your career in psychology: Putting your graduate degree to work* (pp. 231–244). Hoboken, NJ: Wiley-Blackwell.

Internet

Lloyd, M. M. (2004). *Marky Lloyd's careers in psychology page.* Retrieved November 1, 2009 from http://www.psychwww.com/careers/index.htm

What if you're citing a book chapter in an edited book? List it as follows:

- List the chapter author's last name and first initial.
- The year of publication follows, in parentheses, followed by a period.
- The title of the chapter follows, with only the first word capitalized, ending with a period.
- Next indicate the editors and book by writing, "In" and listing the editors by first initial and last name, followed by "Ed." or "Eds." in parentheses, followed by a comma. Then list the title of the book, capitalizing only the first word.
- Provide the page numbers in parentheses, signified by "pp." Note that this is the only time that "pp" is used in APA style.
- Finally, provide the place of publication, followed by a colon, and the publisher.
- Electronic books include a DOI which should be listed after the period following publisher, with doi and a colon listed in lowercase letters.
- The first example in Table 6.1 lists a sole authored chapter in a book edited by two people. The second example illustrates two authors and two editors, and the third example lists three authors and three editors.

List Internet sources as follows:

- Cite Internet sources by the author's last name (if no author appears, then cite the organization; if there is no author or organization, the article title moves to the position of author).
- Indicate the year of publication (if listed) in parentheses. If the year of publication is not listed, then use "n.d." to indicate no date, in parentheses.
- The title of the page appears next, in italics (with only the first word capitalized).
- Next, list the date that you retrieved the information and the Internet address (don't use a period after the Internet address).
- Note that the *Publication Manual* includes different reference styles for blog posts, online forum/discussion group posts, and messages occurring on electronic mailing lists. Learn more by perusing the *Publication Manual* or ask your instructor for assistance.

EXERCISE 6.2
Practice Preparing Reference Lists

1. Conduct a PsycINFO search on the topic of your choice. Identify seven publications. Of these, at least one must be a journal article and another must be a book chapter.
2. Construct a reference list.

3. Seek feedback from your professor.
4. APA style is challenging and most beginning writers make errors. What kinds of errors did you make? Correct your reference list.
5. Locate three more publications and try again.

Writing an empirical paper entails using a highly structured, scientific style. The sample paper at the end of this chapter illustrates how to format your empirical paper. Use Checklist 6.1 to help you determine whether your paper meets the major guidelines set by APA style. At first the elements of an empirical paper—and the formal style of writing—may seem foreign. With practice you will find that writing comes more easily and perhaps you will come to see the value in clear, concise scientific communication. It likely will not be as easy as the other forms of writing you have undertaken to date, but the ability to write in a formal style and with precision will suit you well in your career.

CHECKLIST 6.1
APA Style Checklist

- ❏ Have you used 1-inch margins?
- ❏ Have you double spaced the document?
- ❏ Have you used a running head and number on every page?
- ❏ Is the running head no longer than fifty characters?
- ❏ Have you checked for typos?
- ❏ Have you used 5–7 space paragraph indents?
- ❏ Is your title no longer than twelve words?
- ❏ Did you include your name and affiliation below the title and centered on the page and line?
- ❏ Does the abstract appear on a new page, without indentation, headed by the word "Abstract" centered?
- ❏ Is the abstract no longer than 120–150 words?
- ❏ Does the introduction begin on a new page, headed by the paper's title?
- ❏ Do the method and other sections appear immediately after the last section (no page break)?
- ❏ Have you used the past tense in writing the introduction, method, and results sections?
- ❏ Have you reported the effect size?
- ❏ Have you organized the results into paragraphs and subsections?
- ❏ Did you italicize mathematical symbols, use numbers rather than words, and capitalize the names of independent variables?
- ❏ Did you report the value for nonsignificant results without interpreting them?
- ❏ Did you interpret all significant results?

❑ Did you explain interactions?
❑ Did you create tables to summarize all data?
❑ Did you create figures to illustrate interactions?
❑ In the discussion section, have you used the past tense to describe results and present tense to discuss conclusions?
❑ Have you included all authors' names in the first in-text citation?
❑ Have you used "and" to link authors' names in text?
❑ Have you used & to link authors' names in parenthetical citations?
❑ Did you include the year in parenthetical citations?
❑ Did you begin the reference list on a new page, headed by the word "References" centered?
❑ Are the references listed in alphabetical order?
❑ Is the first line of each reference flush with the left margin and the subsequent lines hanging indented (i.e., tab-indented)?
❑ Are tables listed on a different page?
❑ Have you cited only work that you have read?

SUGGESTED READINGS

American Psychological Association. (2010). *Publication manual of the American Psychological Association.* Washington, DC: Author.

Mitchell, H. L., & Jolley, J. M. (2009). *Writing for psychology.* Belmont, CA: Wadsworth.

Rosnow, R. L., & Rosnow, M. (2008). *Writing papers in psychology.* Belmont, CA: Wadsworth.

Sternberg, R. J. (2003). *The psychologist's companion: A guide to scientific writing for students and researchers.* Cambridge, England: Cambridge University Press.

Szuchman, L. T. (2010). *Writing with style: APA style made easy.* Belmont, CA: Wadsworth.

INTERNET RESOURCES

APA Style Online

http://www.apastyle.org

This site from the American Psychological Association presents an overview of APA style, along with answers to frequently asked questions.

The Elements of Style

http://www.bartleby.com/141/index.html

This Web site gives you access to Strunk and White's classic volume on how to write clearly and concisely.

How to Write a Research Report in Psychology

http://www.psych.upenn.edu/~baron/labrep.html

At this site you'll find an overview of the sections in an empirical paper, with additional advice on grammar.

JOURNAL EXERCISES

My Question

Free write about your research project. Don't use your notes or readings, but write as much as you can about your project. What is your research question? How did it evolve? Where did you get the idea? How is your study an improvement over prior studies? Why is your study important?

My Findings

Tell a story about your research project. What did you set out to do, and what did you find? Try to explain what your statistical analyses tested. Pretend that you're explaining your project to a friend or a high school student. How would you explain your results in a way that a student could understand?

Implications

Without looking at your notes or readings, free write about the possible implications of your study. Be grandiose and try to think about far-reaching implications for laws, social policy, regulations, education, and so on.

If I Could Do It All Over

Pretend that you are going to revise your study and start from the beginning. What would you do differently? Why?

Appendix 1 Sample Paper

Running head: TEMPLATE PAPER

My Paper: A Template from Which to Work

Jane J. Smith

Your State University

Template Paper 2

Abstract

The abstract should be self-explanatory, self-contained, and should not

exceed 120 words. Describe the problem under investigation, the major

hypotheses, participants, materials, and procedure. Summarize the results

1 inch   1 inch

and conclusions, indicating the implications or applications. A good abstract

interests readers and convinces them that the study is worth reading.

My Paper: A Template from Which to Work

Begin the introduction with a general statement about your topic area. Consider your readers and attempt to pique their interest. Use the funnel effect in the first paragraph of your introduction so that you begin with general statements, each one becoming more narrowly focused, until you end with a statement of the problem under study.

A second paragraph of the introduction might explain the importance of the research question. What is its theoretical or applied relevance?

After introducing the problem, the second component of the introduction section provides a literature review of what is known about the topic. What has prior research shown? What are the limitations in prior research? How is your study an extension of prior research? As you write the literature review, cite only those studies that are most pertinent to your research question (and use appropriate documentation, as described in Chapter 5). The literature review is typically several pages long.

End the introductory section with a clear statement of the purpose and rationale of your study. Discuss hypotheses and set the stage for the Method section.

Method

The method section explains how the study was conducted. Provide enough detail so that a reader could replicate your research. Typically the methods section contains several sections: participants; apparatus, materials, or measures; and procedure.

Notice that three levels of headings are used. The first is written in upper and lower case, centered. The second level of headings is written in upper and lower case letters, flush left, and italicized. The third level of headings is indented and italicized, with only the first letter of the first word capitalized, and is followed by a period. Headings may be used to organize your introduction section. Review the *Publication Manual* to learn more about the use of headings.

Participants

The participants section describes the characteristics of the participants and explains how they were selected. Explain any demographic details that might affect your study, including age, sex, ethnicity, geographic location, and number of participants assigned to each treatment group. Report any inducements to participate (e.g., money, extra credit).

Apparatus/Measures

Depending on your study, this section might be entitled apparatus, materials, or measures. Briefly describe the equipment or instruments used in the study. If the equipment is a manufactured item, include information on the manufacturer and the model number. If you developed an apparatus or materials for your study, describe them in enough detail so that a reader could reproduce them. If standardized tests or measures were used, describe them, their psychometric properties (e.g., reliability and validity), and how they were coded or scored.

Procedure

Describe each step in conducting the study. Clearly describe what happened to participants from the time they walked into the lab to when they

Template Paper 5

left, the beginning to the end of the study. Describe your methods and any control features of the design such as counterbalancing or the use of control groups. What instructions were provided to participants? How were participants debriefed at the end of the study?

Results

Indent the first sentence and begin your results section by explaining the main findings. Follow up by explaining the analyses in detail. Report all relevant results, even those that are counter to your hypothesis. As you report tests of statistical significance, include the name of the test, degrees of freedom, and significance level. Provide enough detail to justify the conclusions that you will make in the discussion section. Provide tables to display complex sets of data (e.g., means and standard deviations, the results of complex analyses). For information on how to construct tables, see the *Publication Manual*.

Discussion

Begin the discussion section by reiterating the purpose of the study. Provide a statement on the support of your original hypotheses. Next, examine your findings. Explain what the results mean, consider them in the context of the literature, and discuss their implications. Identify possible limitations of your study. Close with a discussion of venues for future research.

Template Paper 6

References

Note that the reference section includes only articles that were cited in your study. List the references in alphabetical order. See Table 1 for sample article, book, and Internet references. Further examples of references appear in the *Publication Manual*.

What Can I Do With a Bachelor's Degree in Psychology?

Chapter Outline

As a psychology major, you're in good company because each year, psychology is consistently among the top five most popular bachelor's degrees awarded (National Center for Education Statistics, 2009). In the 2006–2007 academic year, over 90,000 students earned bachelor's degrees in psychology (National Center for Education Statistics, 2009). Why are so many students attracted to psychology? Psychology courses cover a range of fascinating topics, such as how we think, learn, use our memory, feel emotions, cope with adversity, change throughout our lives, and more. Much of what we study in psychology is directly relevant to our everyday life. We all seek to understand human behavior and the environment around us.

Many undergraduate students choose psychology because of their desires to become psychologists or to work with people. However, a bachelor's degree in psychology will not qualify you to be a psychologist. Becoming a psychologist typically requires a doctoral degree, which entails several years of education, training, and supervision beyond the bachelor's degree.

So why major in psychology? Although a baccalaureate in psychology won't qualify you to formally practice psychology, you'll learn skills that are applicable to a variety of jobs, including some that allow you to work with people. This chapter describes the skills that employers seek, the kinds of jobs that bachelor's degree graduates in psychology hold, and how you can cultivate useful skills and enhance your employability.

SKILLS AND ABILITIES SOUGHT BY EMPLOYERS

A bachelor's degree in psychology cultivates skills that are the foundation for a variety of career paths in the mental health professions, science, and business. When considering possible careers, evaluate and think carefully about the skills and knowledge that you've acquired over the college years. It may help for you to reconsider your answers to the exercises in Chapter 2. A thorough understanding of your talents and proficiencies is particularly important because it is unlikely that you will see classified ads listing "Psychology Majors Wanted." While it is rare to see classified ads explicitly recruiting psychology majors, don't be fooled. Your major has helped you to develop a host of skills that employers want. It's up to you to identify those skills and educate employers.

What do employers look for in a new hire? Table 7.1 lists the most desirable qualities in prospective employees, according to surveys of a broad sample of employers. Carefully examine the list, and you'll quickly notice that interpersonal skills—including the abilities to communicate, influence others, and work in groups—are highly valued. These results indicate that "people skills" typical of psychology majors, honed through course work, practica, and extracurricular activities, provide an upper hand in the job market.

TABLE 7.1   TEN MOST DESIRABLE QUALITIES IN PROSPECTIVE EMPLOYEES

Quality	Description
1. Communication skills	Writing, public speaking skills, social skills
2. Motivation/influence	Commitment to life-long learning, ability to meet challenges
3. Teamwork skills	Ability to work with others
4. Leadership abilities	Ability to lead groups, communicate, and work effectively with others
5. GPA/academic abilities	Broad education, good grades
6. Interpersonal skills	Interact well with others, social skills
7. Flexibility/adaptability	Can cope with change and tolerate stress
8. Technical skills	Computer skills, Internet skills
9. Honesty/integrity	Ethics, personal responsibility
10. Analytical skills/problem solving	Reasoning and thinking abilities

Source: Adapted from National Association of Colleges and Employers, 2009.

Many other surveys have yielded similar results. Following is a compilation of the conclusions of these studies, providing a detailed description of the skills employers seek in prospective employees (Appleby, 2000; Grocer & Kohout, 1997; Edwards and Smith, 1988; Landrum & Davis2000; Lloyd & Kennedy, 1997; Sheetz, 1995).

- **Communication and Interpersonal Skills.** Listening skills and the ability to communicate clearly, concisely, and logically are important. Group skills, the ability to share responsibility with others, conflict management, and an appreciation of individual differences are desired by employers.
- **Thinking and Problem-Solving Skills.** Successful employees have good judgment and decision-making skills. They can apply information to solve problems and analyze problems on the basis of personal experience and psychological principles. Analytical and decision-making skills are important because many of today's jobs require higher levels of complex critical thinking than ever before.
- **Information Acquisition and Synthesis Skills.** Successful employees understand how they absorb and retain information. They know how to learn, where to find information, and how to evaluate and use it. A commitment to learning is essential in today's marketplace.
- **Reading and Writing Skills.** The abilities to extract important ideas from reading and to document them are valued by employers.

Strong writing skills, such as the ability to write reports, proposals, and summaries, are useful.

- **Career-Related Work Experience.** Successful job applicants have obtained hands-on, practical experience through cooperative education, internships, practica, part-time jobs, or summer work experience. They can apply their school-based knowledge in practical settings.
- **Psychological Knowledge.** Employers often desire specific knowledge from psychology graduates, such as how attitudes are formed and changed, or how people think, solve problems, and process information. Also useful is an understanding of group dynamics and knowing how people perceive and sense their environment.
- **Data Analysis Skills.** Employers seek prospective employees with computational skills, the ability to reason numerically, and the ability to identify problems in data. Graduates who can collect, record, and report statistical information will find success.
- **Computer Literacy.** Knowledge of computer applications—including word processing, spreadsheet, and database software—and familiarity with the Internet and e-mail are essential.
- **Self-Management.** Employers desire personal qualities and traits such as self-esteem, confidence, and social skills. Self-management skills such as the ability to set and pursue goals, tolerate stress, control one's emotions, and engage in appropriate behavior are sought.
- **Adaptability.** Employers seek employees who are adaptable, flexible, and capable of handling multiple tasks. A broad knowledge base outside the field of psychology provides the background to enhance your adaptability. The ability to utilize resources in order to effectively complete tasks (e.g., creating a schedule, writing a budget, assigning space, and managing others) is essential. Employers also value the ability to tolerate ambiguity—the fact that often there is not a clear right or wrong answer or approach to a problem. Instead, successful employees adapt to the situation and carefully evaluate options to determine the best approach for a given situation.

Now that you have a general understanding of what employers seek, consider the goals of psychology education, as discussed in Chapter 1. The goals of undergraduate education in psychology match employers' expectations well. Over the course of your undergraduate years you will not be able to achieve every one of these skills or abilities, but you will gain proficiency in many of them.

Where should you focus the most attention? What skills should you seek to develop? Consider what employers expect specifically from psychology graduates. Table 7.2 lists employers' views of the top five most useful skills and knowledge areas attained specifically by psychology students. Perhaps what's most important to take away from these results is the fact that employers will

| TABLE 7.2 | USEFUL SKILLS AND KNOWLEDGE GAINED BY PSYCHOLOGY STUDENTS, AS RATED BY EMPLOYERS |

Skills

1. Writing proposals and reports
2. Ability to identify problems and suggest solutions based on research findings and knowledge of psychology
3. Conducting interviews
4. Doing statistical analyses

Knowledge Areas

1. Attitude and opinion formation and change
2. Principles and techniques of personnel selection
3. How people think, solve problems, and process information
4. Group dynamics and structure
5. How the physical environment influences our feelings and actions

Source: Adapted from Edwards & Smith, 1988.

expect you to know something about your major (Landrum & Davis, 2010). While cramming may get you through an exam, you probably won't retain the material well enough to satisfy an employer who needs your expertise. (See Chapter 4 for study tips to help you more effectively learn and retain material.)

So where do you focus your energy? First, consider your own strengths and weaknesses (reviewing the assessments you completed in Chapter 2 may help). Seek improvement in the areas you identify as weaknesses. Second, focus on the two components of the psychology major desired most by employers: people skills and research skills. People skills include knowledge and an understanding of psychological principles and group dynamics, as well as interpersonal skills—self-management skills. Employers also value research skills such as report writing, the ability to carry out a research project, and the ability to conduct statistical analyses. The blend of liberal arts and science is what makes the psychology major unique, and it's what makes you very employable.

JOBS FOR PSYCHOLOGY MAJORS

Contrary to popular belief, most students who graduate with a bachelor's degree in psychology do not go to graduate school (Borden & Rajecki, 2000). It has been estimated that about one-quarter of psychology undergraduate degree recipients attend graduate school immediately after graduation (Tsapogas, 2004). Instead, psychology baccalaureates head into the job market and find success. According to the National Science Foundation (2009), only 7 percent of 2003, 2004, and 2005 psychology bachelor's degree recipients were unemployed in 2006. Most bachelor's degree recipients in psychology work in jobs that are not directly related to psychology (although an understanding of human behavior obviously is helpful in most positions; Borden & Rajecki, 2000; Finney, Snell, & Sebby, 1989; Keyes & Hogberg, 1990; Littlepage, Perry, & Hodge, 1990). About one-half of psychology graduates work in business settings, 20 percent in education, 15 percent in government, and 12 percent in nonprofit settings (National Science Foundation, 2009). Table 7.3 lists common jobs that psychology majors have obtained after graduation. It is not a complete list; many other opportunities are out there waiting for you.

Psychology majors obtain jobs that require people skills (the ability to communicate effectively with others) and research skills (the ability to identify problems and locate, analyze, and apply information to solve problems). All jobs entail both types of skills but in differing degrees. Your job options are varied if you think creatively and focus on your skills. As you consider job options and look for a position, remember that many people do not understand psychology. It is your responsibility to educate them about how your degree has prepared you for a position with their organization or company. Following is a sampling of jobs, according to the degree that they emphasize research skills and people skills, but remember that all jobs tap both sets of competencies.

Job Settings that Emphasize Research Skills

The particular research-oriented skills valued by employers vary by setting, employer, and experience level. Research tasks include administrative work, data collection, data entry, data analysis, and interpretation and dissemination. The term *data*, however, should be conceptualized broadly and not as quantitative data that you enter in SPSS or another statistics program. Data refers to information. Employers look for employees who can manipulate, interpret, and apply information. Many employment settings emphasize research skills, and employers tend to view liberal arts majors, and especially psychology majors, favorably (McGovern & Carr, 1989). Graduates who obtain positions in business often work in human resources departments, public relations, retail, and advertising.

Public Relations   Public relations professionals work in businesses, government, universities, hospitals, schools, and other organizations to build and maintain positive relationships with the public. An entry-level position usually entails assisting a public relations professional work to improve the

TABLE 7.3   POSITIONS OBTAINED BY PSYCHOLOGY MAJORS

Business	Education/Academic	Social
Administrative assistant	Administration	Activities coordinator
Affirmative action officer	Child care provider	Behavioral specialist
Advertising trainee	Child care worker/ supervisor	Career counselor
Benefits manager		Case worker
Claims specialist	Data management	Child protection worker
Community relations officer	Laboratory assistant	Clinical coordinator
Customer relations	Parent/family education	Community outreach worker
Data management	Preschool teacher	
Employee recruitment	Public opinion surveyor	Corrections officer
Employee counselor	Research assistant	Counselor assistant
Human resources coordinator/ manager/specialist	Teaching assistant	Crisis intervention counselor
Labor relations manager/ specialist		Employment counselor
		Group home attendant
Loan officer		Occupational therapist
Management trainee		Probation officer
Marketing		Program manager
Personnel manager/officer		Rehabilitation counselor
Product and services research		Residence counselor
Programs/events coordination		Mental health assistant
Public relations		Social service assistant
Retail sales management		Social worker assistant
Sales representative		Social worker
Special features writing/ reporting		Substance abuse counselor
Staff training and development		Youth counselor
Trainer/training officer		

Source: Adapted from DeGalan & Lambert, 1995; Fretz, 1976; Lloyd, 1997A; University of Texas at Austin, 2000.

organization's communication with the community; with consumer, employee, and public interest groups; and with the media. Part of the job entails inform-ing the community and media about an organization's policies, activities, and accomplishments; but public relations specialists also must keep an organiza-tion's management and administrative personnel aware of the attitudes and concerns of the public and special interest groups. Public relations work is information-laden in the sense that it entails gathering information about how a client, organization, or product is perceived, using it to craft a message, and then gathering data to determine the effectiveness of the communication. Public relations activities include setting up speaking engagements for management, helping to prepare speeches, and assisting in planning conferences and presentations. Titles include public relations specialist, information officer, press secretary, communications specialist, public affairs specialist, and others. Entry-level titles are usually labeled as *assistant*.

Advertising   There are many different kinds of entry-level positions in advertising. Assistant account coordinators work in the account management department, which identifies and solicits new clients, and ensures that clients' advertising needs are met. Assistant media planners work in the media department, which places ads; they study what people read and watch in order to determine where to place advertising, and then attempt to place the right ad at the right time to reach the intended audience. Assistant media buyers help media buyers secure ad time and space and ensure that the advertisements appear as planned and according to the intended budget. There are also many administrative positions within advertising firms, as described below.

Administrative Assistant   Administrative assistants, also known as executive assistants or executive secretaries, engage in office management functions and support executive staff. Activities include word processing, scheduling meetings and appointments, and maintaining files. They may conduct research to support a particular project, manage databases, create reports, and oversee projects. In addition to coordinating administrative and information management activities within an office, many administrative assistants train and orient new staff. The responsibilities vary with the employer, setting, and employee competencies. Employees who are capable, motivated, and take initiative are likely to be awarded greater responsibilities and challenges.

Computer Support Specialist   A computer support specialist provides technical assistance to users of hardware, software, and computer systems, acting as a troubleshooter who interprets problems and provides technical support for hardware, software, and systems. Computer support specialists work in at least two capacities: *technical support specialists* and *help-desk technicians*. Technical support specialists are employed by companies to help employees solve computer-related problems. They respond to inquiries from users, diagnose and solve problems, and may install, modify, clean, and repair computer hardware and software. Help-desk technicians answer telephone calls and e-mail inquiries from customers seeking technical assistance for a given hardware or software product. They help users by listening, asking questions to diagnose the problem, and walking the user through steps to solve the problem. Many companies consult help-desk technicians about customers' experiences with the product, what gives them the most trouble, and other customer concerns.

Job Settings that Emphasize People Skills

Make no mistake, people skills are a part of every job. That said, some jobs require more contact with people and more interpersonal skills.

Retail Worker   Of workers in the United States, about one-fifth are employed in the retail sector (U.S. Bureau of Labor Statistics, 2004). Retail sales workers sell goods, provide customer service, and help buyers make informed purchases. Many large retail stores have management training programs in which a worker learns about all aspects of the business and is then placed as an assistant manager or store manager. An understanding of consumer behavior is important in order to deliver the appropriate sale techniques to achieve success. As one advances in retail to supervisor status, he or she becomes responsible for managing the activity of part or all of a store, including managing staff, tracking inventory, marketing products, devising techniques to attract customers, and promoting sales and good customer relations.

Human Resources Worker   Careers in human resources focus on helping employers work with their employees. Human resource positions encompass many titles (personnel administrator, employment specialist, human resources coordinator/specialist/manager, affirmative action coordinator, employee relations manager) and serve various functions: employment and placement, wage and salary administration, training and development, benefits administration, research, and information management. For example, human resources personnel work to attract the most qualified employees, match them to the jobs for which they are best suited, and help them to succeed in their jobs. Activities include recruiting and interviewing potential employees, training and development of workers to help them develop and enhance their morale and performance, organization development (helping companies and businesses deal with change), and career development (helping employees manage their careers; DeGalan & Lambert, 1995). Human resources personnel often collect applications and resumes for jobs, assemble applicant files, perform background checks, orient new employees, educate employees about salary and benefits, and assess departmental needs for staffing. Entry-level positions usually include the title *assistant*, and the duties typically involve assisting a more senior human resources professional. Human resources positions involve not only working with people but also a great deal of paperwork and information management; accurate record keeping about employment salary and benefits is essential to the work of human resources personnel.

Human Services Worker   This category of positions includes various job titles such as social services worker, case management worker, social work assistant, community support worker, alcohol and substance abuse counselor, mental health worker, community outreach worker, life skills counselor, child care worker, and gerontology aide (U.S. Bureau of Labor Statistics, 2004). Each of these positions is a paraprofessional position, or "a support role that overlaps with job duties and responsibilities of a psychologist; however, the paraprofessional does not have the education, responsibility, nor salary of the psychologist" (Landrum & Davis 2000, p. 17). Human services workers provide direct and indirect services to clients. Typical duties include assessing clients' needs and eligibility for services, helping clients obtain services (such as food stamps, Medicaid, and other human services programs), and providing emotional support (U.S. Bureau of Labor Statistics, 2004). In communities, group homes, or government-supported housing programs, human services workers assist clients in need of counseling, assist adults with daily living skills, and organize group activities. Turnover is often high in these positions because the jobs are challenging and the pay low. Advancement, additional opportunities, and pay raises come with a master's degree.

Police Officer   Police officers have lots of contact with the public—people skills are an essential part of a successful officer's toolbox. Typical activities of police officers include maintaining regular patrols, responding to calls for service, directing traffic as needed, investigating a crime scene, or providing first aid to an accident victim (U.S. Bureau of Labor Statistics, 2009). As an officer is promoted through the ranks, he or she takes on more leadership responsibilities; for example, to a position as a detective with the primary responsibility of investigating crime scenes. Skills in observation, attention to detail, and critical thinking—all part of the psychology major's repertoire—make for successful police officers.

Each of the careers we have discussed requires both research and people skills, to varying degrees. Each entails a different set of duties that tap competencies that psychology majors develop. What can you expect to earn with your bachelor's degree? Salaries vary by occupation, region, and experience. The 2008 median weekly earnings for all employed persons with bachelor's degrees (regardless of major or job experience) was $1,012 ($52,624 annually) (U.S. Bureau of Labor Statistics, 2009). The average starting salary for all bachelor's degree recipients in 2009 was $48,515. The average starting salary for psychology majors of the class 2009 was $34,573 (National Association of Colleges and Employers, 2009). Work experience has a favorable effect on salary; with experience, your salary will increase. Table 7.4 presents employment data from the *Occupational Outlook Handbook* (U.S. Bureau of Labor Statistics, 2009). Also, complete Exercise 7.1 to explore additional careers.

EXERCISE 7.1
Career Research Exercise

Consider the jobs discussed in this chapter as a starting point. There are many other types of jobs out there for psychology graduates. Conduct some research to learn about a job that sounds interesting to you.

1. What is this job? What are typical titles?
2. Describe the nature of the work
   a. List at least three job duties or work tasks performed in this occupation.
   b. What kind of work would someone be doing if he or she were hired as a college graduate with no prior experience in this field?
   c. What other occupations are related to this job?
   d. What is the history of this occupation, and what does it do for society?
3. Training/licensing/certification and other qualifications
   a. What is the lowest level of education needed for entry into this occupation?
   b. What is the most desirable education level?
   c. Is special licensing or certification required? If so, please explain.
   d. Which major(s) courses of study or training are most desirable?
   e. What kinds of skills are needed? Please be as specific as possible.
   f. Does this occupation have specific physical requirements and/or desirable personal traits (friendliness, patience, etc.)? If so, please describe them.
4. Advancement and job outlook
   a. What are the opportunities for advancement in this job?
   b. What is the turnover rate for employees in this occupation?
   c. List at least three kinds of organizations that employ people in this occupation.
   d. What is the projected employment outlook for this occupation?
5. Salary and benefits
   a. What is the potential salary range for this occupation?
   b. What other benefits are generally associated with this job?

Source: Adapted from Nauta, 2002.

TABLE

7.4

PSYCHOLOGY-RELATED POSITIONS: TITLES, SALARY, AND OUTLOOK

Area	Titles	Median Salary in 2006	Outlook through 2016
Preschool teacher/Child care worker	Preschool teacher	$22,680	Increase as much as the average
Corrections officer	—	$35,760	Increase faster than the average
*Counselor	Rehabilitation counselor	$34,380–$47,530	Increase much faster than the average
	Employment or career counselor		
	Mental health counselor		
	Gerontology counselor		
Human resource workers	Human resources specialist	$33,750–$50,230	Increase faster than the average
	Benefits analyst		
	Personnel officer assistant		
	Training specialist		
Human service workers and assistants	Social service worker	$25,580–$34,040	Increase much faster than the average
	Case management worker		
	Social work assistant		
	Community support worker		

TABLE 7.4

PSYCHOLOGY-RELATED POSITIONS: TITLES, SALARY, AND OUTLOOK (CONTINUED)

	Alcohol or drug abuse counselor		
	Gerontology aide		
	Mental health worker		
	Life skills counselor		
*Occupational therapy assistant	—	$25,020–$42,060	Increase much faster than the average
*Social worker	Child welfare social worker	$35,310–$37,480	Increase faster than the average
	Family services social worker		
	Child or adult protective services social worker		
	Health care social worker		
	Occupational social worker		
	Gerontology social worker		

*Typically requires additional course work/experience.
Source: Adapted from U.S. Bureau of Laborstatistics, 2009.

ACQUIRE USEFUL SKILLS AND ENHANCE YOUR EMPLOYABILITY

As you've seen, the psychology major is quite useful, with its blend of liberal arts and science, but you cannot rest on your laurels. Regardless of your major, obtaining a job and entering a career requires preparation and planning, and this is especially true in difficult economies. To enhance your marketability and help your psychology education work for you, you must plan your career goals. This is a difficult task, but try to think about where you'd like to be in a few years. The counseling center or career development center at your school can help you to select your goals through personality, ability, and vocational interest assessments and counseling. The career development center may also offer alumni contacts who can tell you about their experiences and offer advice. Once you have a potential career path in mind, complete Exercise 7.2 to learn more about your fit to this career and how to plan your education accordingly.

EXERCISE 7.2
Plan Your Career

1. Identify one (or two) specific occupations for which you are preparing.
   a. What is the work environment of a person employed in this area (e.g., workload, hours, deadlines, travel)?
   b. Why is this occupation a good fit for you in terms of your characteristics, skills, interests, abilities, and values? (Refer back to Chapter 2.)
   c. How much and what kind of education will you need for this career?
2. Examine your course catalogue and the materials that the psychology department provides to its majors at your school. What skills can you develop if you take full advantage of these opportunities during your undergraduate years?
3. What electives should you choose to prepare yourself for your chosen career? Electives are a way to help you to develop the knowledge and skills that you will need to succeed in your chosen career. Choose your electives wisely to demonstrate that you are a person who knows what you want to do and who has made wise choices in preparation for that goal. For example, if you were considering a career working with juvenile offenders, appropriate electives might include classes in the departments of criminal justice, sociology, social work, public policy, communications, human development, anthropology (e.g., ethnic identity, social and cultural behavior, urban anthropology), and English (e.g., literature for adolescents).

4. Identify opportunities for outside-of-class experience, through research, internships, or work experience. The psychology department course catalog and Web site, your advisor, and the career services office at your school can provide assistance with this task.
   a. Describe the activity.
   b. When do you make contact and whom do you contact?
   c. How will this experience enhance your education? What will you learn? What skills will you gain? What are the outcomes of this experience?

After you've considered where you'd like to be, that is, your ultimate career goal, take a few elective courses outside of psychology that are specific to your goals. For example, if you plan to enter the business world, a course in management or accounting certainly wouldn't hurt. If you would like a job in human services, take courses in social work, communication, criminal justice, sociology, or anthropology. Regardless of your career plans, classes and experiences that enhance your communication skills (e.g., courses in writing, speech, and communications; writing for the campus newspaper) are a good investment because employers view communication skills favorably (Edwards and Smith, 1988; Grocer & Kohout, 1997; Landrum & Davis 2000; Lloyd & Kennedy, 1997; National Association of Colleges and Employers, 2000).

Seek research experience by assisting professors with their research or by developing an independent research project. Research experience demonstrates your ability to work independently, and sharpens your analytic and critical thinking skills. It also provides employers with evidence of your motivation, initiative, and willingness to go beyond basic requirements.

Secure an internship or practicum for hands-on experience. Internships provide wonderful opportunities for learning and training that you can use later. Another advantage of an internship is that it lets you sample a potential career. Do you really want to work with people? Your internship experiences may surprise you. The career center at your school can place you with an internship that provides valuable hands-on experience. In addition, internships can lead to contacts in the field, a possible offer for paid employment after graduation, and someone who can provide a reference or recommendation based on your ability to apply your knowledge of psychology in a real-world setting. In addition to, or in place of, an internship, seek work experience. Plenty of part-time and summer jobs allow you to hone your interpersonal skills and try out potential careers.

Extracurricular activities can help you develop useful skills and enhance your marketability. Similar to internships and work experience, extracurricular activities can give you opportunities to test career paths, develop contacts, and work on your communication skills. In addition, employers value volunteer work for campus and community organizations because it shows that you're a good citizen. Extracurricular participation gives employers evidence about your leadership skills, your ability to work effectively in a group, and your initiative and motivation. Finally, be open to new possibilities. Flexibility is an important life skill; it is critical to coping and optimal development throughout adulthood. Employers also rate adaptability as highly desired in new employees (National Association of Colleges and Employers, 2000). Keep an open mind and explore multiple possibilities to find a job that you'll love.

SUGGESTED READINGS

Kuther, T. L., & Morgan, R. D. (2010). *Careers in Psychology: Opportunities in a changing world.* Belmont, CA: Wadsworth.

Landrum, R. E. (2009). *Finding jobs with a psychology bachelor's degree: Expert advice for launching your career.* Washington DC: APA.

Morgan, B. L., & Korschgen, A. J. (2009). *Majoring in psych? Career options for psychology undergraduates.* Needham Heights, MA: Allyn and Bacon.

INTERNET RESOURCES

Occupational Outlook Handbook

http://www.bls.gov/OCO/

Provides national data on a variety of careers in order to assist individuals making decisions about their careers. It is revised every two years.

Occupational Information Network Resource Center

http://www.onetcenter.org/

Administered and sponsored by the U.S. Department of Labor's Employment and Training Administration, this site contains career exploration tools, testing and assessment guides, occupational listings, and more.

Psychology Careers for the 21st Century

http://www.apa.org/careers/resources/guides/careers.pdf

This American Psychological Association brochure describes the field of psychology, including employment settings, job outlook, and career preparation.

Careers in Psychology

http://www.psywww.com/careers/index.htm

Dr. Margaret Lloyd's Web site discusses entry-level and graduate-level careers in psychology, as well as how to prepare for them.

Pursuing Psychology Career Page

http://www.uni.edu/walsh/linda1.html

Dr. Linda Weber provides a list of links to excellent materials on career development and resources for psychology majors.

Psi Chi: The International Honor Society in Psychology

http://www.psichi.org

The Psi Chi Web site offers a variety of resources for psychology students, including full-text access to all of the articles published in *Eye on Psi Chi*, the organization's quarterly newsletter. Articles cover areas in psychology, career preparation, personal growth, and more.

JOURNAL EXERCISES

Dream Job

Describe your dream job. What does it entail? What skills are required? How can you work toward your dream?

My Strengths and Weaknesses

Consider the skills that a liberal arts degree builds as well as the skills employers seek. Identify your strengths. What do you do well? What do you enjoy? What are your weaknesses? How do you feel about your weaknesses? How might you strengthen these areas?

Considering Life After College

Taking classes, studying for exams, writing papers—sometimes students forget to think about the big picture. By now you likely have thought about what you would like to do after graduation. Now consider how your post-graduation life will differ from your present experience. How will you spend your time? Is there anything about college that you will miss? What won't you miss? Transitions from one phase of life to another, like from college to work, are exciting but also stressful. What can you do now to prepare? What types of activities might ease your transition to work?

Finding a Job with Your Bachelor's Degree

Chapter Outline

As the saying goes, "time flies when you're having fun." Before you know it, graduation will be here. If you've decided to seek employment with your bachelor's degree, start planning early and hone your job-seeking skills. This chapter discusses how to find a job with your bachelor's degree, including where to look, how to construct a resume, the importance of cover letters, interviewing, and more.

FIND JOB OPENINGS AND COMPLETE APPLICATIONS

The first stop on your job search should be the career services office at your college, where you'll find skilled professionals who can help you with all aspects of the job search. Career services offices have a variety of resources for locating available positions, including books, databases, and lists of employers who have contacted them seeking to employ college students and recent graduates.

Peruse the job ads in your local newspaper; many newspapers maintain searchable online databases of job ads. The Internet is a valuable resource for locating positions, as many Web sites specialize in listing job ads. The Internet Resources section at the end of this chapter offers a few examples of comprehensive job sites, but also use a search engine to locate other site listings. Contact the human resources department of major businesses, corporations, and agencies in your area to inquire about job openings. Many businesses and organizations advertise jobs on their Web pages, typically linked from the Human Resources Web page or on a page called "Employment Opportunities."

Remember the most important job-hunting resource of all: You! Applicants commonly overlook their own personal networks when scouting for available positions. Through school, friends (and their parents), part-time jobs, and internships, you've already made many connections. Tap into these professional connections. If you've completed an internship or practicum, you may already have a foot in the door and a potential employer has already had a peek at your work habits. Even if the organization where you did your internship is not hiring additional staff, your supervisor probably has outside contacts. Your personal connections are valuable for locating job openings because most jobs are not advertised in newspapers or other ads. You can learn about these unadvertised positions only by word of mouth. Networking—establishing connections—will help you to become more knowledgeable about positions within the hidden job market.

As you apply for jobs you'll find that many employers require applicants to complete a job application form or even a large packet of forms. Take care in completing job applications because they reveal a great deal about you. Your job application tells potential employers about your work habits, your ability to follow instructions, your personality and character, your personal achievements and job performance, and your potential to succeed (Landrum & Davis, 2000). Neatness, spelling, and grammar count, regardless of the position to which you apply. A sloppy application tells employers that they can expect carelessness and sloppiness from you. Be honest and accurate, and remember to ask the people you plan to list as references beforehand (notify them each time they are listed and, if you begin a second job search in the future, ask again). Some applications include personality inventories and other kinds of psychological assessments. Be truthful. Finally, many job applications do not instruct applicants to include a resume, but you should always supplement your application with a copy of your resume because it lists all of your relevant experiences and highlights your strengths.

EXERCISE 8.1
Deconstructing Job Ads

Conduct a search on a job search Web site, such as those listed at the end of this chapter. Locate one or two job ads that appeal to you.

1. What is the job?
2. What are the demographic details, such as location?
3. What are the education and experience requirements listed?
4. What skills are needed to succeed in the job? If the ad does not list them (and it likely will not), brainstorm what skills would be coveted by the employer.
5. Consider the assessments that you conducted throughout this book. What is your skill set? How does it compare with that needed for the job?
6. What skills might you improve to enhance your fit to the job?
7. How would you sell yourself to the employer?

PREPARE YOUR RESUME

A resume is a summary of your educational history, work experience, and career objectives. Employers always expect to see a resume (even if it isn't stated in the advertisement). As you prepare your resume, remember that it is often the only impression that an employer has of you. It is a chance to present your strengths, to communicate that you have valuable skills, and to emphasize the aspects of your educational and employment background that make you unique. Writing a resume may seem overwhelming, but you'll soon see that it is a simple matter of showcasing your skills.

Before you write, reevaluate your skills and abilities. Review the self-assessments that you completed in Chapter 2. Outline your skills and abilities as well as your work experience and extracurricular activities to make it easier to prepare a thorough resume. As you assess your skills, keep in mind the qualities that employers seek, as shown in Checklist 8.1. How many of these items match your abilities? Highlight your strengths.

CHECKLIST 8.1
Skills and Qualities that Employers Seek

- ❏ Public speaking
- ❏ Writing (e.g., reports and proposals)
- ❏ Problem identification and solving
- ❏ Small group and teamwork skills
- ❏ Interpersonal and communication skills (including listening)
- ❏ Leadership skills
- ❏ Motivation
- ❏ Flexibility
- ❏ Tolerance for ambiguity
- ❏ Organizational skills
- ❏ Desire and willingness to learn
- ❏ Survey construction and methodology
- ❏ Statistics and mathematical reasoning
- ❏ Understanding of human cognition and behavior
- ❏ Understanding of how attitudes form and change

Source: Adapted from Edwards & Smith, 1988; Landrum et al., 2003.

A resume is your ticket through the door; its purpose is to convince an employer to interview you, but most employers glance at a resume for only 20–30 seconds (Krannich, 2005). If the initial scan of your resume doesn't catch the employer's attention, the opportunity is lost. How do you make it past the 20-second test? Consider the main question that employers ask themselves as they read resumes: Why should I learn more about this applicant? Keep this question in mind as you prepare your resume, answer it, and you'll have a unique resume that will get you to the next stage of the job hunt.

Parts of the Resume

The chronological resume is most commonly used. It is easy for employers to understand and read because it discusses the chronological progression of your career. A brief description of the content of each section of the chronological resume follows; a sample chronological resume appears in Box 8.1.

SAMPLE CHRONOLOGICAL RESUME

CHRISTINE JONES

Student Dorms #321
Your University
Purchase, NY 11234
(914) 555-1414
Jones@yourstateu.edu

77 Pleasant Street
Pleasantville, NY 11245
(914) 555-6677
Fax (914) 555-9999

EDUCATION: Your University, Purchase, NY
Bachelor of Arts in Psychology, May 2011
Minor: Communications

EXPERIENCE: *Resident Assistant,* Your University, Purchase, NY,
May 2009–Present

Assisted the director of a 360-resident living unit on
campus in creating and implementing policies and
procedures for managing the residence. Developed
and presented programs on a variety of subjects
including alcohol awareness, career development,
leadership, and safety.

Intern, Purchase Daily News, Purchase, NY, August
2008–May 2009

Researched and wrote weekly articles on breaking news.
Interviewed and researched local residents for weekly
"Local Profile" articles.

Cashier, Purchase Delicatessen, Purchase, NY, June
2007–August 2009

Assisted customers in locating products, operated
computerized cash register, handled large sums
of cash, stocked shelves, and monitored store
inventory.

ACTIVITIES: *Theater Society*, active member, two years, chorus member
in three plays

Psychology Club, active member, three years, organized
fund raisers, participated in tutoring groups, and invited
local speakers to club meetings

REFERENCES: Available upon request

Heading/Contact Information   All of your contact information should go at the top of your resume. Include your name, permanent address (this is particularly important if you live on campus and are moving home after graduation), phone (with area code), fax (if available), and e-mail. Use a professional e-mail address rather than a fun, personal e-mail address (silly usernames such as "Butterflygirl," "Temptress," or "JediMaster," are not professional). If possible, use your last name and first initial as your e-mail address. Include your Web site address only if the Web site reflects your professional ambitions.

Education   Report the name of the degree that you received or will receive (AS, BS, BA, etc.), institution name and address, month and year of graduation, major, minor/concentration, grade point average (only if it is higher than 3.0), and academic honors, if applicable.

Experience   Discuss your work experience. List your most recent job first and work your way backward. For each job, indicate the position title, company or organization name and address, and dates of employment. Include all relevant employment experiences: part-time work, internships, cooperative education, or self-employment. Recruiters are interested in the skills that you've developed, not whether or how much you were paid. For each position, briefly describe your duties and responsibilities as they relate to the position you are seeking, and emphasize specific skills and achievements. Use active words to describe your duties and the results that you produced. Table 8.1 provides a list of action verbs to help you construct this section of your resume.

Activities and Affiliations   List any professional affiliations (e.g., student affiliate of the American Psychological Association) that are relevant to the objective stated on your resume. Include activities and awards only if they are significant experiences that speak to your capacities as an employee (such as leadership experience). If you can draw a valid connection between your professional goal and the activity, keep it in. If not, take it out.

Make your resume as professional looking as possible. Be concise; a new graduate's resume should be no more than one page in length. Carefully proofread your resume because typographical, spelling, and grammar errors are unacceptable and will cost you an interview. Print your resume on white or off-white paper, using a laser printer. Review Box 8.1 for a sample resume. See Checklist 8.2 for more resume tips. Also note that many employers request that applicants upload electronic resumes to their Web site or e-mail them to the human resources department. Convert your resume to a pdf file so that the formatting is retained regardless of what computer system the employer uses. Appearances count, so check your resume pdf file for errors in formatting even if the copy in your word processing file is flawless.

TABLE
8.1

ACTION VERBS TO SPICE UP YOUR RESUME

Achieved	Completed	Earned	Informed	Oversaw	Served
Acquired	Composed	Edited	Initiated	Participated	Showed
Acted	Computed	Eliminated	Innovated	Performed	Simplified
Adapted	Conceptualized	Empowered	Installed	Persuaded	Sketched
Administered	Condensed	Encouraged	Instituted	Planned	Sold
Advised	Conducted	Enforced	Instructed	Predicted	Solved
Allocated	Consolidated	Ensured	Integrated	Prepared	Staffed
Analyzed	Constructed	Established	Interpreted	Presented	Streamlined
Applied	Consulted	Estimated	Introduced	Processed	Studied
Arranged	Contributed	Evaluated	Invented	Produced	Submitted
Assembled	Controlled	Examined	Investigated	Projected	Summarized
Assessed	Converted	Expanded	Learned	Proposed	Supervised
Assisted	Counseled	Expedited	Lectured	Qualified	Supported
Attained	Created	Facilitated	Led	Quantified	Synthesized
Averted	Coordinated	Financed	Maintained	Questioned	Systematized
Balanced	Decided	Formulated	Managed	Realized	Tabulated
Briefed	Decreased	Gathered	Mapped	Received	Taught
Budgeted	Defined	Generated	Marketed	Recommended	Tested
Built	Demonstrated	Guided	Measured	Recorded	Trained
Calculated	Designed	Handled	Met	Reduced	Translated
Clarified	Determined	Headed	Modified	Reinforced	Undertook
Classified	Developed	Helped	Monitored	Repaired	Updated
Coached	Devised	Identified	Motivated	Represented	Utilized
Collaborated	Diagnosed	Illustrated	Negotiated	Researched	Verified
Collected	Directed	Implemented	Observed	Resolved	Wrote
Communicated	Discovered	Improved	Obtained	Reviewed	
Compared	Documented	Improvised	Operated	Revised	
Compiled	Drafted	Increased	Organized	Scheduled	

Source: Appleby, 1997; DeGalan & Lambert, 1995; Lock, 1988.

Exercise 8.2

Write Your Resume

Writing a resume is easy if you break it down into steps and take your time. Begin with the most challenging part, experience.

1. List all of the jobs that you have had, along with the dates of employment.
2. What did each job entail? Free write about your activities, responsibilities, and everything you did. What were you particularly good at? Identify achievements.
3. Condense each description into 1–2 sentences.
4. Identify action words to describe each job and further condense each job description into one sentence.
5. Format the experience section of your resume.
6. Prepare the heading and education sections of your resume.
7. List relevant activities and affiliations.
8. Format your resume.
9. Spell check your resume.
10. Get feedback on your resume.

Checklist 8.2

Resume Checklist

❏   Clearly communicate your purpose and value.
❏   Communicate your strongest points first.
❏   Don't make statements that you can't document.
❏   Be direct, succinct, and expressive with language.
❏   Don't use lengthy sentences and descriptions; this is the only time that sentence fragments are acceptable, but use them judiciously.
❏   Don't use the passive voice.
❏   Don't change the tense of verbs throughout the resume.
❏   Confine your information to one page.
❏   Use space to organize your resume; it should not appear cramped.
❏   Aim for overall visual balance on the page.
❏   Use a font size of 10 to 14 points.
❏   Choose a simple typeface and stick to it (i.e., don't change fonts).
❏   Use ample spacing and bold for emphasis (but don't overdo it).
❏   Don't fold or staple your resume.
❏   Check spelling, grammar, and punctuation.
❏   Proofread.
❏   Ask someone else to proofread.

❑   Get outside help. Get feedback from two or three people, including someone who regularly evaluates resumes and hires employees.
❑   Do not include your reference information on your resume (see sample).
❑   Before giving their names to a potential employer, ask your references if they are willing to serve as references.

Source: Appleby, 1997; DeGalan & Lambert, 1995; Krannich, 2005.

The Cover Letter

The cover letter is an introduction to your resume that enables you to tailor your application to the prospective employer. Your cover letter must be concise and explain what you can offer an employer. It should include no more than three paragraphs. Begin by briefly stating your reason for writing (e.g., "to apply for the research assistant position advertised in the *Daily News*"). Then explain what you can offer an employer. Highlight the most important aspects of your background that are relevant to the position and/or organization. Finally, provide contact information (a phone number and e-mail address), thank the reader, and reiterate your interest in the position.

Remember that the cover letter is an introduction that should motivate the reader to examine your resume. An effective cover letter is written with the needs of the audience (i.e., prospective employer) in mind. Before writing a cover letter, ask yourself, What is the purpose of this letter? What are the needs of the reader? What benefits will an employer gain from me? How can I maintain the reader's interest? How can I end the letter persuasively, so that the reader will want to examine my resume and contact me? Be explicit and communicate what you can do for the employer, not what the job will do for you. Checklist 8.3 provides tips for writing your cover letter. If you are submitting your resume by e-mail, shorten your cover letter to simply identify the position to which you are applying and why you are a good fit (in about 2–3 sentences).

CHECKLIST 8.3
Cover Letter Checklist

❑   Address the letter to an individual, using the person's name and title. If answering a blind newspaper advertisement, use the following salutation: "To Whom It May Concern."
❑   Indicate the position for which you are applying and explain why you are qualified to fill it.

❏ Include a phone number where you can be reached.
❏ Ask someone to proofread your letter for spelling, grammar, and punctuation errors.
❏ Indicate how your education and work skills are transferable and relevant to the position for which you are applying.
❏ Keep a copy of each cover letter for your records; write notes from any phone conversations that might occur on your copy of the cover letter.
❏ Make a connection to the company through a person you know, some information you've researched, or a specific interest.

Source: Adapted from Appleby, 1997; DeGalan & Lambert, 1995; Krannich, 2005.

INTERVIEW

Congratulations! If you have been asked to come for an interview, you have made it past the first round of reviews and have an opportunity to land the position. The interview is the most important criterion for hiring; it beats out grades, related work experience, and recommendations (Krannich, 2005). The interview helps companies to identify which applicants they'd like to take a closer look at and which are out of the running. Often second, and sometimes even third, interviews occur. This is your chance to impress the prospective employer. How do you do it? Display good communication skills, clearly defined professional goals, and an honest, outgoing personality (Appleby, 1999). Interviews are stressful, but you can increase your confidence by being thoroughly prepared.

Prepare

Understand the purpose of the interview, and keep the interviewer's objectives in mind. From your perspective, the purpose of the job interview is to get a second interview or job offer; but for employers, the purpose of the job interview is to whittle down the list of applicants to one or two finalists. The interviewer is interested in answering several questions:

- Why does this person want to work for us?
- What position is this person suited for?
- What are his or her qualifications?
- Why should I hire him or her?
- Does this person meet my employment needs?
- Is he or she trustworthy?

Because many applicants apply for each position, the interviewer often looks for reasons why you should not be hired. Interviewers are interested in identifying your weaknesses. Your job is to communicate your strengths. This means that you must understand yourself, but you also must understand the company or organization to which you are applying in order to determine how to package your strengths in order to appeal to the interviewer.

Research the company. What is the relative size and growth of the industry? What product lines or services are offered? Where is the headquarters? Identify the competition. Be familiar with any recent items in the news. Try to predict what will be asked during the interview, and prepare answers. Table 8.2 presents common questions asked during interviews. You also will be judged on the questions you ask. Ask thoughtful and intelligent questions about the company and position. Table 8.3 provides sample questions that an applicant might ask on an interview.

What to Wear

It may not be politically correct, but physical appearance counts. Dress appropriately for your interview because your appearance communicates messages about your level of seriousness and professionalism. During the first five minutes of an interview, interviewers make initial judgments or create expectations about your professionalism and "fit" for a position based on your appearance and demeanor. Use this to your advantage by dressing appropriately. Even if you are applying to a company with a casual dress code, dress up for the interview to communicate your enthusiasm for the position.

Whether you're a man or a woman, you can't go wrong with a classic navy or grey suit. Men should wear a white or blue oxford shirt with an understated tie. Women should wear a modest blouse, with understated hair and makeup. Keep jewelry to a minimum: a watch, simple earrings (for women only), and a ring. Err toward the conservative side, as you want to be remembered for what you say and not what you're wearing. Remember that these are merely general rules. You might want to see how others in your field dress for appropriate cues. You can't go wrong if you dress for the position, wearing attire that you might wear to work, but a little bit dressier.

During the Interview

Be enthusiastic. Remember that your interviewer is committed to his or her position and the company, and wants to hire someone who is similarly committed. Demonstrate your enthusiasm by discussing what you've learned from your research and preparation. Ask questions to fill in any gaps in your understanding. Convey a sense of long-term interest by asking about opportunities for further professional education and advancement.

TABLE 8.2 COMMON INTERVIEW QUESTIONS

What do you hope to be doing five or ten years from now?

Why did you apply for this job?

Tell me about yourself.

What are your strengths and weaknesses?

What can you offer to us, and what can we offer to you?

What are the two or three accomplishments in your life that have given you the greatest satisfaction?

Do you work well under pressure?

Have you ever held any supervisory or leadership roles?

What do you like to do in your spare time?

What other jobs are you applying for?

Is there anything else we should know about you?

Why do you feel that you will be successful in this position?

What courses did you like best? Least? Why?

What did you learn or gain from your part-time and summer job experience?

What are your plans for graduate study?

Why did you choose your major?

What can a psychology major do for this organization?

If you could do it all again, what would you change about your education?

Did you do the best you could in school? Why or why not?

Why did you leave your last employer?

What job did you like the most? The least? Why?

Have you ever been fired?

Why do you want to join our organization?

Why should we hire you?

When will you be ready to work?

What do you want to do with your life?

Do you have any actual work experience?

How would you describe your ideal job?

Are you a team player? Explain.

What motivates you?

Tell me about some of your recent goals and what you did to achieve them.

Have you ever had a conflict with a boss or professor? How did you resolve it?

If I were to ask one of your professors to describe you, what would he or she say?

Why did you choose to attend your college?

What qualities do you feel a successful manager should have?

What do you know about our company?

What kind of salary are you looking for?

Source: Appleby 1997; DeGalan & Lambert, 1995; Krannich, 2005; Landrum & Davis, 2000.

TABLE 8.3	QUESTIONS TO ASK DURING AN INTERVIEW

Tell me about the duties and responsibilities of this job.

How long has this position been in the company?

What would be the ideal type of person for this position?

What kinds of skills or personality characteristics are ideal for this position?

Whom would I be working with?

What am I expected to accomplish during the first year?

How would I be evaluated?

Are promotions and raises tied to performance criteria?

What is unique about working for this company?

What does the future look like for this company?

Source: Appleby, 1997; DeGalan & Lambert, 1995; Krannich, 2005.

Throughout the interview, be aware of your body language and limit fidgeting to a minimum. Lean very slightly toward the interviewer to communicate your interest in what he or she is saying (Krannich, 2005). Maintain eye contact to convey interest and trustworthiness. Smile to convey your positive attitude. Don't forget that your tone of voice can indicate how interested you are in the interview and the organization. Following are some other helpful tips for acing interviews:

- Bring a copy of your resume. It comes in handy if you have to fill in applications and provides initial information for your interviewer.
- Allow the interviewer to direct the conversation.
- Answer questions in a clear and positive manner.
- Never speak negatively about former employers or colleagues, no matter what.
- Let the interviewer lead the conversation toward salary and benefits. Try not to focus your interest on these issues (at least not during the initial interview).
- When discussing salary, be flexible.
- If the employer doesn't say when you'll hear about their decision, ask when you can call to follow up.
- Thank the employer for the interview.

Above all, remember that employers anticipate applicants to be on their best behavior during an interview. They recognize that any perceived flaws, such as arrogance, impoliteness, or poor listening skills, will likely be more apparent when the applicant becomes an employee. Be self-aware because any negative interactions or ambivalent signals can stop your application in its tracks.

Thank-You Note

Immediately after your interview, send a thank-you note. Few applicants do, so you'll stand out (Appleby, 1997; Krannich, 2005). Once upon a time applicants sent thank-you notes via snail mail. Today, e-mail is suitable (although a timely snail mail card signifies extra effort on the part of the applicant). Express your appreciation for the opportunity to meet the employer and for his or her time and consideration. Restate your interest, and highlight any noteworthy points made in your conversation. Be brief.

The Job Offer

Usually job offers are made over the phone or in person (e.g., toward the end of an interview). No matter how the offer is delivered, you're likely to be surprised. The most appropriate response to an offer in person or by phone is to ask any questions that come to mind, and then request time (a day or two) to think about the offer.

Before accepting an offer, be sure that you understand the conditions and elements of the job. In many cases, salaries for entry-level positions leave little room for negotiation. Take your lead from the employer as to whether the salary is negotiable. If the salary is lower than you hoped and it isn't negotiable, you must decide whether you're still willing to accept the position, and what, if anything, would make it more attractive. As you think about whether to accept the job offer, consider the scope of the position, how it fits your career goals, opportunities for professional growth, and pragmatic issues (geographic location, benefits, salary, work hours, etc.). If you decide to accept the offer, be sure to inform any employers still actively considering you. Also contact your references to inform them of your new job as well as to thank them for their assistance.

If you decide not to accept the job, notify the employer as soon as possible, by telephone. Timeliness is important because other applicants also are waiting for a response. Be polite, thank the employer for the offer, and wish him or her success. Follow up with a polite e-mail as well, which ensures that your reply is recorded.

SUGGESTED READINGS

Beshara, T. (2008). *Acing the interview: How to ask and answer the questions that will get you the job.* New York, NY: AMACOM.

Bolles, R .N. (2009). *What color is your parachute? A practical manual for job-hunters and career-changers.* Berkeley, CA: Ten Speed Press.

DeGalan, J., & Lambert, S. (2006). *Great jobs for psychology majors.* Chicago, IL: VGM Career Horizons.

Fry, R. (2001). *Your first resume: For students and anyone preparing to enter today's tough job market.* Manassas Park, VA: Impact Publications.

Greene, B. (2008). *Get the interview every time: Fortune 500 hiring professionals' tips for writing winning resumes and cover letters.* Chicago, IL: Dearborn Trade.

INTERNET RESOURCES

Job Hunter's Bible

http://www.jobhuntersbible.com/

Richard Bolles, author of *What Color Is Your Parachute? A Practical Manual for Job-Hunters and Career-Changers*, maintains this site of job hunting and career development resources.

Quintessential Careers

http://www.quintcareers.com

This Web site offers an extensive online guide to job hunting and career exploration, complete with resources on resumes, cover letters, interviewing, and more.

College Grad Job Hunter

http://www.collegegrad.com/

This is a job site designed for college students and others who are just getting started in the world of work.

JobWeb

http://www.jobweb.com

Here you'll find links to job search guides, articles, and other valuable resources on the Web.

MonsterCollege.com

http://www.monstercollege.com

This site features job search tools, articles, a salary search center, and more.

JOURNAL EXERCISES

Who Am I?

Who are you? What are your interests, skills, abilities, and aspirations? Free write about yourself and your goals. After you complete this exercise, look back over the exercises in Chapter 2. Do you notice anything different, or can you add anything to your responses?

Think Ahead

Try to imagine your ideal life five years from now. What are you doing? Where do you live? How do you spend your days?

Interview Preparation

In preparation for an interview, take notes on the prospective employer. What kinds of questions might the interviewer ask? How might you respond? Which of your characteristics match the job description well? Which might need some work?

WHAT CAN I DO WITH A GRADUATE DEGREE IN PSYCHOLOGY?

CHAPTER OUTLINE

Armed with a blend of liberal arts skills, most psychology majors successfully enter the workforce following graduation. About 28 percent of graduates continue their education at the graduate level (National Science Foundation, 2009). Graduate education imparts specialized knowledge for students who have already obtained bachelor's degrees. During college, psychology majors are exposed to all subfields of psychology and obtain a broad knowledge of the field. Graduate study, in contrast, entails specializing in one subfield of psychology, such as experimental psychology, for example. Graduate study imparts depth of knowledge. As we have discussed, employers value psychology majors' broad background in the liberal arts, science, and psychological knowledge. Graduate study is not necessary to find employment. Some careers, though, require a graduate degree.

Graduate Degrees

The Master's Degree

In 2007, over 21,000 master's degrees were awarded in psychology (National Center for Education Statistics, 2009), making the master's degree much more popular than the doctoral degree in psychology, with about 5,000 degrees awarded in 2007. Why do more students pursue master's degrees than doctoral degrees?

Master's degrees are quick   Relative to doctoral degrees, that is. A master's degree typically takes two years to earn, as compared with five to eight for a doctorate (Actkinson, 2000). Students with families must also consider how the length of graduate study will affect the family unit. Doctoral programs place students under great stress for an extended period of time. Some students may not be able or willing to place long-term stress on their families.

Master's degrees are cheap   Again, this is relative to doctoral degrees. A master's degree is expensive, both in tuition and in salary lost while attending school, but it is much less expensive than a doctoral degree (largely because it takes less time to graduate).

Master's programs are more widely available   Many more colleges offer master's programs than doctoral programs. A doctoral program may not be available in a given geographical location, and students may not be able or willing to relocate to attend graduate school (Actkinson, 2000).

Master's programs have less stringent admissions requirements   The acceptance rate for U.S. doctoral programs is typically 20 percent, versus about 60 percent for master's programs in psychology (Pate, 2001). Master's programs in psychology typically require a GPA of 2.9, minimum verbal GRE score of 473, and quantitative GRE score of 476. Doctoral programs in psychology most often require a GPA of 3.1, verbal GRE score of 535, and quantitative GRE score of 540 (Pate, 2001).

Master's programs often offer flexible enrollment   Master's programs are more likely than are doctoral programs to offer part-time study, which allows time for employment and family responsibilities. In addition, most doctoral programs allow for entry only in the fall semester, whereas master's programs often allow spring admissions (Actkinson, 2000).

Master's programs provide sufficient training and credentials   Many students pursue master's degrees because "a master's degree provides sufficient training and credentials for a large number of employment arenas: there are many career opportunities for master's degree holders" (APA, 2007, p. 53). With changes in health care reimbursement, there is a growing preference for hiring master's-level clinicians instead of pricier doctoral-level clinicians (Actkinson, 2000; Humphreys, 1996). In addition, master's-level practitioners can be licensed or certified as counselors or marriage and family therapists in all states. (Check the specific guidelines for your state to ensure that you obtain the necessary education and applied experience.)

Master's programs expand your intellectual horizons   Finally, some students are motivated to seek a master's degree simply because they want more education for its own sake (Peters, 1992).

Despite these benefits, myths abound about the master's degree because students and advisors often know little about master's degrees in psychology and related fields (Actkinson, 2000). What can you do with a master's degree? Depending on the program and curriculum, a master's degree enables graduates to (a) teach psychology in high school (other certification may be needed); (b) become more competitive for management, leadership, and consulting positions in government and industry; (c) practice counseling (credentials vary by state); (d) practice school psychology (certification/licensure requirements vary by state); and (e) obtain data management and analysis positions in government, industry (e.g., insurance, pharmaceutical, and manufacturing companies), and nonprofit organizations.

Master's-level professionals in psychology are employed in a variety of settings, including:

- Educational settings: elementary or secondary school, school system district offices, special education, and vocational or adult education
- Human services settings: counseling and guidance centers, student counseling centers, nursing homes, substance abuse facilities, mental

retardation facilities, developmental disability facilities, head injury facilities, and other community social services agencies
- Business and government: consulting firms, private research organizations, government research, corporations, small business, criminal justice system, military, government agencies, and nonprofit organizations
- Hospitals and clinics: outpatient mental health clinics, community mental health centers, and HMO and other managed care settings (Singleton, Tate, & Kohout, 2003a)

Perhaps the confusion about master's degrees lies in questions about whether master's-trained professionals can practice psychotherapy. Recognize that the term *psychologist* is regulated by state licensing boards; in order to use the title of "psychologist," you must have a doctoral degree, appropriate supervised experience, and pass a test (Lloyd, 2000). A master's degree will not qualify you to be a psychologist. However, master's-level professionals may conduct individual counseling and therapy by obtaining certification appropriate to their level of education and experience. Specifically, master's-level professionals in psychology can be licensed in all states as marriage and family therapists and/or licensed professional counselors and sometimes as clinical social workers. States differ in regulations and requirements, so learn about the requirements in your state to ensure that you obtain all the necessary experience while in school.

Most states permit several forms of licensure for master's-trained individuals, usually as counselors, which provides a great deal of autonomy (Actkinson, 2000). Master's-level counselors and social workers (with degrees in psychology, counseling, or social work) conduct many of the same services as those with doctoral degrees: They provide assessment and intervention services in community-based programs, public and private institutions, and programs dealing with special problems such as substance abuse, spouse abuse, crisis intervention, and vocational rehabilitation (Himelein, 1999). In institutional settings, master's degree holders may work as behavior change specialists who design and implement programs to serve special populations. Finally, if you're considering a graduate degree for the purpose of setting up a private practice, be aware that many licensed mental health workers, including social workers and psychologists, find it difficult to maintain a private practice because it entails more than therapy. Private practice requires marketing, bookkeeping, and interacting with insurance companies. Some practitioners leave private practice for financial reasons because they cannot compete with health maintenance organizations (HMOs) for patients (Himelein, 1999; Humphreys, 1996).

If you choose a master's degree in psychology, expect to complete two years of full-time graduate study. Requirements for service-oriented subfields such as clinical, counseling, and school psychology usually include experience in an applied setting. Research-oriented subfields such as experimental or developmental psychology usually require a master's thesis based on a research project. Some programs require students to pass a comprehensive exam that evaluates students' knowledge and reasoning skills. As you examine graduate programs, consider the kinds of experiences that occur outside of the classroom. Specifically, consider the "integrative experiences that help the student pull together knowledge learned in courses and translate it into practice. . . .[and]… summative experiences which test the student's knowledge and ability to do this integration on a higher than undergraduate level" (Peters, 1992, p. 112). Examples of integrative experiences include internships, practica, and other research and or field work. Examples of summative experiences include comprehensive examinations, theses, and research projects. In addition to psychology, there are many other fields in which master's-level practitioners can help people, as shown in Table 9.1.

The Doctoral Degree

A master's degree may allow you to work directly with people, but if you're planning on conducting research or teaching at the college level, a doctoral degree is essential. A doctoral degree provides a greater range of flexibility and autonomy, but it usually requires five to seven years of graduate work to complete. In clinical or counseling psychology, the requirement for the doctoral degree generally includes a year or more of internship or supervised experience. A doctoral degree requires a great commitment of time.

Why do students seek doctoral degrees? Generally students pursue doctoral degrees for any of the following reasons: (a) to teach college, (b) to conduct research in a university or private organization in industry or business, (c) to be licensed as a psychologist and practice psychology independently, or (d) to engage in a variety of consulting roles allowing autonomy. Most psychologists engage in more than one of these roles. For example, a college professor doesn't spend all of his or her time in class. Other activities include advising students, conducting research, and writing scholarly papers and books. With a doctoral degree, a psychologist may also serve as a consultant to private agencies or businesses, or may have a private psychotherapy practice.

As you consider pursuing a doctoral degree—the highest academic degree attainable—one of the first decisions to make is whether to pursue a PhD, PsyD, or EdD. What's with all the letters? These are three different kinds of doctoral degrees that a psychology student may pursue. The PhD refers to the doctor of philosophy. Like the master's degree, the PhD is awarded in many fields. It is a research degree that culminates in a dissertation based on original research. If you're considering pursing a PhD in psychology, note that courses in quantitative research methods and statistics, including the use of computers, are an integral part of graduate study and are needed to complete the dissertation (Lloyd, 1997b). The PhD in clinical or counseling psychology is a flexible degree—it trains people for research, teaching, writing, and clinical practice.

TABLE
9.1

MASTER'S DEGREES IN OTHER HELPING FIELDS

	Activities	Education
Social Work	As a profession, social work is dedicated to helping people to adapt and function as best they can in their environment. Social workers provide direct services or therapy, serving individuals, families, and communities. They work in hospitals, clinics, schools, correctional facilities, specialized programs, and private practice. Social workers assist clients in identifying problems, issues, and concerns, help them to consider and implement effective solutions, and guide them in locating reliable resources.	The master of social work (MSW) enables degree holders to practice therapy independently, because they are eligible for licensure in all states. The MSW requires two to three years of study, depending on the program and when the supervised internship (of 900 hours for licensure) is scheduled.
Counseling	There are many different types of counselors, but all help people who are experiencing personal, family, or mental health problems. Counselors also help people make educational and career decisions. Counselors work in schools, colleges, health care facilities, job training, career development centers, social agencies, correctional institutions, residential care centers, drug and alcohol rehabilitation programs, state and government agencies, group practice, and private practice.	Typically, a master's degree in counseling requires two years of coursework, including 600 hours of supervised clinical experience. Master's degree holders in counseling may conduct therapy independently and may seek licensure or certification.
Occupational Therapy	Occupational therapists work with clients who are experiencing disabilities (emotional, mental, physical, and developmental) that influence their occupational performance or well-being. Occupational therapists assess physical, mental, and emotional deficiencies, and counsel patients to help them improve their ability to function in their daily environments. For example, an occupational therapist might help a client to improve basic motor functions or reasoning abilities, as well as help him or her to compensate for permanent losses of function. Occupational therapists obtain positions in hospitals, offices and clinics of occupational therapists and other health practitioners, school systems, home health agencies, nursing homes, community mental health centers, adult day care programs, job training services, and residential care facilities.	All fifty states regulate occupational therapy, meaning that graduates must obtain licensure. Since 2007, the minimum educational requirement for entry into this field is a master's degree in occupational therapy.
Speech Pathology	Speech pathologists assess, diagnose, and treat communication disabilities such as stuttering, or impaired language. They work with clients who have difficulty understanding and producing language, including clients with cognitive	A master's degree in speech pathology (approximately two years

(Continued)

TABLE 9.1	MASTER'S DEGREES IN OTHER HELPING FIELDS (CONTINUED)	
	Activities	**Education**
	communication impairments such as attention and memory disorders. Speech pathologists help clients to develop and regain language (e.g., assist with making speech sounds). Their work also involves counseling clients and families to help them to better understand the disorder and treatment. Speech pathologists provide direct clinical services in schools, nursing homes, mental health centers, private practices, and medical settings, often as part of a team of allied health professionals.	of coursework) is required for entry into the profession. Nearly all states require speech pathologists to be licensed, with 300–375 hours of supervised clinical experience required for licensure (varying by state).

The PsyD refers to the doctor of psychology. It is offered only in clinical and counseling psychology and is considered a professional degree, much like a JD (doctor of jurisprudence, a lawyer's degree). How is the PsyD different from the PhD? The main difference is that a PhD has a greater emphasis on research, with more required courses in methodology and statistics. The PhD degree prepares graduates for research as well as practice, while the PsyD prepares graduates to be consumers of research (Lloyd, 1997b). The PsyD is usually based on practical and applied work, as well as on examinations. The dissertation, if required, is usually a theoretical paper. The PsyD is for those who aim to engage in clinical practice rather than conduct research.

The doctor of education (EdD), a third doctoral option for psychology students, is not as common as the PhD and PsyD. The EdD is offered in departments of education, rather than psychology. According to Lloyd (1997b), the research requirements for many EdD programs are not as rigorous as PhD programs. Psychologists sometimes view the EdD degree as inferior because it is rarely offered by a psychology department and frequently offers less training in the principles of psychology than PhD and PsyD degrees. Nevertheless, many administrative positions in college and university settings do not discriminate between applicants with an EdD and a PhD degree (Himelein, 1999).

GRADUATE-LEVEL CAREERS IN PSYCHOLOGY

Graduate education opens the door to many opportunities. What follows is a sampling of possible careers, but note that no one program will prepare you for all of these careers. Before you decide on a graduate degree and program, it's important to consider all the types of careers that you might enjoy and choose a degree and program that will not limit your options.

Teaching Careers

Many students seek a graduate degree in order to teach at a high school, two-year, or four-year college. Master's degree holders may teach psychology in a high school (although additional certification may be necessary, depending on the state) or community college setting. In recent years, faculty positions at two-year and community colleges have become more competitive; many are held by doctoral degree holders. Similarly, although master's degree holders may be hired to teach at four-year colleges on a part-time basis, they are unlikely to be hired for full-time positions (Peters, 1992).

If your goal is to teach at the college level, it's in your best interest to pursue a doctoral degree, which will provide you with the most opportunities for employment, mobility, and advancement as a faculty member (Actkinson, 2000; Lloyd, 2000). Graduates with doctoral degrees may teach undergraduate, master's, and doctoral students in a variety of educational settings, including universities, professional schools, and medical schools. When you consider a career as a professor, recognize that there is more to the professorate than lecturing in front of a classroom each day. Working in the classroom is only the most obvious thing a professor does. A professor's career entails many roles, usually including research and service to the campus and community (advising, committee work, administrative work). During a typical week, a professor may give lectures, spend time writing an article or book, conduct statistical analyses and continue with his or her research, conduct literature searches, sit in on faculty meetings, advise students, write letters of recommendation, spend time grading papers, give a talk at a professional meeting, engage in consulting work, serve as an advisor for community agencies, and much more.

Research Careers

A graduate degree in psychology is excellent preparation for a career in research. Research psychologists conduct basic and applied studies of human behavior and may participate in research programs sponsored by universities, government, and private organizations (Kuther & Morgan, 2010). For example, a psychologist working in a university or hospital-based clinic might study smoking cessation; another working in a traumatic brain injury center might study the effects of particular kinds of brain injuries on behavior as well as resilience to brain injury and rehabilitation strategies. Some psychologists work in military research programs, examining the effects of exposure to trauma, for example, while others act as research and development officers at pharmaceutical companies and businesses (Lloyd, 2000). Medical schools are emerging as an important employment setting for research psychologists who conduct research and teach medical students. Fields such as anatomy, biochemistry, physiology, pharmacology, and microbiology are merging; as a result, interdisciplinary study is playing an increasingly important role in university life and is leading to more research (and teaching) opportunities for psychologists outside of psychology departments (Balster, 1995). Many research positions are available to master's degree holders, especially in business and private organizations. Particularly in academic settings, the doctoral degree offers more flexibility, opportunities for advancement, and opportunities to serve as the primary investigator of federal grants (Lloyd, 2000).

Master's degree recipients in research-oriented fields such as quantitative psychology, developmental psychology, general psychology, and experimental psychology have developed useful methodological and quantitative skills. They are often employed in research positions in university research centers as well as in government, business, and private organizations. Others seek entry into doctoral programs.

Service Delivery (Practice)

Graduate degree holders have a variety of opportunities to engage in service delivery. Mental health professionals with graduate degrees, including clinical and counseling psychologists, engage in a variety of practice activities including, but often not limited to (a) conducting psychotherapy with persons who have psychological disorders, crises, or problems of living; (b) administering and interpreting psychological tests of personality, intellect, and vocational aptitude; (c) facilitating psychoeducational and psychotherapy groups; (d) giving talks or workshops on specialty areas; (e) directing and administrating mental health programs; (f) supervising the clinical work of other therapists; and (g) responding to crises or emergency situations (Himelein, 1999; U.S. Bureau of Labor Statistics, 2009).

All states permit several forms of licensure for master's-trained individuals, usually as counselors, which provides a great deal of autonomy (Actkinson, 2000). If you're considering a master's in clinical or counseling psychology with the intention of setting up an independent practice, carefully research your options beforehand because some clinical and counseling master's programs meet the requirements to seek licensure as counselors or marriage and family therapists (Levant, Moldawsky, & Stigall, 2000). Be sure to do your homework so that you're not disappointed later. Finally, although some school psychologists practice with a master's degree, national certification as a school psychologist (from the National Association of School Psychologists) requires a more advanced degree called a specialist's degree (Rittle, 2000). A specialist's degree falls between the master's and doctoral degrees and typically takes from an extra semester to a year of study to complete. Because 75 percent of nondoctoral school psychologists hold a specialist's degree, and it's required for certification, you should plan on taking the time to earn this degree if you're interested in school psychology (Himelein, 1999).

Practicing with a Master's Degree

1. Opportunities to practice therapy with a master's degree vary by state. Research the requirements of your state. Under what conditions may an individual with a master's in psychology practice? What types of credentialing or licensure are necessary?
2. What other types of master's degrees offer practice opportunities in your state?
3. If you were to pursue a master's degree with the intent of practicing, which degree would you choose and why?
4. Based on your research, with how much independence can an individual with a master's degree practice in your state?

Non-Academic Careers

Administration   Graduate degree holders in psychology and related fields work as managers and administrators in hospitals, mental health clinics, government agencies, schools, universities, businesses, and nonprofit organizations, where they may administrate research and applied activities (Bat-Chava, 2000). The ability to effectively administrate in each of these settings is enhanced by the research skills obtained in graduate school. Research skills are essential for evaluating programs and making decisions based on evaluations. Many administrative positions can be obtained with a master's degree and some experience, especially in smaller institutions and organizations. As in other applied careers, additional opportunities are available to doctoral-level administrators.

Consulting   Graduate degree holders in psychology often are hired by organizations to provide consultative services on problems in their area of expertise. Consultative services can include designing a marketing survey, organizing outpatient mental health services, conducting individual assessments, providing expert testimony to a court, and designing Web pages, as well as many other activities.

Health psychologists, for example, may be hired as consultants to design and implement programs to help people become healthier, stop smoking, lose weight, or manage stress. Some consultants work in policy: They conduct, interpret, and disseminate research to help national planners and policy makers reach decisions (Flattau, 1998). Trial consultants work in several areas: They may help with jury selection, work with witnesses, or develop effective trial strategy in order to shape juror perceptions (Stapp, 1996). Those trained in forensic or clinical psychology may conduct clinical work in corrections settings, serve as consultants for trial lawyers or as expert witnesses in jury trials, and conduct assessments that are used in trials. As in the other areas that we've discussed, some opportunities are available to master's degree holders, and additional opportunities for advancement are open to doctoral holders.

Business/Human Resources   Many graduate degree holders find a home in business, where they select and train employees, engage in human resources development, and develop employee assistance programs. Typical activities include designing and validating assessment instruments; determining the fairness of assessment and vocational tests, particularly for minority applicants; and creating work environments in public and private settings that maximize employee satisfaction (U.S. Bureau of Labor Statistics, 2004).

The research skills honed in graduate school are applicable and valued in many corporate settings, for example, market research (Garfein, 1997). Like other research psychologists, market researchers design studies, construct questionnaires and other research instruments, analyze data, draw conclusions, and write reports. However, instead of conducting and publishing research to advance theory, a market researcher conducts applied research in an effort to help clients become more productive, competitive, and profitable (Krauss, 1996). Business holds a variety of opportunities for master's degree holders because, unlike many other applied careers, doctoral degrees do not necessarily offer much of an advantage over master's degrees. For both master's and doctoral degree holders, advancement becomes possible with additional work experience.

EXERCISE 9.2
Exploring Psychology Specializations

1. Identify two areas of specialization in psychology that interest you. Why do these areas interest you? What are typical topics of study within these areas?
2. What kinds of jobs do individuals with master's degrees in these areas hold? Include information about typical settings, salary, and more.
3. What kinds of jobs do individuals with doctoral degrees in these areas hold? Include information about typical settings, salary, and more.
4. How has what you have learned about this specialization influenced your views about graduate study in this area? Is a graduate degree a good career option? Which degree offers more opportunities? Conduct a cost analysis of the pros and cons of seeking a master's degree versus doctoral degree in this specialization.

Publishing   Journalism and publishing offer new opportunities for advanced degree holders in psychology. Some psychologists pursue careers as acquisitions editors. An acquisitions editor works for a publishing company and engages in a variety of tasks, including reading book proposals, interpreting reviews of proposals, deciding whether to offer book contracts to authors, approaching potential authors with book ideas, discussing works in progress with authors, negotiating journal-publishing agreements with professional societies, and working on practical issues in publishing such as the design of book covers (Amsel, 1997). Positions in publishing offer important opportunities for master's degree holders with interests in writing and the ability to think critically and solve problems effectively. More advanced positions in publishing are held by doctoral degree holders and master's degree recipients with experience in the field.

WHAT CAN YOU EXPECT TO EARN WITH A GRADUATE DEGREE?

Table 9.2 illustrates starting salaries for full-time positions among 2001 and 2002 master's degree recipients in psychology, adjusted for inflation. Table 9.3 lists the 2009 median salaries among all master's degree holders

| TABLE 9.2 | STARTING SALARIES FOR FULL-TIME EMPLOYMENT POSITIONS AMONG 2001 AND 2002 MASTER'S DEGREE RECIPIENTS IN PSYCHOLOGY ADJUSTED FOR 2009 |

Setting	Median Salary 2009 (2002)
Direct Human Services	
Clinical Psychology	35,900 (30,000)
Counseling Psychology	39,494 (33,000)
School Psychology	49,367 (41,250)
Administration of Human Services Delivery	38,297 (32,000)
Applied Psychology Settings	57,440 (48,000)
Research	43,683 (36,500)
Administrative Positions	41,781 (34,911)
Other	48,829 (40,800)

Source: Adapted from Singleton et al., 2003A.

TABLE 9.3   2009 MEDIAN SALARIES OF ALL MASTER'S-LEVEL PSYCHOLOGISTS

Position	Median Salary
Faculty Positions	45,000
Research Positions	57,500
Direct Human Services	52,322
Administration of Human Services	54,000
Other Administration	79,800
Applied Psychology	80,000

Source: Adapted from Michalski, Finno, Kohout, & Wicherski, 2009.

TABLE 9.4   STARTING SALARIES FOR FULL-TIME EMPLOYMENT POSITIONS AMONG DOCTORAL DEGREE RECIPIENTS IN PSYCHOLOGY

Setting	Median
Assistant Professor	49,091
Educational Administration	67,000
Research Positions	55,000
Research Administration	52,000
Direct Human Services	
Clinical Psychology	52,000
Counseling Psychology	51,000
School Psychology	61,172
Administration of Human Services	60,000
Applied Psychology	68,000
Other Administrative Positions	66,000

Source: Adapted from Wicherski & Kohout, 2007.

in psychology (regardless of when the degree was conferred). Table 9.4 presents data on the starting salaries of employed 2005 doctoral degree recipients in psychology. Table 9.5 lists the median salaries of all doctoral-level psychologists.

TABLE 9.5   2003 MEDIAN SALARIES OF ALL DOCTORAL LEVEL PSYCHOLOGISTS

Position	Median Salary
Professor	62,000
Educational Administration	97,000
Research Positions	78,000
Administration of Research	95,000
Direct Human Services	
Clinical Psychology	75,000
Counseling Psychology	65,500
School Psychology	75,500
Administration of Human Services	75,000
Applied Psychology	
Industrial/Organizational Psychology	105,000
Other Areas of Psychology	92,500
Administration of Applied Psychology	110,000
Other Administrative Positions	100,500

Source: Adapted from Pate, Frincke, & Kohout, 2005.

THE CHANGING ROLES OF PSYCHOLOGISTS

Concern about the supply and demand of psychologists has grown over the last two decades along with the growth of the number of psychologists proportional to the population and growth in the number of doctoral programs in the United States (Cummings, 1995; Frank & Ross, 1995; Robiner & Crew, 2000). As the number of psychologists increases, some are concerned that supply is exceeding demand. For example, internships, a required part of doctoral training for clinicians, are becoming more difficult to secure. Each year nearly one-quarter of students are not matched to an internship site.

With changes to health insurance, such as the movement towards managed care and other legislation, the role of psychologists in fostering mental health may change. For example, solo independent practice, once very popular, is economically unfeasible for many psychologists who instead gravitate towards group practice (Cummings, 1995; Hersch, 1995). As master's-trained professionals take on larger roles in mental health care delivery, some fear that doctoral-level clinical psychologists are "being underbid by master's-level social workers, marriage and family counselors, and psychological assistants, and will be increasingly supplanted in the role of psychotherapist by these master's-level professionals" (Humphreys, 1996, p. 190). Humphreys (1996) warns that psychologists will experience what has already happened in psychiatry: "Psychiatrists are still involved in psychotherapy, their role has become circumscribed . . . cost-conscious payers prefer not to pay psychiatrist's fee for anything other than what only a psychiatrist can do . . . such as brief diagnostic assessment and prescription of medications" (p. 192). Cummings (1995) predicts that similar economic factors will force psychologists out of psychotherapy practice as well.

What do all these dire warnings mean? Should you give up on a doctoral degree in clinical or counseling psychology? No! Each of the doomsayers has received a substantial amount of criticism. We don't know where the field is going and how opportunities for psychologists will change in the coming years, but the Occupational Outlook Handbook reports that employment of psychologists is expected to increase faster than the average through 2016 (U.S. Bureau of Labor Statistics, 2009). These warnings are provided as encouragement for you to enter the field with your eyes open. There are many opportunities for new psychologists; however, the new psychologists who will be most successful in the coming years are those who have an open mind to change and who are not afraid to explore new and nontraditional avenues.

SUGGESTED READINGS

Davis, S. F., Giordano, P J., & Licht, C. A. (2009). *Your career in psychology: Putting your graduate degree to work.* Hoboken, NJ: Wiley.

Kuther, T. L., & Morgan, R. (2010). *Careers in psychology: Opportunities in a changing world.* Pacific Grove, CA: Wadsworth.

Morgan, R. D., Kuther, T. L., & Habben, C. J. (2004). *Life after graduate school: Opportunities and advice from new psychologists.* (Edited book) New York: Psychology Press.

Sternberg, R. J. (2006). *Career paths in psychology: Where your degree can take you.* Washington, DC: American Psychological Association.

INTERNET RESOURCES

Interesting Careers in Psychology

http://www.apa.org/careers/resources/profiles/index.aspx

Interested in a nonacademic career in psychology? Check out the links to case studies on this page.

♂

Fields of Psychology

http://www.psichi.org/pubs/search.aspx?category1=12

Psi Chi, the International Honor Society in Psychology, presents links to articles about a
variety of career areas in psychology.

Early Career Psychologists

http://www.apa.org/earlycareer/

The American Psychological Association provides resources and links for new psychologists. Get a feel for the field by visiting this site.

Psychology: Scientific Problem Solvers . . . Careers for the Twenty-First Century

http://www.apa.org/students/brochure/brochurenew.pdf

This American Psychological Association brochure describes the field of psychology,
including employment settings, job outlook, and career preparation.

JOURNAL EXERCISES

Is Graduate School Necessary?

Look through your journal and review past entries. Considering all that you've
learned about yourself, what type of career would make you happy? Now
consider the information in this chapter. Will a graduate degree help you to
achieve your goals? Be honest with yourself.

Other Applications

Imagine that you went to graduate school and earned a doctoral degree in
psychology, but you will not practice therapy. What would you do? What other
activities of psychologists appeal to you, aside from therapy?

Considering Fields

Choose two or three psychology subfields. What is most interesting about the
subfield? What are the drawbacks? Identify two career options for each. How
well do these careers fit your interests and skills? Can you see yourself working in each? Why or why not?

Applying to Graduate School in Psychology

Chapter Outline

By now you have learned that psychology majors have a host of skills that employers want. Contrary to common lay belief, a bachelor's degree in psychology does not automatically commit you to years of graduate study. Graduate study is not for everyone and, as we have discussed, a graduate degree is not necessary for you to be employable. Should you decide to apply to graduate school, however, you must focus your energy because the application process is arduous and highly competitive, with about 20 percent of applicants gaining admission to doctoral programs and about 60 percent to master's programs. In this chapter we discuss the process of applying to graduate school and how to succeed in a difficult market.

SHOULD YOU GO TO GRADUATE SCHOOL?

Graduate study isn't the right choice for everyone. Is it right for you? Only you can answer that question. Review Chapter 2 and reflect on your interests, goals, dreams, and abilities. What kind of career do you want? Is it necessary for you to go to grad school to achieve your goals? Are there alternative ways of achieving them? Be honest with yourself. As we discussed in Chapters 7 and 9, if you would like to work with people, there are many alternatives to a doctoral degree in psychology (and some are preferable over a psychology degree for reasons of time and expense). Complete Quiz 10.1 and then consider its results.

Quiz 10.1
Is Graduate School for You?

Answer the following questions honestly (that's the hard part!).
1. Are you ready to live in near poverty for the next two to seven years?
2. Does the thought of studying all the time make you ill?
3. Is writing term papers fun?
4. Does public speaking bother (or even terrify) you?
5. Do you like to read psychology books or articles even if they are not assigned?
6. Do you put off studying for tests or writing papers as long as possible?
7. Do you enjoy reading and studying?
8. Do you hate library research?
9. Will you give up a social opportunity (like a party) to study for a test or to finish a paper?

10. Are you sick of school?
11. Can you concentrate and study for hours at a time?
12. Are your grades mainly Bs or lower?
13. Do you read recent issues of psychology journals?
14. Are there other careers aside from psychology that you'd like to explore?
15. Did you earn an A or B in statistics?
16. Does research bore you?
17. Are you comfortable competing against other students?
18. Do you frequently hand assignments in late or forget to do them?

Scoring:
Assign one point for each odd item to which you answered yes and one point for each even item to which you answered no. Sum the points to obtain a total score. Higher scores indicate a greater potential for graduate study.

Reflection:
How did you score? Given your score, how well do you think your characteristics and habits match those of successful graduate students? Is graduate study a realistic match to your characteristics? Why or why not?

Adapted from Appleby, 1997; Fretz & Stang, 1988; Keith-Spiegel & Wiederman, 2000.

Are you considering graduate study for the right reasons?

Some people attend graduate school for the love of learning; others seek career advancement. Can you fulfill your goals with your bachelor's degree, or is a master's degree needed? If you're considering pursuing a doctorate, why? Some students focus on the desire to be called "Doctor"—the prestige. A graduate degree is certainly prestigious, but that shouldn't be the only reason for attending grad school. Are you willing to take on a heavy workload for many years to earn the degree? Are you willing to put much of your personal life on hold? Incur debt? Remember that just because your faculty advisor has a PhD doesn't mean that you need to earn one to be happy or respected. This is a personal decision. If you decide to attend graduate school, choose the level of education, whether master's or doctoral degree, that offers the training and course work to prepare you for the career to which you aspire.

Are you prepared for the academic demands of graduate study?

Generally it is expected that students will maintain at least a 3.0 average during graduate school. Some programs deny funding to students with less than a 3.33 average. Consider your undergraduate psychology coursework. How comfortable did you feel with these courses? Do you like writing papers? How about library research? Students who choose to attend graduate school tend to be more satisfied with their undergraduate courses than students who do not. Do you have good academic habits? Can you juggle multiple tasks, projects, and papers? Can you manage time effectively? Look back over your responses to the assessments in Chapter 4. What did they reveal about your academic habits? Are your habits suited for graduate study?

Are you prepared to take graduate-level methodology and statistics courses? If you are weak in math, you may not be able to complete the basic statistical requirements for psychology. If you like math and performed well in your math courses (for example, with grades of B or higher), then you will be better able to handle graduate-level math. Before you rule out graduate school based on these math requirements, do a little soul searching. Is your ability in math really weak, or do you just think so? Perhaps if you adjust your studying strategies, or devote more time to it, you'll find that you're better at math than you think.

Do you have the motivation for two or more years of school?

Graduate school entails a greater commitment than undergrad. You must enjoy and excel at reading, writing, and analyzing information. Gone are the days of skipping classes, waiting until the last minute to write papers, and late-night partying. Excelling in college may have come easily, but you likely will find graduate school to be quite different. You'll be surrounded by students who performed just as well and even better than you did in college. The bar is set much higher, and you'll need to work harder and more consistently than ever before. Speak with professors and graduate students to get a better idea of what's involved in graduate study. Most first-year graduate students are overwhelmed and remark that they had no idea what they were getting into. Seek a first-year student's perspective for a reality check (and read the letter from a new graduate student in Box 10.1).

Do you have the personal characteristics needed to succeed in graduate school?

Self-reliance, a desire to excel, commitment to scholarship, intellectual curiosity, and emotional stability are necessary to successfully navigate the rigor, stress, and often impersonal nature of graduate school. As shown in Table 10.1, faculty rate a range of characteristics as important for success in graduate school, some skill-based (like research and counseling ability), others more intrinsic (like empathy and discipline). A quick perusal of the list reveals that hard work, social skills, and writing skills are vital to success in graduate school. Therefore, you should work on developing not only academic skills but also interpersonal (teamwork) and intrapersonal (emotional

BOX

10.1   LETTER FROM A FIRST-YEAR GRADUATE STUDENT

Dear Potential Graduate Student:

I'm currently enrolled in Your State University's developmental psychology PhD program. I'm writing to provide advice about how to prepare for admissions and what grad school is really like.

As an undergraduate, there are many things you should do to prepare for graduate school. In selecting courses, take extra mathematics and science classes because graduate schools are looking for students with well rounded backgrounds. Balance should also be reflected in your choice of major courses. Don't focus only on the fun classes (e.g., social, clinical, child); take the harder psychology classes too (e.g., physiological psychology, perception, learning theory).

Try to obtain additional research experience beyond the methodology requirements. Speak to faculty about research opportunities if you are genuinely interested. Many faculty members are very interested in student research; however, you need to express your desire. Thus, it is important to develop relationships with faculty members with whom you share interests because they can serve as role models or mentors.

It is also important to develop a solid background and understanding of statistics (especially if you're interested in a clinical program because they are the most competitive). Consider taking additional statistics courses from the mathematics department because they will improve your standing. In addition to monitoring your course selection, save all of your class notes and books from your major courses. They will be helpful in preparing for the GRE as well as later reference.

It's crucial that you prepare for the GRE. The GRE scores are not only used as entry criteria; competitive financial aid packages and assistantships are allocated on the basis of these scores. Therefore you should do the best that you can to qualify for financial assistance. When applying to graduate school, be sure that you and each school that you apply to are a good fit. Don't apply hoping to be accepted anywhere. Consider the philosophy/orientation of the school with your career goals in mind or you might be unpleasantly surprised. For example, one student in our research-oriented developmental program recently dropped out because she had the false impression that she would be able to have a private practice providing clinical services with this degree. Learn more about current students' career goals and those of successful graduates.

As an undergraduate, I wish I had spoken with someone about what graduate school is really like. Grad school requires a higher level of dedication, time, professionalism, and maturity. Successful grad students constantly study or work on research, 8 hours per day, 6–7 days per week. In most graduate schools, professors don't read the material to you, nor do they interpret it for you. Rather, you are required to read, understand, and discuss it intelligently. It's a whole other world from the innocence of undergraduate work. It's a lot of work and a life change, but I'm glad I'm here.

TABLE 10.1	TOP 15 CHARACTERISTICS THAT DESCRIBE A SUCCESSFUL GRADUATE STUDENT

1. Working hard
2. Getting along with others
3. Writing ability
4. Clinical and counseling skills
5. Doing research
6. Handling stress
7. Discipline
8. Good grades
9. High intelligence
10. Empathy
11. Establishing a relationship with a mentor
12. Getting along with peers
13. Broad knowledge of psychology
14. Specialized knowledge in one or two areas of psychology
15. Reflecting program values

Source: Adapted from Descutner & Thelen, 1989.

intelligence and self management) skills. Learn how to manage stress because professors prefer to work with students who are emotionally mature, can consistently produce quality work, and can meet deadlines in an emotionally stable manner.

Finally, consider Fretz and Stang's warning (1988):

> Graduate work takes initiative, independence, perseverance, acceptance of responsibility, and a general freedom from emotional conflict and anxiety. The benefits of going to graduate school, especially a top-ranked school, are enormous, but they demand a high price in sweat and anxiety. . . . Succeeding in graduate school requires years of single-minded dedication, much energy, individual initiative, and responsible independent study. (pp. 79–80)

Does this sound overwhelming? That's a normal response. This information is not meant to change your mind, but to provide a more realistic picture of what attending graduate school really entails. Going to graduate school affects the rest of your life. There are both pros and cons to continuing your education. Seek information from multiple sources—this book, the career counseling center, graduate students, professors, and your family. Take your time with the decision. More importantly, trust your judgment and have faith that you'll make the choice that's best for you.

Selecting Graduate Programs

As you'll soon see, pursuing graduate study in psychology entails many decisions. You'll confront decisions about type of degree, training models, and then among the many graduate programs themselves.

Differentiate Among Training Models and Degrees

Graduate programs in psychology follow one of three basic models of training. Choose a program whose model best fits with your interests, because most psychologists engage in the same type of activities that they experienced in their graduate program of study.

Research-Scientist Model   Programs that follow a research-scientist model focus on molding students into scholars who will make new discoveries and advance the knowledge in their field. From a historical perspective, this was the first training model to emerge as it characterizes the emphases of the PhD, or doctor of philosophy degree. Most of your college professors hold this degree; it is conferred in nearly all academic fields. The PhD in psychology provides training in experimental methods, methodological skill, and a background in a particular specialty area. Individuals trained in the research-scientist model conduct original research, teach, and write about their research findings, typically in the core academic areas of psychology such as experimental, social and personality, quantitative, physiological, and developmental psychology. PhD recipients tend to be employed as researchers or college and university professors, and some work as consultants or conduct research for the government or corporations.

Scientist-Practitioner Model   Programs adopting the scientist-practitioner model seek to train scholars who integrate their research training with human service; graduates engage in practice activities and conduct applied and basic research. This model is commonly found in PhD programs in clinical, counseling, school, and industrial psychology. Similar to the research-scientist model, students trained in the scientist-practitioner model receive training in research and methodology, but they take more courses in applied areas and complete more internships and practica than do students trained in the research-scientist model. Graduates trained in the scientist-practitioner model may be employed by hospitals and clinical practices; teach in colleges and universities; work in medical centers, mental health centers, and inindustry and government; and may own private practices. The extent to which a particular psychologist engages in each of these activities depends on his or her job setting and commitment to research; most practicing clinicians do little to no research.

Professional Psychologist-Practitioner Model   Graduate programs that adopt the professional psychologist-practitioner model train students to provide psychological services and award the PsyD, a practitioner degree that emphasizes clinical training or the professional model of training. The PsyD and the practitioner model of training place greater emphasis on clinical practice than in the scientist-practitioner model, and much less emphasis on research. PsyD programs train students to be consumers of research rather than producers of it.

PsyD programs tend to be larger than PhD programs, so more students are accepted and your chances of acceptance are much higher. One study found that accredited PhD programs in clinical psychology had acceptance rates of about 6 percent and accredited PsyD programs in clinical psychology had acceptance rates of about 39 percent (Pate, 2001). The PsyD degree often is offered at private or professional schools and is generally more expensive than a PhD. Most funding for PhD students comes from faculty research grants; little research is conducted in PsyD programs, so there are fewer opportunities for funding. Professional programs train students to be educated consumers of research rather than generators of research. Because there is less emphasis on research, PsyD students earn their degrees a little quicker; however, they usually graduate with more debt than do PhD students.

Practice-oriented students often find the curricula of professional programs to be better aligned with their own interests and career aspirations than those of traditional scientist-practitioner programs. Although some have argued that the PhD is more prestigious than the PsyD (Buskist & Shurburne, 1996) and the PhD may be more flexible in terms of career options because of its research basis, you should choose the degree that will prepare you for the career you desire. If you're interested in practicing psychology and do not want to teach in a university setting or conduct research, the PsyD may be for you. Graduates from professional schools are at a disadvantage only when they apply for positions in research or academic settings. Understand your interests, abilities, and professional goals in order to choose a training model and degree that will prepare you for the career you desire.

Gather Information on Graduate Programs

Before you spend a great deal of time gathering information about graduate programs, consider your priorities. Where does graduate school fit in your life? Are there geographic restrictions on where you live? What will you specialize in? This is a crucial question. Unlike college, where you majored in psychology, a general degree, graduate school entails specializing in a particular area of psychology. Carefully consider your area of specialization (e.g., clinical, experimental, developmental, school, and others) because that will determine to which schools and programs you'll apply as well as your likelihood of gaining admission to a program.

How do you choose? Examine your responses to the assessments in this book as well as your journal entries. Consider your interests. Do you want to work with people? In a laboratory? Teach college? Conduct research? What were your favorite classes in college? On what topics have you written term papers? Seek advice from professors in your department, especially from those in the areas in which you wish to specialize. Chapter 1 notes the major specialty areas of psychology. In order to apply to graduate school, you must choose an area in which to specialize. Take your time in making this decision because it will shape your education and career.

Once you have a specialty area(s) in mind, it's time to gather program information. How do you get information about programs? Rely on a variety of resources, in print and online. Several books offer information about programs; many resources are also available on the Internet. Peterson's publishes a set of educational guidebooks each year; look for the volume entitled *Graduate Studies in Social Sciences and Social Work*. Most college libraries have a copy. The Peterson's guidebook is organized by field, with universities listed alphabetically. This is a good general guide to help you find out about existing programs and their general requirements; compare the listed admission requirements with your own GPA and GRE scores for an initial glimpse of what programs are within your range.

One of the best sources of information about graduate programs is the APA *Guide to Graduate Study in Psychology.* It describes every psychology graduate program in the United States and Canada. Organized alphabetically by state and by school and updated every two years, this guide provides the following information: criteria for admission; program emphasis; number of faculty; enrollments; and additional admissions information, including the average GPA and GRE scores for each school. Most campus bookstores keep this volume in stock or will order it for you.

Peruse the bookshelves at the college bookstore and library, and you'll find several other guides. A list of helpful print and online resources is provided at the end of this chapter. Note that the material in each of these printed resources is usually at least two years old because of the time required to print and distribute books. The American Psychological Association Web site has an online searchable database of graduate programs that contains the most up-to-date information about programs. A three-month subscription to the database costs about $20; visit http://www.apa.org/grad-study/ for more information. Once you have a list of programs, your next step is to gather more detailed information. Visit the school's Web site to get more information about admissions, and possibly an online application, as well as to review the department and program home page for additional information.

Evaluate Graduate Programs

All too often when I ask students where they want to go to school, they respond, "Anywhere that takes me." It's understandable that students want to get into graduate school, but it's also important to be an educated consumer. While the admissions committee evaluates you as a potential student, you should evaluate the program to see whether it fits your needs. Is it someplace where you can spend the next few years? Take the time to carefully review and evaluate each graduate program. As you read the information about graduate programs, you'll probably notice that there are differences among departments in goals, program philosophies, theoretical orientations, facilities, and resources. What are you looking for as you peruse the volumes of information obtained through your research? Basically you're looking to see how well each program matches your goals and aspirations—the "fit" between you and the graduate program. How do you determine fit? As you examine a graduate program, consider the areas listed in the following sections. How well does each program fulfill your expectations of what graduate training should entail?

Department Emphasis and Program Philosophy   What are the program goals? Do they fit with your own? Is the department heavily research oriented, or is it more theoretical or applied? What's the program's theoretical orientation (e.g., cognitive-behavioral, psychoanalytic)? Is the program oriented toward producing researchers? Is it heavily oriented toward theory? Are theory and practice united? Where does the program fall on the scientist-practitioner continuum? Consider:

1. **Faculty research interests and publications.** Do you share interests with any of the faculty? Do the faculty publish often and in refereed journals? Look up faculty members in PsycINFO to learn more about their work.
2. **Teaching goals and style.** Can you find any information about how classes are run? Look at the Web site. Do faculty have their own Web pages? Do any of these Web pages describe classes or provide resources for students? Try to find out what it's like to be a student in the program. Does it appear to be a student-oriented program?
3. **Information about students and graduates.** Where do graduates go? Do they find jobs in academia, practice, or the "real world"? Do students present at conferences or publish in journals?
4. **Course offerings.** Look over the program course book and requirements to get a feel for what courses you'll take and what you'll learn. This gives you a chance to see some of the program's inner workings, so that you're not surprised once you're admitted.

Program Quality   Program quality is difficult to assess because some factors are somewhat subjective. Here are some considerations in evaluating program quality.

1. **Attrition**. What is the attrition rate? Some programs select only a handful of the top students and lose a few of them; other programs take in more students than they can effectively manage and lose many of them. Some programs use comprehensive exams to weed out students.
2. **Time to completion.** What is the average time to completion of the degree? In psychology, five to seven years is a normal range. If a program's average time to completion is close to seven years or beyond, you should examine it more closely to determine why.
3. **Logistical resources.** Are there adequate computer facilities, library resources, money for travel to conferences, and other forms of support?
4. **Financial support.** Are research and teaching assistantships used to fund students? Does it appear to be a quality program? To help you evaluate the overall quality of the program, Checklist 10.1 presents some characteristics of quality PhD programs.

CHECKLIST 10.1
Characteristics of a Quality PhD Program

❏   Program faculty work closely with students
❏   Faculty regularly publish in their fields and make conferences at the regional, state, national, and international levels
❏   Faculty publish with students and graduates
❏   Program is accredited by APA (if clinical, counseling, or school)
❏   Program emphasizes research productivity
❏   Program faculty are tenured or tenure track
❏   Department is large enough to have faculty who represent the major areas in psychology
❏   Program is able to support or partially support students through assistantships and other means
❏   Program has adequate facilities for research and practica

Source: Buskist & Shurburne, 1996; Keith-Spiegel & Wiederman, 2000.

In addition to program quality, consider the prestige of the department. How much does prestige matter? That depends on what you hope to do with your degree. There generally is a correlation between departmental prestige and job quality (Peters, 1992). Doctoral recipients from prestigious departments are more likely to land prestigious jobs (e.g., at research institutions) than are those from less distinguished institutions. Advisors and mentors in prestigious graduate departments often have excellent reputations and important connections that can help you advance in your career. Powerful mentors can write persuasive letters of recommendation, lend authority to student papers, and pull strings because their old classmates, friends, and former students often hold prestigious positions. Though you should also note that powerful mentors often are very busy, so you may have little direct contact with them.

Accreditation   Many programs advertise that they are APA accredited. What does that mean? The American Psychological Association (APA) is a national association of psychologists. One of APA's many activities is to evaluate practice-oriented psychology programs to ensure that the educational criteria meet the public's needs. APA accredits doctoral programs in the practice areas of clinical, school, counseling, and combined professional-scientific psychology (for example, some programs in applied developmental psychology seek accreditation).

In order to be accredited, a program must meet the minimum standards for clinical training established by APA. The criteria include faculty credentials, specific course work, eligibility for state licensure, adequate research and clinical opportunities, and internships for clinical and counseling students. A site visit confirms that these requirements are met, and they must be maintained over time. If you are applying to clinical, counseling, or school programs, it is in your best interest to be sure that they are accredited because a degree from an APA-approved program carries more weight; students from accredited programs are more successful in competing for clinical internships and jobs. In fact, many states *require* doctoral degrees from APA programs for licensure. Note that programs in scientist-nonpractice areas, such as experimental and social psychology, are not part of the APA accreditation program. Research programs that do not prepare students to practice psychology are not accredited.

THE APPLICATION

Once you have narrowed your choice of programs, you're ready to begin the application. Apply to enough programs to have a reasonable chance of being accepted, given your credentials. There is a great deal of competition for entry into doctoral programs in psychology. Plan on applying to six to ten programs and possibly more if you're applying to particularly selective programs (especially in clinical psychology). This can quickly become expensive; application fees are over $50 for most programs. In addition to investing money, plan on investing a significant amount of time on each application. Table 10.2 provides a timeline for applying to graduate school. Now, let's examine the typical components of a graduate application.

TABLE
10.2

TIMELINE FOR APPLYING TO GRADUATE SCHOOL

Sophomore Year

❑ Take a least one more math and science course beyond the general requirements.

❑ Learn about the research interests of the faculty at your school, read their articles, and get to know those whose work interests you.

❑ Request to assist professors with their research.

❑ Seek research experiences in psychology.

❑ Make contact with graduate students in psychology who you may know. Ask them what graduate student life is like and what kind of study load you can expect in various specialties in psychology. Your professors may be able to help you locate graduate students, or you can check with the Career Services or the Alumni Offices.

❑ Find out about regional psychological meetings, such as the meetings of the Eastern Psychological Association or Midwestern Psychological Association, which are usually held in late March, April, or early May. Check the American Psychological Association Web site (http://www.apa.org/about/organizations/regionals.aspx) for links to each association.

Junior Year

❑ Take note of professors' research interests and talk with them about research opportunities.

❑ Participate in an independent research project with a faculty member. Talk with your professors about research opportunities.

❑ Get information about GREs; use study guides to prepare.

❑ Take the GRE in the spring.

❑ Some programs require the MAT—learn about the requirements of the programs to which you plan to apply.

❑ If you are interested in the clinical or counseling areas of psychology, get practical experience.

❑ Learn about graduate programs and begin considering programs to which to apply.

Summer Before Your Senior Year

❑ Examine graduate programs online. Request bulletins, brochures, financial aid forms, and departmental application forms from the schools to which you may eventually apply. Many schools place these materials online or have online request forms.

❑ Prepare and register for the GRE Psychology Test. Check the registration deadlines and be sure not to miss them.

❑ Begin drafting your resume.

Beginning of Your Senior Year

❑ Check with your advisor and the registrar to determine that you have fulfilled all graduation and departmental requirements.

❑ Ask professors for their opinions on what courses you should take beyond requirements to help you prepare for graduate school.

❑ Take a list of your graduate school choices to your professors, and ask them to recommend the schools they think would be most appropriate for you. Take copies of your resume and transcript with you, and ask them if they will write letters of recommendation for you when the time comes.

(Continued)

TABLE 10.2 TIMELINE FOR APPLYING TO GRADUATE SCHOOL (CONTINUED)

❑ If you haven't already taken the GRE General Test and GRE Psychology Test, do so.

❑ If you are applying for financial aid, pick up the necessary forms now. The same goes for fellowships and scholarships. The deadlines may be earlier than the actual applications for admission.

November of Your Senior Year

❑ Narrow down your list of graduate schools to which to apply (seek faculty assistance).

❑ List each school, noting the application deadline and what each school requires for a complete application.

❑ Ask your professors for letters of recommendation. Some prefer a deadline to work by, so be prepared to offer a firm date by which they should have the recommendation finished and sent. If they are writing directly to the school (that is, the letter is not returned in a sealed envelope to you in order for it to be placed with your application materials), be sure to offer to pay for the postage. Provide them with a copy of your resume, a list of activities, clubs, or organizations you've been involved with, and talk to them about your future goals. Give them a clear sense of where you are headed and what you intend to do in graduate school and after.

❑ Begin working on your personal statement. Always show it to at least one other person before you type it on the application and send it. Show it to someone who knows you and who is a good judge of writing skills. Be sure to write the statement carefully, answering the questions each graduate school wants you to comment on.

❑ Request that GRE and MAT scores be sent to all the schools to which you are applying.

December of Your Senior Year

❑ Finish application materials and mail them at least two weeks in advance of the deadline. Be sure to include letters of recommendation (if the school requests they be sent with your application) and the necessary application fees.

❑ If you are submitting the applications online, do so several days in advance. (Do not wait for the last minute as computer problems happen!)

❑ Keep photocopies of every application.

❑ Check back with the professors who are sending in your letters of recommendation themselves to make sure they have finished them and have sent them.

❑ Request that the Registrar's office and the financial aid office send out official transcripts to all the schools to which you are applying. Do this early as it often requires ten working days to send a transcript request.

❑ Be sure that GRE and MAT scores were sent to all schools to which you are applying.

Late January–April

❑ Follow up to confirm that your completed applications and all letters of recommendation were received.

❑ Most schools send a postcard upon receipt of each application. Keep track of these. If you don't receive a postcard or letter, contact the admissions office by e-mail or phone to ensure that your application has been received before the deadline.

❑ Thank those who wrote letters of recommendation.

❑ Attend any interviews to which you are invited.

(Continued)

TABLE 10.2	TIMELINE FOR APPLYING TO GRADUATE SCHOOL (CONTINUED)

March–April

❑ Accept and decline offers.

❑ When declining an offer, be sure to telephone the schools whose offers you are declining to let them know that you appreciate the offer but have decided not to accept it. Schools wait for your decision in order to accept alternates.

❑ If you accept an offer, you have until April 15th to change your mind—after that, any reason besides illness, change of career plans, or dire circumstances will not impress the graduate school whose offer you accepted. You should not accept any other offer until you have officially separated from your first acceptance.

❑ Call or write people who wrote you letters of recommendation and inform them of the outcome, thanking them for their help.

EXERCISE 10.1

Your Personal Timeline for Applying to Graduate School

Construct your personal timeline for applying to graduate school. Table 10.2 provides a generalized timeline. Consider your own situation.

1. How much time do you have? Are you a sophomore, junior, or senior?
2. What coursework do you need to become competitive?
3. What out-of-class experiences do you need?
4. What is your timeframe for obtaining these experiences?
5. When will you apply to graduate school? Identify the steps that you will take in applying and your timeline.

Graduate Record Exam: General Test

The Graduate Record Exam (GRE) is a standardized test that all applicants to graduate programs must complete. The GRE General Test is an aptitude test that measures a variety of skills, acquired over the high school and college years, that are thought to predict success in graduate school. The GRE is only one of several criteria that graduate schools use to evaluate your application, but it is one of the most important. This is particularly true if your college GPA is not as high as you'd like. Exceptional GRE scores can open up new opportunities for grad school. Similarly, low GRE scores can cast doubt on a very good GPA.

The GRE General Test yields three scores: verbal ability, quantitative ability, and analytical ability. As shown in Table 10.3, the verbal section

TABLE
10.3   **OVERVIEW OF THE GRADUATE RECORD EXAM (GRE)**

GRE Verbal Section

Overview

You will be asked to read passages and analyze information obtained from your reading, analyze sentences and the relationships among component parts of sentences, as well as recognize relationships between words and concepts within written material. The topics that comprise the reading comprehension sections are meant to be answered without any particular knowledge or expertise other than the general knowledge and skills that an average graduate is presumed to have. Excelling on the verbal section of the GRE requires an advanced vocabulary.

Types of Questions

1. **Analogies** examine your ability to understand the relationship that exists between the words in a word pair and recognize a parallel relationship among other word pairs. This requires determining how two words are related and then determining what word pair provided displays a similar relationship.
2. **Antonyms** test Antonyms test your knowledge of vocabulary and your ability to identify the opposite of a given concept.
3. **Reading comprehension** measures your ability to read analytically. You're asked to explore a written passage from several perspectives, recognize elements that are explicitly stated and inferred, and understand the assumptions underlying the passage as well as the implications of those assumptions. Reading comprehension questions assess six types of information: identify the main idea, identify explicitly stated information, identify implied ideas, apply the author's ideas to other situations, identify the author's logic or persuasive techniques, and identify the attitudinal tone of the passage.
4. **Sentence completion** questions measure your ability to use syntax and grammar cues to understand the meaning of a sentence. This task requires that you analyze the parts of the incomplete sentence and determine which word or set of words can be substituted for the blank space in the sentence.

GRE Quantitative Section

Overview

The quantitative section measures basic mathematical skills, understanding of mathematical concepts, and quantitative reasning. The quantitative section does not require mathematic skills beyond the high school level (e.g., arithmetic, algebra, geometry, and data analysis); but calculators are not permitted, so you must be prepared to complete problems only with the help of a pencil and scratch paper.

Types of Questions

1. **Problem solving** questions are word problems that assess your understanding of, and ability to apply, arithmetic, algebra, and geometry.
2. **Quantitative comparison** questions ask you to compare two quantities, one in column a and one in column b. Your task is to determine if they are equal, if one is larger than the other, or if not enough information is presented to make the determination.
3. **Data analysis** questions require use of basic descriptive statistics, the ability to interpret data in graphs and tables, and elementary probability. Questions emphasize the "ability to synthesize information, select appropriate data for answering a question, and to determine whether or not the data provided are sufficient to answer a given question" (GRE Bulletin, p. 8).

(Continued)

TABLE 10.3	OVERVIEW OF THE GRADUATE RECORD EXAM (GRE) (CONTINUED)

GRE Analytical Writing Section

Overview	The analytical writing section examines your ability to communicate complex ideas clearly and effectively, support your ideas, examine claims and supporting evidence, sustain a focused and coherent discussion, and effectively use the elements of standard written English.
Subsections	1. **Present Your Perspective on an Issue:** In this 45-minute task, you are presented with an issue of general interest and asked to address it from any perspective, providing reasons and examples to support your views. Your job is to construct an argument and support it with reasons and examples.
	2. **Analyze an Argument:** This 30-minute task presents you with an argument. Your task is to critique the argument, assess its claims, and conclude whether it is reasoned.

assesses your ability to understand and analyze written material. The quantitative section tests basic math skills and your ability to understand and apply quantitative skills to solve problems. The analytical writing section examines critical thinking and analytical writing skills. No specific content knowledge is assessed. It examines your ability to explain and support complex ideas, and engage in focused and coherent discussion and analysis of arguments. The verbal and quantitative subtests yield scores ranging from 200 to 800. Graduate schools consider the verbal and quantitative sections to be particularly important in making decisions about applicants. Therefore, the total GRE score usually refers to the quantitative and verbal scores summed to a total of 1,600 possible points. The analytical writing section is the most recent addition to the GRE and is scored on a 0–6 point scale (in half point increments).

The GRE General Test is administered by computer year-round. Plan to take the GRE well in advance of application due dates. Generally you should take it in the spring or summer before you apply to grad school. Remember that it takes several weeks for scores to be reported to schools—if you take the GRE too late in the fall, the scores may not arrive in time for your application to be considered. Also, you will want to have enough time to retake it if necessary. You can always retake the GRE, but remember that you're allowed to take it only once per calendar month. Because all prior scores are sent to the institutions that you're applying to, never take the GRE as practice.

The GRE General Test will take two and one-quarter hours to complete, but allow an extra hour and one-half for reading instructions and taking tutorials. The verbal section consists of thirty multiple choice questions that are answered within thirty minutes. That's not a lot of time, so it's important to be familiar with the test so that you can work quickly and efficiently. In other words, practice beforehand using the *Powerprep* software provided by the Educational Testing Service, maker of the GRE Test (http://www.ets.org/gre/general/prepare). Also examine the books and Web sites recommended at the end of this chapter.

Like the other sections of the GRE General, the essay tasks are delivered on the computer. The GRE software contains a simple word processor that includes basic functions like cut and paste, insert text, delete, and undo, but does not include spelling or grammar checkers. Practice using the word processor on *Powerprep*, the practice software sent to you when you register for the GRE (and downloadable from the GRE Web site at http://www.ets.org/gre/general/prepare).

What score should you aim for? There is tremendous variation among programs, but most PsyD programs require a minimum score of 540 on each subtest; most scientist-practitioner programs require 580; and most research programs require 600 (Mayne et al., 1994). Norcross (1997) reports a mean total for GRE scores of incoming graduate students of 1,206 for doctoral programs and 1,033 for master's programs. Generally, more competitive programs require higher minimum GRE scores. The average GRE scores for incoming students are listed in the program materials, in APA's *Guide to Graduate Study in Psychology*, and in the annual program rankings provided by *US News and World Report*. Review Table 10.4 for additional tips for preparing for and taking the GRE.

GRE Psychology Test

Many, but not all doctoral programs require that applicants take the Psychology Test. The GRE Psychology Test consists of about 215 multiple choice questions that tap information from the core psychology courses required in most undergraduate programs. The questions are drawn from commonly offered courses at the undergraduate level and are designed to measure what an undergraduate Psychology major who plans to attend graduate school should know about the field of Psychology. Questions cover the following categories of content:

- Experimental psychology topics (about 40 percent of the test), including learning, language, memory, thinking, sensation and perception, physiological psychology, ethology, and comparative psychology.
- Clinical and social topics (about 43 percent of the test), including clinical and abnormal, developmental, personality, and social psychology.
- General psychology topics (about 17 percent of the test), such as the history of psychology, measurement, research designs, and statistics (Matlin & Kalat, 2001).

TABLE

10.4 **GRE TIPS**

Preparation: Well Before Test Day

❑ Know the test. Your GRE preparation should emphasize getting to know the test and the types of questions that will appear. Be familiar with the time limit for each section and how many questions each section includes.

❑ Know the directions for each question beforehand to save time, but remember that the directions for the GRE Test might be slightly different from the ones in your study material. Be sure to always read the instructions—quickly.

❑ Download *GRE Powerprep Software — Test Preparation for the GRE General Test,* free software provided by the makers of the GRE. According to the online description, *Powerprep* "includes test tutorials, practice questions with explanations, and two actual computer-adaptive tests for the verbal and quantitative sections. The software also includes sample topics and essays for the analytical writing section, and advice on how to write effective essays for the Issue and Argument tasks. *Powerprep* lets you practice writing essays under simulated GRE testing conditions with the same GRE word processing and testing tools that appear on the test" (at http://www.gre.org/faqnew.html).

❑ Try a practice test under conditions similar to the actual GRE. Based on your practice score, devise a study plan to help you brush up on vocabulary, reading comprehension, analogies, algebra, and geometry.

❑ Download sample GRE tests.

❑ Buy a GRE review book—and use it.

Test Day: Logistics

❑ Get enough sleep the night before. Don't study the night before. Instead, have a quiet night at home and do something that you find relaxing and enjoyable.

❑ Eat breakfast. Make sure that you're not hungry during the test, which can affect your performance.

❑ Wear comfortable clothes and bring a sweater in case the test center is cold.

❑ Arrive at the test center at least thirty minutes early to complete any paperwork. If you arrive late, you may not be admitted and will not be refunded. Remember to bring at least two forms of identification (with at least one containing a photo and signature). For more information about identification requirements and policies, consult the GRE Bulletin.

❑ If you're taking the GRE at a test center other than at your college or university, do a test drive the week before to learn where the center is and how long it takes to get there because it's important that you arrive at the test center thirty minutes beforehand.

Test Day: During the Exam

❑ Your practice should make you familiar with the test and the amount of time you need to tackle each type of question. Don't get stuck on one particular question for too long because you'll lose time and may miss easier questions later on.

❑ Don't rush. The GRE isn't a race, so use your time judiciously, devoting just enough time to each question to get it done and maximize your score in the limited time allotted.

❑ The questions at the beginning of the exam are more important than those toward the end. Because the GRE is computer adaptive, the difficulty level of the questions you receive later are determined by those you've correctly answered before.

❑ If you don't know the answer to a question, eliminate alternatives that cannot be the answer to narrow down your guesses to two or three alternatives and improve the odds of choosing correctly.

❑ Don't leave questions unanswered because there is no penalty for wrong answers.

❑ Be very sure of your answer before proceeding because the Computer-Adaptive Test (CAT) for GRE does not permit you to return to a question once you have attempted it. You cannot leave the difficult questions for later nor can you check your answers towards the end even if you have extra time. So pace yourself properly and be very certain of your answers.

Since the GRE Psychology Test is designed to sample a broad range of topics in psychology, the best way to prepare is by studying an upper-level introductory psychology textbook. Ask a faculty member for guidance in selecting an appropriate textbook to use.

Unlike the General Test, the GRE Psychology Test is administered only by pencil and paper three times a year: in April, November, and December. Ideally, you should take the GRE Psychology Test in April so that you have time to retake it, if needed. If you are taking it as a senior, take it in November, not December, to allow enough time for scores to be reported. Register for the GRE Psychology Test online or by mail using the address and registration form found in the GRE Bulletin (both at http://www.ets.org/gre). Remember that seats are assigned on a first-come first-served basis, so register early.

When you register for the GRE, you'll select among several test administration centers at colleges, universities, and testing centers. For a complete list of testing centers, consult the GRE Web site. The instructions regarding arriving early and bringing proper identification provided earlier for the GRE General Test also apply to the GRE Psychology Test. The test takes up to three and one-half hours to complete.

Although the GRE scores are an important part of your application, remember that graduate admissions committees consider many other factors. Many programs will accept students with lower GRE scores if they have strengths in other areas, such as research. How do you communicate your strengths to graduate admissions committees? Admissions essays and personal statements offer you an opportunity to speak directly to the committee.

Admissions Essays and Personal Statements

The admissions essay or personal statement often is the most difficult part of the application; this is because the task is somewhat ambiguous, yet very important. It's your chance to present yourself as an individual, a person behind the GPA and GRE scores. Because most of the other applicants have similar academic credentials, admissions committees need the additional information contained in admissions essays to narrow the pool of applicants. Your essays will provide information about your ability to write, to stick to the task at hand, and to persuade readers. Your essay will also inform the admissions committee about your interests, career aspirations, and values. This is the place where you can stand out.

As you consider your essay, consider the other side of the admissions equation: What do graduate programs look for in applicants? Consider the factors in Table 10.5. It appears that graduate programs want applicants who are

TABLE 10.5	IMPORTANT CRITERIA FOR EVALUATING APPLICANTS (AS RATED BY FACULTY MEMBERS)

1 The fit or match between the applicant's interests and skills and the program's goals

2 Research experience (especially research resulting in the publication in a scholarly journal of a paper presented at a professional conference)

3 Interest expressed by one or more members of the selection committee in working with a particular applicant

4 The clarity, focus, and content of the applicant's admission essays

5 Experience as a research assistant

6 Writing skills

7 Knowledge about, and interest in, the program

8 Number of statistics, research methodology, and hard science courses taken

9 Prestige and status of faculty in undergraduate department, especially of those who are writing letters of recommendation

10 Potential for success as judged by interview

11 Honors and merit scholarships

Adapted from Bonifazi, Crespi, & Rieker, 1997; Keith-Spiegel, Tabachnick, & Spiegel, 1994.

interested in the program, have research experience, and have a background in statistics, methodology, and science.

A large part of acceptance is whether you appear to be capable of fulfilling the needs of others; "Because graduate faculties must be diverse enough to represent the breadth of the discipline within the department, any given faculty member may not have a single colleague in his or her area of expertise. The remedy for such isolation and frustration is, of course, to attract students who will share an appetite for the professor's area" (Keith-Spiegel & Wiederman, 2000, p. 39). Faculty look for applicants who share their interests and are prepared to engage in collaborative research or scholarship. In addition, scholarly productivity in the form of publications in scholarly journals is the primary criterion by which faculty are evaluated and rewarded. Therefore, it's important for faculty to find students who fit their needs, who can work with them, and who enhance their productivity and reputation. Faculty want students who will thrive and bring respect to their program long after graduation. That's why it is important for you to know as much as possible about the program and faculty, so that you can present yourself effectively.

Essay Topics   So what exactly do you write about? Usually programs give applicants a question or two to answer, or a specific topic on which to write. Keith-Spiegel and Wiederman (2000) have noted that there is a remarkable similarity among essay topics requested by graduate programs. Most questions posed by graduate programs fall into one of several categories (Keith-Spiegel & Widerman, 2000):

- Career plans. What are your long-term career goals? Where do you see yourself ten years from now?
- General interest areas. What academic or professional areas interest you?
- Research experiences. Discuss areas in which you might like to do research, research experiences you have had, or both. Describe your research interests.
- Academic objectives. Why are you undertaking graduate study? Describe how graduate training is necessary for your goals.
- Clinical or other field experience. Describe your clinical experience. How have your field experiences shaped your career goals?
- Academic background and achievements. Discuss your academic background.
- Personal. Is there anything in your background that you think would be relevant in our evaluation of applicants? Describe your life up to now: family, friends, home, school, work, and particularly those experiences most relevant to your interests in psychology Use this information to write an autobiographical sketch that portrays your fit with your chosen career and graduate program.
- Personal and professional development. Describe your values and your approach to life

Although there are many similarities among essay topics, you should not write a generic essay. Tailor your essay to the specific question and the program. The "old days" of writing a statement on a typewriter and then photocopying it are long gone. Saving your essay on a computer permits you to revise it and tailor it to each program. Be sure to save each version of your essay. Many essays ask the applicant to discuss how the program or faculty match his or her individual needs. This means that you must demonstrate that you have researched the program and are familiar with its faculty and curriculum. Explain how the program will prepare you for the career you desire, offering specific examples. While writing your essay, remember that your goal is to come across as someone with the potential to succeed in graduate school.

Length and Content   Your essay should be about one and one-half to two single-spaced pages long. Shorter statements provide too little information and longer ones tend to become wordy. Readers will assess the content of your essay and your ability to express yourself effectively and succinctly. Be extra careful to not include spelling or grammatical errors. Attention to detail is critical.

Be careful about the content of your essay. As Bottoms and Nysse (1999) advise, "Do not misinterpret the meaning of *personal* in the phrase *personal statement!*" The essay is a professional essay, not a place to discuss your own mental health, experiences with therapy, or heartaches. Instead explain the experiences that have prepared you for graduate school and have led to your decision to apply to graduate school. Use concrete examples whenever possible. Your essay should include at least these four components: your previous research experience, research interests, relevant experience, and career goals (Bottoms & Nysse, 1999).

Discuss the details of your involvement with previous research. Who supervised the work? Was the research completed as part of a course requirement, for class credit, or as an independent study? Discuss the purpose of the research, including the theory, method, and results. Explain your role. Rather than merely explaining that you entered data for Dr. Smith's research study, for example, show that you have worked to understand the purpose of the research. If the research resulted in class papers, conference presentations, or publications, mention that. If you were an author on a conference presentation or publication, include a copy in your application packet. Discuss how your attitude about research has changed as a result of the experience.

Discuss the areas of psychology that most interest you now. You've already chosen graduate programs to which you'll apply based on the fit between your and the faculty's research interests. For each program, identify faculty whose research interests you and tailor your personal statement so that it will entice faculty with whom you'd like to work. This entails doing your homework first. Read the faculty members' Web pages and locate articles they have published. Explain what interests you about the professor's work. State your preferred research interests but also that you are open to studying related areas (if that is true). You are more likely to be accepted at a particular program if you discuss the research interests of several faculty (because not all professors look for new students each year).

Your statement should also include other relevant experience that pertains to your decision to go to graduate school or makes you qualified for graduate school. Internship experiences and volunteer experiences are included here. Avoid personal, emotional self disclosures. Explain what you would like to do after graduation. What kind of career do you envision after receiving your degree? Illustrate how the specific program will prepare you for the career that you desire. Personal details that you include about yourself should be relevant to your ability to be a successful graduate student and reflect maturity, adaptability, and motivation.

Writing as Process   Writing your admissions essay is a process, not a discrete event. The first step involves preparation—gathering the information needed to compose the essay that sets you apart from the rest. Conduct a thorough self-assessment. Leave yourself plenty of time; you don't want to rush this process of self-exploration. Look back over your journal entries, especially your responses to the exercises in Chapter 2. Then sit down with a pad, or at the keyboard, and begin writing. Don't censor yourself in any way. Just write what feels natural. Begin taking notes on what drives you. Describe your hopes, dreams, and aspirations. What do you hope to gain from graduate study? Granted, not all of this information will make it into the essay, but your goal at this point is to brainstorm.

EXERCISE 10.2

Admissions Essay Prep

Prepare to write your admissions essay by examining your personal history. Identify as much of your personal history as possible so that you can carefully sift through and sort out events and personal items that will strengthen your essay. List and explain:

- Hobbies
- Projects you've completed
- Jobs you've held
- Responsibilities
- Personal and academic accomplishments
- Challenges and hurdles that you've overcome
- Life events that motivate your education
- People who have influenced you or motivated you
- Traits, work habits, and attitudes that will insure your success

Carefully consider your academic record and personal accomplishments. How do the attitudes, values, and personal qualities that you've listed correspond to these experiences? Try to pair them up. For example, your curiosity and thirst for knowledge may have led you to conduct independent research with a professor. Consider how each pair of attitudes, personal qualities, and experiences show that you're prepared to excel in graduate school.

Once you have a master list, carefully examine the information. Remember that the information you choose to present can portray you as a positive and upbeat person or as a tired and discouraged student. Think about the image you want to portray, and revise your master list accordingly. Use the revised list as a basis for all of your admissions essays. Remember to be forthcoming about your weaknesses. If your early academic record is weak, explain why. Bright people will be evaluating your application, and they'll spot weaknesses. Don't force them to make assumptions about you. Instead, discuss your weaknesses and explain how you've overcome them.

There's still more information to consider for your admissions essays. Tailor your essay to each program. Show that you're interested and that you've taken the time to learn about each program. Put all of that research you've done on programs to good use. Reread the program brochure; check the Web site; gather all information possible to help you determine what the admissions committee is looking for from potential students. Take careful notes on each program, observing where your personal interests, qualities, and accomplishments coincide. If you're truly interested in the graduate programs to which you're applying (and with a $50 application fee for most schools, you should be interested), take the time to tailor your essay to each program. One size clearly does not fit all.

As you write your essay, occasionally stop to make sure that you're answering the question posed by the admissions committee. Think about the question, the central theme asked, and how it corresponds to your master list of experiences and personal qualities. Some applications offer a string of questions. Pay attention to your responses, and try to avoid being redundant. Remember that this is your chance to present your strengths and really shine. Take advantage of it. Discuss your accomplishments, describe valuable experiences, and emphasize the positive. Show that you're motivated. The committee is composed of professionals who have read hundreds, even thousands of such statements over the years. Make yours stand out.

Letters of Recommendation

Every graduate program requires applicants to submit letters of recommendation. Don't underestimate the importance of these letters. While your transcript, standardized test scores, and admissions essay are vital components of your application, an excellent letter of recommendation can make up for weaknesses in any of these areas. The letters of recommendation give admissions committees information that isn't found elsewhere in the application. What is a letter of recommendation? It's a letter, written by a faculty member, that discusses the personal qualities, accomplishments, and experiences that make you unique and perfect for the programs to which you've applied.

Who Should You Ask? Most graduate programs require two or more letters of recommendation. Deciding who will write your recommendation letters often is difficult. Consider faculty members, administrators, internship or co-operative education supervisors, and employers. But remember that it's faculty who will be reading the recommendation letters (and they've been through graduate school), so faculty tend to write the most credible recommendation letters.

Appleby, Keenan, and Mauer (1999) examined recommendation forms from the application packages of 143 graduate programs in clinical,

TABLE 10.6	TOP CHARACTERISTICS ASSESSED BY RECOMMENDATION FORMS (APPLEBY, KEENAN, & MAUER, 1999)

Motivation

Intellectual/scholarly ability

Research skills

Emotional stability and maturity

Writing skills

Speaking skills

Teaching skills or potential

Ability to work with others

Creativity

Knowledge of area of study

experimental, and industrial-organizational psychology. The applicant characteristics that recommenders were requested to discuss and rank were identified and categorized. About 40 percent of the 802 characteristics referred to personal characteristics, about one third referred to acquired skills, and about one quarter referred to intellectual abilities or knowledge. The top characteristics that recommendation forms asked faculty to discuss are listed in Table 10.6. As you can see, grad programs are interested in more than your academic abilities.

The persons you ask to write your letters should:

- Know you well
- Have known you long enough to write with authority
- Know your work
- Describe your work positively
- Have a high opinion of you
- Know where you are applying
- Know your educational and career goals
- Be able to favorably compare you with your peers
- Be well known
- Be able to write a good letter

Keep in mind that no one person will satisfy all of these criteria. Aim for a set of letters covering the range of your skills. Letters should include your academic and scholastic skills, research abilities and experiences, and applied experiences (e.g., co-operative education, internships, related work experience). When you approach potential recommenders, ask if they know you well enough to write a meaningful letter. Pay attention to their demeanor. If you sense reluctance, thank them and ask someone else. Remember that it is best to ask early in the semester. As the end of the semester approaches, faculty may hesitate because of time constraints.

Help Your Referees   The best thing you can do to ensure that your letters cover all the bases is to provide your referees (those who will write your letters of recommendation) with all the necessary information. Don't assume that they will remember anything about you. I know, you're quite memorable, but think about what it must be like to have 150 or more students each semester. Give them the information you'd like included. Make an appointment to speak with each of your referees. Give them plenty of time (three to four weeks at minimum). Provide a file with all of your background information:

- Transcript
- Resume or vita
- GRE scores
- Courses you've taken with them and grades that you've earned
- Research experiences
- Internship and other applied experiences
- Honor societies to which you belong
- Awards you've won
- Work experience
- Professional goals
- Due date for the application
- Copy of the application recommendation forms

Confidentiality   The recommendation forms supplied by graduate programs require you to decide whether to waive or retain your rights to see the recommendations. As you decide whether to retain your rights, remember that confidential letters tend to carry more weight with admissions committees. In addition, many faculty members will not write a recommendation letter unless it is confidential. Other faculty may provide you with a copy of the letter, even if it is confidential. If you are unsure of your decision, discuss it with your referees. As the application deadline approaches, check back with your recommenders to ensure that the letters were sent on time (but don't nag). Contacting the graduate programs to inquire whether your materials were received is also appropriate.

Now What?

Now that you've submitted your applications, patience is essential. It is easy to start ruminating over the status of your application and wonder, "Do they like me? Am I good enough? Will I get in? Why haven't I heard anything?" Don't let these destructive thoughts overwhelm you. Instead, focus on what you can control—your schoolwork. Remember school? You've still got to graduate, and you don't want to let your grades slip now.

Should you ever make contact with graduate programs? If you have not been notified that your application file is complete, a call or e-mail to the admissions office is appropriate to determine that your application is complete. Incomplete files are not considered for admission, and not all programs notify applicants of incomplete files.

When can you expect to hear from programs? Every program has a different method and style of handling admissions. Some programs review applications and make decisions early, and others wait. How quickly applications are reviewed depends on a variety of factors including the number of applications received, how many people are on the committee, academic demands, conferences, holidays, how well the members of the committee work together, and so on. Most programs inform applicants of their status by mid-April, but you might hear from programs earlier or later.

THE INTERVIEW

Some programs conduct phone interviews, some conduct on-site interviews, and some don't interview at all. What happens if you're invited to interview? How do you prepare? What are admission committees looking for? The interview gives admission committees an opportunity to meet candidates and see the people behind the GPAs and GRE scores. It's a chance for them to meet you, to see how you react under pressure, and to assess your verbal and non-verbal communication skills. The interview might range from half an hour with one or two faculty to a full day or more filled with meetings with students and faculty. Activities might range from small group discussions to larger group interviews and even social hours or parties.

How do you prepare for the interview? Learn as much about the program as possible. Review the program description, department Web site, and faculty Web sites. Understand the program's emphasis, and be aware of the faculty's research interests. Consider how you will answer common interview questions, such as the following:

- Why are you interested in our program?
- What do you know about our program?
- What are your career goals?
- Why did you choose a career in psychology?
- What are your research interests? Describe your research experience. Regarding research, what are your strengths and weaknesses?
- What are your academic strengths? What was your favorite course, and why?

- What do you like best about yourself?
- Whom would you like to work with? Why?
- Describe the accomplishment you're most proud of.
- If you were to begin a research project now, what would be the topic?
- Describe your theoretical orientation.
- Discuss your experiences in clinical settings. Evaluate your clinical abilities.
- What are your strengths and weaknesses?
- Tell us about yourself.

Consider how you might answer each of these questions, but don't memorize answers. Instead, be prepared to speak extemporaneously so that you're ready for interview curveballs. To gain confidence, practice with family or friends, or in front of the mirror.

Don't forget that this is your opportunity to ask questions too. In fact, admissions committees expect you to ask questions, so prepare some thoughtful questions about the program, faculty, and students. Use this opportunity to learn about the program and whether it meets your needs. During your visit, try to get a sense of the department's emotional climate. What do graduate students call professors? Doctor? Or do they use first names? Are students competitive with one another? Try to get a sense of whether the atmosphere matches your personality. Is it excessively formal? Would you be happy there?

BEING ACCEPTED

You've received good news. Congratulations! Most programs inform applicants of their acceptance from March through early April. In most cases, your decision on whether to accept an offer is due by April 15. Once you decline an offer, it can be passed along to someone else who is waiting, so do not hold onto offers that you don't plan on accepting. As soon as you have two offers, decide which to decline. Each time you receive a new offer, decline your least preferred offer so that you're not holding onto offers that you don't intend to accept. How do you decide which to decline? Consider your priorities. Know what you are accepting (and declining). Don't be surprised because you made assumptions about financial support, housing, or assistantships. Instead, ask questions and confirm your understanding. Compare acceptance packages to decide among programs. Don't be afraid to do some negotiating, because they've decided that they want you. Help them make it possible for you to accept by explaining any financial limitations that might impede accepting their offer. How do you decline a graduate program? E-mail or fax a letter explaining that you appreciate their interest but will not be accepting their offer. Mail a hard copy of the letter as well.

DEALING WITH REJECTION

What if you're rejected? It is difficult to be told that you are not among a program's top choices. From a statistical standpoint, you have lots of company; most competitive doctoral programs receive ten to fifty times as many applicants as they can take. You may find it particularly difficult if you were invited for an interview. As many as 75 percent of applicants invited for interviews are not accepted.

Why are students rejected? Most simply, because there aren't enough slots; graduate programs in psychology receive far more applications from qualified candidates than they can accept. Why were you eliminated by a particular program? There is no way to tell, but in many cases applicants are rejected because they didn't fit the program. For example, an applicant to a research-scientist program who didn't read the program materials carefully might be rejected for indicating an interest in practicing therapy.

You might find it difficult to inform family, friends, and professors of the bad news, but it is essential that you seek social support. Allow yourself to feel upset and acknowledge your feelings, and then move forward. If you are rejected by every program you've applied to, reassess your goals, but don't necessarily give up.

- Did you select schools carefully, paying attention to fit?
- Did you apply to enough programs?
- Did you complete all parts of each application?
- Did you spend enough time on your essays?
- Did you have research experience?
- Did you have field experience?
- Did you know your referees well, and did they have something to write about?
- Were most of your applications to highly competitive programs?

Your answers to these questions may help you determine whether to reapply to a greater range of programs next year, or to apply to a master's program instead, as either a first step towards the doctoral degree or as an ends in itself. Or you may want to choose another career path. If you are firmly committed to attending graduate school in psychology, consider reapplying next year; but don't send out the same application. Use the next few months to improve your academic record, seek research experience, and get to know professors. Apply to a wider range of schools (including "safety" schools), select programs more carefully, and thoroughly research each program.

Suggested Readings

American Psychological Association (2007). *Getting in: A step-by-step plan for gaining admission to graduate school in psychology.* Washington, DC: Author.

American Psychological Association (2008). *Graduate study in psychology: 2009 Edition.* Washington, DC: Author.

Keith-Spiegel, P., & Weiderman, M. W. (2000). *Complete guide to graduate school admission: Psychology, counseling, and related professions.* Mahwah, NJ: Erlbaum.

Kracen, A. C. (2008). *Applying to graduate school in psychology.* Washington, DC: APA.

Kuther, T. L. (2004). *Getting into graduate school in psychology and related fields: Your guide to success.* Springfield, IN: C. Charles Thomas.

Norcross, J. G., Sayette, M. A., & Mayne, T. J., (2008). *Insider's guide to graduate programs in clinical and counseling psychology.* New York: Guilford.

Princeton Review (2009). *Cracking the GRE 2010.* New York: Random House.

Internet Resources

Applying to Graduate School

http://www.psichi.org/pubs/search.aspx?category1=7

At this site, you'll find articles about all aspects of the graduate admissions process; from Psi Chi, the International Honor Society in Psychology.

GRE Homepage

http://www.ets.org/gre

Get information about the GRE from the source.

Psychology Graduate Applicant's Portal

http://www.psychgrad.org/

This site provides extensive coverage of all aspects of graduate admissions.

About Graduate School

http://gradschool.about.com

I maintain this site, which is part of the About.com network. Here, you'll find information for graduate school applicants, current students, postdoctoral fellows, and faculty in all disciplines, including psychology.

JOURNAL EXERCISES

Why Graduate School?

Where does graduate education fit into your life? What goals will it help to accomplish? What are the costs of graduate school? It is sometimes said that as one door of opportunity opens, another closes. What door will close when you enter graduate school? What will you miss out on in your years of graduate study?

Comparing Jobs Across Degrees

Choose an area of psychology that interests you and brainstorm two to three jobs that fall within that content area. Identify jobs for bachelor's, master's, and doctoral degree recipients. How do the jobs and types of tasks change with the level of education? What do you think about each of these options?

Where Do I Stand and What Must I Do?

Imagine that you are to apply to graduate school. What steps are entailed? What preparation is needed? Do you have the necessary academic, research, and/or applied experiences? What are your strengths as an applicant? Weaknesses? Everyone can improve in some area. Consider ways of addressing the weaknesses in your application.

References

Actkinson, T. R. (2000). Master's and myth: Little-known information about a popular degree. *Eye on Psi Chi, 4*(2), 19–21, 23, 25.

American Psychological Association. (2002). *Ethical standards of psychologists and code of conduct*. Washington, DC: Author.

American Psychological Association. (2007). *Getting in: A step-by-step plan for gaining admission to graduate school in psychology*. Washington, DC: Author.

American Psychological Association. (2010). *Publication manual of the American Psychological Association*. Washington, DC: Author.

Amsel, J. (1997). *An interesting career in psychology: Acquisitions editor*. Retrieved February 1, 2001, from http://www.apa.org/science/ic-amsel.html

Anderson, E. R. (2006). *How to choose a major and career*. Capital University. Retrieved November 9, 2009, from http://www.capital.edu/Resources/Files/career-planning/MajorCareerBooklet2005.pdf

Appleby, D. (1997). *The handbook of psychology*. New York: Longman.

Appleby, D. (1999). Choosing a mentor. *Eye on Psi Chi, 3*(3), 38–39.

Appleby, D. (2000). Job skills valued by employers who interview psychology majors. *Eye on Psi Chi, 4*(3), 17.

Appleby, D. (2001). The covert curriculum: The lifelong learning skills you can learn in college. *Eye on Psi Chi, 5*(3), 28.

Appleby, D., Keenan, J., & Mauer, B. (1999). Applicant characteristics valued by graduate programs in psychology. *Eye on Psi Chi, 3*(3), 39.

Austin, J. T., & Calderon, R. F. (1996). Writing in APA style: Why and how. In F. Leong & J. Austin (Eds.), *The psychology research handbook: A guide for graduate students and research assistants* (pp. 265–281). Thousand Oaks, CA: Sage.

Balster, R. L. (1995). An interesting career in psychology: A research psychologist in a medical school. *Psychological Science Agenda*. Retrieved April 12, 2002, from http://www.apa.org/science/ic-balster.html

Bare, J. K. (1988). A liberal education. In P. J. Woods (Ed.), *Is psychology for them? A guide to undergraduate advising* (pp. 39–41). Washington, DC: American Psychological Association.

Bat-Chava, Y. (2000). *An interesting career in psychology: Research director for a non-profit organization.* Retrieved February 1, 2001, from http://www.apa.org/science/ic-bat-chava.html

Bonifazi, D. Z., Crespi, S. D., & Rieker, P. (1997). Value of a master's degree for gaining admission to doctoral programs in psychology. *Teaching of Psychology, 24,* 176–182.

Borden, V. M. H., & Rajecki, D. W. (2000). First-year employment outcomes of psychology baccalaureates: Relatedness, preparedness, and prospects. *Teaching of Psychology, 27,* 164–168.

Bornstein, M. H., & Arterberry, M. E. (1999). Perceptual development. In M. H. Bornstein & M. E. Lamb (Eds.), *Developmental psychology: An advanced textbook* (pp. 231–274). Mahwah, NJ: Erlbaum.

Bottoms, B. L., & Nysse, K. L. (1999). Applying to graduate school: Writing a compelling personal statement. *Eye on Psi Chi, 4*(1), 20–22.

Bureau of Labor Statistics. (2004). *Wholesale and retail trade. Industry at a glance.* Retrieved January1, 2005, from http://www.bls.gov/iag/wholeretailtrade.htm

Bureau of Labor Statistics. (2009). *Occupational outlook handbook.* Washington, DC: Author.

Buskist, W., & Shurburne, T. R. (1996). *Preparing for graduate study in psychology: 101 questions and answers.* Needham Heights, MA: Allyn & Bacon.

Christensen, A., & Jacobson, N. S. (1994). Who (or what) can do psychotherapy: The status and challenge of nonprofessional therapies. *Psychological Science, 5,* 8–12.

Cummings, N. A. (1995). Impact of managed care on employment and training: A primer for survival. *Professional Psychology: Research and Practice, 26,* 10–15.

Davis, S. F. (1995). The value of collaborative scholarship with undergraduates. *Psi Chi Newsletter, 21*(1), 12–13.

DeGalan, J., & Lambert, S. (1995). *Great jobs for psychology majors.* Chicago: VGM Career Horizons.

Descutner, C. J., & Thelen, M. H. (1989). Graduate student and faculty perspectives about graduate school. *Teaching of Psychology, 16,* 58–60.

Dunn, D. S., McCarthy, M. A., Baker, S., Halonen, J. S., & Hill, G. W. (2007). Quality benchmarks in undergraduate psychology programs. *American Psychologist, 62*(7), 650–670.

Edwards, J., & Smith, K. (1988). What skills and knowledge do potential employers value in baccalaureate psychologists? In P. J. Woods (Ed.), *Is psychology for them? A guide to undergraduate advising* (pp. 102–111). Washington, DC: American Psychological Association.

Finney, P., Snell, W., & Sebby, R. (1989). Assessment of academic, personal, and career development of alumni from Southeast Missouri State University. *Teaching of Psychology, 16,* 173–177.

Flattau, P. E. (1998). *An interesting career in psychology: Policy scientist as an independent consultant.* Retrieved February 1, 2001, from http://www.apa.org/science/ic-flattau.html

Frank, R. G., & Ross, M. J. (1995). The changing workforce: The role of health psychology. *Health Psychology, 14,* 519–525.

Fretz, B. R. (1976). Finding careers with a bachelor's degree in psychology. *Psi Chi Newsletter, 2,* 5–9.

Fretz, B. R., & Stang, D. J. (1988). *Preparing for graduate study in psychology: Not for seniors only!* Washington, DC: American Psychological Association.

Fry, R. (1991). *Manage your time.* Hawthorne, NJ: Career Press.

Garfein, R. (1997). *An interesting career in psychology: International market research consultant.* Retrieved February 1, 2001, from http://www.apa.org/science/ic-garfein.html

Grocer, S., & Kohout, J. (1997). *The 1995 APA survey of 1992 psychology baccalaureate recipients.* Retrieved August 21, 2000, from http://research.apa.org/95survey/homepage.html

Grover, S. F. (2006). Undergraduate research: Getting involved and getting into graduate school (a student's perspective). *Eye on Psi Chi, 11*(1), 18–20.

Halpern, D. F. (2009). *Undergraduate education in psychology: A blueprint for the future of the discipline.* Washington, DC: American Psychological Association.

Hersch, L. (1995). Adapting to health care reform and managed care: Three strategies for survival and growth. *Professional Psychology: Research & Practice, 26,* 16–26.

Himelein, M. J. (1999). A student's guide to careers in the helping professions. *Office of Teaching Resources in Psychology.* Retrieved January 3, 2001, from http://www.lemoyne.edu/OTRP/otrpresources/helping.html

Holland, J. L. (1959). A theory of vocational choice. *Journal of Counseling Psychology, 6,* 35–45.

Holland, J. L. (1994). *Self-directed search.* Retrieved July 5, 2001, from http://www.self-directed-search.com

Humphreys, K. (1996). Clinical psychologists as psychotherapists: History, future, and alternatives. *American Psychologist, 51,* 190–197.

Jalbert, N. L. (1998). Publication and award opportunities for undergraduate students. *Office of Teaching Resources in Psychology.* Retrieved August 8, 2001, from http://www.lemoyne.edu/OTRP/otrpresources/otrp_undergrad.html

Jessen, B. C. (1988). Field experience for undergraduate psychology students. In P. J. Woods (Ed.), *Is psychology for them? A guide to undergraduate advising* (pp. 79–84). Washington, DC: American Psychological Association.

Kahn, N. B. (1992). *More learning in less time: A guide for students, professionals, career changers, and lifelong learners.* Berkeley, CA: Ten Speed Press.

Karlin, N. J. (2000). Creating an effective conference presentation. *Eye on Psi Chi, 4*(2), 26–27.

Keith-Spiegel, P., Tabachnick, B. G., & Spiegel, G. B. (1994). When demand exceeds supply: Second order criteria used by graduate school selection committees. *Teaching of Psychology, 21,* 79–81.

Keith-Spiegel, P., & Wiederman, M. W. (2000). *The complete guide to graduate school admission: Psychology, counseling, and related professions.* Mahwah, NJ: Erlbaum.

Keyesm, B. J., & Hogberg, D. K. (1990). Undergraduate psychology alumni: Gender and cohort differences in course usefulness, post baccalaureate education, and career paths. *Teaching of Psychology, 17,* 101–105.

Kierniesky, N. C. (1992). Specialization of the undergraduate major. *American Psychologist, 47,* 1146–1147.

Krannich, R. I. (2005). *Nail that resume: Great tips for creating dynamite resumes.* Woodbridge, VA: Impact Publishers.

Krauss, S. K. (1996). *An interesting career in psychology: Market research consultant.* Retrieved February 1, 2001, from http://www.apa.org/science/ic-kraus.html

Kuther, T. L., & Morgan, R. (2010). *Careers in psychology: Opportunities in a changing world (3rd ed.).* Pacific Grove, CA: Thomson/Wadsworth.

Landrum, E. (2008). Evaluating the undergraduate research assistantship experience. *Eye on Psi Chi, 12*(3), 32–33.

Landrum, E., & Davis, S. (2010). *The psychology major: Career options and strategies for success.* Upper Saddle River, NJ: Prentice Hall.

Landrum, R. E., Harrold, R., & Davis, S. F. (2003). What employers want from psychology graduates. *Teaching of Psychology, 30,* 131–133.

Levant, R. F., Moldawsky, S., & Stigall, T. T. (2000). The evolving profession of psychology: Comment on Hays-Thomas' (2000) 'The silent conversation,' *Professional Psychology Research and Practice, 31,* 346–348.

Littlepage, G., Perry, S., & Hodge, H. (1990). Career experiences of bachelor's degree recipients: Comparison of psychology and other majors. *Journal of Employment Counseling, 27,* 50–59.

Lloyd, M. A. (1997a). *Entry level positions obtained by psychology majors.* Retrieved August 18, 2000, from http://www.psywww.com/careers/entry.htm

Lloyd, M. A. (1997b). *Graduate school options for psychology majors.* Retrieved February 15, 2001, from http://www.psywww.com/careers/options.htm

Lloyd, M. A. (2000). *Master's- and doctoral-level careers in psychology and related areas.* Retrieved February 1, 2000, from http://www.psychwww.com/careers/masters.htm

Lloyd, M. A., & Kennedy, J. H. (1997). *Skills employers seek.* Retrieved August 20, 2000, from http://www.psywww.com/careers/skills.htm

LoCicero, A., & Hancock, J. (2000). Preparing students for success in fieldwork. *Teaching of Psychology, 27,* 117–120.

Lock, R. D. (1988). *Taking charge of your career direction.* Pacific Grove, CA: Brooks/Cole.

Matlin, M. W., & Kalat, J. W. (2001). Demystifying the GRE psychology test: A brief guide for students. *Eye on Psi Chi, 5*(1), 22–25.

Mayne, T. J., Norcross, J. C., & Sayette, M. A. (1994). Admission requirements, acceptance rates, and financial assistance in clinical psychology programs. *American Psychologist, 12,* 806–811.

McGovern, T. V., & Carr, K. F. (1989). Carving out the niche: A review of alumni surveys on undergraduate psychology majors. *Teaching of Psychology, 16,* 52–57.

McGovern, T. V., Furumoto, L., Halpern, D. F., Kimble, G. A., & McKeachie, W. J. (1991). Liberal education, study in depth, and the arts and sciences major—Psychology. *American Psychologist, 46,* 598–605.

Meyer, M. (1985). *The little, brown guide to writing research papers.* Glenville, IL: Scott, Foresman and Company.

Michalski, D., Finno, A. A., Kohout, J. L., & Wicherski, M. (2009). *2009 APA salary survey: Master's-level respondents.* Washington, DC: APA Center for Workforce Studies.

National Association of Colleges and Employers. (2000). *Ideal candidate has top-notch interpersonal skills, say employers.* Retrieved August 19, 2000, from http://www.naceweb.org/press/display.cfm/2000/pr011800.htm

National Association of Colleges and Employers. (2009). *Salary survey.* Bethlehem, Pennsylvania: Author.

National Center for Education Statistics. (2009). *Digest of education 2008.* Washington, DC: Author.

National Science Foundation. (2009). *Women, minorities, and persons with disabilities in science and engineering: Employment.* Retrieved November 1, 2009, from http://www.nsf.gov/statistics/wmpd/employ.cfm

Norcross, J. C. (1997). GREs and GPAs: The numbers game in graduate admissions. *Eye on Psi Chi, 1*(2), 10–11.

Pate, W. E. (2001). *Analyses of data from graduate study in psychology: 1999–2000.* Retrieved January19, 2005, from http://research.apa.org/grad00contents.html

Pate, W. E., Frincke, J. L., & Kohout, J. L. (2005). *Salaries in psychology 2003.* Retrieved July 29, 2008, from http://research.apa.org/03salary/homepage.html

Pauk, W., & Fiore, J. (2000). *Succeed in college!* New York: Harper & Row.

Peters, R. L. (1992). *Getting what you came for: The smart student's guide to earning a master's or a PhD.* New York: Noonday Press.

Powell, J. L. (2000). Creative outlets for student research or what do I do now that my study is completed? *Eye on Psi Chi, 4*(2), 28–29.

Psi Chi. (2000). *Tips for paper/poster presentations.* Retrieved May 18, 2001, from http://www.psichi.org/content/conventions/tps.asp

Rittle, R. (2000). *Career options with a master's degree.* Retrieved February 1, 2001, from http://www.nsm.iup.edu/pc/jobs3ma.html

Robiner, W. N., & Crew, D. P. (2000). Rightsizing the workforce of psychologists in health care: Trends from licensing boards, training programs, and managed care. *Professional Psychology: Research and Practice, 31*, 245–263.

Robinson, F. P. (1970). *Effective study.* New York: Harper & Row.

Rosnow, R. L., & Rosnow, M. (2008). *Writing papers in psychology.* Belmont, CA: Wadsworth.

Scott, J. M., Koch, R. E., Scott, G. M., & Garrison, S. M. (1999). *The psychology student writer's manual.* Upper Saddle River, NJ: Prentice Hall.

Seligman, M. E. P. (1995). The effectiveness of psychotherapy: The consumer reports study. *American Psychologist, 50*, 965–974.

Sheetz, P. I. (1995). *Recruiting Trends: 1995–1996.* East Lansing, MI: Collegiate Employment Research Institute, Michigan State University.

Singleton, D., Tate, A. C., & Kohout, J. L. (2003a) *2002 master's, specialist's, and related degrees employment survey.* Retrieved January19, 2005, from http://research.apa.org/mes2004contents.html

Singleton, D., Tate, A. C., & Kohout, J. L. (2003b). *Salaries in psychology, 2001: Report of the 2001 APA salary survey.* Retrieved January19, 2005, from http://research.apa.org/01salary/index.html

Sleigh, M. J., & Ritzer, D. M. (2007). Undergraduate research experience: Preparation for the job market. *Eye on Psi Chi, 11*(3), 27–30.

Society of Research and Child Development. (1999). *Ethical standards for research with children.* Ann Arbor, MI: Society for Research in Child Development.

Stapp, J. (1996). *An interesting career in psychology: Trial consultant.* Retrieved February 1, 2001, from http://www.apa.org/science/ic-stapp.html

Sternberg, R. J. (1993). *The psychologist's companion.* New York: Cambridge University Press.

Taylor, M. S. (1988). Effects of college internships on individual participants. *Journal of Applied Psychology, 73,* 393–401.

Tsapogas, J. (2004). Employment outcomes of recent science and engineering graduates vary by field of degree and sector of employment. *Science Resources Statistics Info Brief.* Retrieved December 31, 2004, from http://www.nsf.gov/sbe/srs/infbrief/nsf04316/start.htm

University of Tennessee (n.d.). *Major and career information.* Retrieved July 5, 2001, from http://career.utk.edu/students/holland/holland.asp

University of Texas at Austin. (2000). *Career opportunities for psychology majors.* Retrieved August 18, 2000, from http://cwis.uta.edu/psychology/dept/careers.htm

US Bureau of Labor Statistics. (2009). *Current population survey.* Washington, DC: US Dept of Labor.

Wicherski, M., Michalski, D., & Kohout, J. (2009). *2007 Doctorate employment survey.* Washington, DC: APA Center for Workforce Studies.

Wicherski, W., & Kohout, J. (2007). *2005 Doctorate employment survey.* Washington, DC: APA Center for Psychology Workforce Analysis and Research.

Winter, D. G., McClelland, D. C., & Stewart, A. J. (1981). *A new case for the liberal arts: Assessing institutional goals and student development.* San Francisco: Jossey-Bass.

Index

Careers in Psychology
Opportunities in a Changing World

Third Edition

Tara L. Kuther
Western Connecticut State University

Robert D. Morgan
Texas Tech University

CLINICAL AND COUNSELING PSYCHOLOGY

CHAPTER GUIDE

Clinical Psychology

Counseling Psychology

Other Mental Health Professions

Opportunities with a Bachelor's Degree

Human Services Worker

Social Worker

Substance Abuse Counselor

Opportunities with a Graduate Degree

Graduate Education and Training Considerations

Practice

Program Development and Evaluation

Administration

Suggested Readings

Web Resources

Checklist: Is Clinical or Counseling Psychology for You?

Did you know that about 61 percent of psychology doctoral graduates are from the subfields of clinical, counseling, or school psychology (American Psychological Association Center for Workforce Studies, 2008)? Clearly, mental health service providers comprise the largest subfields in psychology. Why are these subfields so popular? Many students explain their career choices by stating simply,

"I want to help people." The mental health service provider subfields afford students opportunities to gain specialized skills and knowledge that can assist people suffering from mental illness, emotional or behavioral problems, or other psychological distress. Because the mental health service field is so large, we'll discuss it within the next two chapters; in this chapter we examine clinical and counseling psychology, and in Chapter 4 we'll explore the subfield of school psychology. Do clinical and counseling psychologists do the same thing? Do they have the same jobs? If not, how are they different? These are important questions for students at the baccalaureate, masters, and doctoral levels considering careers as mental health service providers.

Before reviewing the two subdisciplines of clinical and counseling psychology, it is worth exploring the question of how are they different. Results of empirical research suggested that there are few quantitative differences between clinical psychology Ph.D., Psy.D., and counseling psychology Ph.D. programs (Morgan & Cohen, in press). In fact, there appear to be greater discrepancies within each specialty than between the two specialties of clinical and counseling psychology (Cobb et al., 2004; Morgan & Cohen, in press). Nevertheless, subtle differences exist in training requirements (see Morgan & Cohen, in press, for a detailed description of these differences) as well as historical and philosophical differences (see Roger & Stone, n.d.).

CLINICAL PSYCHOLOGY

Clinical psychology is the integration of science, theory, and practice to explain and understand, predict, and alleviate psychological problems and distress, as well as promote healthy human development (American Psychological Association Society of Clinical Psychology, n.d.). Assessment and diagnosis, intervention or treatment, consultation, research, and application of ethical and professional principles are the necessary skills developed by training in clinical psychology (Resnick, 1991). In other words, clinical psychologists work to help people alleviate distress or to improve their functioning via (1) psychological practice, or the provision of services such as assessment, diagnosis, and treatment (for example, psychotherapy); (2) consultation; or (3) by conducting research aimed at understanding human phenomena with the goal of helping people. But where are clinical psychologists found and how do they spend their time?

Primary employment settings of clinical psychologists include: private practice (40%), university settings (19%), hospital settings (9%), outpatient clinics and community mental health centers (8%), medical schools (9%), Veteran's Administrative (VA) Medical Centers (3%), and "other" settings such as correctional facilities, child and family services, rehabilitation centers, and so on (11%) (Norcross, Karg, & Prochaska; 1997). Clinical psychologists spend approximately 37% of their time involved in direct client intervention (for example, psychotherapy) and approximately 15% of their time in assessment- and diagnostic-related activities (Norcross et al., 1997). Somewhat less frequent activities of clinical psychologists include administrative responsibilities (11%), research/writing activities (10%), teaching (9%), supervision of other mental health service providers (7%), and professional consultation (7%) (Norcross et al., 1997).

COUNSELING PSYCHOLOGY

Counseling psychologists, like their clinical psychology colleagues, work to alleviate distress and emotional or behavioral difficulties associated with psychological problems; however, counseling psychology maintains an equal focus on helping people improve their well-being across the lifespan, including emotional, social, vocational, health-related, developmental, and organizational concerns (Society of Counseling Psychology, Division 17: American Psychological Association, n.d.). Additionally, counseling psychologists have been instrumental in sensitizing psychologists to an understanding and appreciation of human diversity, particularly as multicultural issues relate to human functioning. Defined more simply, counseling psychology is a field of study that works to improve human functioning, either by enhancing current functioning or by alleviating distress.

The roots of counseling psychology can be found in five unifying themes: (1) focus on intact or normative functioning rather than profoundly disturbed functioning; (2) focus on client's assets and strengths, and positive mental health; (3) emphasis on brief interventions (for example, counseling sessions of fewer than 15 sessions); (4) emphasis on person-environment interactions, rather than focus on person or environment as separate entities; and (5) emphasis on educational and career development and vocational environments (Gelso & Fretz, 2001). It is not surprising then, that based on these unifying themes, counseling psychologists are more likely to identify themselves primarily as clinical practitioners (48%) than other professional roles such as academicians (28%), administrators (11%), consultants (6%), and researchers (3%) (Watkins, Lopez, Campbell, & Himmel, 1986); however, like their clinical psychology colleagues, counseling psychologists are employed in a variety of settings: colleges and universities, including university counseling centers; private practice; community mental health centers; psychiatric hospitals; medical facilities; correctional facilities; VA medical centers; health maintenance organizations; family services; business and consulting firms; and rehabilitation agencies.

OTHER MENTAL HEALTH PROFESSIONS

It is also worth noting that there are mental health professions that are not based in the discipline of psychology. That is, some mental health training does not have psychology as the disciplinary root. Many students may find marriage and family therapy (MFT) programs, rehabilitation or rehabilitation counseling programs, social work programs, or addictions counseling programs a better fit for their career interests (for more information see: American Association of Marriage and Family Therapy, 2002; American Counseling Association, 2008; National Association of Social Workers, 2008; and National Rehabilitation Counseling Association, n.d.). A student in one of these programs may earn a doctoral-level degree (for example, Ph.D., Ed.D.), but a terminal masters degree (M.S. or M.A.) is more common. Licensure as a mental health professional (for example, Licensed Professional Counselor, LPC; Licensed Master Social Worker, LMSW) is then typically required to provide counseling or related clinical services.

Overlap exists between marriage and family therapy, rehabilitation counseling, social work, and clinical and counseling psychology, in the form of professional services provided and employment settings. The primary distinction with regard to clinical services is that psychologists are trained to administer and interpret psychological tests. Additionally, psychology-based programs at the masters and doctoral levels typically place greater emphasis on conducting research. This is not to say that students in other mental health programs are not trained in research—they are, particularly at the doctoral level; however, research appears to be more heavily emphasized in clinical and counseling psychology training programs than in social work programs. Regarding employment settings, these mental health professionals overlap with clinical and counseling psychologists and will be found in: community mental health centers, psychiatric hospitals, private practice, medical facilities, correctional facilities, family services, and rehabilitation agencies.

OPPORTUNITIES WITH A BACHELOR'S DEGREE

Although a graduate degree is the entry-level degree to practice professional psychology, several opportunities to help people exist for undergraduate psychology majors who choose not to pursue graduate education. Let's take a look at service opportunities for bachelor's degree holders in psychology.

HUMAN SERVICES WORKER

Human services workers occupy a range of positions, including social service worker, case management aide, social work assistant, community support worker, mental health aide, community outreach worker, life skills counselor, and gerontology aide (Bureau of Labor Statistics, 2008). These positions are paraprofessional positions with "a support role that overlaps with job duties and responsibilities of a psychologist; however, the paraprofessional does not have the education, responsibility, nor salary of the psychologist" (Landrum, Davis, & Landrum, 2000, p. 17). Human services workers provide services, both direct and indirect, to clients that typically include: assessing clients' needs and eligibility for services, helping clients obtain services (for example, food stamps, Medicaid, transportation, and other human services programs), and providing emotional support (Bureau of Labor Statistics, 2008). In community settings (such as group homes or government-supported housing programs), human services workers assist clients in need of counseling, assist with daily living skills, and organize group activities. In clinical settings (for example, psychiatric hospitals, outpatient clinics), human services workers support clients participation in treatment plans, assist with daily living skills, help clients communicate more effectively, and promote social functioning (Bureau of Labor Statistics, 2008).

Advantages to a position in human services are the opportunity to help others in need, as well as a steady job market. In fact, human services positions are expected to increase much faster than the average for all occupations through 2016, with an expected growth rate of 36 percent (Bureau of Labor Statistics, 2008). Unfortunately, long hours, difficult cases, and low income often lead to burnout. In 2006, the median salary of human services workers was $25,580, with a range of $20,350 to $32,440 for the middle 50 percent, and a peak salary of approximately $40,780 for human services workers (Bureau of Labor Statistics, 2008).

Notably, positions with local and state governments tend to offer better salaries than individual or family service agencies, vocational rehabilitation agencies, or residential mental health, substance abuse and mental retardation facilities (Bureau of Labor Statistics, 2008).

SOCIAL WORKER

Although a degree in social work is sometimes a prerequisite, entry-level social worker positions often can be obtained with a bachelor's degree in psychology. Social workers aim to help people improve their lives through counseling and identifying needed resources (such as housing or food stamps). Frequent duties include individual and group counseling sessions, identifying federal and state program assistance as needed (for example, housing assistance, disability benefits, food stamps, and so on) (Bureau of Labor Statistics, 2008). Social workers are employed in a variety of settings: hospitals, schools, community mental health centers, social service agencies, and courts and correctional institutions; thus, social workers can seek settings that best suit their needs and abilities.

Salaries for social workers tend to be moderate, with a median yearly salary in the mid-thirties (approximately $35,000); however, salaries are quite variable depending on education, location and agency with a median salary range of $32,490 to $48,420 (note that higher salaries are likely for positions at the masters degree level; Bureau of Labor Statistics, 2008). Other benefits of this career choice include an increasing job market (expected to increase by 22 percent by 2016; Bureau of Labor Statistics, 2008) and the satisfaction of helping people at the grassroots level. A primary limitation of this career is the stress or feelings of helplessness resulting from difficulty identifying or securing appropriate resources for clients.

Although it is possible to obtain many social work positions with a bachelor's degree, continuing education in the form of a part-time masters program will increase your job security, opportunities for advancement, and ability to start a private practice. Salary will also increase with increased education. All states have licensing or certification requirements for private practice and the use of the title "social worker." Standards for licensing vary by state, so it's a good idea to check with your school's career development office and the Association of Social Work Boards (http://www.aswb.org/), to ensure that you are not disappointed.

SUBSTANCE ABUSE COUNSELOR

Although most counseling professions require graduate degrees (at least a masters degree) for employment, substance abuse counselors are a common exception. Substance abuse counselors provide counseling or rehabilitation services in residential treatment programs or as part of comprehensive outpatient substance abuse programs. The substance abuse counselor often is the primary therapist working with clients on their alcohol or drug dependence or abuse. Substance abuse counselors may spend their days facilitating therapy groups (particularly focused on educating clients about addiction and its related problems), as well as meeting individually with clients. Individual sessions allow therapists one-on-one time to focus on a client's specific problems.

The demand for drug and alcohol abuse counselors is strong, with an expected growth of 34 percent by 2016 (Bureau of Labor Statistics, 2008). Salaries for substance abuse counselors are consistent with other undergraduate positions listed in this chapter, with a median 2006 income of $34,040 per year, with the middle 50 percent earning between $27,330 and $42,650 (Bureau of Labor Statistics, 2008). It should be noted, however, that similar to social worker positions, higher salaries for substance abuse counselors are likely for positions that require a masters degree. Job availability and salary varies across the country, so examine the range of opportunities in your desired location as you plan for a career as a substance abuse counselor.

As with other mental health positions, one of the primary benefits of this career lies in the opportunity to help disturbed people who are in desperate need of help. In addition, the opportunity to enter the helping field at the baccalaureate level is attractive for students who want to enter the mental health profession but don't want to go to graduate school. Limitations of this career choice include the

TABLE 3.1	PREPARATION FOR B.A.–LEVEL CAREERS RELATED TO CLINICAL AND COUNSELING PSYCHOLOGY

Coursework
   Abnormal Psychology or Psychopathology
   Communications
   Community Mental Health
   Developmental Psychology
   Family Systems
   Interviewing, Counseling, or Helping Skills
   Professional Issues
   Psychological Assessment
   Psychopharmacology
   Social Work
   Substance Abuse
   Writing

Applied Experiences: Volunteer, intern/practica, or paid part-time positions in any of the following settings
   Any Mental Health Setting
   Big Brother/Big Sister Programs
   Boys and Girls Club
   Inpatient Psychiatric Unit
   Mental Retardation Facility
   Residential Treatment Facilities
   Substance Abuse Center

Research Experiences: Experiences studying and participating in research in any of the following areas*
   Abnormal Behavior
   Psychopathology
   Substance Abuse
   Specific Disorders (for example, Schizophrenia, Bipolar Disorder, Depression, Anxiety)
   Any treatment-, assessment-, or diagnostic-oriented research

*Note that the content area of the research is less important than the experience itself, which enhances reasoning, quantitative, writing, and organizational skills.

difficulty of professional advancement at the bachelor's degree level and the challenges of working with substance abusers, who often are resistant clients and can be difficult to work with.

Substance abuse counselors often are employed at the associate or bachelor's level, with certification. The requirements for certification as a drug and alcohol abuse counselor vary by state. Most states require the completion of four courses in drug and alcohol abuse counseling and 300 to 600 hours of supervised training. For more information about certification as a drug and alcohol abuse counselor, contact the National Association of Alcoholism and Drug Abuse Counselors (NAADAC) at http://www.naadac.org.

Although applied career opportunities exist for students who earn a bachelor's degree in psychology, many more opportunities exist for those earning a graduate degree. For example, students completing their masters (MA, MS), Ph.D., or Psy.D. may pursue applied careers as practitioners, program developers or evaluators, or consultants.

OPPORTUNITIES WITH A GRADUATE DEGREE

Your career options and financial prospects in clinical- and counseling-related careers expand dramatically with a graduate degree in psychology. Before we discuss graduate-level careers for students with interests in clinical and counseling psychology, let's take a look at graduate training and related issues. Students interested in these fields have several choices with regard to training. Following our discussion of graduate education in clinical and counseling psychology, we discuss three career trajectories for applied psychologists: practice, program development and evaluation, and administration.

GRADUATE EDUCATION AND TRAINING CONSIDERATIONS

Do your homework before entering graduate programs in counseling or clinical psychology. The most successful students are those who enter programs that are right for them (meaning, there is a good fit between the type of graduate program and their professional interests). As you read this book, you will realize there are many different types of programs available to you—clinical and counseling, but also non-service fields such as experimental or cognitive psychology. In this chapter, we examine the issue of choosing a graduate program in clinical and counseling psychology, but recognize that the decision-making process is similar in other fields (see Chapter 14 for more about applying to graduate school). Critically evaluate programs in light of your interests and career goals. Ask yourself:

- Do I understand the differences between the various programs? (How are clinical and counseling psychology different? What is a combined program?)
- What type of degree program is right for me (for example, Ph.D. or Psy.D.)?
- How do I get licensed after graduation?
- Are there other practice-related issues of which I should be aware?

DIFFERENTIATING CLINICAL AND COUNSELING PSYCHOLOGY.   Although the fields of counseling and clinical psychology overlap significantly (Cobb et al., 2004), subtle differences may be gleaned from the definitions provided earlier in this chapter.

It has commonly been suggested that one difference between the two disciplines is that clinical psychology is based on the medical model (meaning, assess, diagnose, and treat an ailment) whereas counseling psychology is less pathology-focused, favoring a holistic perspective emphasizing all aspects of a client's life. Not surprisingly, counseling psychologists, compared to their clinical psychology counterparts, tend to work with healthier individuals who are experiencing less psychopathology or distress (Norcross, Sayette, Mayne, Karg, & Turkson, 1998).

Consistent with a holistic perspective across the lifespan, counseling psychologists are more likely to conduct career and vocational assessments, whereas clinical psychologists, who focus on assessment and diagnosing pathology for treatment purposes (meaning, the medical model), are more likely to receive training in projective personality assessment (for example, the Rorschach or Thematic Apperception Test [TAT]) (Norcross, et al., 1998). Counseling psychologists tend to be employed in university counseling centers more often than clinical psychologists, whereas clinical psychologists are more likely to be employed in hospital settings (Gaddy, Charlot-Swilley, Nelson, & Reich, 1995; Watkins, et al., 1986). Another difference between the disciplines of clinical and counseling psychology is found in therapists' theoretical orientations. Clinical psychologists are more likely to endorse a behavioral or psychodynamic theoretical orientation, whereas their counseling psychology colleagues are more likely to endorse a person-centered (or Rogerian) theoretical orientation (Norcross, Prochaska, & Gallagher, 1989a; 1989b; Watkins et al., 1986).

With regard to training, results of empirical research suggest that there are few differences in clinical psychology Ph.D., Psy.D., and counseling psychology Ph.D. programs (Morgan & Cohen, in press). Two important differences are, first, that counseling psychologists are more likely to receive training in group psychotherapy than are clinical psychologists (Weinstein & Rossini, 1999) and, second, that counseling psychology programs tend to rely on external practicum sites for their graduate students, whereas clinical psychology programs are more likely to have in-house training clinics (meaning, psychology clinics operated by the department, which offers graduate student therapists opportunities to provide psychological services under close supervision of the faculty) (Morgan & Cohen, in press; Romans, Boswell, Carlozzi, & Ferguson, 1995). Given the few differences between training in clinical and counseling psychology, there appears to be more variation within each specialty than between the two specialties (Cobb et al., 2004; Morgan & Cohen, in press). Despite this, there are subtle differences in training requirements (see Morgan & Cohen, in press, for a detailed description of these differences) as well as historical and philosophical differences (see Roger & Stone, n.d.). Carefully evaluate each subdiscipline and each program to determine how each fit your interests and needs.

OPPORTUNITIES FOR GRADUATE EDUCATION.   If you're planning to seek graduate training in clinical or counseling psychology, understand that there is a large discrepancy in the number of graduate programs for each discipline. There are 232 American Psychological Association (APA)–accredited doctoral programs in clinical psychology compared to 72 APA–accredited doctoral programs in counseling psychology (American Psychological Association, 2007). It is not surprising that clinical psychology students accounted for 47 percent of all psychology doctorate degrees granted in 2003 (Center for Psychology Workforce Analysis and Research, 2008).

Both clinical and counseling psychology programs remain very competitive for admission, with an average admission rate of 6 percent for clinical psychology programs and 8 percent for counseling psychology programs (Norcross et al., 1998).

Admission criteria for clinical and counseling psychology programs are very similar, with some differences. Clinical psychology programs tend to require slightly higher verbal and quantitative Graduate Record Examination (GRE) scores than do counseling programs (Norcross et al., 1998). Another significant difference is in the percentage of students admitted with a masters degree versus a bachelor's degree. Counseling psychology programs are much more likely to admit a student who has already obtained a masters degree than are clinical psychology Ph.D. programs, which tend to admit students who have a bachelor's degree (Norcross et al., 1998). Counseling psychology programs also appear to be more ethnically diverse than their clinical counterparts (Morgan & Cohen, in press).

Somewhat less common than clinical and counseling programs are combined programs that integrate training from two or three of the subfields (counseling, school, and clinical psychology programs) without distinguishing among the disciplines. In other words, students in combined programs are trained in the principles of each of the specified subfields (for example, both clinical and school subfields). It should be noted that all combined programs are not alike; some integrate all three of the applied psychology disciplines (clinical, school, and counseling), whereas other programs incorporate either clinical or counseling psychology with school psychology. Although fewer combined programs (N = 11; American Psychological Association, 2007) exist compared to traditional counseling and clinical psychology programs, combined programs may offer increased diversity and a broader-based training experience for students; however, this has not been empirically examined.

PH.D. VERSUS PSY.D. DEGREES.   There are two types of doctoral degrees that a student interested in clinical psychology may obtain: the Ph.D. and Psy.D. How can we distinguish between these degrees? The first level of distinction can be found in their history. Generally speaking, the history of the Psy.D. is in training practitioners; thus, graduate training focuses more heavily on service provision than research. The history of the Ph.D., on the other hand, is based equally on science and practice (that is, the Boulder model), and so Ph.D. programs provide a greater focus on research skills than do Psy.D. programs. Students earning a Ph.D. complete a doctoral dissertation based in empirical research, whereas only a written project is often sufficient to complete requirements for the Psy.D. Alternatively, students in Psy.D. programs often accrue many more hours of clinical experience than do students in Ph.D. programs. So how do you know which degree is for you?

Consider two key issues. First, what do you hope to be doing in ten years? Although programs offering both the Ph.D. and Psy.D. train students to be clinicians, Ph.D. programs are more likely to train students to be scientists. If you're interested in becoming a practitioner and seek a program that emphasizes practice, the Psy.D. may fit your needs. However, if you're interested in developing your skills as a scientific researcher as well as your clinical skills, then the Ph.D. is in order. Which degree you choose is your decision, but recognize that there are very few noticeable differences in applicant quality between students in Psy.D. versus Ph.D. programs (Norcross et al., 1998). In other words, both options are highly competitive.

The second issue to consider is whether you prefer to attend a professional school or a more traditional university. The majority, albeit not all, of Psy.D. programs are housed in professional schools, whereas programs offering the Ph.D. are primarily housed in major state or private universities. What's the difference? We've already discussed the educational differences between the Ph.D. and Psy.D., but there's one more difference to consider: finances. Universities and private school based Ph.D. programs generally are less expensive and offer more funding to students (Norcross, Castle, Sayette, & Mayne, 2004). Professional schools, on the other hand, are not only more expensive but also tend to offer less financial assistance in the form of research and teaching assistantships (Norcross et al., 1998; 2004). While you should not base your decision solely on finances, it's important that you understand the economic realities of graduate education. For more information about graduate education, see Chapter 14.

LICENSURE.   The title of "psychologist" is protected; in order to provide psychological services (meaning, therapy, assessment, consultation) as a psychologist, you must be licensed in the state in which you wish to practice. Each state has a slightly different path to licensure; however, the basic process is roughly equivalent for all states.

First, a potential licensee must complete a doctoral program in clinical or counseling psychology (in a small minority of states, masters-level psychologists can seek licensure). Most states require that the doctoral degree is obtained in a program accredited by the APA, thereby certifying its rigor and training emphases, but it is possible in some states to seek licensure with a degree from a program that is not APA-accredited.

In addition to a doctoral degree, at least two years of supervised practice are required. Most students complete the first year as part of their degree requirements, the one-year full-time internship (or a two-year part-time internship) in which they receive supervision for providing psychological services (for example, therapy, assessment, crisis intervention). After completion of the doctoral degree (including completion of the internship), the licensee must acquire an additional year of supervised experience. This experience can be in the form of a formal postdoctoral program, but it can also be less structured (for example, in a private practice setting) as long as it includes providing psychological services under the supervision of a doctoral-level licensed psychologist.

After all degree and supervision requirements are met, the next step is to apply for licensure, which entails a national written examination and a jurisprudence examination. The national examination is multiple-choice, covering a broad range of issues and topics relevant to the practice of psychology. Because this is a national examination, the test is written for licensure applicants in all states and is thus of a generalist nature. A 70 percent accuracy rate is necessary to pass in most states, although states vary slightly in score requirements. The jurisprudence examination is also a written test; however, it is specific to the ethical code and licensure laws of each state. Thus, if you're applying for licensure in California, you will be asked questions regarding California law and its ethical code, but if you're applying for licensure in New York, you'll answer questions about New York statutes and ethics code.

After completion of the written examinations, many states require an additional oral examination in which licensees are presented with a case vignette and asked questions regarding diagnosis, treatment planning, and ethical concerns, as well as what multicultural issues might impact the case. As you can see, the process of obtaining licensure is time-consuming; it's also costly. For example, for one of the authors, the expense of pursuing licensure from start to finish cost approximately $1,300 (in 2000; adjusted for inflation, about $1,600 in 2007) after the examination and application fees. Furthermore, the expense and time commitment increases if a licensee doesn't pass a particular examination and therefore must repeat it (people fail the exams for various reasons). Despite the challenge of seeking licensure, it enables you to earn your stripes, so to speak. With licensure you are eligible to practice psychology without supervision.

INNOVATIVE TRAINING OPPORTUNITIES. Technological advances (for example, telemedicine), marketplace demands (such as managed care or prescription privileges for psychologists), and informational gains (for example, empirically-supported practice, formerly referred to as empirically based practice) continue to alter the face of psychology with the potential to profoundly impact the future of psychological practice. Two current issues that are gaining increased attention in psychology are prescription privileges and telemedicine or telehealth.

Prescriptive authority for mental health professionals has historically been limited to physicians and psychiatric nurses; however, psychologists in the United States military and several states recently gained prescription privileges, the ability to prescribe psychotropic medications to clients independent of psychiatrists or physicians. This opportunity not only meets a mental health service need in these agencies, states, or territories (for example, legislation was initiated in New Mexico because of a drought of psychiatrists in rural areas), but also creates many new practice and research opportunities for psychologists.

Similarly, the delivery of psychological services via computer networks is referred to as *behavioral medicine, telehealth,* or *telemental health* and is significantly expanding professional practice opportunities. In telehealth, a psychologist remains in one location and provides a psychological service (for example, therapy) to a client in a hospital, prison, or community agency in another location. This practice significantly alters the service delivery area of psychologists and may afford clients care from a specialist whom they would otherwise be unable to visit.

As relatively new and innovative practice strategies, many issues (including ethical and legal issues) must be navigated regarding training and competency in prescription authority as well as telehealth; however, for the innovative student the doors are wide open. If you have interests in these or other innovative opportunities, seek specialized experiences during graduate school that will best facilitate your future opportunities. For example, you may elect to complete coursework in psychopharmacology and seek practicum placements that require collaboration with psychiatrists. You might seek practicum opportunities in hospitals that rely on telehealth, or complete elective coursework in computer science to become as familiar as possible with computer technology. These are just a couple of examples of the myriad professional opportunities currently evolving in psychology, and students planning on pursuing a graduate degree in psychology are strongly encouraged to maintain an open mind and to seek innovative opportunities that may enhance future career possibilities.

PRACTICE

Undoubtedly, the greatest number of applied psychologists use their knowledge and skills as practitioners. Practitioners work in a variety of settings including private practices, hospitals, community mental health centers, schools, university or college counseling centers, criminal justice settings, and specialty clinics, to name just a few examples. In addition to selecting the setting where they will practice, psychologists also have an opportunity to decide if they want to specialize in a particular kind of client or problem. For example, some practitioners prefer to specialize in forensic or sports psychology practices, whereas other psychologists prefer to specialize in a particular type of presenting problem (for example, depression, anxiety, relationships).

One of the primary benefits of a graduate degree in clinical or counseling psychology is the flexibility to pursue career opportunities that match one's own interests and skills or abilities. Advanced degrees also afford practitioners salaries that are competitive with other psychology-related positions. In 2003, the median salary of all clinical psychologists (regardless of experience) was $75,000, and counseling psychologists earned a median salary of $65,000 (Pate, Frincke, & Kohout, 2005), varying by geographic location, setting, and clientele.

Another benefit for those interested in the practice of psychology is the expansion of the field. Psychology continues to break new ground and recent advances include delivering mental health services via telehealth and legislated prescription privileges. Although the days of seeing individual clients in one's private office are not extinct, neither is this type of service delivery necessarily the all-encompassing method of mental health services in the future. This is exciting for current students; innovative opportunities abound for those of you with imagination and foresight.

PROGRAM DEVELOPMENT AND EVALUATION

In addition to direct service delivery, clinical and counseling psychologists often pursue career opportunities in program development and evaluation. Psychologists may choose to develop the programs that schools or community placements offer, for example, rather than being the practitioner who provides the service.

Careers in program development and evaluation offer several benefits that practitioners don't always have. First is the opportunity to identify and develop the types of programs that are warranted for a particular agency or type of client. Working at the grassroots level such as this can be extremely rewarding, especially when a program is successful in helping the intended audience. Second, program developers avoid the stress of daily service provision to clients. On the other hand, psychologists involved in program development may miss the intimate contact and satisfaction from client progress that practitioners experience regularly. Typically, psychologists who take positions in program evaluation work as research associates at nonprofit organizations or as consultants. In 2007, research associates and consultants in private companies and government earned $85,000 and $77,000, respectively, with 2 to 4 years of experience. Those in nonprofit organizations, with 5 to 9 years of experience, earned $76,000 (American Psychological Association 2008).

ADMINISTRATION

ADMINISTRATIVE CAREERS.   In addition to careers in practice or as researchers, many clinical and counseling psychologists choose careers in administration. Administrators may be specialists who manage clinical services, or generalists who manage an entire agency or organization (Bureau of Labor Statistics, 2008). Administrators are responsible for overseeing the operation of an agency, including staffing and budget issues, healthcare delivery systems and technological advances, as well as daily operations (for example, mental health service delivery). If you're interested in a career in administration, take additional coursework in business administration, finance, and management.

Psychologists work in administrative roles within hospitals and clinics, community mental health centers and community organizations, correctional and rehabilitation centers, and nursing homes, to name just a few examples. Administrative positions in medical and mental health settings offer an attractive salary, with a median salary of $73,340 in 2006 with a slightly higher salary for those in general medical settings, and slightly less for those in outpatient service centers (Bureau of Labor Statistics, 2008). Another benefit of an administrative career is the direct influence administrators have on the services an organization delivers and the care clients or patients receive. On the other hand, administrative work typically requires long hours and job-related stress, particularly when dealing with personnel and budgetary issues (Bureau of Labor Statistics, 2008).

In this chapter we've covered just a few of the myriad possibilities available with a graduate degree in clinical or counseling psychology. Opportunities also exist for careers in writing and publishing (Chapter 13), research and academia (Chapter 13), corrections (Chapter 5), public health (Chapter 6), consulting (Chapter 9), marketing (Chapter 11), and social policy (Chapter 12), to name just a few.

SUGGESTED READINGS

Brown, S. D. & Lent, R. W. (Eds.). (2008). *Handbook of counseling psychology* (4th ed.) New York: Wiley.

Collison, B. B., & Garfield, N. J. (1996). *Careers in counseling and human services*. New York: Taylor & Francis.

Gelso, C., & Fretz, B. (2001). *Counseling psychology* (2nd ed.). Orlando: Harcourt.

Ginsberg, L. H. (2000). *Careers in social work*. Boston: Allyn & Bacon.

Kuther, T. L., Habben, C. J. & Morgan, R. D. (2005). "Today's new psychologist: Traditional and emerging career paths". In R. D. Morgan, T. L. Kuther & C. Habben (Eds.), *Life after graduate school in psychology: Insider's advice from new psychologists* (pp. 1–11). New York: Psychology Press.

Landrum, R. E. (2001). *I'm getting my bachelor's degree in psychology—what can I do with it? Eye on Psi Chi, 6*, 22–24.

Morgan, B. L. & Korschgen, A. (2001). *Majoring in psych? Career options for psychology undergraduates* (2nd ed.). Boston: Allyn & Bacon.

Srebalus, D. J. & Brown, D. (2000). *Guide to the helping professions*. Boston: Allyn & Bacon.

Woody, R. H. & Robertson, M. H. (1997). *A Career in clinical psychology: From training to employment*. Madison, CT: International Universities Press.

WEB RESOURCES

Division 12 of the American Psychological Association (Society of Clinical Psychology)
http://www.apa.org/divisions/div12/homepage.html

Society of Counseling Psychology (Division 17) of the American Psychological Association
http://www.div17.org/

So You're Considering Graduate Study in Clinical Psychology
http://www.wcas.northwestern.edu/psych/undergraduate/clinical.html

Marky Lloyd's Careers in Psychology Page
http://www.psywww.com/careers/

Choices: Careers in Social Work
http://www.naswdc.org/pubs/choices/choices.htm

Appreciating the PsyD: The Facts
http://www.psichi.org/pubs/articles/article_171.asp

Clinical versus Counseling Psychology: What's the Diff?
http://www.psichi.org/pubs/articles/article_73.asp

Counseling Psychology: Making Lives Better
http://www.psichi.org/pubs/articles/article_97.asp

CHECKLIST: IS CLINICAL OR COUNSELING PSYCHOLOGY FOR YOU?

Do you:

- ☐ Like working with people?
- ☐ Have an interest in helping people with problems?
- ☐ Want to work with healthy people to improve their current functioning?
- ☐ Have an interest in why people do the things they do?
- ☐ Have an interest in identifying people's abilities or personality functioning?
- ☐ Think you would enjoy working in a hospital, clinic, university counseling center, or other health care setting?
- ☐ Find that you are a person others feel comfortable talking to about their problems?
- ☐ Find yourself interested in other people's problems?
- ☐ Have good listening skills and avoid tuning out when people talk about their lives?
- ☐ Have an interest in mental illness?
- ☐ Enjoy reading about abnormal psychology?
- ☐ Enjoy reading research about mental illness?
- ☐ Think you would enjoy a career providing psychotherapy and assessment?
- ☐ Have an interest in applied research that can be used to better people's lives?
- ☐ Keep secrets and protect information that others feel is personal?
- ☐ Find that people consider you trustworthy?
- ☐ Have compassion and feel for other people when they are suffering?

Scoring: The more boxes you checked, the more likely it is that you're a good match for clinical or counseling psychology.

School Psychology | CHAPTER 4

As we have discussed, the majority of psychology graduate students specialize in the mental health service provider subfields (American Psychological Association Research Office, 2003). We have discussed the fields of clinical and counseling psychology; school psychology is a third mental health service provider subfield of psychology. School psychology offers unique training and professional opportunities that diverge from those of counseling and clinical psychology.

School psychology overlaps with clinical and counseling psychology with regard to job activities, but school psychologists work with a more specific population. Trained in both psychology and education (Silva, 2003), school psychologists work with children, families, and school systems (American Psychological Association Division 16, 2005). Consistent with the title "school psychologist," the majority of school psychologists are found in school districts or school systems. School psychologists are also employed in clinics (such as community mental health centers), medical centers, correctional facilities, colleges and universities, and private practices.

School psychologists provide assessment and treatment services for children and families, consult with teachers and school officials, develop and evaluate programs, conduct research, and promote health in children and adolescents (American Psychological Association Division 16, 2005; Trull, 2004). School psychologists work with children and adolescents who present a broad array of psychological needs that are of a developmental or school-related nature. Approximately one in five children and adolescents experience significant mental health problems during their school years (Costello et al., 1996), and typical presenting problems school psychologists work with include: fears about starting school, time management and study skills deficits, family and relationship problems, psychopathology (such as depression or anxiety), drug and alcohol problems, developmental and life stage problems (for example, sexuality, college, and work issues), and concerns regarding academic aptitude and intellectual abilities (Silva, 2003). The school psychologist's task is to help families, teachers, and the educational system understand and resolve these problems while promoting the child's overall health and development.

OPPORTUNITIES WITH A BACHELOR'S DEGREE

Many psychology students are interested in working with and helping children and adolescents. If these are your interests, consider a career in teaching, school counseling, or childcare.

TEACHER

Few career paths enable you to have as much day-to-day contact with children as teaching. Teachers clearly need an understanding of behavior, learning, and development. If you're interested in a position where you can make a difference in the lives of others, consider teaching.

Given your school experiences, you're probably aware of the teaching duties required of teachers, but there are many other duties and obligations that occupy a teacher's day. Teachers are responsible for supervising study halls, homerooms, and extracurricular activities, all of which provide extended contact with students and therefore afford teachers the opportunity to identify physical or mental health problems and refer the child for the appropriate services. Thus, a background in psychology may assist teachers, not only in their work in the classroom but also in identifying and helping students who are experiencing problems.

Salaries for public educators are respectable, with an average income between $43,580 and $48,690 (Bureau of Labor Statistics, 2008), which is based on a nine-month salary ($58,106 to $64,920 extrapolated to 12 months). Note that salaries vary with geographical location and school system, but a career as a teacher can afford financial stability. In addition to a comfortable salary, an important benefit of a teaching career is parallel to that of the college professor: time off.

Schools routinely allow for traditional holidays (such as Thanksgiving), with extended holiday leave around Christmas (approximately two weeks) as well as spring and (of increasing frequency) fall breaks. So, during the nine-month academic year, it is reasonable that an educator may expect to receive anywhere from two to four weeks of time off. In addition, as the educator is tied to a nine-month salary, summers are unaccounted for. This allows for extra vacation time, pursuit of additional occupational interests, family time, or any other number of ways in which you wish to spend time.

As we've indicated, the primary benefit of a career as a schoolteacher may be the opportunity to be involved in and influence the lives of the children or adolescents who will lead our country into the future. As a schoolteacher, you'll have the opportunity to make a difference in a young person's life. The primary drawback to a career as a schoolteacher is the limited availability for professional advancement. Although some opportunities exist for advancement (for example, administration, teaching mentor), these positions are less common than teaching positions and require additional education. Thus, most schoolteachers remain in the classroom for the majority of their careers, which may lead to burnout for some.

If you're considering a career as a schoolteacher, understand that all teaching positions require the completion of a bachelor's degree and an approved teacher education program, plus certification, which is obtained after completing a specified number of courses in education and passing a standardized exam. An education major usually is not required as long as the required classes and experiences are obtained. Many universities offer a one-year program for bachelor's degree holders who wish to re-specialize and become teachers. The exact requirements for becoming a teacher vary by state, so consult your advisor and the Education Department at your college or university.

CHILDCARE WORKER

Students who are interested in school psychology often seek positions as childcare workers in childcare centers, nursery schools, preschools, public schools, private homes, and after-school programs. Childcare workers care for children and engage them in activities that promote their development while their parents are at work. They teach children and stimulate physical, emotional, intellectual, and social development (Bureau of Labor Statistics, 2008). They keep records on children's progress and maintain contact with parents to discuss children's needs and progress. In other words, childcare workers provide children with care and opportunities to learn through play and more formal activities. As a childcare worker, you'll prepare day-to-day and long-term schedules of activities that include quiet and active time, and individual and group play.

Childcare is strenuous work that can be physically and emotionally taxing (Bureau of Labor Statistics, 2008). Although childcare workers interact with parents or guardians, the majority of the work is with children. Thus, the work requires high energy with frequent bending and stooping as well as lifting of children in times of need (for example, the child who is sad when his parent drops him off). The work may become routine and hours may be long because childcare centers are open year-round and typically have extended hours to allow time for child drop-off and pickup that is flexible for parents' schedules (Bureau of Labor Statistics, 2008).

An important disadvantage to a career in childcare is that there is a high degree of burnout and employee turnover. In a large childcare center or preschool, you might advance to a supervisory or administrative position; however, other opportunities for advancement are limited. Other disadvantages of a career in childcare are dealing with children who have behavioral problems and working with difficult parents (unless difficult family situations and childhood behavioral problems are a specialty or interest of yours).

Nevertheless, few careers are as intrinsically rewarding as that of a childcare worker. Few careers allow for greater influence in the learning, growth, and development of children. The working conditions will vary by agency or employment setting (for example, one's own home versus an agency), and turnover in childcare work is high. High turnover, however, creates excellent job opportunities for those recently graduating from college and may provide a professional stepping-stone to other opportunities or career paths (Bureau of Labor Statistics, 2008).

Unfortunately, childcare workers often earn income that is low relative to their education (Whitebrook & Phillips, 1999). The median salary for a child worker in 2006 was $17,630; however, salary is contingent upon education and experience such that employees with more education typically receive higher salaries (Bureau of Labor Statistics, 2008). Salaries also vary by setting (for example, public or private childcare, home-based or center-based) and geographic location. In 2008, a typical daycare teacher earned a median salary of $27,294 (Salary.com, 2008). Unfortunately, benefits are also relatively poor (Bureau of Labor Statistics, 2008). For many, however, the disadvantages of a career in childcare are outweighed by the joy they experience in helping young children grow and flourish.

If childcare interests you, take additional courses in child development and early childhood education. It's essential that you develop an understanding of normative childhood development because childcare providers often help to identify children with disabilities or special needs. A career in childcare can be demanding because you must be enthusiastic, alert, and have lots of physical energy and endurance (for lifting, holding, carrying, and playing with all those kids!). Good communication skills with children and parents are important, and childcare workers must be able to anticipate problems and act to promote children's welfare.

TEACHER ASSISTANT

Teacher assistants typically perform a combination of instructional and clerical duties (for example, monitoring students in non-academic activities such as recess and eating) to allow teachers more time for lesson planning and teaching (Bureau of Labor Statistics, 2008). Assistant teaching is a rewarding career with opportunities to significantly impact the learning and well-being of children without the daily responsibilities of developing lesson plans and serving as the principal monitor and communicator of student progress to administrators and parents.

Teaching assistant positions offer a stable employment opportunity with solid growth, as teaching assistant positions are expected to grow by 10 percent by 2016 (Bureau of Labor Statistics, 2008). Although salaries for teaching assistants tend to be low with a median 2006 income of $20,740 (Bureau of Labor Statistics, 2008), increased salaries are available with increased education and experience. Furthermore, upper levels of teaching assistant salaries are not substantially below those of first-year teachers, who have a mean salary of $31,753 (American Federation of Teachers, 2007).

EARLY CHILDHOOD BEHAVIORAL SPECIALIST

Early childhood behavioral specialists develop behavioral interventions for children, generally from infancy to seven years-of-age, experiencing a variety of behavioral difficulties. Behavioral interventions are developed in consultation with parents, daycare providers, and early childhood teachers, and include observations of the child in his or her natural environments, including home and childcare or educational settings. Children served may suffer from serious mental disorders (for example, autism, Asperger's syndrome, or attention deficit/hyperactivity disorder), or evidence severe acting-out behavior (such as aggression or self-injurious behavior). Early childhood behavioral specialists will work with parents, other family members, and the identified child to implement planned interventions.

Although many early childhood behavioral specialist positions require a masters degree, many positions are available for graduates with a bachelor's degree. Early childhood behavioral specialists understand theories of childhood development, including social, emotional, cognitive, and other verbal and non-verbal domains, and are grounded in theories of early childhood interventions.

TABLE 4.1	PREPARATION FOR B.A.–LEVEL CAREERS RELATED TO SCHOOL PSYCHOLOGY

Coursework

    Abnormal Psychology/Child Psychopathology

    Child Psychology

    Communications

    Developmental Psychology

    Early Interventions

    Education courses focusing on assessment and intervention

    Family Systems

    Human Development/Child Development in non-psychology departments

    Math

    Other courses related to practical application of psychology for children

    Professional Issues

    Special education courses

    Writing

Applied Experiences: Volunteer, intern, or paid part-time positions in any of the following settings

    Any Child/Adolescent Mental Health Setting

    Big Brother/Big Sister Programs

    Child/Adolescent Psychiatric Unit

continued

TABLE 4.1	CONTINUED

Day Care and Preschool Settings
Head Start
Mental Retardation Facility for Children
Boys and Girls Club
Residential Treatment Facilities for Children with Behavioral Disorders
Teaching Assistant (Particularly in Special education)

Research Experiences: Experiences studying and participating in research in any of the following areas*

Child Psychology or Child Psychopathology
Early Intervention
Childhood Behavioral Problems
Education

*Note that the content area of the research is less important than the experience itself, which enhances reasoning, quantitative, writing, and organizational skills.

Advantages of this career choice include a strong employment outlook, as "Early childhood mental health specialists are desperately needed" (Bryans, 1999). Furthermore, salaries are very competitive in this field, as graduates with a bachelor's degree in psychology can expect to earn approximately $38,995 (PayScale, 2008). Disadvantages of this job are the emotionally taxing client load which often includes abused and neglected children; however, opportunities for significant progress are available that can be extremely professionally and personally rewarding.

OPPORTUNITIES WITH A GRADUATE DEGREE

If you're interested in school psychology and desire a wide range of professional opportunities, consider earning a graduate degree in school psychology or school counseling (often available through departments of education). Training in school psychology emphasizes mental health services (such as assessment and counseling), child development, school organization, and learning/behavior and motivation theory (Silva, 2003). Like their counseling and clinical psychology counterparts, many school psychologists earn doctoral degrees; however, a school psychologist may practice with a masters degree and/or receive national certification (from the National Association of School Psychologists) as a school psychologist, which requires a more advanced degree called a specialist's degree. A specialist's degree falls between the masters and doctoral degrees and typically adds from an extra semester to an extra year of study beyond the masters degree. Because a specialist's degree is required for certification, if you're interested in school psychology at the masters degree level, plan on taking the time to earn the specialist's degree. Now let's take a look at graduate-level careers in school psychology.

SCHOOL PSYCHOLOGIST

Although school psychologists are known for their work in schools, they are found in a variety of settings and in private practice.

SCHOOL SETTINGS. The primary responsibilities of the school psychologist in a public or private school setting are to provide consultation, assessment, intervention and prevention, educational or training services, and research and program development (Silva, 2003).

Consultation and educational services are primary tasks of the school psychologist in a school setting (Bardon, 1989). School psychologists consult with administrators, teachers, and parents to help them better understand how child development affects learning and behavior (Silva, 2003). For example, a school psychologist in a school setting may facilitate coordination between parents and the school system to ensure that all parties are promoting the best interest of the child. Similarly, educational services are offered to administrators, teachers, and parents to facilitate effective learning environments and address problem behaviors. Educational services may take the form of classroom management techniques, teaching educators new learning strategies or ways to identify at-risk children.

Assessment is also an emphasis of the school psychologist in school settings (Bardon, 1989). School psychologists use a myriad of instruments and techniques to evaluate the nature of a student's problem and identify the most appropriate intervention. School psychologists may be asked to evaluate students' academic skills and learning aptitudes, personality and emotional development, social skills, learning environment and school climate, eligibility for special education, and effectiveness of intervention strategies (Silva, 2003). In other words, although school psychologists provide direct services (such as counseling), they more typically assess a problem and then teach other people (for example, parents, teachers) more directly involved with the student how to be helpful to the child.

School psychologists also provide direct services via preventive and intervention strategies. Prevention strategies are designed to identify at-risk children and provide services to prevent the onset of learning or behavioral problems. Prevention services that school psychologists may provide include: program development and teacher education for identifying children at risk for learning disorders or mental health problems, skills training for parents and teachers to cope with disruptive behavior, developing school initiatives to facilitate school safety (for example, preventing bullying and aggression), and facilitating tolerance of individual differences and diversity (Silva, 2003). Intervention services, on the other hand, are designed to help children who already have learning or behavioral problems. Examples of intervention services a school psychologist may provide include: individual or group counseling, skills training (for example, social skills, time management, study skills, problem-solving skills, coping strategies), crisis management, grief counseling, family therapy, and substance abuse counseling.

Finally, school psychologists may be involved in research and program development within school settings. School psychologists evaluate the effectiveness of their services, academic programs, and behavior management systems, as well as develop new programs (for example, best practices) to facilitate student learning and development or for educational reform or restructuring (Silva, 2003).

Salaries for school psychologists in elementary and secondary school settings are comparable to counseling and clinical psychologists, with school psychologists earning a 2006 median salary of approximately $61,290 annually (Bureau of Labor Statistics, 2008; see Chapter 3 for more information on salaries in the applied areas of psychology, including clinical and counseling psychology). A primary benefit for the psychologist in a school setting is flexibility. Because school psychologists engage in a range of activities, they have diverse daily schedules and routines. An additional advantage is that psychologists in school settings adhere to the academic schedule, which affords extended leaves for winter holidays, fall and spring breaks, and summer breaks. Some school districts may employ their psychologists throughout the summer, although this usually includes increased pay.

A disadvantage for psychologists working in the school system is lack of access to colleagues. Most school districts employ one school psychologist (although this is tied to the size of the school district, with larger districts employing more school psychologists), so a sense of professional isolation may occur. One school psychologist may be responsible for all students in the district and across all grade levels, which can easily amount to overseeing the needs of hundreds and perhaps greater than a thousand students spread across several schools, requiring frequent travel between settings. Traveling among schools can leave some school psychologists feeling that they lack a "home base;" however, this diversity and travel between schools may be refreshing for some, preventing feelings of boredom or staleness.

PRIVATE PRACTICE. School psychologists in private practice engage in similar activities to those in school settings. Although some psychologists debate the appropriateness of school psychologists in private practice, a child's behaviors at school are not always directly related to the school or educational system. Thus, private practitioners are equally capable of providing consultation, assessment, and prevention and intervention services for learning and behavioral problems as are psychologists employed in school settings. Therefore, school psychologists in both private practice and school settings provide similar services and perform similar tasks.

Alternatively, school psychologists in private practice have unique advantages over their counterparts in the schools. First, school psychologists in private practice have greater flexibility in the scheduling of their appointments, with the exception that many students will not be seen until after 4:00 P.M., which often requires evening work. Nevertheless, this schedule may prove desirable for individuals who aren't "morning people." Second, school psychologists in private practice spend less time traveling from school to school and are more likely to see clients in their office. Thus, they have a central office from which to work and are less distracted by shuffling about. Finally, school psychologists in private practice are not limited in their clientele by an agency. Therefore, they have opportunities to branch out and provide other services (for example, relationship counseling, individual counseling to non-students) if they receive the appropriate training and supervision. Salary for school psychologists in private offices may also be slightly higher than for those working in elementary and secondary school settings.

A limitation for the private practitioner is the lack of availability and access to a child's learning environment. Whereas a school psychologist employed in a school setting has immediate access to a child and the classroom, the private practitioner must seek permission and approval from the school to observe a classroom and must wait for the student to be transported to his or her office. An additional disadvantage for the private practitioner is the overhead cost of maintaining a private practice (for example, office space, clerical assistance, and so on). Psychologists in school settings have little to no overhead costs, because the school district provides office space, computer access or computing services for report writing, and testing materials. The private practitioner must cover these expenses as business costs.

OTHER SETTINGS.   In addition to school settings and private practice, school psychologists are found in many other settings, including clinics and hospitals, criminal justice settings, universities and medical schools, businesses, and residential settings (see D'Amato and Dean, 1989, for a review of school psychologists in these settings). Similar to graduate degrees in counseling and clinical psychology, a graduate degree in school psychology affords great flexibility with regard to professional settings and responsibilities. Regardless of where a school psychologist works, however, he or she focuses on providing services that help students (children, adolescents, or adults) succeed academically, emotionally, and socially (Silva, 2003) by engaging in consulting and educational services, providing assessments, developing prevention and intervention programs, and conducting research.

SCHOOL COUNSELOR

Remember the school counselor in your high school—a trusted professional who would help you or your friends when you needed information about colleges and college admissions, or who offered assistance in times of need, or who simply offered a friendly smile and a comfortable place to talk about "stuff" that was occurring in your life? This, in essence, is the career of the school counselor.

As described in the Occupational Outlook Handbook (Bureau of Labor Statistics, 2008), school counselors help students understand and cope with social, behavioral, and personal problems. School counselors use counseling skills to emphasize prevention of problems before they arise, as well as skill development to enhance personal, social, and academic growth. School counselors may provide special services such as substance abuse prevention programs, conflict management, and parenting education training, as well as supervising peer counseling programs.

School counselors may work with individuals, small groups, or entire classes. Although this job description may appear to overlap with the school psychologist's, the school counselor is vastly different. Whereas school psychologists work with children with special needs, school counselors are available for all children and maintain regular school hours to help students as they navigate the educational process. Furthermore, unlike school psychologists, school counselors typically have less formal training in psychopathology, assessment, and counseling skills. When students are encountering severe problems or distress (academic, personal, behavior, social) the student is referred to the school psychologist, who has specialized training to deal with such issues.

Career opportunities for the school counselor are very good. The job outlook for school counselors is expected to remain steady through 2016 (Bureau of Labor Statistics, 2008). Other advantages of a career as a school counselor include the salary and work schedule. School counselors earn salaries with a 2006 median income of $53,750 (Bureau of Labor Statistics, 2008); however, it should be noted that this annual salary is typically based only on a nine- or ten-month contract. An additional benefit is the work schedule. School counselors, like teachers, have two or three months off every year to pursue other interests or other employment. In addition, they receive generous vacation packages that include major holidays, as well as spring and fall breaks, and an extended Christmas break.

A few states allow bachelor's degree holders to work as school counselors; however, all states require school counselors to hold state school counseling certification (Bureau of Labor Statistics, 2008), which usually requires additional training and credentialing beyond the bachelor's degree. The amount of education varies and some can be completed as part of the bachelor's degree. Some states require public school counselors to have both counseling and teaching certificates (Bureau of Labor Statistics, 2008). The opportunities available to you will vary by geographic location, as there are substantial differences in requirements across the nation. A growing number of states require school counselors to hold masters degrees in school counseling (usually available within departments of education). If you're considering a career as a school counselor, look into the education and certification requirements in your state (the American School Counselor Association is a great place to start your research: http://www.schoolcounselor.org/).

SUGGESTED READINGS

Burden, K. (2000). Psychology in education and instruction. In K. Pawlik & M. R. Rosenzweig, (Eds.), *International handbook of psychology* (pp. 466–78). Thousand Oaks, CA: Sage.

Esquivel, G. B., Lopez, E. C., & Nahari, S. G. (2007) *Handbook of multicultural school psychology: An interdisciplinary perspective*. Mahwah, NJ: Erlbaum.

Fagan, T. K., & Warden, P. G. (Ed.). (1996). *Historical encyclopedia of school psychology*. Westport, CT: Greenwood Publishing Group.

Gilman, R., & Teague, T. L. (2005). School psychologists in nontraditional settings: Alternative roles and functions in psychological service delivery. In R. D. Morgan, T. L. Kuther, & C. Habben (Eds.), *Life after graduate school in psychology: Insider's advice from new psychologists* (pp. 167–180). New York: Psychology Press.

Jimerson, S. R., Oakland, T., & Farrell, P. T. (2006). *The handbook of international school psychology*. Thousand Oaks: Sage.

Moffatt, C. V., & Moffatt, T. L. (1999). *How to get a teaching job*. Boston: Allyn & Bacon.

Renolds, C. B., Gutkin, T. B. (1999). *The handbook of school psychology* (3rd ed.). New York: Wiley.

Saklofske D. H., & Janzen, H. L. (1993). Contemporary issues in school psychology. In K. S. Dobson & D. J. C. Dobson (Ed.), *Professional psychology in Canada* (pp. 313–50). Seattle: Hogrefe & Huber.

Talley, R. C., Kubiszyn, T., Brassard, M., & Short, R. J. (Eds.). (1996). *Making psychologists in schools indispensable: Critical questions & emerging perspectives*. Washington, DC: American Psychological Association.

WEB RESOURCES

American Academy of Child & Adolescent Psychiatry (AACAP)
http://www.aacap.org/

Canadian Association of School Psychologists (CASP)
http://www.stemnet.nf.ca/casp/

Division 16 of the American Psychological Association (School Psychology)
http://www.indiana.edu/~div16/index.html

Division of Educational and Child Psychology of the British Psychological Society
http://www.bps.org.uk/decp/decp_home.cfm

European Agency for Development in Special Needs Education
http://www.european-agency.org/

International School Psychology Association (ISPA)
http://www.ispaweb.org

National Association of School Psychologists (NASP)
http://www.nasponline.org/

American School Counselor Association
http://www.schoolcounselor.org/

Selections from: A Complete Guide to the Advanced Study in and the Profession of School Psychology
http://www-gse.berkeley.edu/program/sp/html/spguide.html

Becoming a School Psychologist
http://www.nasponline.org/certification/becoming.aspx

CHECKLIST: IS SCHOOL PSYCHOLOGY FOR YOU?

Do you:

☐ Want to work with healthy people to improve their current functioning?
☐ Find that you are a person others feel comfortable talking to about their problems?
☐ Have good listening skills and avoid tuning out when people talk about their lives?
☐ Think you would enjoy a career providing assessment?
☐ Have an interest in applied research that can be used to better people's lives?
☐ Keep secrets and protect information that others feel is personal?
☐ Find that people consider you trustworthy?
☐ Have compassion and feel for other people when they are suffering?
☐ Have a preference for working with children, rather than adults?
☐ Have an interest in working in a school system?
☐ Prefer identifying the source of peoples' problems rather than working with them directly to resolve their problems?
☐ Enjoy working with children?
☐ Have the courage to report people who abuse children?
☐ Like to see children succeed?
☐ Enjoy developmental psychology?
☐ Enjoy watching children play?
☐ Consider children and their problems to be as important as adult problems?

Scoring: The more boxes you checked, the more likely it is that you're a good match for a school psychology career.

5 | LEGAL AND FORENSIC PSYCHOLOGY

Arriving at a crime scene with badge in hand, analyzing the scene, exploring the intimacies of the alleged offender's life, and ultimately assisting in the offender's apprehension—certainly this must be the interface of psychology and the law, right?

It is not surprising that when we think about careers in psychology and law, forensic psychology, especially criminal profiling, comes to mind. Based on our experiences, an increasing number of psychology majors express the desire to become forensic psychologists, consequently more courses are being offered in psychology and law (Bartol & Bartol, 2004; Liss, 1992). But what exactly is a forensic psychologist? Popular films like *Silence of the Lambs* and television shows like *Profiler* depict forensic psychology as an action-packed career of apprehending dangerous criminals. Understandably, these exciting dramas pique the interest of many psychology students. Although the media portrays forensic psychology and careers in psychology and law as action-packed, this is rarely the case. So, then, what is the field of psychology and law? This chapter explores career opportunities for students at all educational levels who are interested in psychology and law.

PSYCHOLOGY AND LAW: WHAT IS IT?

Psychologists study human behavior, whereas judges and attorneys study the legal system. Clearly, each discipline is its own distinct field. Yet both disciplines aim at improving the quality of human life. Psychology, for example, studies human behavior to assist people in understanding their own behavior and to maximize human functioning. The law provides a recognized set of rules to ensure that we may all coexist equally. *Psychology and law*, then, is the interface or merging of these two disciplines.

Before we discuss career options in psychology and law, let's consider a further distinction in the field: *forensic psychology*. Forensic psychology is a narrow application of psychology to the legal system. Though many undergraduate students express interest in becoming forensic psychologists with the explicit intent to engage in criminal profiling, understand that criminal profiling is a rare professional activity and very few forensic psychologists do it. Forensic psychology is a mental health discipline, whereas profiling is a criminal investigative technique (American Psychology-Law Society, 2004). Students specifically interested in the opportunity (albeit rare) to be involved in profiling are encouraged to pursue a career in law enforcement.

Although forensic psychology does not typically include profiling activities, it remains a dynamic and challenging field. A forensic psychologist is any psychologist (although usually trained in clinical or counseling psychology) who works within the legal system (Brigham, 1999) including the following settings: secure forensic units, jails, prisons, court-related services and/or community mental health centers, other specialized agencies, and private practice (providing forensic assessment and treatment services). Forensic psychologists are probably best known as practitioners; however, researchers (for example, attorney consultation, jury selection) and educators (for example, in colleges, medical schools, law enforcement agencies) can also be engaged in forensic psychology–related activities. Forensic psychology refers to any application of psychology (by a doctoral-level psychologist) to the legal system, whereas psychology and law also includes broader applications such as social/public policy, trial consultation, and law enforcement, to name just a few.

OPPORTUNITIES WITH A BACHELOR'S DEGREE

A doctorate in psychology is not required to be involved in the legal or the criminal justice system. Bachelor's-level positions that incorporate aspects of psychology and law include law enforcement positions such as police or correctional officers, probation and parole officers, and juvenile detention workers, to name a few. Few professions are as noble or vital to societal functioning as law enforcement and support. Police and correctional officers work within the legal system to enforce the law, and psychology is an important component of their job. This is particularly true today because the mentally ill are increasingly present within the criminal justice system (Condelli, Bradigan, & Holanchock, 1997; Ditton, 1999; Hodgins, 1995; Steadman, Morris, & Dennis, 1995; Torrey, 1995). Police, correctional, probation, and parole officers, and juvenile detention workers are responsible for controlling human behavior and frequently must de-escalate volatile situations. Psychology, with its understanding of human behavior, is clearly essential to their success and safety.

POLICE OFFICER

Policing is one of the most demanding and taxing of all service positions, because officers hold the ultimate responsibility of protecting our lives and property. Depending on seniority and promotional opportunities, typical activities of police officers include: maintaining regular patrols, responding to calls for service, directing traffic as needed (for example, at the scene of a fire), investigating a crime scene, or providing first aid to an accident victim (Bureau of Labor Statistics, 2008). As an officer matures through the police ranks, other opportunities develop. For example, a police officer may be promoted to detective with a primary responsibility of investigating crime scenes. Also, with experience, administrative positions (Sergeant, Captain, Chief of Police) may be available in which an officer can more directly influence or administer policing within a given community. In large police departments, officers usually are assigned to a specific type of duty. Many urban police agencies are becoming more involved in community policing, a practice in which an officer builds relationships with the citizens of local neighborhoods and mobilizes the public to help fight crime. Given the diversity of activities and the direct nature of public service, an understanding of the principles that govern human behavior (psychology) is beneficial to the law enforcement officer.

Unfortunately, salaries in law enforcement aren't commensurate with the level of professional responsibility or job-related stress; however, law enforcement officers earn respectable salaries. For example, the median salary for police officers in 2006 was $47,460 (Bureau of Labor Statistics, 2008). If you are interested in criminal profiling, remember that, with advancement, a police officer may become a detective, and detectives occasionally use profiling as an investigative technique. In addition to increased professional opportunities, promotions carry financial incentives. The median income of police and detective supervisors in 2002 was $69,310 (Bureau of Labor Statistics, 2008). As you might imagine, the primary disadvantage to policing is job-related stress (Anson & Bloom, 1988; Birmingham & Morgan, August, 2001). Other disadvantages include security and safety concerns, as well as the public's occasional negative stereotypes about police officers. Perhaps the primary advantage of law enforcement is that few professions offer such a direct opportunity for public service; rarely does anyone have as great an opportunity to influence others as does the police officer.

CORRECTIONAL OFFICER

Correctional officers are similar to police officers in that they protect public safety as well as being responsible for the safety and well-being of others; in this case, "others" refers to offenders. Once arrested, offenders are housed in jail and prison facilities, and these facilities are stressful (and dangerous) for other inmates as well as staff (Morgan, Van Haveren, & Pearson, 2002). Correctional officers maintain peace in a violent world by monitoring the activities and work assignments of inmates, searching inmates and their living quarters for contraband (such as drugs or weapons), enforcing discipline, settling disputes between conflicting inmates, and maintaining security by routinely inspecting locks, window bars, doors, and gates for malfunction or signs of tampering (Bureau of Labor Statistics, 2008).

Because correctional officers work in the offenders' living environment, it's easy to see why an understanding and healthy appreciation of psychology is beneficial. In a typical day, for example, a correctional officer might resolve a dispute between inmates, console an inmate who has lost a family member and is unable to attend the funeral, and work with inmates on correcting their behavior to increase the likelihood that they will be successful upon release. Correctional officers rely on interpersonal skills and knowledge of human functioning to navigate these difficult situations.

An advantage of this career is the opportunity to serve those typically forgotten by the rest of society as well as protect society from those too dangerous to live in our world. Another advantage is relative job security, given the increasing prison population. However, few occupational environments present as many challenges as a penitentiary. Correctional officers work in a potentially volatile environment, and although this may add a level of excitement and novelty to one's job, stress and burnout are occupational hazards (Anson & Bloom, 1988; Cheek & Miller, 1983; Harris, 1983; Lindquist & Whitehead, 1986; Morgan et al., 2002). Salaries for correctional officers are slightly less than those of police officers with a median salary of $35,760 in 2006 (range, $23,600 to $58,580); however, the job market is strong with expected growth of 16 percent by 2016 (Bureau of Labor Statistics, 2008).

PROBATION AND PAROLE OFFICER

Probation and parole officers also work with offenders within the criminal justice system, but they don't work within correctional settings, nor do they enforce the law like police officers. Rather, probation and parole officers supervise offenders while they are in the community, to ensure that they are in compliance with the stipulations of their parole or probation.

At times, probation and parole officers must enforce the law (for example, when offenders fail to comply with the conditions of their parole or probation and must be returned to prison or the court), but they also aim to assist offenders in getting the help or treatment needed to remain in the free world. These job activities necessitate an understanding of human behavior, and an appreciation of the mental health and psychological needs of offenders. The primary advantage of this career is that, while it is a law enforcement position, it typically affords greater safety than does policing; however, like all law enforcement positions, it is a stressful occupation. Probation and parole officers earn salaries comparable to other law enforcement

TABLE 5.1	PREPARATION FOR B.A.–LEVEL CAREERS RELATED TO PSYCHOLOGY OF LAW AND FORENSIC PSYCHOLOGY

Coursework

Abnormal Psychology or Psychopathology

Communications

Community Mental Health

Criminal Justice or Criminology

Interviewing, Counseling or Helping Skills

Juvenile Delinquency

Law

Professional Issues

Psychological Assessment

Psychopharmacology

Social Work

Substance Abuse

Writing

Applied Experiences: Volunteer, intern, or paid part-time positions in any of the following settings

Any mental health or criminal justice setting

Big Brother/Big Sister Programs

Boys and Girls Club

Inpatient Psychiatric Unit

Juvenile Treatment Facilities

Residential Treatment Facilities

Substance Abuse Center

Research Experiences: Experiences studying and participating in research in any of the following areas*

Antisocial Personality Disorder

Correctional Psychology

Forensic Psychology

Juvenile Delinquency

Study of Abnormal Behavior

Study of Aggressive Behavior

Substance Abuse

*Note that the content area of the research is less important than the experience itself, which enhances reasoning, quantitative, writing, and organizational skills.

officers, with a median salary of $42,500 in 2006 (range, $28,000 to $71,160; Bureau of Labor Statistics, 2006).

JUVENILE DETENTION WORKER

Like correctional officers, juvenile detention workers work within a setting of confinement, but they focus on juveniles (meaning, offenders typically younger than 18 years of age) rather than adults. Juvenile detention workers have many of the same responsibilities as correctional officers and probation or parole officers, but they may have a more desirable work setting because many hold the hope that juveniles can change. It is commonly believed in the adult criminal justice system that "nothing works," and that offenders don't change—that prisons are merely warehouses (Martinson, 1974). This belief isn't accurate because rehabilitation programs do increase the post-release functioning of inmates (Andrews et al., 1990; Andrews & Bonta, 1994; Garrett, 1985; Gendreau & Andrews, 1990; Gendreau & Ross, 1979, 1981; Lipsey, 1992), yet working with juvenile offenders who are stereotypically seen as less hardened offers the perceived potential for effective change. A primary disadvantage of juvenile detention work is coping with juvenile attitudes and impulsivity, which often results in frustration and feelings of futility. Salaries and benefits for the juvenile detention workers are generally consistent with those of correctional officers.

If you're interested in any of these careers in law enforcement, a psychology major will suit you well. Seek additional coursework in criminal justice and political science. Sociology classes in criminology, deviance, the criminal justice system, policing, and corrections can provide background knowledge that will be useful in deciding whether law enforcement is for you. Political science classes on the legal and criminal justice system will provide you with a broader understanding of how the legal and criminal justice systems operate. Also, seek practicum experiences (field experiences taken for course credit) with local police or sheriff's departments, or in the local jail to get some experience and determine whether this really is the career for you.

FORENSIC SCIENCE TECHNICIAN

Forensic science technicians work for or in conjunction with law enforcement agencies to investigate crime scenes and analyze physical evidence to solve crimes (Bureau of Labor Statistics, 2008). Forensic sciences offers an exciting career with opportunities to specialize in specific crime type evidence (for example, DNA analysis, firearm examination) with opportunities to solve crimes and testify in court as an expert witness (Bureau of Labor Statistics, 2008). Although popular media (such as *CSI*) have glamorized forensic sciences, this career choice affords law enforcement agencies a critical criminal investigation technique.

In addition to exciting professional challenges and the opportunity to work high-profile criminal cases, a career in forensic sciences affords a respectable salary with a median 2006 income of $45,323 (Bureau of Labor Statistics, 2008). Also, forensic sciences is a growing profession with employment opportunities predicted to grow much faster than average through 2016 (Bureau of Labor Statistics, 2008). Disadvantages of this career include job stress resulting from law enforcement work (law enforcement is consistently rated as one of the most stressful occupations), testifying as an expert witness, high case loads, and exposure to emotionally disturbing evidence (for example, decomposed or severely traumatized bodies).

OPPORTUNITIES WITH A GRADUATE DEGREE

At the graduate level, there are a variety of career opportunities in psychology and law. Practitioners may conduct forensic assessments, provide treatment services for offenders, or assist law enforcement officers. Research psychologists may seek opportunities to be directly involved in the legal system through trial consultation, or may conduct research that impacts the legal system (for example, research about children's developmental level and their ability to participate in court proceedings). Psychologists of any discipline (such as counseling/clinical, developmental, social, or cognitive) may pursue political careers. Psychologists have been elected to both federal and state legislative bodies (Sullivan, 2001), and opportunities for psychologists to be active in public policy have never been greater. The doctoral degree provides even greater flexibility for those seeking careers in psychology and the law. More specifically, the Ph.D. in psychology (typically in counseling or clinical psychology) affords much greater flexibility in forensic psychology than does the masters degree.

CORRECTIONAL PSYCHOLOGY

As the prison population continues to rise (Boothby & Clements, 2001; Irwin, 1996), correctional psychology is becoming an increasingly frequent career option for many psychologists with forensic interests. In fact, psychologists have been encouraged to seek employment in correctional facilities (Hawk, 1997) and prison and jail settings may become leading employers of psychologists, especially if the current incarceration rate continues to climb. Correctional psychologists report enjoying their jobs (Boothby & Clements, 2001; Ferrell, Morgan, & Winterowd, 2000); however, working in correctional environments is stressful for both inmates (Hassine, 1996; Toch, 1992) and staff (see Morgan et al., 2002), including health professionals (Brodsky, 1982; Inwald, 1982). Nevertheless, correctional mental health can be an enjoyable and rewarding career choice through its opportunity to make a difference with an underrepresented population.

OPTIONS FOR MASTERS DEGREE HOLDERS.   Although the doctorate in psychology is the entry-level degree for many psychology and law-related activities, several options exist for graduates with masters degrees, particularly in forensic psychology. Masters degree holders in clinical and counseling psychology frequently work as treatment providers for offenders in institutional or correctional settings, such as prisons (for example, Boothby & Clements, 2000; Morgan, Winterowd, & Ferrell, 1999). Such correctional settings provide basic mental health services to all inmates and include both assessment and treatment services that focus on symptom reduction and coping within the correctional environment (Morgan, 2002). The hiring of masters-level clinicians is debated (for example, Morgan et al., 1999), but it remains a common practice, particularly for state correctional systems, and affords mental health professionals with job security.

LEGAL AND FORENSIC PSYCHOLOGY   65

An important benefit of correctional mental health is that the salaries are slightly higher than similar entry-level positions in non-correctional settings. While the median salary for a masters-level clinician in 2002 was approximately $32,618 annually (Singleton, Tate, & Kohout, 2003), in corrections, this salary jumps to an average of approximately $40,000 and over (Boothby & Clements, 2000). No specific training beyond psychotherapy and assessment skills is generally required to secure employment in a correctional facility; however, any practicum experience working with offenders or other difficult clients (for example, clients mandated to attend treatment, psychiatric inpatients) is beneficial, even recommended.

OPTIONS FOR DOCTORAL DEGREE HOLDERS.   Similar to masters-level clinicians, doctoral-level psychologists in correctional facilities typically are involved in direct service (Boothby & Clements, 2000), but doctoral-level providers have more opportunities to become involved in rehabilitative efforts through program development (Morgan et al., 1999). In other words, masters-level correctional mental health professionals frequently engage in service delivery, while doctoral-level providers may become more involved in developing specialized programs for offenders and evaluating the effectiveness of these programs. Doctoral-level psychologists in correctional settings generally are compensated well for their time, with a substantial benefits package and a 40-hour work week. Job security is an advantage as the U.S. prison population continues to increase with no slow-down in site. The primary disadvantages of correctional mental health are job-related stress and a potential feeling of dissociation from correctional administrators who have a goal of incarceration (by necessity) as opposed to the rehabilitative preference of most mental health professionals (Morgan et al., 1999).

A scan of classified ads (for example, *The Monitor on Psychology*) indicates that correctional psychology positions are readily available and have been for several years. Whereas masters-level clinicians earn on average $40,000 in correctional settings, their doctoral-level counterparts earn significantly more. In the Federal Bureau of Prisons, for which the doctoral degree is the entry-level degree, the starting salary is approximately $42,000, with an average salary of $61,800 (Boothby & Clements, 2000). Employment in state correctional facilities appears to provide a slightly lower average income for doctoral-level providers ($53,400); however, it was recently noted that California was offering a salary nearing six figures for entry-level psychology positions. No specialized experience beyond doctoral training is required for employment as a correctional psychologist. Nevertheless, field experience is always a plus. If you're interested in this career, consider pursuing internship or postdoctoral experiences in correctional settings (for example, the Federal Bureau of Prisons currently have nine accredited doctoral-level internship sites) or secure forensic institutions.

FORENSIC EXAMINER

Many forensic psychologists seek employment opportunities conducting forensic examinations. In fact, many doctoral-level interns apply to forensic sites to conduct criminal evaluations such as sanity evaluations (Ax & Morgan, 2002). Masters- and doctoral-level psychologists also conduct examinations for other types of court cases, including divorce and child custody, family and children's courts, civil commitment, personal injury cases, and anti-discrimination and entitlement laws (Ackerman, 1999; Melton, Petrila, Poythress, Slobogin, & Lyons, 2007).

Because of such high-profile cases as John Hinckley or the Unabomber, most students are familiar with psychologists' involvement in criminal cases. In criminal cases, psychologists may be asked to assess a defendant's competency to stand trial or mental state at the time of the alleged offense (evaluating the insanity plea); however, other issues may be raised regarding a defendant's competency during the criminal justice process. For example, a defendant's competency to consent to search or seizure, to confess, to plead guilty, to waive the right to counsel, to refuse an insanity defense, to testify, and to be sentenced and executed may also be questioned. (Several sources provide much greater detail on the nature and purpose of these evaluations, including Huss, 2001; Melton et al., 2007.)

Forensic psychologists are also heavily involved in noncriminal cases. Child custody evaluations and personal injury assessments are common forms of noncriminal forensic work. These cases differ from criminal cases in that a person's liberty is not in jeopardy; instead, a plaintiff seeks to obtain something that is in dispute (for example, custody of children, financial compensation for damages in personal injury suits). Child custody evaluations are often requested in divorce proceedings. When this occurs, a psychologist is often asked to assist the court by conducting a child custody evaluation. Such evaluations are requested in approximately 10 percent of custody hearings with the aim of assisting the court by investigating the facts that would be relevant to a judge or jury making a custody decision (Melton et al., 2007).

Psychologists are becoming increasingly involved in personal injury litigation cases (Butcher & Miller, 1999). Personal injury cases include any situation where a person is injured either physically or psychologically, and compensation for damages are sought (Ackerman, 1999). Worker's compensation cases, medical malpractice suits, and sexual harassment cases are just a few of the examples of personal injury cases where a psychological evaluation may be requested as part of the legal process. The role of the psychologist in personal injury cases, in general, is to assist the court in determining if a mental injury occurred as a result of some specific incident. This evaluation is similar to the insanity evaluation, because the examiner conducts a retrospective study (Melton et al., 2007); that is, the examiner determines the plaintiff's mental functioning before and after said incident.

In what setting do forensic examiners work? Many are in private practice, and some criminal forensic psychologists work in state institutions such as secure units, community mental health centers, and hospitals. Entry-level psychologists providing forensic services in hospitals and community settings may begin at approximately $40,000 annually, but salaries tend to vary by state and jurisdiction (American Psychology-Law Society, 2004). Forensic psychologists in private practice typically bill between $100 and $300 per hour (American Psychology-Law Society, 2004), but are without the benefit of a steady income. The primary advantages of forensic evaluation are the job satisfaction that most evaluators experience and the potential to earn a relatively lucrative income. One disadvantage of this career path is the necessity for advanced training beyond academic coursework, such as internship and/or postdoctoral training that specializes in forensic assessments. Another disadvantage is the potential for lawsuits and ethics complaints (for example, Kirkland & Kirkland, 2001) filed against forensic examiners. Even frivolous lawsuits or ethics complaints can be costly in terms of finances, time, stress, and professional image.

In order to conduct forensic evaluations, you must receive training in psychological assessment (for example, personality assessment, intellectual assessment, or mental status examinations), as well as specialized training in forensic issues. Most forensic psychologists receive their training during the predoctoral internship (a field experience obtained while pursuing the doctoral degree) or in specialized postdoctoral training programs where the focus is specific to forensic psychology. There are very few training programs that provide specialized training in forensic psychology practice, so field experience in the form of predoctoral and postdoctoral internships is essential. Some masters-level practitioners receive training in assessment on the job; however, without a doctoral degree and license, independent practice is not possible in most states.

POLICE PSYCHOLOGY

Police psychology has become increasingly necessary in law enforcement (Birmingham & Morgan, 2001) despite law enforcement officers' sometimes negative perceptions towards such services (Max, 2000). Police psychologists provide a variety of services, including: management consultation (consulting on administrative decision making that has agency-wide implications); pre-employment psychological assessments and fitness-for-duty evaluations (evaluations to help determine if a person is suitable for law enforcement work or fit for continued duty); special unit evaluations (assessments to assist with promotional decisions for specialized police assignments such as Special Weapons and Tactics [SWAT], Tactical Response Teams [TRT], and Hostage Negotiation Teams [HNT]); hostage negotiation team consultations (consulting and assisting with hostage negotiations); deadly force incident investigations (assisting with investigations regarding the appropriateness of an officer's use of deadly force); field consultation such as assisting an officer in the apprehension or security of a mentally ill person (Super, 1999); and, less frequently, investigative activities (Bartol, 1996), although investigative activities, such as criminal profiling, appear to be increasing (Bartol & Bartol, 2004).

Stress is a prevalent problem in law enforcement (Anson & Bloom, 1988; Birmingham & Morgan, 2001) and police psychologists provide counseling services to help officers cope with their stress. The most common activity of police psychologists is to provide pre-employment evaluations (Super, 1999). Pre-employment evaluations are requested to determine if would-be officers have the disposition and personality style to cope with stress and serve in the capacity of law enforcer. Typically, police psychologists hold doctoral degrees and may be consultants to law enforcement agencies or may be employed (often actually sworn in as law enforcement officers) by an agency (Bartol, 1996). Entry-level salaries appear commensurate with other entry-level doctoral psychology positions. As with other forensic psychology positions, if you're interested in police psychology, seek specialized training through predoctoral internships or postdoctoral training, because there are few formal opportunities for training in police psychology during graduate school.

TRIAL CONSULTANT

Yet another potential occupational opportunity exists in trial consultation, and is of equal interest for psychological practitioners and other psychologists. In fact, social and cognitive psychologists have particular skills and expertise that translate well to courtroom consultations (American Psychology-Law Society, 2005). *Trial consultation* refers to any service provided to assist in the process of a trial (for example, focus group research; exploratory focus groups; experimental, quasi-experimental, and comparative studies; mock trials; or pretrial case analysis) (Andrews, 2005). Trial consultations usually include case analysis, review of reports and forensic evidence, identification of expert witnesses, development of examination (direct and cross) strategies, and preparation of expert and lay witnesses for testifying (Drogin & Barrett, 2007) with a primary goal of developing a better understanding how the judge or jury will understand and process information (Andrews, 2005).

A trial consultant may conduct research that influences trial process, such as that regarding decision making by the trier-of-fact (meaning, judge or jury), the impact of evidentiary psycholegal research, and eyewitness identification and recall (American Psychology-Law Society, 2004; Andrews, 2005; Huss, 2001). In addition to research, psychologists may advise attorneys regarding jury selection and the effects of courtroom trial procedures on jury decision making (Andrews, 2005; Huss, 2001). For example, trial consultants often use jury simulations or mock jurors (Andrews, 2005; Huss, 2001) to assist attorneys in developing strategies for jury selection, as well as trial strategy itself. Trial consultation occurs in both criminal and civil trials, and although high-profile cases such as the tobacco settlement bring notoriety to this profession, it appears to remain a relatively infrequent occupational consideration for psychologists in training.

The largest advantage of a career as a trial consultant is the potential income; however, it may be difficult initially to establish yourself in the private industry, limiting income in the early years of a career as a trial consultant. Nevertheless, psychologists with appropriate experience and legal connections who are fortunate enough to be hired for high-profile cases have been known to earn incomes in excess of $1,000,000 annually. Remember that this is the high end of the salary spectrum; entry-level positions appear comparable to other entry-level psychological positions. As in most careers, doctoral degrees afford additional opportunities and autonomy over masters degrees.

POLITICS

A bachelor's degree in psychology may enable you to become involved in the political process in a limited fashion. Masters degrees provide similar opportunities; and the Ph.D. provides many more. Psychologists are increasingly politically aware and active. In fact, by 2004, 17 psychologists were serving as United States legislators, 12 in state legislatures, and 5 in Congress (Sullivan, 2005). Although this represents a significant improvement over psychologists' political contributions of the past, much work is yet to be done—or, stated more provocatively, *must* be done. Considering the social and public-policy implications of our work, it is not simply an opportunity; rather, it is our duty, and psychologists should seek to apply the techniques of their trade to meet the larger public needs (DeLeon, 1988). Just as professional (clinical, counseling, or school) psychologists seek to achieve the betterment of the client, so can the political psychologist use psychological principals to the betterment of the public.

What do psychologists do in politics? They may assist in developing briefs, conduct psycholegal research, or become involved in planning strategies and drafting laws. To prepare psychologists for politics, the American Psychological Association developed a congressional fellowship program in 1974. The purpose of this fellowship program is to provide "psychologists with an invaluable public policy learning experience, to contribute to the more effective use of psychological knowledge in government, and to broaden awareness about the value of psychology-government interaction among psychologists and within the federal government" (American Psychology-Law Society, 2005). Psychologists who enroll in this training program spend one year assigned to a member of Congress or a congressional committee and have the opportunity to perform such tasks as assisting in congressional hearings and debates or preparing briefs (American Psychology Association, 2005). Initially, this program was geared exclusively to entry-level psychologists; however, it now targets advanced (senior-level) psychologists as well (Fowler, 1996).

Salaries of psychologists holding political positions are governed by the United States or the state they represent, and vary accordingly. On the high end, a United States senator earns $154,700 (Bureau of Labor Statistics, 2004). Salaries of political employees vary according to level of government and jurisdiction. Entry-level psychologist fellows in the American Psychological Association fellowship program earn approximately $60,000, with the range increasing to $75,000 depending on level of experience (American Psychological Association, 2008). In addition, fellows receive the cost of relocation and/or travel expenses during the fellowship year. Although any United States citizen has the opportunity for political involvement, specialized training such as that provided by the American Psychological Association fellowship program affords psychologists specialized knowledge and experience that is directly applicable to their political interests.

Throughout this chapter we've examined many opportunities for those who are interested in the interface of psychology and law at both the baccalaureate-degree or graduate-degree levels. Crime and social problems remain. Psychologists' specialized training as scientists, and in many cases practitioners, offers opportunities for combating these problems. In many cases, no additional training beyond the traditionally academic is necessary. Furthermore, many of the career options described here offer job security and salaries competitive with comparable positions. While psychology and law rarely includes activities such as analyzing a crime scene or conducting profile analyses, it does afford exciting and rewarding career options.

Suggested Readings

American Psychology-Law Society. (2005). *Careers in psychology and law: Subspecialties in psychology and law: A closer look*. Retrieved July 28, 2008 at http://www.unl.edu/ap-ls/student/careers_closerlook.html.

American Psychology-Law Society. (2004). *Careers in psychology and law: A guide for prospective students*. Retrieved July 28, 2008 at http://www.ap-ls.org/students/careers%20in%20psychology.pdf.

Andrews, C. K. (2005). Trial consulting: Moving psychology into the courtroom. In R. D. Morgan, T. L. Kuther, & C. J. Habben (Eds.), *Life after graduate school in psychology: Insider's advice from new psychologists*. New York: Psychology Press.

Fagan, T., & Ax, R. K. (2003). *Correctional mental health handbook*. Thousand Oaks: Sage.

Huss, M. T. (2001). Psychology and law, now and in the next century: The promise of an emerging area of psychology. In J. S. Halonen & S. F. Davis (Eds.), *The many faces of psychological research in the 21st century*. Society for the Teaching of Psychology: retrieved from http://teachpsych.org/resources/e-books/faces/script/Ch11.htm.

Kuther, T. L. (2004). *Your career in psychology: Psychology and the law*. Belmont, CA: Wadsworth.

Melton, G. B., Petrila, J., Poythress, N. G., & Slobogin, C., Lyons, P. M. (2007). *Psychological evaluations for the courts: A handbook for mental health professionals and lawyers* (3rd ed.). New York: Guilford Press.

Stern, R. (1988). *Law enforcement careers: A complete guide from application to employment*. Tarzana, CA: Lawman Press.

Weiner, I. B. & Hess, A. K. (2006). *The handbook of forensic psychology* (3rd ed.). New York: Wiley.

WEB RESOURCES

American Psychology-Law Society
http://www.unl.edu/ap-ls/

American Society of Trial Consultants
http://www.astcweb.org

Federal Bureau of Prisons
http://www.bop.gov/

Corrections Connection
http://www.corrections.com/

Law and Society Association
http://www.lawandsociety.org/

Mental Health in Corrections Consortium
http://www.forest.edu/mhcca/index.html

National Criminal Justice Reference Service
http://www.ncjrs.org/

National Institute of Corrections
http://www.nicic.org/

National Institute of Justice
http://www.ojp.usdoj.gov/nij/

Police stress
http://www.policefamilies.com/

Police Psychology Online
http://www.policepsych.com

Checklist: Is Legal or Forensic Psychology for You?

Do you:

- ☐ Enjoy shows like *Law and Order*, *CSI*, or *COPS*?
- ☐ Have an interest in politics?
- ☐ Think offenders have rights and should be treated justly and fairly?
- ☐ Think some people are so mentally ill that they shouldn't be punished for the bad things they do?
- ☐ Think you could try to help someone who murdered or raped someone?
- ☐ Think you could try to help someone who abused a child?
- ☐ Like solving puzzles?
- ☐ Like reading about criminal activity in your local newspaper?
- ☐ Like reading biographies about high profile criminals?
- ☐ Think you would like to work in a prison?
- ☐ Like studying about mental illness?
- ☐ Like a good debate?
- ☐ Like people to challenge your thoughts and opinions?
- ☐ Like to write?

Scoring: The more boxes you checked, the more likely it is that legal or forensic psychology is for you.

In 2005, Hurricane Katrina devastated New Orleans and parts of Mississippi, generating feelings of chaos, anxiety, fear, and anger among those in these areas and in the country as a whole. These traumatic events raised health concerns of U.S. citizens effects not only those directly traumatized by the hurricane, but also those exposed to toxins and disease in relief efforts. How do people cope with such life-altering medical situations? What interventions are helpful for those suffering medical complications from disasters, injuries, or other medical hardships? Questions such as these are at the heart of health psychology.

HEALTH PSYCHOLOGY

Health psychology is the study of psychological influences on health, why people become ill, and how people respond when they become ill, as well as the application of preventive strategies and interventions aimed at helping people maintain or improve their health (Taylor, 1999). Health psychologists study the interactive influences of biological, behavioral, and social factors on health and illness (American Psychological Association Division 38, n.d.). In other words, health psychologists examine how our emotions, thoughts, behaviors, and social interactions influence our physical well-being (meaning, health and wellness) and response to illness. Health psychologists study ways to promote healthy behavior (for example help people stop smoking, urge use of sun block, and promote healthy eating). They also study how to prevent and treat illnesses through the use of behavioral management, stress management, and coping techniques. What are the effects of stress? Can stress lead to illness? Health psychologists study the role of psychological and social factors, like stress and social support, in the development of disease.

Before proceeding with our discussion of careers in health psychology, let's first clear up some potentially confusing terminology. Health psychology is a subfield of psychology and has frequently been referred to as *behavioral medicine, medical psychology*, and *psychosomatic medicine*; however, these terms are neither accurate nor appropriate (Belar & Deardorff, 1995). *Behavioral medicine* is the most commonly used alternative term, but it is an interdisciplinary term (including behavioral and biomedical science); psychologists practice psychology, not behavioral medicine (Belar & Deardorff, 1995). Thus, *health psychology* is the most appropriate term for this specialized field and it will be used throughout this chapter.

OPPORTUNITIES WITH A BACHELOR'S DEGREE

If you are interested in health psychology, you'll be glad to know that there are many opportunities for bachelor's degree holders to work in rewarding careers that challenge them to use their general training in psychology as well as specialized knowledge in health psychology. Examples of such careers include recreational therapist, occupational therapy assistant, physical therapy assistant, and health educator.

RECREATIONAL THERAPIST

Recreational therapists provide treatment and recreational activities to individuals with physical or emotional disabilities in a variety of settings, including medical settings, community-based programs (for example, parks and recreation, special education programs for students, adult living programs, community mental health centers), and prisons (Bureau of Labor Statistics, 2008). Recreational therapists are different from recreational workers. Recreational therapists provide treatment services to assist individuals with disabilities or problems and deficits, whereas recreational workers generally work with healthy and/or disabled individuals with emphasis on developing interests rather than treating problems.

Recreational therapists assess and treat individuals with physical or psychological problems. They use standardized assessments and observations, medical records, and collateral information to assess clients' problems and develop treatment strategies targeting physical, mental, or emotional well-being of clients (Bureau of Labor Statistics, 2008). Typical treatment activities include: arts and crafts, animals (meaning, pet therapy), gardening, sports, games, dance and movement, drama, music, and community outings, as well as specific strategies such as stress management and relaxation techniques (Bureau of Labor Statistics, 2008). Recreational therapists frequently are employed in hospitals, nursing homes, community-based programs such as assisted living and outpatient physical and psychiatric rehabilitation facilities, residential and correctional centers, adult daycare facilities, and social service agencies (Bureau of Labor Statistics, 2008).

The median salary for recreational therapists in 2006 was $34,990; however, growth in the field has slowed in recent years (Bureau of Labor Statistics, 2008). Employment opportunities may increase in the future given the rapidly increasing number of aging adults; thus, recreational therapy will remain a viable profession for many. Another benefit of this profession is the opportunity for advancement. Therapists may grow weary of the therapeutic contact and physical energy required to provide recreational therapy on a daily basis, particularly as they themselves age; however, there are opportunities within this profession to advance to supervisory positions or to pursue teaching interests in the field (Bureau of Labor Statistics, 2008). Recreational therapists typically have a bachelor's degree. Psychology's emphasis on understanding behavior, coupled with training in therapeutic recreation, will suit you well in this career.

OCCUPATIONAL THERAPY ASSISTANT

Occupational therapy assistants help occupational therapists provide rehabilitative services to patients with physical, developmental, or psychological impairments (Bureau of Labor Statistics, 2008). Occupational therapy assistants are not limited to working with patients who are attempting to re-enter the labor force; rather, this work is much broader and focuses on any aspect of a patient's life (for example, developing the skills necessary for independent living such as cooking, cleaning, and accessing transportation). Aides to occupational therapists are intimately involved with all aspects of a patient's rehabilitation from disabilities caused by injuries (for example, from an automobile accident); they also help individuals with developmental disabilities (such as mental retardation) to acquire skills for independent living.

Occupational therapy assistants may work with occupational therapists in hospitals, outpatient clinics, and offices. The hours may vary if working in a private medical office to include evenings or weekends in order to be flexible with client schedules; however, in clinics and hospital settings the hours tend to be more traditional (8 A.M. to 5 P.M.). The job outlook for occupational therapy assistants is outstanding with the market for occupational therapists expected to grow more rapidly than the average job over the next eight years (Bureau of Labor Statistics, 2008). Salaries of occupational therapy assistants are competitive, with a median salary of $42,060 (Bureau of Labor Statistics, 2008). One disadvantage of this career choice is the physical demand. Occupational therapy assistants must be strong enough to help lift patients (including overweight patients) as well as to stand, kneel, bend, stoop, and move from station to station for long periods.

Note that a bachelor's degree is not sufficient to be an occupational therapy assistant; the completion of a certificate in occupational therapy is also required (Bureau of Labor Statistics, 2008). It may be advisable to complete two years of college in a field such as psychology, and then work toward the completion of an occupational therapy assistance certificate program. Most states regulate this career option and occupational therapy assistants must pass a national certification examination before being appropriately credentialed to practice. (For more information, consult the American Occupational Therapy Association at http:// www.aota.org.)

Physical Therapy Assistant

A career option that is related to occupational therapy assistant is the physical therapy assistant. Physical therapy assistants assist physical therapists in the provision of treatments and interventions for individuals suffering pain, loss of mobility, or other physical disabilities (Bureau of Labor Statistics, 2008). Although the work is demanding, including necessity of core body strength to assist or physically move patients with mobility issues, this career choice offers hands-on treatment that can be very rewarding. Like the occupational therapist assistant, this occupation may require the attainment of a license as a physical therapist; however, much of the training includes "on-the-job" training (Bureau of Labor Statistics, 2008); thus, a graduate with a major or minor in psychology, with an emphasis on health psychology-related coursework, will be very marketable with specialized training to meet the emotional and motivational needs of patients requiring physical therapy.

The occupational outlook for students interested in a career as a physical therapy assistant is promising as the field is expected to grow much more rapidly than the average job (Bureau of Labor Statistics, 2008). Additionally, income levels are very competitive, with a 2006 median income of $41,360, with the middle 50 percent of employees earning between $33,840 and $49,010 (Bureau of Labor Statistics, 2008).

Health Educator

Health educators educate individuals and communities about healthy lifestyles and wellness (Bureau of Labor Statistics, 2008). In proving education and information, health educators work to prevent illnesses and increase healthy lifestyles. For example, health educators will share knowledge and information on health-related issues such as diet and nutrition, sleep and exercise hygiene, problem behaviors (for example, risky behaviors such as promiscuous sexual behavior, substance abuse), and general health hygiene (for example, dental care, self-examinations for breast or testicular cancer, medical check-ups). Health educators identify needs, with particular attention to cultural groups (Bureau of Labor Statistics, 2008) that may be lacking resources such as geriatric populations, low-income families, or

TABLE 6.1 | PREPARATION FOR BA–LEVEL CAREERS RELATED TO HEALTH PSYCHOLOGY

Coursework
> Abnormal Psychology or Psychopathology
> Anatomy
> Biology
> Epidemiology
> Health (courses in health and wellness at introductory and advanced levels)
> Health Education
> Health Psychology
> Interviewing, Counseling, or Helping Skills
> Mathematics
> Substance Abuse
> Writing

Applied Experiences: Volunteer, intern/practica, or paid part-time positions in any of the following settings
> Any medical setting
> Burn Unit
> Rehabilitation Unit
> University Wellness Center
> Health/Lifestyle Center
> Physical/Occupational Therapy Clinic

Research Experiences: Experiences studying and participating in research in any of the following areas*
> Health Psychology
> Wellness
> Health behaviors such as smoking, obesity
> At-risk behaviors such as unsafe sex, substance abuse
> Sleep disorders
> Behavioral decision making or health decision making

*Note that the content area of the research is less important than the experience itself, which enhances reasoning, quantitative, writing, and organizational skills.

minorities that may be lacking in resources. Health educators will then design and implement educational programs (for example, classes, promotional pamphlets, community activities) to meet the health-related informational need.

A career as a health educator affords many exciting opportunities, including a diverse work setting as health educators typically transition between office and individual or group field placement settings (for example, individual home, community center). A career in health education can also be very rewarding, both professionally and personally, with an opportunity to reach and help marginalized and underserved populations. Additionally, a career in health education necessitates creativity in developing and implementing programs that will impact behavior. Although training and education in health education is likely a prerequisite for a career in health education, a dual major (or minor) in psychology can also make one very competitive. Understanding cultural differences, including attitudes and principles of behavior change, will serve one well when educating and confronting resistance to change that is inevitable when attempting to change behavior. Salary in health education is another benefit, with a median 2006 income of $41,330 (Bureau of Labor Statistics, 2008) and the middle 50 percent earning between $31,300 and $56,580. Finally, health education is a growing industry with a professional growth rate that is expected to be much higher than the average career/job.

Disadvantages to a career as a health educator include an unstable schedule, as many programs will need to be implemented during evening and weekend hours to avoid school and work demands. Additionally, given the nature of the work, some of the targeted clientele, and grassroots-level work, some of the homes and/or community centers encountered are impoverished and lacking in cleanliness; however, such settings offer opportunities for immediate progress.

CAREER AS A HEALTH PSYCHOLOGIST

The specialized nature of a career in health psychology requires training at the doctoral level (meaning, completion of a Ph.D. or Psy.D. program). Health psychologists earn a doctoral degree in psychology, typically clinical or counseling psychology (Belar, 1997), and specialize in health psychology during internship and postdoctoral training.

Because scientific knowledge in health psychology has experienced consider-able growth in the past two decades, there are many career opportunities for health psychologists and the potential to expand clinical practice in this area is dramatic (Belar et al., 2001). In fact, the management of health and disease is one of the most rapidly growing research and practice specialties in professional psychology (Levant et al., 2001). Health psychologists are employed in a myriad of settings, and the professional activities in which they engage often are determined by the setting in which they work. Health psychologists may engage in applied activities (such as providing psychological services for the prevention or treatment of health-related problems and behaviors) or research and academic activities (such as conducting research to investigate health-related issues and behaviors or teaching at a university). Health psychologists are also found in medical settings, such as primary care programs, inpatient medical units, medical schools, and specialized healthcare programs (for example, pain management centers, long-term care facilities, or rehabilitation centers). Let's take a closer look at the settings and activities in which health psychologists engage.

ACADEMIC AND RESEARCH SETTINGS

In academia and research settings, health psychologists teach, conduct research to understand and treat illnesses, and develop preventive and treatment programs to avoid or reduce health-related problems and concerns. Like other professors, health psychologists in academia teach undergraduate and graduate students about the field, and conduct research to expand the field.

Although health psychologists engaged in research are not directly involved in client care, their work often holds profound implications for the care that clients receive. Research conducted by health psychologists provides practitioners with information about lifestyle and personality factors as well as the psychosocial factors that influence health (Sarafino, 2002). Researchers develop and evaluate therapeutic programs aimed at improving healthy functioning or reducing the likelihood of illness (for example, smoking cessation programs), as well as treating existing conditions (for example, stress-reduction programs for persons with coronary heart disease). Thus, researchers have a hand in influencing the health and care of today's medical patient.

Health psychologists who focus on program development actively work to create and assess the efficacy of wellness and health-related programs such as smoking cessation programs, healthy eating and exercising programs, and stress-management programs, to name just a few. The goals of these programs are to increase the well-being and health of individuals in high-risk groups (for example, patients with high blood pressure) or those actively engaged in risky behaviors (for example, smokers).

The benefits and pitfalls of an academic career as well as the credentials and job responsibilities of this career are covered in Chapter 13. We will note here that health psychologists tend to have specialized training which frequently includes postdoctoral experience, which can lead to slightly higher salaries than most other assistant professors.

SERVICE DELIVERY SETTINGS

Health psychology service providers are employed in hospitals, long-term care facilities, rehabilitation centers, medical schools, or private practice. In each of these settings, health psychologists provide assessment and intervention services and usually collaborate with other healthcare professionals such as physicians, dentists, nurses, physician's assistants, dietitians, social workers, pharmacists, physical and occupational therapists, and chaplains (Committee on Education and Training, Division 38, n.d.) in an effort to provide comprehensive and holistic healthcare. The clinical activities of health psychologists generally include assessment activities or prevention/intervention services.

Health psychologists often conduct assessments in conjunction with other medical professionals to determine the etiology (cause of) and correlates of healthy living and health-related problems (Taylor, 1999). Assessments conducted by health psychologists may include cognitive and/or behavioral assessments, psychophysical assessments, personality assessments, demographic surveys and clinical interviews, and other clinical protocols (Committee on Education and Training, Division 38, n.d.).

Treatment services, on the other hand, refers to prevention or intervention services. The goal of prevention is to help people improve their lifestyles and avoid major illnesses or health complications, whereas interventions target existing health-related problems with a focus on helping people cope with or adjust to health-related problems (Kaplan, Sallis, & Patterson, 1993). Examples of preventive care are programs aimed at educating at-risk populations (for example, the "Just Say No to Drugs" program) or the general population about the importance of lifestyle improvements (for example, programs advocating the health benefits of exercise and a proper nutritional diet). Examples of interventions include stress management for medical patients with high blood pressure and pain management for persons who have been injured in an accident. Health psychologists not only design and implement treatment strategies but also conduct research to assess the effectiveness of prevention and intervention programs.

The benefits of a career in health psychology service delivery may include a slightly elevated salary compared to other psychologists, especially when working in medical settings, as well as the opportunity to influence directly the quality of life and wellness of clients in a relatively short period of time (treatment gains in health psychology may be slightly more rapid than treatment gains by psychologists treating other problems or concerns such as severe mental illness). A benefit of becoming a health psychologist in private practice or developing a consulting career is the flexibility in scheduling clients. One limitation of a career choice in health psychology service delivery is the occasional experience of not being well-received by the medical community, where the M.D. is the preferred degree (compared to the Ph.D. or Psy.D. for psychologists). However, psychologists' contributions to wellness and healthy living are becoming increasingly recognized, particularly as the biopsychosocial model of health and illness becomes more widely accepted within the medical community (Sarafino, 2002).

PUBLIC HEALTH SETTINGS

Health psychologists also pursue careers in public health. Psychologists in public health settings will likely be involved in research of health issues, teaching and training future professionals, public health practice and service provision, or consulting with health organizations, professionals, and political leaders (Baskin, 2005). For example, psychologists in public health work may be involved in developing or evaluating programs for public health organizations, or may pursue involvement in social policy. Program developers, as we've discussed, are responsible for developing and implementing health-related programs in communities to promote wellness and healthy living or to treat health-related problems or concerns. Community-based AIDS education and support programs are an example of the type of work in which program developers may be involved. Health psychologists in social policy positions, on the other hand, spend their time developing and drafting legal statutes and proposals in an effort to create federal or state legislation that promotes wellness and health. An example of such legislation is the requirement that tobacco products carry warning labels on their packaging to warn customers of the health risks associated with tobacco products.

A primary benefit of seeking employment as a health psychologist in public health is the opportunity to influence directly the services available to communities and persons in need. Unfortunately, the time to develop and implement services can be extensive, and that can be very frustrating when there are people in need or there is an urgent problem to be addressed. Salaries in public health are comparable to other psychology-related positions discussed in this text. (For more information on policy-related careers, see Chapter 12.)

The field of health psychology offers knowledge and training that is relevant at both the bachelor's and graduate levels. At the bachelor's level, careers tend to be multi-disciplinary. If you are interested in pursuing a health-related position with your baccalaureate degree, supplement your academic training in psychology with courses in other health areas such as health education, nutrition, and safety. Careers at the doctoral level are more specialized. If you are considering a graduate-level career in health psychology, pursue generalist training during graduate school (meaning, clinical or counseling psychology programs), followed by specialized training in health psychology during internship and/or postdoctoral work.

SUGGESTED READINGS

Baskin, M. L. (2005). Public health: Career opportunities for psychologists in public health. In R. D. Morgan, T. L. Kuther, & C. J. Habben (Eds.), *Life after graduate school in psychology: Insider's advice from new psychologists*. New York: Psychology Press.

Belar, C. D., & Deardorff, W. W. (1995). *Clinical health psychology in medical settings: A practitioner's guidebook*. Washington, DC: American Psychological Association.

Boll, T. J., Johnson, S. B., Perry, N., & Rozensky, R. H. (2002). *Handbook of clinical health psychology: Volume 1. Medical disorders and behavioral applications*. Washington, DC: American Psychological Association.

Cohen, L., McChargue, D., & Collins, E. (2003). *The health psychology handbook: Practical issues for the behavioral medicine specialist*. Thousand Oaks, CA: Sage.

WEB RESOURCES

American Psychological Association, Division of Health Psychology (Division 38)
http://www.health-psych.org/

Society of Behavioral Medicine
http://www.sbm.org/

Health Psychology and Rehabilitation
http://www.healthpsych.com/

The Health Psychology Network
http://www.healthpsychology.net/

Careers in Health Psychology
http://www.wcupa.edu/_ACADEMICS/sch_cas.psy/Career_Paths/Health/Career02.htm

CHECKLIST: IS HEALTH PSYCHOLOGY FOR YOU?

Do you:

☐ Want to work in a medical setting?
☐ Want to better understand medical problems?
☐ Want to conduct research with the aim of helping people with health problems?
☐ Enjoy reading about health problems or concerns?
☐ Find satisfaction in the recent tobacco settlements?
☐ Want to help people live healthier lives?
☐ Want to understand the effects of stress and lifestyle choices on health?
☐ Have interest in the growing health concerns across the globe?
☐ Want to understand how the mind influences the body?

Scoring: The more boxes you checked, the more likely it is that health or sport psychology is a good match for you.

SPORT PSYCHOLOGY | CHAPTER 7

The events of September 11, 2001 created chaos in New York City and Washington, D.C., as well as fear, anxiety, anger, and a myriad of other feelings and emotions for all citizens of the United States. Following the terrorist attacks on New York and Washington in 2001, all major sporting events were canceled in the days that followed, and debate ensued about the role of athletics for morale and patriotism of U.S. citizens (for example, do sports—watching and playing—help us deal with life-altering events and stressors?). Three days later the first Major League Baseball games were held. How did professional athletes remain focused on their sports while the remainder of the country, and world, was focused on the devastation of New York and Washington? What psychological factors underlie the performance of expert athletes? Questions such as these are at the heart of sport psychology.

WHAT IS SPORT PSYCHOLOGY?

Sport psychology is the "study of the psychological aspects of sport" (Anderson, 2000, p. xiii); however, sport psychology isn't limited to sports and may include any type of physical activity or exercise (American Psychological Association Division 47, 2007). Thus, sport psychology services may address any aspect of athletes' or performers' lives, competitive or otherwise, to assist them in their performance and life endeavors (Anderson, 2000).

Sport psychologists examine topics such as the ways an athlete can use visualization techniques to improve performance, ways to manage performance anxiety, and ways athletes on sports teams can cooperate to work more effectively together. Like other psychologists, some sport psychologists conduct research in academic, clinical, government, and business settings. Others engage in clinical or consulting practice, helping individuals and teams improve their athletic performance, and training coaches to help them become more efficient and productive in leading athletic teams. It is easy to see why students are intrigued by sport psychology: the philosophy and principles of improving performance work for more than just athletes—they are effective beyond the field as well.

OPPORTUNITIES WITH A BACHELOR'S DEGREE

If you are interested in sport psychology, you'll be glad to know that there are many opportunities for bachelor's degree holders to work in rewarding careers that challenge them to use their general training in psychology as well as any specialized knowledge in sports. It should be noted that a history as an athlete is not a prerequisite for a career in the sport psychology arena; however, former athletes may find such careers highly rewarding as they are able to remain close to competitions and the athletes competing in sports. There are a wide variety of sports-related careers at the bachelor's degree level for which psychology majors will find themselves competitive, with just a few examples including careers as fitness instructors and recreational workers, physical education teachers, sport instructors and coaches, and sport reporters.

FITNESS INSTRUCTOR AND RECREATIONAL WORKER

Fitness instructors and recreational workers develop, plan, organize, and direct recreational activities (such as aerobics, arts and crafts, performing arts, camping, or recreational sports) for both healthy and disabled (physically or psychologically) persons (Bureau of Labor Statistics, 2008). In other words, fitness instructors and recreational workers are not limited to a specific clientele or persons with particular health-related issues. Fitness instructors and recreational workers are employed in educational and university settings, nursing homes, park and recreational centers, community activity centers, health clubs and fitness centers, and medical and rehabilitation centers. Although fitness instructors and recreational workers often major in recreational studies (such as leisure studies or parks and recreation) or related fields (for example, health sciences) (Bureau of Labor Statistics, 2008), psychology majors, particularly when accompanied by a dual major or minor in recreational studies or related fields, are highly competitive for this career because of psychology's broad based training in human development and motivation which are important skills in fitness and recreational work.

Typical activities of fitness and recreational workers will vary depending on agency type and clientele. For example, directors of parks and recreational programs spend the majority of their time developing and managing recreational programs in parks, playgrounds, and other child-oriented settings (Bureau of Labor Statistics, 2008). They may be responsible for park and recreational budgets, but also have an opportunity for direct involvement with program participants. Camp counselors, on the other hand, are recreational workers who "lead and instruct" children and adolescents in outdoor activities such as swimming and boating, horseback riding, camping, hiking, sports, music, drama, art, and computers (Bureau of Labor Statistics, 2008). Recreational workers may also assume more of a therapeutic role in residential camps where they provide assistance in skill building to individuals lacking daily living skills, social skills, and problem-solving skills. Fitness workers, on the other hand, coach groups or individuals in sporting or exercise activities with the goal of developing skills or promoting physical fitness and healthy living (Bureau of Labor Statistics, 2008).

Median salaries for recreational workers ($20,470) and fitness instructors ($25,910) are modest for entry-level positions (Bureau of Labor Statistics, 2008). However, one of the benefits of these careers is the opportunity to advance to supervisory positions or to pursue self-employment as a personal trainer, both of which offer salary increases. The job market for fitness instructors is very favorable; however, positions for recreational workers tend to be more competitive (Bureau of Labor Statistics, 2008). Advantages of these jobs include the employment setting; the nature of the work necessitates much time spent outdoors in parks, the wilderness, or near water, as well as other unique employment settings including tourist and vacation getaway spots. Imagine the enjoyment of working as a recreational worker on a cruise ship, on an island resort in the Bahamas, or at a secluded mountain spa. Although such positions remain highly coveted, and therefore competitive, such opportunities do exist. Another benefit is health-related—a fitness career will require you to maintain your fitness. As mentioned, the primary limitation of this career choice is the modest salary and the competition for entry-level positions for recreational workers; however, recognize that those with a bachelor's degree will most likely fare better, because many applicants for recreational positions will be applying with an associate degree or high-school diploma.

PHYSICAL EDUCATION TEACHER

Physical education (PE) teachers, employed in school settings, rarely major in psychology; however, training in psychology (for example, a double major or minor in psychology) may prove to be a great asset to PE teachers. A thorough review of the role of psychology in academic and school settings is discussed in Chapters 3 and 4, including discussion of the career choice of teacher. Here we focus on the benefit to PE teachers of specialized information in sport psychology. Course work in health and sport psychology at the undergraduate level is particularly beneficial to PE teachers in their roles as educators, trainers, and coaches. A foundation in psychology provides the necessary tools and principals to motivate students as well as to access the best learning strategies (for example, principles of reinforcement and overlearning for skill development). In addition, PE teachers are rarely restricted to the gym; thus, your degree in psychology, especially with a focus on sport psychology, may make you more competitive as you market yourself dually as a teacher of physical education as well as psychology-related classes. The salary, advantages, and disadvantages for a PE teacher are similar to those of other educators; we refer you to Chapter 4 for a review of this information.

Sport Instructors and Coaches

With increased interest in youth sports, a growing field is sport instruction. Sport instructors work with individuals or a team of athletes to enhance skills. Sport instructors typically function in a consultant role, whereby they are hired to teach particular skills (for example, hitting coach for Little League baseball players, serving coach for youth tennis players, and so on). Coaches, on the other hand, are hired to lead a team (for example, baseball or football) or group of athletes (for example, golfers or cross-country runners) into competition. Whereas sport instructors work with people of all ages involved in sport, coaches are generally employed at the middle-school level and above. In middle and elementary schools, coaches are often dual-hires, meaning that they are hired both to teach a subject matter and to coach an athletic team (in the cases of smaller school districts, coaches may coach multiple team sports).

A bachelor's degree in psychology offers many advantages for sport instructors and coaches. The study of human behavior, including attitudes and motivation, will assist sport instructors and coaches trying to motivate athletes to improve. Additionally, studying psychology, including learning and motivation, will provide those in this field with the necessary knowledge to best teach athletes. Athletes of all ages and levels learn differently. The astute sport instructor or coach is able to modify his or her teaching style to best reach athletes. A bachelor's degree in psychology offers such a skill set and knowledge. Additionally, a bachelor's degree in psychology affords coaches the opportunity to teach diverse and interesting courses (for example, psychology, family studies, sociology) at the high-school level, a potential advantage in the hiring process in school districts that must juggle multiple demands with a hire—meaning, hire a coach that can also teach.

Sport instructor and coaching careers offer many benefits. First, the typical athlete is highly motivated and eager to improve; thus, resistance is generally minimal. Sport instructors and coaches frequently work outdoors, which is attractive for many, and the constant movement and teaching require some level of fitness, so opportunities for long-term fitness are good. Finally, sport instructors and coaches typically instruct or coach in sports of their choice, so interest remains high. Unfortunately, salaries in sport instruction and coaching are often low, especially in the early years of one's career, as it takes time to develop a reputation. The median annual income for coaches is $26,950; however, salaries will typically rise substantially as one moves up the athletic hierarchy (high-school coaches typically earn more than middle-school coaches; college coaches typically earn more than high-school coaches; professional coaches typically earn more than college coaches) (Bureau of Labor Statistics, 2008). Another disadvantage to a career in sport instruction or coaching is irregular work hours (Bureau of Labor Statistics, 2008). Sport instructors and coaches often can't begin their work day until after school hours, when athletes are available. Additionally, they must frequently attend events in the evenings and weekends. Lastly, coaches typically have small travel budgets.

Sport Reporter

Although a degree in journalism is often a prerequisite for a career as a sport reporter (including television or paper outlets), a minor in psychology is advantageous. Specifically, the writing, statistics, and analyzing of data that is required in the field of psychology affords excellent training for sport reporting. Sport reporters gather information (data), prepare stories (analogous to writing a research paper based on the obtained data), and publish or broadcast the information (similar to

TABLE 7.1	PREPARATION FOR BA–LEVEL CAREERS RELATED TO SPORT PSYCHOLOGY

Coursework

    Abnormal Psychology or Psychopathology
    Biology
    Communication
    Exercise and Sport Science
    Interviewing, Counseling, or Helping Skills
    Physical Health
    Principles of Sport Coaching
    Psychology of Motivation (or Attitudes)
    Sport Management
    Sport Psychology

Applied Experiences: Volunteer, intern/practica, or paid part-time positions in any of the following settings

    University Athletic Department
    Youth/Adult Sports Programs (for example, Little League, Parks and Recreation)
    University Recreational Center

Research Experiences: Experiences studying and participating in research in any of the following areas*

    Sport Psychology
    Exercise Psychology
    Leadership
    Goal setting
    Performance enhancement
    Motivation

*Note that the content area of the research is less important than the experience itself, which enhances reasoning, quantitative, writing, and organizational skills.

published psychological reports or professional presentations at a research conference). With increased media focus on celebrity-athlete behavior, a background in psychology, specifically social psychology with focus on group behavior, attitudes, and decision making, offers compelling insights into individual and team behavior. Thus, when editors request a special report on why a sport team engaged in a certain type of behavior or bonded better than other teams, a background in psychology may offer the advantage to get the special assignment.

Work hours vary by season (for example, the fall and winter include many weekend hours as collegiate and high-school football games, volleyball matches, basketball games, and wrestling matches, for example, typically occur on weekends). Additionally, the work schedule is frequently hectic (Bureau of Labor Statistics, 2008) as reporters struggle to meet deadlines for on-air reporting, often with minimal preparation, or for newspapers to go to press. A career as a sport reporter, however, offers the potential for great excitement as coverage of sporting events will often include highly contested and riveting games or competitions. Sport reporters are often very close to the action with a close-up of the stress and strain endured by the athletes. Income for sport reporters is respectable, with a median income in 2006 of $33,470, with the middle 50 percent earning between $24,370 and $51,700 (Bureau of Labor Statistics, 2008).

CAREER AS A SPORT PSYCHOLOGIST

Sport psychology is a "stimulating" field offering a variety of career opportunities (Carter, 2005). Educational requirements for sport psychology generally are more flexible than for other psychology careers. Academic degrees may be earned from departments of physical education, psychology, counseling, or sport science. In fact, sport psychology is a multi-disciplinary field, and course work should be taken in psychology and counseling, and also in courses such as exercise physiology, sport sociology, and biomechanics (Van Raalte & Williams, 1994). Although many employment opportunities for sport psychologists require the completion of a doctoral degree, some opportunities exist for individuals with a masters degree. (Note, however, that masters-level professionals will encounter a more limited and competitive job market.) Regardless of the educational track being pursued, specialized training (for example, internships) should be sought that provide training and experience in the field of sport psychology, yet such opportunities are limited.

Sport psychologists have three primary roles: practice, research, and teaching (Van Raalte & Williams, 1994). However, sport psychology is a highly specialized field which has lent itself to less career diversity than other areas of psychology. The vast majority of sport psychologists are employed in academic settings (47 percent) and private practice (37 percent) (Meyers, Coleman, Whelan, & Mehlenbeck, 2001). The following sections discuss the various settings in which sport psychologists work.

ACADEMIC AND RESEARCH SETTINGS

Within academia, sport psychologists may be affiliated with departments of psychology, sport exercise programs, and physical education programs. Not surprisingly, within academia the majority of their time is spent in teaching and research activities, with some time available for consulting or service delivery activities (Meyers et al., 2001). The aim of sport psychology research is to identify the effects of athletic participation (including exercise and other physical activities) on development, health, and overall well-being throughout the lifespan (Van Raalte & Williams, 1994). Much of this research focuses on strategies for improving athletic performance; however, sport psychologists also are interested in the overall life functioning of athletes and performers. Therefore, issues of life satisfaction, vocational plans for retired athletes, and relationship issues are a few examples of the varied research interests of sport psychologists.

As is true with other psychological specialties, academic careers in sport psychology afford the opportunity to collaborate with other professionals. Also of benefit is the potential for access to an athletic population via college sports teams, as well as flexibility of schedule to pursue practice or consultation interests. In fact, many collegiate athletic departments are moving to a model of hiring full-time sport psychologists, which affords great opportunity for research collaborations and the development of consultation relationships. The primary pitfall for academically inclined sport psychologists is the job demand, as there appear to be a limited number of available positions within higher-education settings during any given year, and competition is at a premium. However, this is true of most academic positions within and outside of psychology. Academic salaries of sport psychologists are consistent with other academic psychologists (Meyers et al., 2001).

PRACTICE SETTINGS

The goal of the practicing sport psychologist is to use psychological principles to help athletes and performers achieve optimal physical performance (American Psychological Association Division 47, 2007). This increased performance is accomplished through techniques such as relaxation, imagery, goal setting, and self-talk (Anderson, 2000). Relaxation strategies are taught to athletes and performers to reduce anxiety and stress in order to maximize performance (Sherman & Poczwardowski, 2000). Sport psychologists direct athletes to use imagery (Simmons, 2000) and self-talk (Perry & Marsh, 2000) before, during, and after an event to improve their focus and mental clarity with the expectation of improved performance. Goal setting is used with athletes and performers to increase their sense of self-control and to enhance performance over the long term (Marchant, 2000).

Sport psychologists tend to enjoy a flexible work environment. A sport psychologist may see an athlete in the office but may also travel to the relevant athletic arena for service delivery. For example, a sport psychologist may work with a golfer at the driving range or putting green to implement focusing strategies previously discussed in the office. A sport psychologist working with a basketball player may meet the client at the arena to implement relaxation strategies while the athlete shoots free throws. Thus, careers in sport psychology require flexibility and often creativity for service delivery. Sport psychologists who provide services are employed in university counseling centers, sports medicine clinics, consulting agencies, and in private practice.

Sport psychologists who work in private practice provide clients with performance enhancement, life-skills training, organizational consulting, psychotherapy and counseling interventions, and rehabilitation (Danish, Petit-pas, & Hale, 1993). Private practice, however, tends to be less financially successful and stable for sport psychologists than is academia; practitioners often must supplement their income (Meyers et al., 2001) by providing non-sports-related psychological services. Once supplemented however, the income of sport psychologists in private practice appears equivalent to other psychologists in private practice. Furthermore, sport psychologists who are fortunate enough to be affiliated with collegiate or professional teams and athletes are likely to have higher incomes than sport psychologists not working with elite athletes and their teams.

Throughout this chapter, we have seen that sport psychology offers knowledge and training that is relevant to many careers. If you are interested in pursuing a sports-related position with your baccalaureate degree, supplement your academic training in psychology with courses in other health- and recreation-related areas such as health education, nutrition, and safety. Careers at the doctoral level are more specialized. If you are considering a graduate-level career in sport psychology, recognize that there are few sport psychology programs. Most sport psychologists have degrees in clinical or counseling psychology and have specialized in sport psychology after graduate school. If a career as a sport psychologist appeals to you, pursue generalist training during graduate school (meaning, clinical or counseling psychology programs), followed by specialized training in health or sport psychology during internship or postdoctoral work.

SUGGESTED READINGS

Anderson, M. B. (Ed.) (2000). *Doing sport psychology.* Champaign, IL: Human Kinetics.
Carter, J. E. (2005). Sport psychology: Locker room confessions. In R. D. Morgan, T. L.Kuther, & C. J. Habben (Eds.), *Life after graduate school in psychology: Insider's advice from new psychologists.* New York: Psychology Press.
Cox, R. H. (2006). *Sport psychology: Concepts and applications.* New York: McGraw Hill.
Van Raalte, J. L., & Brewer, B. W. (2002). *Exploring sport and exercise psychology* (2nd ed.). Washington, DC: American Psychological Association.

WEB RESOURCES

Association for the Advancement of Applied Sport Psychology
http://www.aaasponline.org/

European Federation of Sport Psychology
http://www.fepsac.org

Sport Psychology OverSite
http://www-personal.umich.edu/~bing/oversite/sportpsych.html

Athletic Insight: The Online Journal of Sports Psychology
http://www.athleticinsight.com/

Sports and Performance Psychology
http://www.shpm.com/articles/sports/index.shtml

The International Society of Sport Psychology
http://www.issponline.org

CHECKLIST: IS SPORT PSYCHOLOGY FOR YOU?

Do you:

- ☐ Want to help people maximize their physical capabilities?
- ☐ Enjoy working with athletes? Want to help people live healthier lives?
- ☐ Enjoy sports?
- ☐ Want to work with athletes?
- ☐ Like conducting research?
- ☐ Want to learn more about athletic performance?
- ☐ Often wonder why some people succeed whereas others fail?
- ☐ Want to understand how the mind influences the body?

Scoring: The more boxes you checked, the more likely it is that sport psychology is a good match for you.

CHAPTER **8** | BIOPSYCHOLOGY, COGNITIVE NEUROPSYCHOLOGY, AND CLINICAL NEUROPSYCHOLOGY

CHAPTER GUIDE

Do children act aggressively because they inherited an aggressive gene or do they learn aggressive behavior early in life? Are quiet people born shy or do they develop shyness in response to their early environment? You have undoubtedly been asked to think about such "nature versus nurture" issues by now in your college education and you've probably found it difficult to develop satisfactory answers. Don't worry, you're not alone! In fact, an entire field of psychology is devoted to one aspect of these questions—the study of the biological bases of behavior.

Technological breakthroughs are rapidly advancing scientific knowledge in the biological sciences (for example, DNA research, cloning, stem cell research). What do these advances mean for psychology? With increased technology and refined research methods we are able to identify more accurately the biological processes and neurological functioning that impacts human behavior. Thus, biopsychology, cognitive neuropsychology, and clinical neuropsychology have enormous potential for altering our understanding of human behavior, not only to increase our knowledge base but also to influence how psychology is applied in the real world. Before discussing applications of biopsychology, cognitive neuropsychology, and clinical neuropsychology, let's spend some time defining the fields.

BIOPSYCHOLOGY, COGNITIVE NEUROPSYCHOLOGY AND CLINICAL NEUROPSYCHOLOGY

Biopsychology, or physiological psychology, is the branch of psychology that studies the relationship between biology and behavior (Myers, 2004). Biopsychology integrates various areas of neuroscience (for example, neuroanatomy, the study of the structure of the nervous system; neurochemistry, the study of the chemical composition of neural activity; neuroendocrinology, the study of the interplay between the nervous system and endocrine system; neuropathology, the study of disorders that affect the nervous system; and neuropharmacology, the study of how drugs affect neural activity) to explain the biological bases of behavior. For example, a biopsychologist might study how genetics and experience interact to influence behavior. Others study the influence of hormones and other chemicals on behavior (for example, is there a "love" hormone? or does gambling or other risky behaviors release endorphins into the bloodstream?). Biopsychologists predominantly are researchers and academicians, employed by universities, government, research institutes, and pharmaceutical companies.

Cognitive neuropsychology is a branch of cognitive psychology that aims to understand cognition from the perspective of the brain—it represents the merge of cognitive psychology and biopsychology. Cognitive neuropsychologists study the brain to understand the neural bases of mental processes like thinking, memory, attention, and language (Carpenter, 2001). A cognitive neuropsychologist may use brain imaging techniques to study what happens in people's brains when they tackle math problems (see for example Murray, 2000). How does the brain of someone with dyslexia function differently from a typical brain? What areas of the brain are responsible for language, short-term memory, or decision making? Cognitive neuropsychologists conduct research to examine how neural activity translates into mental activity: How do collections of neurons communicate, and how do we interpret that communication as thought? As you might guess, cognitive neuropsychology is primarily a research-oriented field and cognitive neuropsychologists are found in a variety of research and academic settings.

Whereas cognitive neuropsychology represents the joining of cognitive psychology and biopsychology, *clinical neuropsychology* applies findings from biopsychology within clinical and counseling contexts. Clinical neuropsychology is the application of psychological assessments and interventions based upon the study of the central nervous system (American Psychological Association Division of Clinical Neuropsychology, 1989). In other words, clinical neuropsychology integrates biopsychology and clinical/counseling psychology to assist clients suffering from brain dysfunction (for example, a patient suffering memory loss following a traumatic brain injury).

Clinical neuropsychologists conduct neuropsychological assessments to identify the extent of brain damage or severity of impairment in clients. They also develop interventions to help clients adapt or regain function in order to maximize the potential for independent living and quality of life. Like other psychologists, clinical neuropsychologists are employed in applied settings such as medical hospitals, clinics, and private practice, and in academic positions within university settings or research positions in academia, government, or industry.

OPPORTUNITIES WITH A BACHELOR'S DEGREE

Although much training in biopsychology or neuropsychology occurs at the graduate level, students with interests at the baccalaureate level have many career options available to them, including science technician, psychiatric aide, psychiatric technician, clinical laboratory technician, and pharmacy technician. These positions provide students an opportunity to apply their knowledge of psychology along with their knowledge and interest in biopsychology.

SCIENCE TECHNICIAN

Science technicians are involved in laboratory research and "use the principles and theories of science and mathematics to solve problems in research and development" (Bureau of Labor Statistics, 2008). They are a scientist's "hands," so to speak. They maintain scientific laboratories, operate and maintain laboratory instruments and equipment, monitor experiments, make observations and record data, and work with scientists who are forming conclusions based on experiments and lab work. There are many different kinds of technicians, because many fields require technical assistance. Thus, professional titles are designated according to the specific field (for example, agricultural technician, forensic science technician, nuclear technician) (Bureau of Labor Statistics, 2008). Bachelor's degree holders in psychology with interests in biopsychology may choose positions as *biological technicians* or *research technicians*.

In collaboration with biologists, biological technicians study living organisms and may be involved in medical or pharmaceutical research, microbiological or biotechnological laboratories (Bureau of Labor Statistics, 2008). Examples of such research include studying cures for physiological diseases (for example, Alzheimer's or AIDS) or analyzing organic substances and the effects of chemicals on the treatment of mental illness. Other research technicians may assist biopsychologists with their research. Science technicians typically work in research laboratories; however, they may occasionally work in other settings (for example, the "laboratory" of a forensic science technician may be the crime scene under investigation) (Bureau of Labor Statistics, 2008).

The job outlook for science technicians is expected to remain steady through 2016 (Bureau of Labor Statistics, 2008). Competitive salaries are one of the advantages of a career as a science technician. For example, in 2006, biological technicians working in government settings earned an average salary of $40,629 for physical science technicians (Bureau of Labor Statistics, 2008). Similar to other career fields, science technician salaries fluctuate with employer (private employers tend to pay more than the government) and type of science work (forensic science technicians earn slightly more than biological technicians). In addition to salary, the perks of this job include a comfortable work environment (laboratories are typically made to be comfortable), casual dress codes (the laboratory can get messy, so most science technicians wear jeans and casual clothing to work), and a 40-hour work week with normal business hours. The primary disadvantage of this career is the limited opportunity to develop and design research projects of your own interest. Although science technicians may have input into the research on which they are working, the employer or agency being served will typically determine the focus of research studies. If you're interested in this career choice, supplement your biopsychology training with additional research and laboratory-related coursework, such as biology, chemistry, and physics. The more laboratory experience you have, the greater your marketability.

Psychiatric Technician

A career as a psychiatric technician involves assisting psychiatrists or other mental health professionals in their care of mentally ill or emotionally disturbed patients. A psychiatric technician follows both a physician's instructions and hospital procedures, monitors patients' physical and emotional well-being, reports to medical staff, and may also provide therapeutic services and administer medications. (Bureau of Labor Statistics, 2008). Psychiatric technicians may also develop specialized skills, such as providing biofeedback in a clinic or for a private practitioner or providing EEG services in a sleep disorders clinic.

Rewards of a career as a psychiatric technician include direct work with clients, the chance to make a difference in someone's life, and the opportunity to work with an interdisciplinary team (Jobprofiles, 2003). Unfortunately, this career can be stressful, with limited job opportunities and few opportunities for advancement. Compared to other healthcare professionals, salaries in this field are marginal; as a psychiatric technician, you can expect to earn an entry salary of approximately $27,865 (salary.com, 2008). If you're interested in becoming a psychiatric technician, supplement your psychology coursework with courses in nursing and seek certification as a psychiatric technician (available through many colleges and universities).

Clinical Laboratory Technologist or Technician

Graduates with biopsychology interests sometimes obtain positions within clinical laboratories, as clinical laboratory technicians or clinical laboratory technologists, where they play a vital role in detecting, diagnosing, and treating diseases through their work analyzing a patient's physical samples (for example, body fluids, tissues, and cells) (Bureau of Labor Statistics, 2008). Clinical laboratory technicians conduct work similar to science technicians. They work under the supervision of laboratory technologists or managers and assist in the medical process. Clinical laboratory technicians maintain the laboratory, prepare specimens, and conduct basic tests either manually or with automated analyzers (Bureau of Labor Statistics, 2008).

Clinical laboratory technologists supervise technicians and perform sophisticated medical testing, including "chemical, biological, hematological, immunological, microscopic, and bacteriological tests" (Bureau of Labor Statistics, 2008). In other words, clinical laboratory technologists conduct all of the sophisticated medical tests that your physician orders when you visit for a routine exam (for example, blood glucose and cholesterol levels) or if he or she suspects that you are ill (for example, searching for microscopic signs of pathology in blood and tissue samples). Clinical laboratory technologists "make cultures of body fluid and tissue samples to determine the presence of bacteria, fungi, parasites, or other microorganisms" (Bureau of Labor Statistics, 2008).

The job outlook for clinical laboratory workers over the next ten years is excellent, with more job openings than qualified professionals to fill them (Bureau of Labor Statistics, 2008). As a clinical laboratory technologist you can expect to earn approximately $49,700 per year (Bureau of Labor Statistics, 2008). Disadvantages to a clinical laboratory career include the physical hazards: as a clinical laboratory worker, you may handle infectious agents. In addition, clinical laboratory personnel often are exposed to fumes for significant time periods, and spend a significant portion of their work day on their feet.

If you're considering a position within a clinical laboratory setting, understand that your psychology degree will enable you to pursue a position as a technician. For a technologist position, take additional courses in biology, chemistry, and medical technology to be competitive for this career option. Understand that some states require laboratory personnel to be certified, registered, or licensed (Bureau of Labor Statistics, 2008), so contact your state department of health for more information.

PHARMACY TECHNICIAN

Pharmacy technicians often work in retail pharmacies, where they help pharmacists distribute medication and information to customers. Pharmacy technicians verify customer and prescription information, perform the many clerical duties that arise within a pharmacy, and prepare medications for patients, including counting medications and preparing bottle labels (Bureau of Labor Statistics, 2008).

Benefits of a career as a pharmacy technician include a very good job market, that is expected to increase more rapidly than average for both full-time and part-time work (Bureau of Labor Statistics, 2008), and an opportunity to work directly with the public (public relations are an important aspect of this career). A career as a pharmacy technician also typically offers a very comfortable work environment plus regular business hours. However, salaries for pharmacy technicians are modest, with a median salary in 2006 of approximately $25,625. Additionally, opportunities for job advancement are limited. Higher salaries are

TABLE 8.1	PREPARATION FOR BA–LEVEL CAREERS RELATED TO BIOPSYCHOLOGY, COGNITIVE NEUROPSYCHOLOGY, AND CLINICAL NEUROPSYCHOLOGY

Coursework
  Abnormal Psychology
  Anatomy
  Biopsychology
  Brain and Behavior
  Chemistry
  Cognitive Psychology
  Genetics
  Math
  Microbiology
  Neuropsychology
  Psychological Assessment
  Writing

Applied Experiences: Volunteer, intern, or paid part-time positions in any of the following settings
  Doctor's Office
  Hospital
  Mental Retardation Facility
  Pharmaceutical Company
  Pharmacy (as an aide behind the counter)

Research Experiences: Experiences studying and participating in research in any of the following areas*
  Biology
  Chemistry
  Cognitive Psychology
  Neuropsychology
  Psychopathology

---

*Note that the content area of the research is less important than the experience itself, which enhances reasoning, quantitative, writing, and organizational skills.

available for those employed in hospital and grocery store pharmacies (Bureau of Labor Statistics, 2008).

Although formal pharmacy technician programs and certification are available, and preferred by many employers, many pharmacy technicians are trained on the job (Bureau of Labor Statistics, 2008); thus, psychology graduates with emphasis in biopsychology should find themselves very marketable for this career. Nevertheless, supplemental course work in chemistry is likely to enhance your application. Once employed (or prior to employment if you're trying to maximize your credentials) you may want to pursue certification via the Pharmacy Technician Certification Board that administers a national exam for certification (Bureau of Labor Statistics, 2008, visit http://www.ptcb.org/). Although this examination and certification are voluntary in most states, some states require certification, and a particular pharmacy/ pharmacist may prefer or require it.

OPPORTUNITIES WITH A GRADUATE DEGREE

A graduate degree in biopsychology, cognitive neuropsychology, or clinical neuropsychology is versatile, provides training for a career in teaching or research, and also enables the pursuit of applied interests. Although some opportunities are available to masters degree holders, if you're interested in applied work, a doctoral degree is preferred. You may obtain a doctoral degree in biopsychology, cognitive neuropsychology, or cognitive psychology within a program that specializes in cognitive neuropsychology, or in clinical/counseling psychology followed by specialized training in clinical neuropsychology during the yearlong internship and/or postdoctoral training.

As is true for all psychologists, biopsychologists, cognitive neuropsychologists, and clinical neuropsychologists often find employment in academic settings. We discuss academic careers in detail in Chapter 13, but biopsychologists, clinical neuropsychologists, and cognitive neuropsychologists in academia face a challenge that is often specific to their fields: They usually require expensive laboratory equipment to conduct their research. Thus, getting a laboratory established and functioning can be problematic because significant space and money are required. Although a university may provide funds to assist new faculty in developing a psychophysiological or neuroanatomy lab, additional funds are often required to fully establish and maintain the laboratory. These psychologists spend a great deal of time writing grants to find their work, yet grant writing is time consuming and detracts from the research and publication that new professors are expected to do. Once received, however, grants offer faculty many perks, including increased salary via summer pay, course release time, paid research assistants, and status within the department. For more on academic careers, see Chapter 13. Let's take a closer look at the work of biopsychologists, cognitive neuropsychologists, and clinical neuropsychologists outside of academia.

PHARMACEUTICAL AND BIOTECHNOLOGY RESEARCH

In addition to academia, biopsychologists, clinical neuropsychologists, and cognitive neuropsychologists may pursue research careers in pharmaceutical or biotechnology companies (as well as within government settings, as described in Chapter 13). Researchers with pharmaceutical companies work to develop medications and evaluate the effectiveness of existing medicines. Researchers in biotechnology manipulate biological organisms to make products (for example, food products and medicines) to benefit the human race (Levine, 2002). Psychologists employed in biotechnology agencies or companies may evaluate the effectiveness of a product or assist in developing new products.

A research career with a pharmaceutical or biotechnology company can be very rewarding because you'll have the opportunity to develop and evaluate products, whether food or medicine, designed to benefit people. Starting salaries for researchers with established pharmaceutical companies are typically well above other entry-level positions. You may expect to begin your first job earning more than $80,000 per year, with a rise to six figures expected in a short period of time (personal communication with Lee Cohen, July 29, 2008). On the other hand, research positions with pharmaceutical and biotechnology companies can be stressful because fluctuations in the stock market and product development continually push developers and evaluators to produce new and better products. In this career your work is never done, as you will always be looking for ways to improve current products or produce new, more effective products.

PRACTICE

Of the subfields discussed in this chapter, clinical neuropsychology most lends itself to an applied career. The most common practice of clinical neuropsychologists is neuropsychological diagnostic assessment to identify the extent of brain damage or severity of impairment. They may, for example, be asked to conduct an evaluation to discriminate between neurological and psychiatric symptoms, to identify a neurological disorder or help distinguish between different neurological conditions, or to assist in the localizing of a lesion site (Lezak, 2004). Other reasons for neuropsychological assessments include patient care and planning (including cognitive capacities), rehabilitation and treatment evaluations, and research purposes (Lezak, 2004).

The goals of clinical neuropsychological assessment are different from those of the general psychological evaluation. In the neuropsychological evaluation, four primary goals exist: (1) to locate and diagnose cortical damage or dysfunction; (2) to facilitate patient treatment and rehabilitation; (3) to identify the presence of mild disturbance that is unrecognized in other examination procedures; and (4) to examine brain dysfunction in clients with a preexisting condition (Kolb & Whishaw, 2003). Aside from these goals, the neuropsychological assessment serves four primary functions in the treatment of mental health patients and includes diagnosis, treatment planning, rehabilitational evaluations, and research (Lezak, 2004).

As psychologists, clinical neuropsychologists are interested in behavior; behavior in this career refers to cognition, emotionality, and executive functioning. According to Lezak (2004), cognition includes receptive functions (meaning, the ability to "select, acquire, classify, and integrate information") and includes expressive functions (for example, speaking), memory, constructional abilities (for example, building blocks), attention and concentration, consciousness, and mentation (speed of mental activities). *Emotionality* refers to personality or emotional changes that occur following a brain injury. Finally, Lezak (2004) refers to *executive functioning* as the abilities that contribute to the expression of behavior (meaning, functions that enable a person to engage in independent, goal-directed, and self-serving behavior). Referral questions may include one or any combination of these behaviors, and the type of neuropsychological evaluation conducted is determined by the referral question.

Examination procedures may include any or all of the following: a clinical interview, detailed case history, mental status examination, standardized neuropsychological assessments (e.g., Hallstead-Reitan Battery, Luria-Nebraska Neuropsychological Battery), standardized psychological instruments such as intelligence tests (for example, Wechsler Adult Intelligence Scale III, Wechsler Intelligence Scale for Children–IV, Stanford-Binet Intelligence Scale–Fifth Edition), memory tests (Wechsler Memory Scale–III), other brief examination instruments to assess specific deficits (for example, Rey Auditory-Verbal Learning Test, Rey-Osterrieth Complex Figure Test, Finger Tapping Test), personality assessment (Minnesota Multiphasic Personality

Inventory–2), and vocational/occupational assessments. A thorough clinical neuro-psychological assessment can be completed in as little as 4 to 6 hours, but may require as much as 8 to 12 hours of testing. Thus, neuropsychologists in full-time practice may spend the majority of their time conducting and reporting the results of their assessments.

Clinical neuropsychologists may also be involved in providing treatment and rehabilitation services. Thus, they can provide therapeutic services to help patients adapt to their injuries or develop new skills to compensate for lost abilities. Although psychotherapy or counseling is occasionally implemented to assist pa-tients and their families struggling to cope with the life-altering effects of a brain injury, therapeutic services implemented by clinical neuropsychologists are typically cognitive in nature. In other words, the behaviors previously discussed as the targets of neuropsychological evaluations are the same behaviors that will be treated fol-lowing a brain injury. For example, a patient suffering from short-term memory loss due to a cardiovascular accident (such as a stroke) may by presented with memory strategies (for example, developing chunking strategies where information is remembered in chunks rather than individual units of information). In addition, the patient may be encouraged to participate in a game (for example, "concentra-tion" or the "memory" card game) that requires remembering information during the course of play.

Interventions, particularly rehabilitation, are becoming a primary role for clinical neuropsychologists (Golden, Zillmer, & Spiers, 1992). Rehabilitation psychology is the application of psychosocial principals to people with physical, sensory, cognitive, developmental, or emotional difficulties (American Psychological Association Division 22, n.d.) with a goal of helping clients "relearn" lost functions or develop new func-tions, or altering the environment to maximize quality of life (Golden et al., 1992).

An applied career as a clinical neuropsychologist has many benefits. First, clini-cal neuropsychology is a very specialized field that typically allows for hourly billing at a rate greater than general psychological billing; thus, salaries of clinical neuropsychologists are often greater those of nonspecialized psychologists (see Chapter 3 for a review of applied psychology salaries). In addition, clinical neurop-sychologists are often afforded special status in medical settings because they work in conjunction with physicians and of all psychological professionals are the most closely aligned with the medical field. They may even be required to be present dur-ing brain surgery, for example, to map cognitive function, or to locate a lesion or a particular cognitive function. Finally, clinical neuropsychology training affords a psychologist flexibility with regard to employment settings, and clinical neuropsy-chologists are employed in medical settings (for example, hospitals, rehabilitation centers, specialty medical clinics, medical schools), private practice, private and public agencies, and other settings typical of the counseling and clinical psycholo-gist without clinical neuropsychological training.

A primary drawback to an applied career as a clinical neuropsychologist is the amount of time spent writing reports. For every evaluation conducted, the clinical neuropsychologist must write a report, and these reports can be quite lengthy and time-intensive. For example, you may expect to spend anywhere from 1 to 6 hours for a single report (personal communication with Dan Johnson on October 27, 2005). Another disadvantage is the stress of continued work with severely injured people, including children. Automobile accidents, violent crime, and terrorism are a few examples of the types of incidents that lead to neurological damage, and clinical neuropsychologists must deal with these issues and their effects on an ongoing basis. On a positive note, clinical neuropsychology is one of the most rapidly growing fields in professional psychology, and it will continue to be as our society continues to age. In fact, many consider clinical neuropsychology to be one of the leading careers for psychologists in the twenty-first century.

Suggested Readings

Adams, R. L., Parsons, O. A., & Culbertson, J. L. (Eds.). (1996). *Neuropsychology for clinical practice: Etiology, assessment, and treatment.* Washington DC: American Psychological Association.

Frank, R. G., & Elliott, T. R. (Eds.). (2000). *Handbook of rehabilitation psychology.* Washington, DC: American Psychological Association.

Kolb, B. & Whishaw, I. Q. (2008). *Fundamentals of human neuropsychology* (5th ed.). New York: Bedford, Freeman, & Worth Publishers.

Lezak (2004). *Neuropsychological assessment* (4th ed.). New York: Oxford University Press.

Myers, D. G. (2004). *Psychology* (6th ed). New York: Worth.

Snyder, P. J. (2008). An interesting career in psychology: A neuropsychologist prospers in the pharmaceutical industry. Retrieved on July 29, 2008 from http://www.apa.org/science/ic-snyder.html.

Snyder, P. J., & Nassbaum, P. D. (Eds.). (2005). *Clinical neuropsychology: A pocket handbook for assessment.* Washington, DC: American Psychological Association.

Web Resources

Biopsychology.org
http://www.biopsychology.org/

American Board of Clinical Neuropsychology
http://www.theabcn.org/

American Academy of Clinical Neuropsychology
http://www.theaacn.org/

American Board of Professional Neuropsychology
http://abpn.net/

International Neuropsychological Society
http://www.the-ins.org/

National Academy of Neuropsychology
http://nanonline.org/

Behavioral Neuroscience and Comparative Psychology
http://www.apa.org/divisions/div6/

Rehabilitation Psychology
http://www.div22.org/

Clinical Neuropsychology
http://www.div40.org/

Neuropsychology Central
http://www.neuropsychologycentral.com/

Neuropsychology Homepage
http://www.tbidoc.com/

CHECKLIST: IS BIOPSYCHOLOGY, CLINICAL NEUROPSYCHOLOGY, OR COGNITIVE NEUROPSYCHOLOGY FOR YOU?

Do you:

- ☐ Enjoy biology classes?
- ☐ Remember dissecting frogs in biology class as a pleasant or non-aversive experience?
- ☐ Enjoy reading about the functions of the human brain?
- ☐ Get excited about human anatomy and biological functioning?
- ☐ Think you would enjoy conducting research aimed at identifying specific brain functioning?
- ☐ Want to work in a medical setting with brain-injured patients?
- ☐ Enjoy solving complex puzzles?
- ☐ Want to work in a hospital?
- ☐ Have an interest in technology?
- ☐ Believe that much of human behavior has a biological cause or component?
- ☐ Want to conduct neurological assessments?
- ☐ Want to help people overcome brain injuries and neurological problems?
- ☐ Like science?
- ☐ Want to go to graduate school?
- ☐ Do you want to conduct research (for example, psychosurgery) with animals?

Scoring: The more boxes you checked, the more likely it is that a career in biopsychology, neuropsychology, or cognitive neuropsychology is for you.

CAREERS FOR STUDENTS WITH INTERESTS IN INDUSTRIAL, ORGANIZATIONAL, AND HUMAN FACTORS PSYCHOLOGY

CHAPTER 9

CHAPTER GUIDE

Industrial Psychology

Selection and Placement of Employees

Training and Development of Employees

Performance Evaluation of Employees

Participation in Applying and Adhering to Laws and Litigation

Organizational Psychology

Improve Job Satisfaction and Quality of Work Life

Improve Leadership

Promote Organizational Development

Human Factors

Opportunities with a Bachelor's Degree

Human Resources Jobs

Commercial or Industrial Design Assistant

Administrative Assistant and Office Manager

Opportunities with a Graduate Degree

Human Resources

Consultant

Usability Specialist

Environmental Designer

Suggested Readings

Web Resources

Checklist: Is Work Psychology for You?

As you likely are aware by now, psychology—the study of human behavior—can inform all fields. Psychology offers important applications to business settings. Several subdisciplines of psychology address the needs of business and industry: industrial psychology, organizational psychology, and human factors psychology. Collectively, these areas are referred to as "work psychology" (Patterson, 2001). Degree holders in psychology work with owners, managers, and employees of business and industry to select, train, and manage employees, design and market products, and organize work environments. Those with interests in industrial and organizational psychology apply psychological principles to the workplace, and those with interests in human factors psychology apply psychological principles in the design of equipment, work spaces, and computer software. In this chapter, you'll learn about each of these areas of psychology and explore careers that combine psychology with business and industry.

INDUSTRIAL PSYCHOLOGY

Industrial psychology, sometimes called *personnel psychology*, is the study of individual behavior in work settings. A career as an industrial psychologist entails one or more of the following activities. Note that many of these activities may be conducted by persons with various levels of training, from a bachelor's degree with considerable work experience to a doctoral-trained industrial psychologist; however, the most advanced positions tend to be held by doctoral-level industrial psychologists.

SELECTION AND PLACEMENT OF EMPLOYEES

Careful selection and appropriate placement of employees promotes their job satisfaction and productivity. An industrial psychologist employs a scientific approach toward selecting and placing employees. Degree holders with interest and experience in industrial psychology conduct job analyses to determine the specific tasks a job entails and the individual abilities and characteristics needed to be successful. With advanced training in industrial psychology, professionals create, validate, and choose tests and interviews that are administered to job applicants to determine whether they should be hired and where they should be placed (Kasserman, 2005; Kuther, 2005). Placing employees entails identifying what jobs are most compatible with an employee's skills and interests, as assessed through questionnaires and interviews (Muchinsky, 2006). After placing employees into jobs, the emphasis shifts to following up with employees to determine how well the assessment tests predict later job performance.

TRAINING AND DEVELOPMENT OF EMPLOYEES

Industrial psychology is applied in training and development of employees, specifically, in conducting needs analyses to determine the skills and technical needs of employees and developing training programs to impart those skills. Professionals with training in industrial psychology create assessment centers, collections of questionnaires, vignettes to assess problem-solving skills, and simulated work situations to determine an employee's skills and abilities (Aamodt, 2007; Tenopyr, 1997). Training needs may include assisting new employees during their transition to the workplace, updating current employees' technical skills, preparing employees for new responsibilities, and providing diversity training to retrain employees' attitudes, prejudices, and stereotypes (Muchinsky, 2006; Kasserman, 2005; Scrader, 2002). Training in industrial psychology also aids professionals in devising methods for evaluating the effectiveness of training programs.

PERFORMANCE EVALUATION OF EMPLOYEES

The first step in performance evaluation entails determining the criteria or standards by which employees will be evaluated. What defines employee success? Training in industrial psychology helps professionals choose, create, and validate methods for measuring the criteria that underlie employee success. They assess employees' abilities and performance, providing feedback and documentation about the quality and quantity of an employee's work to support pay increases and promotions (Aamodt, 2007; Muchinsky, 2006). Specialists in performance evaluation also train supervisors to evaluate employee performance and to communicate the results to employees.

PARTICIPATION IN APPLYING AND ADHERING TO LAWS AND LITIGATION

Industrial psychology examines how legal issues relate to the workplace (for example, selecting, hiring, and promoting employees). Professionals with training in industrial psychology create policies and conduct regular training workshops to promote a positive work environment and to prevent harassment and other issues that contribute to a hostile work environment. When companies are faced with layoffs they often seek advice from professionals with training in industrial psychology regarding how to act with fairness and sensitivity in order to avoid litigation from disgruntled former employees (Murray, 2002).

When devising employee selection, placement, and training procedures, industrial psychology professionals must learn a great deal about civil rights laws and build compliance with the laws into their efforts (Aamodt, 2007; Tenopyr, 1997). They must understand the legal context for personnel decisions and assist their employers in making personnel decisions that are legal. Individuals with training in industrial psychology may advise the company's attorneys and explain the science behind a company's hiring and promotion policies (meaning, the validity of the assessment tests and interviews). They often assist company attorneys in preparing for litigation in response to complaints from employees and former employees under the various federal, state, and local civil rights acts (Tenopyr, 1997). As expert court witnesses, professionals with advanced training and experience in industrial psychology persuade judges and juries that work was done correctly. Some might work as expert witnesses on employment-related cases, such as those concerning discrimination. In those cases the psychologist analyzes the information to determine whether discrimination has taken place and testifies concerning the results of the analysis (Weiner, 2001).

ORGANIZATIONAL PSYCHOLOGY

The distinction between industrial and organizational psychology is fuzzy because practicing industrial and organizational psychologists often share job descriptions and duties (and many graduate programs are labeled as Industrial-Organization Psychology); therefore, the two areas are often referred to as industrial/organizational psychology. As we've discussed, industrial psychologists traditionally focus on the individual worker: selection, placement, training, and evaluation. The organizational psychologist works at the organizational level to understand how workers function in the organization and how the organization functions as a whole. The following sections discuss activities typically ascribed to organizational psychologists. As with our discussion of industrial psychology, many of these activities may be conducted by persons with various levels of training, from a bachelor's degree with considerable work experience to a doctoral-trained organizational psychologist; however, the most advanced positions tend to be held by doctoral-level organizational psychologists.

IMPROVE JOB SATISFACTION AND QUALITY OF WORK LIFE

Professionals with interests in organizational psychology determine what factors contribute to a healthy and productive work force. They examine job satisfaction and study factors associated with it, such as employee turnover, absenteeism, age, pay, motivation, and attitudes toward the organization. They develop and evaluate systems to promote job satisfaction by rewarding good performance and redesigning jobs to make them more challenging, meaningful, and satisfying to employees (Muchinsky, 2006). Promoting job satisfaction entails understanding workers' needs and creating incentives that build job commitment and loyalty. For example, professionals with training in organizational psychology might attempt to understand how Generation Y workers are different from the generations that came before them and how companies can tailor employee incentives to maximize their satisfaction (Cohen, 2002). They also study how employee services (for example, office-based childcare, gym facilities) influence morale, job satisfaction, and productivity.

IMPROVE LEADERSHIP

Organizational psychologists study leadership: What makes a good leader? They identify characteristics of effective leaders and determine the types of leaders who are most effective in particular positions. People with training in organizational psychology create individual and group training programs to improve the leadership and communication skills of supervisors and managers (Williams, 2005). With advanced training in organizational psychology, some professionals act as executive coaches, working one-on-one with individuals to help them become better leaders and business people (Kilburg, 1996; Witherspoon & White, 1996).

PROMOTE ORGANIZATIONAL DEVELOPMENT

Professionals with training in organizational psychology help companies analyze the organization's functioning and determine when changes are needed. They help organizations make changes, transition to new ways of managing things, and accept change. Organizations grow and change over time. Organizational development entails studying growth, directing it, and facilitating it (Muchinsky, 2006).

Professionals in organizational psychology act as change agents who identify problems, study potential solutions, and make recommendations (Aamodt, 2004; Kasserman, 2005; Tenopyr, 1997). They might examine and refine business procedures, such as developing a paperwork processing plan that is concise, consistent, and without unnecessary steps. Professionals with training in organizational psychology help organizations manage and resolve interpersonal problems (Williams, 2005), such as using conflict-resolution skills to work out a solution for feuding departments or team members. Another task might entail examining the lines of authority or communication and redesigning them when necessary. Industrial and organizational psychology is applicable to all work settings—business, consulting firms, government, the military, and university.

HUMAN FACTORS

Human factors psychology, sometimes called engineering psychology, is concerned with the interaction between humans and their environments, and especially humans and machines. Human factors professionals design work environments to optimize productivity, employee satisfaction, and safety, and limit stress, fatigue, and error. Some specialize in human and computer interaction, or study how people interact with computers in order to improve computer applications and hardware designs (Chapman, 2005; Day, 1996). A human factors professional might study how to make Web sites more user-friendly (Clay, 2000), or engage in device testing, new product design, and developing warnings and labeling for products (Callan, 2004). Others may conduct research and develop programs in military command, aircraft and ship control systems, or Internet systems (Callan, 2004).

People with interests in human factors often study error prevention and management (the study of human error) in order to predict and prevent errors through excellent design. An understanding of how people use products and the common mistakes that people are likely to make aids in designing products that prevent error and misuse. For example, a professional might work to reduce human error in medicine by improving the accessibility of software for recording patient information, streamlining reporting procedures, or adding cross-checks before surgeries or other medical procedures are conducted (Kao & Thomas, 2008; Woods, 2002). Another area of work is in managing traffic, looking for ways to reduce accidents and injury, death, and property losses on highways. Human factors is also important in promoting aviation safety and preventing pilot error (Landwehr, 2001; Lauber, 1997; Tyler, 2000). Human factors professionals can play a role in improving national security by deterring future terrorist threats directed towards air travel because they analyze and have tools to evaluate proposed changes in equipment, procedures, and regulations, and study how they impact efficiency of people operating them and the system as a whole (Callan, 2004; Hart, 2002).

Ergonomics, the study of work environments and how to modify them to enhance productivity, is an important subarea of human factors. Ergonomic professionals adapt work environments, including computer interfaces and other equipment, to compensate for the limitations and qualities of people, increasing safety and reducing accidents. They study the effects of environmental factors such as light, noise, temperature, and work schedules (for example, night shifts or compressed work weeks) on worker safety, productivity, and satisfaction (Muchinsky, 2006). Others work to improve the safety and comfort of spaces. For example, investigating the capacity and comfort of aircraft seating and studying the user interface of anything with which an airline customer will interact (Landwehr, 2001).

OPPORTUNITIES WITH A BACHELOR'S DEGREE

A bachelor's degree prepares graduates for a variety of entry-level positions within business and industry. Because of the solid liberal arts background, psychology majors with interests in business are excellent matches for positions in human resource departments and can serve as assistants in other fields, as described in the following sections.

HUMAN RESOURCES JOBS

Human resources departments, also known as personnel departments, are responsible for managing an organization's employees: recruitment, placement, administering salaries and benefits, training, and conducting research on employee needs and satisfaction. Human resources personnel work to attract the most qualified employees, match them to the jobs for which they are best suited, help them to succeed in their jobs, and ensure that the organization complies with labor laws. Depending on your interests and experience, there are a variety of positions at all levels of education within human resource departments located in businesses, government, and private and nonprofit agencies. Recognize that the level of opportunities, responsibilities, and autonomy varies with expertise, experience, and education. Entry-level employees likely will not serve all functions described, but they will have the opportunity to learn and the potential to grow into positions with more responsibility.

HUMAN RESOURCE GENERALIST.   Human resource generalists engage in all aspects of managing personnel, including recruitment, placement, training, and development.

Often they also administer salary and benefits, and develop personnel policies that conform to labor laws. Entry-level generalist positions typically fall under the following titles: *human resource assistant, human resource specialist, personnel assistant, personnel specialist,* or *employee relations specialist.* They are more likely to be found in small businesses and organizations with few employees.

EMPLOYMENT, RECRUITMENT, AND PLACEMENT SPECIALIST.   The job description of an employment, recruitment, and placement specialist includes recruiting personnel, collecting applications and résumés for jobs, assembling applicant files, performing background checks, interviewing applicants, administering pre-employment assessments and tests, and placing employees. In short, they are involved in hiring employees. They also orient new employees, educate employees about salary and benefits, and assess departmental needs for staffing. Entry-level positions for recent graduates will likely entail more paper-based activities such as filing, organizing applicant files, and so on. More advanced activities and responsibilities, such as interviewing, come with experience. Common titles for entry-level positions include *interviewer, recruiter, employment representative,* or *EEO (equal employment and opportunity) specialist.*

TRAINING AND DEVELOPMENT SPECIALIST.   Training and development specialists conduct training sessions, provide on-the-job training, and maintain records of employee participation in training and development programs. They help employees improve their knowledge and skills (such as sales techniques, safety guidelines, and productivity), and assist supervisors and managers to improve their interpersonal skills in dealing with employees. More advanced training and development positions involve human resource planning and organizational development. For example, a training specialist might create a leadership development program to develop employees' leadership potential and prepare them for promotion and advancement. Entry-level positions in this area include *training specialist* and *orientation specialist.* Some might include the title of *assistant.*

COMPENSATION AND BENEFITS SPECIALIST.   Compensation and benefits specialists engage in job analysis, write job descriptions, collect and organize information about an organization's benefits programs, administer benefits plans, and monitor costs. Typical titles include *benefits analyst, compensation specialist,* and *salary administrator.* Entry-level positions often include the title of *assistant* and generally include fewer responsibilities and entail providing support to supervisors.

EVALUATING CAREERS IN HUMAN RESOURCES.   A career in human resources offers many advantages, including an office environment, a 40-hour work week, and opportunities for advancement with a bachelor's degree and job experience. As a human resources employee, you'll have the opportunity to directly help people, solve practical problems, and use your knowledge of psychology. You will interact with a wide range of people, which will require flexibility, patience, and excellent communication skills. Sometimes the "people" part of the job can be stressful and challenging. For example, you may deal with employees who are angry over changes in work conditions or who have been laid off. Human resources positions also entail

| TABLE 9.1 | SAMPLE HUMAN RESOURCE POSITIONS AND SALARIES (ADAPTED FROM SALARY.COM, 2008) |

Title	Median 2008 Salary
Benefits Analyst	$45,946
Employee Relations Specialist	$45,750
Human Resources Assistant	$38,537
Human Resources Generalist	$46,590
Recruiter	$41,015
Training Specialist	$43,302

administrative work that requires attention to detail and can sometimes be tedious. Although entry-level positions in human resources are highly competitive, the field is expected to grow more rapidly than the average (16 percent) for all occupations through 2016 (Bureau of Labor Statistics, 2008) and human resources positions offer comfortable salaries, as shown in Table 9.1.

If you are interested in pursuing a career in human resources, psychology offers a solid background in communication skills, statistics, research methods, presentation skills, and human behavior. Additional courses in communication, writing, business administration, labor law, and accounting will enhance your employability. Seek an internship to obtain experience and make contacts that can help you find a human resources position after graduation.

COMMERCIAL OR INDUSTRIAL DESIGN ASSISTANT

An assistant to a commercial or industrial designer helps in designing products and equipment, such as airplanes, cars, children's toys, computer equipment, furniture, home appliances, and medical, office, and recreational equipment. A designer combines artistic talent with research on customer needs, ways products are used, the consumer market, and production materials and methods to create a design that is functional, appealing, and competitive with others in the marketplace. An assistant to a designer conducts research and engages in support functions related to the designer's needs. Depending on the particular field or industry, design assistants may help designers in planning packaging and containers for products such as foods, beverages, toiletries, or medicine, or might assist in creating and designing packaging, illustrations, or advertising for manufactured materials. Design assistants help the designer to coordinate design concepts among engineering, marketing, production, and sales departments in order to produce a product that is safe, well-designed, and marketable.

Designers and design assistants are employed by manufacturers, corporations, and design firms. They tend to work regular 40-hour weeks in an office setting. At the entry level, design assistants often provide administrative support including clerical tasks; as they demonstrate competence, assistants will take on more design-related tasks.

The market for design assistants is expected to grow as rapidly as the average through the year 2016; however, competition is keen (Bureau of Labor Statistics,

2008). In 2008, the median entry-level salary in design was $35,000 (American Institute of Graphic Arts, 2003). If you're interested in becoming a design assistant, creativity is essential and sketching ability will help you to advance to design positions. Psychology's emphasis on research methods and problem solving will suit you well in this field. In addition, take courses in merchandising, business administration, and marketing, and seek training in art—especially a course in computer-aided design (CAD).

ADMINISTRATIVE ASSISTANT AND OFFICE MANAGER

Traditionally the administrative assistant was a secretary who spent her (as the majority were women) days typing memos on an old-fashioned typewriter (the machine in which you roll the paper in and each letter is stamped onto the page as you press the keys). Today's administrative assistants (also known as *executive assistants* or *executive secretaries*) tend to engage in office management functions and support executive staff. Increasingly, office automatization and executives' use of word processing software has relieved administrative assistants from typing. In addition to coordinating administrative and information management activities within an office, many administrative assistants train and orient new staff, and conduct research on the Internet. Administrative assistants schedule meetings and appointments, maintain files, conduct research, manage databases, create reports, and manage projects.

Office managers, sometimes titled *administrative services managers*, oversee various components of an office, varying from administrative assistance and reception services to data processing, conference planning, payroll, and other office functions. The responsibilities will vary with the position and organization, but the role is to oversee office functions.

Employment of administrative assistants and administrative services managers is expected to grow about as rapidly as the average for all occupations through 2016 (Bureau of Labor Statistics, 2008). An administrative assistant position offers several advantages, including an office environment, a 40-hour work week, and the opportunity to help others solve practical problems. Administrative services manager positions have similar advantages as well as the opportunity to lead others, have relative autonomy, and the ability to show creativity in solving office problems. Salaries for administrative assistants and administrative services managers are competitive. In 2008, the median salary for administrative assistants was $39,568; half of administrative assistants earn between $34,985 and $44,152 (Salary.com, 2008). In 2008, the median salary for all administrative services managers, regardless of education or experience, was $71,922; half earn between $60,965 and $82,880 (Salary.com, 2008). Salaries rise with experience. Administrative positions can entail stress, especially when the office is trying to meet a deadline or if a boss expects the assistant to run personal errands. Managing administrative staff can be particularly stressful because it entails coordinating the activities of several employees in order to achieve goals, and requires excellent interpersonal and planning skills. Skills in organization, communication, research, and stress management, as well as understanding of human behavior, leadership, and groups, make the psychology major competitive for administrative assistant and manager positions.

TABLE 9.2	PREPARATION FOR BA–LEVEL CAREERS RELATED TO INDUSTRIAL, ORGANIZATIONAL, AND HUMAN FACTORS PSYCHOLOGY

Coursework

Human Resources Positions
- Accounting
- Business Administration
- Communication
- Economics
- Human Resources Management
- Labor Economics
- Labor Law
- Management Information Systems or Database Applications in Business
- Organizational Behavior
- Writing

Commercial or Industrial Design Assistant Positions
- Advertising
- Architecture
- Art: Sketching, Design, and Computer-Aided Design (CAD)
- Business Administration
- Engineering
- Industrial Design
- Marketing
- Mathematics
- Product/Brand Management
- Certification in art and design from the National Association of Schools of Art and Design is available at some institutions (about 250 in the U.S.)

Administrative Assistant and Office Manager Positions
- Accounting
- Business Administration
- Business Law
- Communication
- Finance
- Human Resources Management
- Management Information Systems or Database Applications in Business
- Purchasing and Sales
- Writing

Applied Experiences: Volunteer, intern, or paid part-time positions in any of the following settings
- Advertising Department
- Any Office Setting
- Architect
- Human Resources Department
- Leadership programs
- Product design firm
- Engineering firm

Research Experiences: Experiences studying and participating in research in any of the following areas*
- Human factors
- Industrial psychology
- Management and leadership
- Organizational behavior
- Social psychology

*Note that the content area of the research is less important than the experience itself, which enhances reasoning, quantitative, writing, and organizational skills.

OPPORTUNITIES WITH A GRADUATE DEGREE

Although a bachelor's degree in psychology prepares graduates for entry-level jobs, graduate degree holders have more opportunities for advancement. A masters degree can serve as the basis for supervisory and advanced opportunities in human resources, usability, and market research fields. Doctoral degrees offer additional opportunities, especially in upper management, consulting, and product design and development careers. Masters degree holders who have extensive experience often obtain positions comparable to those of doctoral degree holders.

HUMAN RESOURCES

Graduate degree holders may work in any of the human resources career tracks that we have discussed, with additional responsibilities and compensation. A graduate degree enables the employee to engage in management and executive functions within human resources departments.

Human resource generalists with graduate degrees are involved with all human resource activities, including designing and administering human resources policies, collecting and analyzing data, making recommendations to management, and taking leadership roles on projects. Similarly, graduates who specialize in *employment, recruitment, and placement* design assessment techniques to select and place employees, collect data on the effectiveness of the assessments, and supervise other workers. Graduate degree holders specialized in *training and development* create training programs, conduct research on the effectiveness of those programs, and supervise other workers. Other human resources professionals specialize in the training and development needs of the organization as a whole; these professionals often are called *organizational development specialists*. With additional experience, graduate degree holders move on to managerial positions, as well as more advanced positions that entail overseeing all human resources functions within an organization, such as human resources manager or human resources director. Salaries for human resources positions for graduate degree holders are shown in Table 9.3.

CONSULTANT

Consultant is an umbrella term for a variety of individuals who engage in problem solving within organizations. Consultants specialize in a variety of areas, including management of employees or an organization's resources, strategy development and long range planning, training, organizational development, and recruitment. Consultants in each of these areas engage in the same basic task: they advise organizations on how to solve problems, such as researching a new market, reorganizing a company's structure, hiring top executives, or improving productivity. Consultants offer their clients perspective and insight (an understanding of the big picture and the problem at hand), analysis (an examination of potential solutions), and recommendations (a strategic plan to address the problem) (Boulakia, 1998; Kasserman, 2005). In other words, consultants solve business problems by applying a scientific approach through testing hypotheses and analyzing data (McCracken, 1998).

TABLE 9.3 | SAMPLE HUMAN RESOURCE POSITIONS AND SALARIES FOR GRADUATE DEGREE HOLDERS (ADAPTED FROM SALARY.COM, 2008)

Title	Median 2008 Salary
Advanced Human Resources Positions	
Employee Relations Specialist	$71,188
Human Resources Generalist	$68,848
Organizational Development Specialist	$76,263
Executive Recruiter	$75,124
Training Specialist	$64,575
Managerial Positions	
Employee Relations Manager	$82,768
Human Resources Manager	$81,100
Organizational Development Manager	$97,627
Recruiting Manager	$83,650
Training Manager	$78,712

There are many different types of consultants. *Management consultants* analyze ways to make an organization more competitive and efficient (Bureau of Labor Statistics, 2008). *Search consultants* are high-level recruiters, often called "head hunters," who use their knowledge of industrial psychology to recruit, assess, and place employees in top positions. *Organizational development consultants* help companies with team building, training, dealing with change, and professional development. Marketing consultants help companies advertise and market products and services. *Mediation consultants* help organizations to solve interpersonal conflicts in the workplace (meaning, conflicts among individuals, and within and between departments and teams) and teach communication and conflict management skills. Some consultants emphasize developing leadership skills in executives; recently, these consultants have been referred to as *executive coaches* (Kilburg, 1996). An executive coach helps an executive identify personal strengths and weaknesses, and works to enhance an executive's skills and promote growth (Witherspoon & White, 1996).

Advanced analytical skills developed in graduate school make graduate degree holders well suited to careers in consulting. They understand how to analyze data, manage databases, and present data simply and elegantly through the use of tables and graphs. Their knowledge of computer software and statistics is an asset to any organization, and their communication skills, honed through writing papers, theses, and dissertations, as well as making conference presentations, are valuable in the office setting (Sebestyen, 2000).

There are many advantages to a career in consulting. It is a great way to learn about business because most firms offer plenty of opportunities for professional development through training workshops, seminars, and mentoring programs. (McCracken, 1998; Montell, 1999). As a consultant you'll collaborate with talented colleagues from a variety of educational and experiential backgrounds. You'll be challenged to devise and implement useful solutions to real problems (Smith, 1997). As a recent graduate, you likely will find that your lack of experience is an important challenge to doing your job, so you will find yourself working hard to catch up (Hedge & Borman, 2008). The pace is quick and the problems constantly change: One day you might analyze the potential market for a new product and the next day consider reorganizing the management structure of an organization. The main disadvantage of a career in consulting is that it often requires long hours and travel; however, the salary makes up for the long hours. In 2008, the median annual salary for consultants to businesses and organizations, across all education levels, was $82,658, with 25 percent earning less than $71,068 and 75 percent earning more than $94,249 (Salary.com, 2008).

Among doctoral-level industrial/organizational psychologists sampled who work at consulting firms, the median salary for consultants with 5 to 9 years of experience in 2007 was $110,000, with 50 percent earning between $96,500 and $148,500 (American Psychological Association, 2008). The median starting salary for psychologists from other subfields who work at consulting firms was $85,000 for those with 2 to 4 years of experience and $120,000 for those with 5 to 10 years of experience, with 50 percent earning between $75,000 and $125,000 and $100,000 and $130,000, respectively (American Psychological Association 2008). Finally, consulting careers are expected to grow much more rapidly than the average for all occupations through 2016 (Bureau of Labor Statistics, 2008); the field is expected to grow by 78 percent, making consulting the most rapidly growing industry.

USABILITY SPECIALIST

Many professionals with graduate degrees in industrial/organizational or human factors psychology obtain positions in product design and development, often specializing in promoting product usability, or ease and pleasure of use. Usable, or user-friendly, products are easy for users to learn how to use, are efficient and memorable, minimize errors, and are pleasing or satisfying to use (Aamodt, 2004). Usability specialists ensure that product designs fit users. They work with all kinds of products: toys, computer hardware and software, electronic equipment, cars, and more.

The understanding of human capacities and limitations that comes with a graduate degree in psychology is excellent preparation for a career in usability applied to product design and production (Day, 1996). Usability specialists serve as user advocates in that their goal is to create products that meet the needs of the user. They research a product, create product prototypes, and test and modify them based on input from potential users. For example, in designing the interior of an automobile, they might create a life-size prototype in which all of the instruments and controls can be moved (for example, by attaching them with Velcro). Potential users then provide feedback on the best location for each of the instruments and controls, moving them as necessary. Other usability specialists conduct usability studies to create aircraft that meet pilots' needs and thereby reduce pilot error (Lauber, 1997; Tyler, 2000). Psychologists are also employed by NASA and contribute to the operation of the space shuttle by applying information about how people think and perceive sensory stimuli into the design of equipment and controls used to pilot space craft (McCann, 2001).

Usability research also takes place in the computer software industry. Knowledge of cognitive psychology can be applied to explain why a particular software interface design is confusing for users (Chapman, 2005; Diddams, 1998). Psychologists record and analyze users' behaviors when they try to accomplish a task using a computer software product, such as a spreadsheet program or computer game. For example, how easily can consumers navigate software programs designed to manage pictures? How do they manage their digital photos, and is there a way to improve the ease and speed with which the user can access photographs (Czerwinski, 2002)? Psychologists interview users about their experience with the product: Was it easy to use? What confused them about the interface? The resulting knowledge is used to improve the software design. This problem-solving technique is applied in many contexts. For example, human factors psychologists might assess the credibility of a computer program that simulates medical surgeries, permitting medical students and doctors to practice surgical techniques (Haluck, 2005).

Psychologists who choose careers in product design and development have the opportunity to engage in research that improves people's experiences with products. Their research has practical implications and they get to see the results of their work. A regular 40-hour work week, excellent opportunities for masters-level psychologists, and high rates of compensation are other advantages. The design and development industry is expected to grow as rapidly as the average through 2016 (Bureau of Labor Statistics, 2008). In 2008, the average entry salary for usability practitioners was about $60,000; the average for those with 5 years of experience was about $90,000 (Nielson, 2008).

ENVIRONMENTAL DESIGNER

Professionals trained in industrial/organizational psychology or human factors often work in environmental design. They study the interactive relationship between environments and human behavior and seek to understand why people find some spaces comfortable and others threatening, as well as why some spaces are easier to navigate than others. They then apply this information to design and enhance environments, such as the layout of offices, the design of office buildings and shopping malls, and even the design of neighborhoods and communities, to reduce stress, create more efficiency, and minimize accidents (Winerman, 2004).

Environmental design professionals work for corporations, local and federal governments, and consulting firms. Some participate in city and community planning, designing buildings, and enhancing the interior layout of existing structures. A career in environmental design requires good communication skills and the ability to work as part of a team. Environmental designers who are assigned to large projects will work closely with professionals from many fields, including politicians, architects, urban planners, economists, and engineers, to complete projects. Working with many disciplines can be interesting, but challenging. Good listening and research skills are essential to success in this field, because environmental designers spend lots of time interacting with people—consumers, community members, and other professionals. For example, when a city plans to rebuild a run-down neighborhood, an environmental design professional may interview people who live in the neighborhood to obtain their ideas and perspectives about how to improve the area.

An important advantage of a career in environmental design is the opportunity to be part of a large project and to make a difference. An environmental designer who participates in designing a new community housing project, for example, will find that the work influences residents' day-to-day lives. The teamwork needed to complete large-scale projects can sometimes lead to frustration, because when many people are involved, decisions can take a long time. Also, projects generally take a long time to implement, which can be challenging for someone who is looking for more immediate results from their work. Environmental designers who can take criticism well and deal with pressure without becoming burned out are at a distinct advantage in this stressful field.

Careers in environmental design are expected to increase about as rapidly as average through the year 2016 (Bureau of Labor Statistics, 2008), and salaries are competitive. In 1999, the average salary for a doctoral-level psychologist in environmental design was over $65,000 ($83,506 adjusted for 2008; Conaway, 2000). If you're interested in a career in environmental design, seek additional training in communications, research design and statistics, and related fields such as economics, urban planning, and architecture. Also, seek an internship with an environmental design firm, city planning office, or related placement to obtain hands-on experience in this exciting field.

As we've seen, there are many career opportunities for psychology students with business interests. Many entry-level positions are open to bachelor's degree holders in psychology who have taken coursework and obtained experience in relevant areas. Opportunities expand for graduate degree holders. Remember that these are just a sampling of possible careers; more await your exploration. Finally, note that many other careers described in this book are pertinent to students with interests in industrial, organizational, and human factors psychology. See Chapter 13 to learn about careers in research, publishing, and academia, as well as Chapter 10 for other career options for graduates with quantitative skills.

SUGGESTED READINGS

Aamodt, M. G. (2007). *Applied industrial/organizational psychology.* Pacific Grove, CA: Wadsworth.

Chapman, C. N. (2005). Software user research: Psychologist in the software industry. In R. D. Morgan, T. L. Kuther, & C. J. Habben (Eds.), *Life after graduate school in psychology: Insider's advice from new psychologists* (pp. 211–224). New York: Psychology Press.

Kasserman, J. (2005). Management consultation: Improving organizations. In R. D. Morgan, T. L. Kuther, & C. J. Habben (Eds.), *Life after graduate school in psychology: Insider's advice from new psychologists* (pp. 183–196). New York: Psychology Press.

Kuther, T. L. (2005). *Your career in psychology: Industrial/organizational psychology.* Belmont: Wadsworth.

McKenzie, J. S., Drinan, H. G., & Traynow, W. J. (2001). *Opportunities in human resource management careers.* New York: McGraw-Hill.

Muchinsky, P. M. (2006). *Psychology applied to work*. Pacific Grove, CA: Wadsworth.

Pass, J. (2006). Industrial/Organizational (I/O) psychology as a career: Improving workforce performance and retention. In Sternberg, R. J. *Career paths in psychology: Where your degree can take you*, 2nd ed. Washington, DC: APA.

Pond, S. B. (1999). Industrial-organizational psychology: The psychology of people working together. *Eye on Psi Chi, 3*(3), 34–37.

Salvendy, G. (2006). *Handbook of human factors and ergonomics*. Hoboken, NJ: Wiley.

Tenopyr, M. L. (1997). Improving the workplace: Industrial/organizational psychology as a career. In R. Sternberg (Ed.), *Career paths in psychology: Where your degree can take you* (pp. 185–196). Washington, DC: American Psychological Association.

Wetfeet (2008). *Careers in management consulting*. New York: Wetfeet.com

Williams, S. (2005). Executive management: Helping executives manage their organizations through organizational and market research. In R. D. Morgan, T. L. Kuther, & C. J. Habben (Eds.), *Life after graduate school in psychology: Insider's advice from new psychologists* (pp. 225–238). New York: Psychology Press.

Wolgalter, M. S., & Rogers, W. A. (1998). Human factors/ergonomics: Using psychology to make a better and world. *Eye on Psi Chi, 3*(1), 23–26.

WEB RESOURCES

An Interesting Career in Psychology: Collection of Career Articles
http://www.apa.org/science/nonacad_careers.html

Society for Industrial and Organizational Psychology
http://siop.org/

Professional Industrial Organizational Psychologist Network
http://www.piop.net

Academy of Management
http://www.aomonline.org/

Society for Human Resource Management
http://www.shrm.org/

Human Factors and Ergonomics Society
http://hfes.org/

Getting an Industrial Design Job
http://new.idsa.org/webmodules/articles/articlefiles/GETIDJOB.pdf

Current Trends in Environmental Psychology
http://www.ucm.es/info/Psyap/iaap/evans.htm

Careers in Industrial/Organizational Psychology
http://www.wcupa.edu/_ACADEMICS/sch_cas.psy/Career_Paths/Industrial/Career06.htm

Careers in Consulting
http://jobsearch.about.com/cs/businessjobs/a/consulting.htm

Consulting Career, Job, and Training Information
http://www.careeroverview.com/consulting-careers.html

CHECKLIST: IS WORK PSYCHOLOGY FOR YOU?

Do you:

- ☐ Have an interest in business?
- ☐ Want to understand how psychological methods can improve employee selection and placement?
- ☐ Want to help others gain skills?
- ☐ Want to devise methods to evaluate employees?
- ☐ Want to advise businesses and corporations on personnel policies?
- ☐ Want to promote teamwork in an office environment?
- ☐ Want to study leadership, understand the qualities of an effective leader, and help supervisors and managers to improve their leadership skills?
- ☐ Have an interest in helping organizations make transitions and changes?
- ☐ Have an interest in the way the environment shapes our behavior?
- ☐ Want to design and organize work environments to maximize efficiency?
- ☐ Have good communication skills?
- ☐ Feel comfortable working in groups?
- ☐ Enjoy conducting research?
- ☐ Have the ability to be flexible and deal with ambiguity?

Scoring: The more boxes you checked, the more likely it is that you're a good match for a career in work psychology.

CHAPTER **10** | EXPERIMENTAL, COGNITIVE, AND QUANTITATIVE PSYCHOLOGY AND PSYCHOMETRICS

CHAPTER GUIDE

Number crunching, pocket protectors, lab rats, and IQ tests are just some of the things that come to mind when most psychology students think of experimental, cognitive, and quantitative psychology, and psychometrics. Expertise in statistics and research methodology is valuable, offering graduates some of the most flexible career paths in psychology.

EXPERIMENTAL PSYCHOLOGY

All psychologists learn how to conduct and interpret research, but experimental psychologists specialize in conducting research. Experimental psychologists tend to study research methodology in greater detail than do other psychologists and they apply these methods to study a variety of topics including learning, sensation, perception, human performance, motivation, memory, language, thinking, and communication. Some experimental psychologists study animals to apply what they learn to humans, or simply because animal behavior is interesting.

We usually identify experimental psychologists by the area in which they conduct research (such as perception psychologist or learning psychologist). For example, a sensation and perception psychologist studies the way we use our senses to become aware of the world around us; he or she might study vision, hearing, taste, smell, touch, or all of the senses. A learning psychologist studies processes of learning, such as classical and operant conditioning. There are a wide variety of experimental psychologists, because there are many areas in which to conduct research.

COGNITIVE PSYCHOLOGY

Cognitive psychologists study human cognition: how we take in, store, retrieve, and apply knowledge. They attempt to understand the nature of human thought. How do we attend to the world around us? How do we take in, learn, understand, remember, and use information to make decisions? Cognitive psychologists are interested in topics like attention, visual and auditory perception, memory, reasoning, retrieval and forgetting, and problem solving. They conduct research to extend our knowledge about the mind and to construct theories that explain why our minds work the way they do. Some cognitive psychologists conduct applied research to develop products that people find easy to use (for example, computer software, handheld computer, or remote control, similar to the work of human factors psychologists). Other cognitive psychologists study how people learn in order to develop effective teaching methods. Given the wide range of activities in which humans engage, cognitive psychologists have a great many kinds of decisions and cognitive activities to explain and improve—and a wide range of potential research topics.

QUANTITATIVE PSYCHOLOGY

Quantitative psychology, sometimes called *mathematical psychology*, is the study of research methodology, or methods and techniques for acquiring, analyzing, and applying information. Quantitative psychologists are specialists in designing, conducting, and interpreting experiments. Quantitative psychologists create new methods for analyzing data (for example, statistical tests) and work to develop and test quantitative theories of cognition and behavior (for example, equations and formulas that can account for the range of behavioral phenomena that we see). Today there are mathematical theories of cognition, perception, social interactions, memory, decision making, abnormal behavior, and many other psychological phenomena.

PSYCHOMETRICS

Psychometrics is the science of measuring human characteristics. Psychometricians measure people's behavior, abilities, and potential in the intellectual, emotional, and social realms of functioning. Like quantitative psychologists, psychometricians are well versed in statistics; however, they specialize in measurement (meaning, how do you design a survey that captures the behavior that you intend to study?). Psychometricians create and revise personality tests, intelligence tests, and aptitude tests. They also use these tests to assess people's abilities and level of functioning to assist other psychologists who develop interventions, treatment plans, and diagnostic schemes.

OPPORTUNITIES WITH A BACHELOR'S DEGREE

If you're interested in experimental, cognitive, and quantitative psychology, or psychometrics, there are a variety of career options at the undergraduate level. However, remember that most bachelor's degree holders will begin in entry-level positions that generally entail fewer responsibilities and more clerical, data entry, and supervised work. With experience comes greater autonomy and responsibility, such as that entailed in jobs discussed in the following sections. As with all areas of psychology, graduate degrees open doors to additional career opportunities. Note that the following sections present national data on job growth and salaries; however, availability of jobs and the typical salary that you can expect for each varies by geographic region. Seek advice and do your homework when considering potential careers.

INSURANCE UNDERWRITER

Before an insurance company takes on a new client, whether individual or organizational, an insurance underwriter evaluates the risk of loss, determines the appropriate premium rate, and writes the insurance policy to cover the individuals or organization's risks of loss. An underwriter analyzes information that potential clients provide in insurance applications and supplements the analyses with information from loss control reports, medical reports, and other data to determine if a client is an acceptable risk. The underwriter then determines the appropriate insurance premium to charge. Entry-level positions as underwriters carry the titles of *assistant underwriter* or *underwriter trainee*, with duties and salaries commensurate with experience.

A career as an underwriter offers several advantages: a standard 40-hour work week, quiet office environment, competitive salary, and a measure of job security. Insurance underwriting is not a growth field; employment of underwriters is expected to grow more slowly than average through 2016, but is expected to increase as a growing economy and population expands the insurance needs of businesses and individuals (Bureau of Labor Statistics, 2008). However, insurance is a necessity for both individuals and organizations, so it is a profession that is less vulnerable to economic recessions and layoffs than other fields (Bureau of Labor Statistics, 2008). Finally, underwriting provides a comfortable salary. In 2008, the median salary for an assistant underwriter was $36,082 and median entry-level underwriter salary for life insurance plans was $42,272 and property and casualty plans earned a median salary was $44,430 (Salary.com, 2008). According to the Occupational Outlook Handbook, the median salary for all insurance underwriters was $53,350 in 2006 (Bureau of Labor Statistics, 2008).

Psychology majors have a solid liberal arts background, computer skills, and quantitative abilities that are useful for careers as insurance underwriters. If you're interested in this career, supplement your psychology major with additional courses in statistics, business administration, finance, or accounting. Consider a minor in business administration. Also, consider seeking an internship with an insurance company to learn more about the field.

COMPUTER PROGRAMMER

Computer programmers write the programs, or detailed instructions, that computers follow in performing their functions. They install, test, and debug programs to keep an organization's server and computer systems functional. For example, they might write programs to maintain and control computer systems and networks that permit an organization's computers to communicate with each other and enable an organization's website to function. Computer programmers use technology to solve problems. For example, they may write a new program or adjust existing software in order to assist an organization in performing its mission (for example, write a program to handle a specific job, such tracking inventory). If you are interested in computer programming and understand programming languages like C++, COBOL, or JAVA, a programming career might be for you.

An important advantage of a career in programming is the opportunity for life-long learning. New computer programs and languages rapidly emerge; programmers continually must reevaluate their skills and know the latest technologies. On the other side of the equation, long hours or weekends sometimes are required to meet deadlines or to fix bugs in computer programs. Through 2016, employment of programmers is expected to decline slowly (Bureau of Labor Statistics, 2008). Although overall employment of computer programers is expected to decline, numerous job openings will result from the need to replace programmers who leave the labor force or transfer to other occupations. A typical entry-level programmer earned a median salary of $49,928 in 2007. Median annual earnings of computer programmers were $65,510 in 2006, with the middle 50 percent earning between $49,580 and $85,080 (Bureau of Labor Statistics, 2008).

Psychology students' experience with computers and critical thinking are useful in this field. The analytical approach that cognitive psychologists take towards understanding human problem solving is similar to the methodical step-by-step approach that computer programmers take toward writing computer programs and solving bugs and glitches in programs. Helpful courses to take include mathematics, computer programming, and management information systems. A minor in computer science or management information systems will help you develop proficiency and courses in various programming languages, including C++ and Java, and will demonstrate breadth of knowledge. Employers primarily are interested in programming knowledge, so a degree in computer science isn't necessary if you understand programming languages and have hands-on experience. Seek internship or summer employment opportunities in the field to gain experience and contacts.

COMPUTER SUPPORT SPECIALIST

A computer support specialist provides technical assistance to users of hardware, software, and computer systems, acting as a troubleshooter who interpret problems and provide technical support for hardware, software, and systems. Computer support specialists work in at least two capacities: *technical support specialists* and *help-desk technicians*. Technical support specialists are employed by companies to help employees solve computer-related problems. They respond to inquiries from users, diagnose and solve problems, and may install, modify, clean, and repair computer hardware and software. Help desk technicians answer telephone calls and email inquiries from customers seeking technical assistance for a given hardware or software product. They help users by listening, asking questions to diagnose the problem, and walking the user through steps to solve the problem. Many companies consult help-desk technicians about customers' experiences with the product, what gives them the most trouble, and other customer concerns.

Advantages to careers in computer support include an office environment, excellent job outlook, and high starting salaries. Computer support specialists are projected to increase much more rapidly than the average through 2016 (Bureau of Labor Statistics, 2004). In 2008, a typical help desk technician earned a median salary of $43,319 (Salary.com, 2008); a technical support analyst earned a median salary of $50,586. Psychology majors have computer knowledge, interpersonal skills, and communication skills that are useful for careers in computer support. Completing additional computer classes may increase your marketability.

BUDGET ANALYST

Budget analysts provide data to an organization's management that help them to decide how to allocate an organization's financial resources. Budget analysts develop and analyze an organization's budgets. They analyze spending to determine ways of improving efficiency and increasing an organization's profits. Budget analysts provide advice and technical assistance to managers and department heads in preparing their annual budgets. They examine budgets for accuracy, completeness, and conformance with organizational procedures, objectives, and budgetary limits (Bureau of Labor Statistics, 2004). Throughout the year, budget analysts

TABLE 10.1	PREPARATION FOR BA-LEVEL CAREERS RELATED TO EXPERIMENTAL, COGNITIVE, AND QUANTITATIVE PSYCHOLOGY, AND PSYCHOMETRICS

Coursework

Insurance Underwriter Positions

Accounting
Business Administration
Business Law
Communication
Finance
Statistics
Math
Writing

Computer Programmer Positions

Computer Science
Database Systems such as DB2, Oracle, or Sybase
Management Information Systems
Mathematics
Programming Languages, including C++ and Java

Computer Support Positions

Communication
Computer Science
Computer Software Applications
Information Systems
Writing

Budget Analyst Positions

Accounting
Business Administration
Communication
Economics
Finance
Statistics
Mathematics

Applied Experiences: Volunteer, intern, or paid part-time positions in any of the following settings

Accounting Firm
Evaluation, Measurement, or Assessment Department or Company
Finance Firm
Information Technology Department
Insurance Company

Research Experiences: Experiences studying and participating in research in any of the following areas*

Cognitive Psychology
Experimental Psychology

continued

TABLE 10.1 | CONTINUED

Human Factors
Program Assessment
Psychometrics
Quantitative Psychology
Test Development

*Note that the content area of the research is less important than the experience itself, which enhances reasoning, quantitative, writing, and organizational skills.

monitor the budget to alert management to risks of overspending and avoid financial deficits.

Advantages of a career in budget analysis are the comfortable office setting, relative independence, and comfortable salary. However, long hours and tight, stressful deadlines are common. A bachelor's degree in psychology is sufficient for entry-level positions in budget analysis because psychology majors are skilled in communication, quantitative analysis, and computer use. Additional courses in business, accounting, economics, finance, and statistics are helpful. In 2008, a typical entry-level budget analyst earned a median base salary of $46,926 (Salary.com, 2008). Median annual salary for all budget analysts was $61,430 in 2006 (Bureau of Labor Statistics, 2008). Employment of budget analysts is expected to grow as rapidly as the average rate for all occupations through 2016 (Bureau of Labor Statistics, 2008).

OPPORTUNITIES WITH A GRADUATE DEGREE

The undergraduate psychology degree offers useful preparation to entry-level positions in a variety of areas. As is often the case, a graduate degree serves as preparation for additional and more advanced positions. A graduate degree in experimental psychology, cognitive psychology, quantitative psychology, or psychometrics opens doors to a variety of careers in business settings.

OPERATIONS RESEARCH ANALYST

Operations research (sometimes called *management science*) is a scientific approach to analyzing problems and making decisions. It entails using mathematics, statistics, and computer science to quantify situations and make decisions. Operations research analysts examine how to make products more efficiently, solve problems, and control inventory and distribution of products. They engage in problem solving by studying the problem, gathering data, analyzing it, and coming up with practical solutions. For example, operations research analysts might conduct research to determine the most efficient amount of inventory a business must keep on hand by talking with engineers about production levels, discussing purchasing levels and arrangements, and examining data on storage costs. If you choose a career in operations research analysis, you'll use mathematical modeling on computers to predict the potential outcomes of alternative solutions to a problem in order to determine which is best.

Operations research analysts are found in all work settings (military, government, business, and industry) and under various titles (*operations analyst, management analyst, policy analyst*). As an operations research analyst, you can expect an office environment and high salary, but also stressful deadlines and long hours. Employment of operations research analysts are expected to grow as rapidly as the average (Bureau of Labor Statistics, 2004). The median annual salary of operations research analysts was $64,650 in 2006; 50 percent earned between $48,820 and $85,760 (Bureau of Labor statistics, 2008).

A graduate degree in the quantitative areas of psychology (experimental, quantitative, psychometrics, and even cognitive psychology) offers the mathematical, statistical, and analytical expertise needed for a career in operations research. In addition to quantitative skills, operations research analysts need excellent communication and computer skills, including statistical software packages and programming. Courses in computer science, business, information systems, and management science are useful. An understanding of how the human mind works (for example, thinking and problem solving) is always useful for operations research analysts who want to minimize the effects of human error on their work (meaning, understanding the kinds of mistakes that workers might make can help operations research analysts make useful decisions).

COMPUTER SYSTEMS ANALYST

A computer systems analyst helps a company or organization use its technology resources effectively to achieve its goals, for example, organization by incorporating new technology into existing systems. An organization typically uses a variety of software applications; systems analysts work to make the computer systems within an organization compatible in order to share information. *Systems architects* are computer system analysts who specialize in helping organizations select the software and infrastructure that are the basis for the organization's computing and information management resources. *Systems designers* specialize in designing a system to meet an organization's computing needs by a variety of quantitative and mathematical techniques, such as data modeling, mathematical model building, and information engineering. Some computer systems analysts engage in both architectural and design functions.

Systems analysts work in offices with a standard 40-hour work week, but evening and weekend work is sometimes needed to meet deadlines or resolve problems. Graduate degree holders in experimental, quantitative, and cognitive psychology typically gain experience in computer programming, understand the use of databases, think analytically, work on a number of tasks simultaneously, and can concentrate and pay attention to detail, which are valued by employers of systems analysts. Interpersonal and communication skills, particularly the ability to work as part of a team to tackle large projects, are required. Additional courses in computer science, management information systems, or the use of specific computer software, such as C++, are recommended. Employment of systems analysts is expected to increase much more rapidly than the average for all occupations through 2016; systems analysis is one of the most rapidly growing occupations (Bureau of Labor Statistics, 2008). Salaries for systems analysts are competitive, with a 2005 median annual entry-level salary of $52,528 (Salary.com, 2008). Graduate degree holders are likely to be hired at a higher level. In 2006, the median annual salary for all systems analysts, regardless of experience, was $69,760; the middle 50 percent earned between $54,320 and $87,600 a year (Bureau of Labor Statistics, 2008).

DATABASE ADMINISTRATOR

A database administrator determines how to organize, store, and retrieve data using database management systems. They determine the needs of organizations and users and design, implement, update, test, and repair computer databases. Database administrators are responsible for ensuring database performance, backing up and archiving information, and, increasingly important as computer networks become more interconnected, ensuring database security.

Graduate degrees in quantitative and cognitive areas of psychology offer experience with computer systems and analytic skills that are in demand by employers. If you're interested in a career in database administration, seek experience with popular programs, such as Oracle, SQL, or Sybase. Most colleges and universities offer courses in these programs, but if yours does not, you can seek certification from courses that are developed by software manufacturers, or purchase the software and related books to explore on your own. Also take additional courses in computer science, information science, or management information systems. Employers look for excellent problem solving skills and interpersonal skills, skills that graduate study in psychology imparts.

Advantages of a career in database administration include intellectual challenge and never-ending learning, because technology is constantly changing. Like computer systems analysts, database administrator's work in an office environment, but they often put in long hours to solve problems and debug databases. Database administration is a hot growth field. Employment of database administrators is expected to increase much more rapidly than the average for all occupations through 2016 (Bureau of Labor Statistics, 2008). It also offers a high salary. In 2008, database administrators earned a median salary of $82,594 (Salary.com, 2008).

ACTUARY

Actuaries use statistics and mathematical models to estimate the statistical probability of particular types of risk, such as death, injury, property loss, or financial risk. Most actuaries are employed by insurance companies. They gather and analyze data to determine who will and will not receive insurance coverage, as well as the price to charge for insurance that will cover claims and ensure profitability. Some actuaries are employed in finance industries to help organizations manage credit or plan new investment tools to help their company compete against others. Actuaries are also employed as consultants, engaging in similar functions, but usually on a contractual basis.

The strong background in mathematics and statistics that graduate degree holders in psychometrics or experimental, cognitive, and quantitative psychology obtain is excellent for a career as an actuary. Actuaries also require strong communication and computer skills, including spreadsheets, databases, and statistical analysis software. Knowledge of computer programming languages, such as

Visual Basic for Applications, SAS, or SQL, is useful. Additional courses in business, economics, and finances will improve your application. If you seek a career as an actuary, be prepared to pass a series of examinations to become certified by Society of Actuaries (SOA), which certifies in the fields of life insurance, health benefits systems, retirement systems, and finance and investment, or the Casualty Actuarial Society (CAS), which certifies actuaries in the property and casualty field, which includes automobile, homeowners, medical malpractice, workers compensation, and personal injury liability. Most actuaries complete licensure exams and become certified while they work and most employers pay some or all of the costs of licensure.

A career as an actuary offers a comfortable office environment, a standard 40-hour work week, and the ability to work autonomously. The employment of actuaries is expected to grow much more rapidly (24 percent) than the average for all occupations through 2016 (Bureau of Labor Statistics, 2008). Actuarial careers have been rated among the top ten careers by *The Wall Street Journal* because they offer high salaries, pleasant working environments, a reasonable job outlook, job security, and reasonable levels of stress (Lee, 2002). According to Salary.com (2008), the typical entry-level actuary earned a median base salary of $55,061 in 2008, with the middle 50 percent earning between $41,976 and $50,796. Median annual earnings of all actuaries were $82,800 in 2006; 50 percent earned between $58,710 and $114,570 (Bureau of Labor Statistics, 2008).

FINANCIAL ANALYST

Financial analysts (also called *security analysts* and *investment analysts*) provide organizations (typically banks, insurance companies, mutual and pension funds, and securities firms) with guidance in making investments. They synthesize financial information by combining data from financial statements, commodity prices, sales, costs, expenses, and tax rates to determine a company's value. They then make recommendations on how to best manage an organization's financial assets and avoid risk.

The broad background in statistics that graduate education in experimental psychology, quantitative psychology, cognitive psychology, or psychometrics provides is an asset to a career in financial analysis. Psychologists in these areas understand how to use mathematics and statistics as a means to an end: to arrive at a practical solution. As a financial analyst, your knowledge of the scientific method will come in handy, because financial analysis entails developing hypotheses and designing tests to validate them using available data, and drawing conclusions (Attfield, 1999). Graduate training offers other benefits to this career, such as experience in giving presentations, strong communication skills, and the ability to work independently. Courses in finance, business administration, accounting, economics, financial analysis methods, or risk management will broaden your knowledge base and demonstrate your interest in applying your statistical skills to financial analysis. Some financial analysts are required to be licensed by the Financial Industry Regulatory Authority (FINRA). Licensure must be sponsored by an employer, so individuals are not expected to be licensed before starting a job.

Advantages of a career in financial analysis include intellectual challenge, comfortable offices, and high salaries. Financial analysts also face long hours, stressful deadlines, and sometimes frequent travel (Attfield, 1999). Financial analysis is a growth occupation; employment of financial analysts is expected to grow much more rapidly (34 percent) than the average for all occupations through 2016 (Bureau of Labor Statistics, 2008). Despite this growth, financial analysis remains a very competitive field. In 2006, the median annual earnings of financial analysts were $66,590 (Bureau of Labor Statistics, 2008). In 2008, a typical entry-level financial analyst earned $46,565 (Salary.com, 2008). A graduate degree may result in a more advanced title and higher entering salary. Annual bonuses increase the salary substantially as they can amount from one-half of to well over the annual salary; however, bonuses fluctuate with the organization's profits.

DATA MINING

Graduate degree holders in quantitative and experimental psychology and psychometrics are especially prepared for careers in data mining. Data mining is the extraction of useful information, or "nuggets," from large databases of information with the use of statistical methods and computational algorithms. It is akin to finding a needle in a haystack, where the needle is critical information that an organization needs and the haystack is the large database with information stored over a long period of time. Data mining entails using statistical analysis to examine large databases for patterns and trends that shed light on consumer habits and potential marketing strategies.

Data mining is used in all industries. For example, discovering new patterns and trends through data mining can help banking executives to "predict with increasing precision how customers will react to interest rate adjustments, which customers will be most receptive to new product offers, which customers present the highest risk for defaulting on a loan, and how to make each customer relationship more profitable" (Fabris, 1998). Data mining professionals, sometimes called *data warehousing professionals* or *database analysts*, are in high demand to develop highly targeted marketing programs, analyze economic trends, detect credit fraud, and forecast financial markets. It is a challenging career that requires analytic thinking and problem-solving skills. If you're interested in a career in data mining, learn about the most popular databases, like SQL, DB2, and Oracle. The main challenges of a career in data mining and data warehousing are the stresses of meeting goals, rolling out database upgrades, learning new analysis techniques, long hours, and analyzing data and drawing conclusions on tight deadlines and with limited budgets and staffs (Smith, 2002). According to *Information Week* (2007) a typical person working in the data mining and warehousing field earned a median base salary of $88,000 in 2007. An entry-level database analyst earned $52,439 in 2008 (Salary.com, 2008). The statistic and research basis of a graduate degree in psychology is likely to result in a higher entry-level salary and title.

As you can see, there are a variety of careers for undergraduate and graduate degree holders that require the statistical expertise of experimental, cognitive, and quantitative psychology and psychometrics. In addition to the careers discussed in this chapter, remember that many individuals with these interests seek careers in research (Chapter 13), teaching (Chapter 4), consulting (Chapter 9), human factors and business (also in Chapter 9), and marketing research (Chapter 11). Quantitative skill is one of the most highly sought skills in the workplace today. Regardless of your career interests, the statistical and methodological knowledge provided by a degree in psychology is excellent preparation for entry-level (for undergraduate degree holders) and more advanced (for masters and doctoral degree holders) quantitative careers.

SUGGESTED READINGS

Bramer, M. (2007). *Principles of data mining*. New York: Springer.

Fitch, T. (2007). *Career opportunities in banking, finance, and insurance*. New York: Checkmark Books.

Henderson, H. (2004). *Career opportunities in computers and cyberspace*. New York: Facts on File.

Hillier, F. S., & Lieberman, G. L. (2005). *Introduction to operation research*. New York: McGraw-Hill.

Liberty, J. (1999). *Complete idiot's guide to a career in computer programming*. New York: Alpha Books.

Schrayer, R. M. (2007). *Opportunities in insurance careers*. New York: McGraw-Hill.

Stair, L., & Stair, L. B. (2002). *Careers in computers*. New York: McGraw-Hill.

Wise, S. (2002). The assessment professional: Making a difference in the 21st century. *Eye on Psi Chi, 6*(3), 20–21.

WEB RESOURCES

Insurance: Overview
http://www.careers-in-finance.com/in.htm

Is a Career in Operations Research/Management Science Right for You?
http://www.informs.org/Edu/Career/booklet.html

Be an Actuary
http://www.beanactuary.org

Data Mining: What Is Data Mining?
http://www.anderson.ucla.edu/faculty/jason.frand/teacher/technologies/palace/datamining.htm

The Data Warehousing Information Center
http://www.dwinfocenter.org/

Budget Analysis as a Career: Information and Opinion from the Budget Analyst
http://www.budgetanalyst.com/careers.htm

Insurance Information Institute
http://www.iii.org/

Institute for Operations Research and the Management Sciences
http://www.informs.org/

CHECKLIST: ARE EXPERIMENTAL, COGNITIVE, OR QUANTITATIVE AREAS OF PSYCHOLOGY FOR YOU?

Do you:

☐ Enjoy conducting research?
☐ Like working with numbers?

☐ Enjoy problem solving?
☐ Like science?
☐ Find computers fun to work with?
☐ Take an analytical approach towards understanding problems?
☐ Know how to use a computer programming language?
☐ Pay attention to detail?
☐ Enjoy writing research reports?
☐ Enjoy intellectual challenges?
☐ Like "fixing" computer problems?
☐ Like math?
☐ Find research methodology courses fun?
☐ Like statistics?
☐ Enjoy using new computer programs?

Scoring: The more boxes you checked, the more likely it is that you're a good match for a career in the experimental or quantitative areas of psychology.

SOCIAL AND CONSUMER PSYCHOLOGY

CHAPTER GUIDE

What causes social problems like interpersonal violence, prejudice, and stereotyping? How do we change people's attitudes? What influences purchasing patterns? Why do people buy what they buy? Social and consumer psychology address a variety of interesting and important questions. Whereas consumer psychology is an applied discipline, social psychologists traditionally find careers in academia, teaching, and conducting research; however, the increasing emphasis on application within social psychology has translated into a variety of new career options.

SOCIAL PSYCHOLOGY

Social psychology is the study of how people interact with each other and the social environment. Social psychologists study personality (for example, why do we act the way that we do?), attitude formation and change, and interpersonal relations such as attraction, prejudice, group dynamics, and aggression. Like many of the other psychologists you've read about, social psychologists engage in both basic and applied research. Basic research advances knowledge about fundamental questions, such as: How does culture and our social environment shape us? The goal of basic research is to advance scientific knowledge; its application value is not inherent to its worth. In other words, basic research results in knowledge for its own sake. Applied research, on the other hand, is conducted to gain insight and solve real world problems. For example, applied social psychologists conduct research on practical questions, such as: How can we reduce aggression among school children? How can we reduce the effects of prejudice in the classroom or office environment? Social psychologists who emphasize basic research are found in academic and research settings, as described in Chapter 13. Social psychologists who are interested in applied questions can be found in the settings described in this chapter as well as in social policy settings (Chapter 12), and business and organizational settings (Chapters 9 and 10).

CONSUMER PSYCHOLOGY

If you're interested in understanding subliminal suggestions and why some commercials and marketing campaigns are more successful than others, consumer psychology may be for you. Consumer psychologists study how we process information and make decisions about purchasing products and services (Beall & Allen, 1997). They use this information to help businesses and organizations improve their marketing and sales strategies (Carpenter, 2000). A consumer psychologist might design a study to evaluate which type of ketchup container (for example, glass or squeezable plastic) consumers are more likely to purchase. They study consumer behavior to aid companies in their marketing strategies. For example, a consumer psychologist might study factors that contribute to the effectiveness of fast-food commercials, conclude that we are more receptive to such commercials when we are hungry, and therefore suggest that fast-food companies place their commercials in the late afternoon, before dinnertime. Consumer psychologists study the effectiveness of different types of sales techniques and provide advice to businesses based on their research. They train salespeople, conduct consumer satisfaction surveys, and study the growth of consumers' emotional attachments to products.

In other words, consumer psychologists attempt "to understand the processes by which consumers search for goods and services, decide which goods and services to purchase, and consume the items they purchase" (Beall & Allen, 1997, p. 199). They try to understand changing needs of consumers and help companies adapt their products and services accordingly. Consumer psychologists are found in business, government, and nonprofit environments, where they work as consultants and employees in departments of marketing research.

OPPORTUNITIES WITH A BACHELOR'S DEGREE

Persuasion is an important topic of study in social and consumer psychology. Perhaps it shouldn't be surprising that bachelor's degree holders with interests in these areas often find work in advertising, real estate, retail, and public relations.

ADVERTISING

Advertising is a broad field that is concerned with helping companies to market their products. There is a variety of positions in this field, at each rank, from entry level to senior executives. Entry-level positions in advertising are typically in the account management and media departments.

The account management department serves as the link between agency and client; it brings the client to the agency and is responsible for ensuring that the various components of the agency work smoothly to ensure that the client's advertising needs are met. The *assistant account manager* (also called an *account coordinator*), an entry-level position, assists the account manager in completing these tasks. Account managers identify and solicit new clients, determining client needs and communicating them to those who create advertisements. Account managers create schedules, enforce deadlines, and help creative staff and management to understand client needs (Wetfeet, 2005a). Social psychological principles underlie much of their work because account managers must have good interpersonal and sales skills, and understand persuasion and attitude formation, in order to attract new clients and assist them in developing marketing plans to advertise their products.

The media department places ads and is responsible for placing the right ad at the right time in order to reach the appropriate audience cheaply and effectively. Entry-level positions in media departments include *assistant media planners* and *assistant media buyers*. Assistant media planners help media planners examine the public's reading and viewing preferences, study the demographics of various types of media (what consumers read and watch), and evaluate the content of newspapers, magazines, and television programs to determine where to place advertising. Assistant media buyers help media buyers buy ad time and space, make sure that ads appear as planned, and create ad budgets. Psychology students bring a host of useful skills to media planning, including a firm grasp of research methods and statistical analysis, plus an understanding of attitude formation and change, which are all essential to studying the public's preferences and designing effective advertisements. The median salary in media planning in 2007 was $47,052 (Salary.com, 2008).

Careers in advertising are fast-paced and exciting. They offer opportunities to exercise creativity, solve problems, engage in research, and advance in the field. To prepare for a career in advertising, take classes in social psychology, consumer psychology, marketing, accounting, advertising, business management, communications, and design. Hone your communication, creative, and organizational skills. The ability to handle stress, work in a team environment, and use technology (for example, Internet research, Web design, computer skills) are essential to this career path.

Seek an advertising internship to gain hands-on experience as well as contacts in the field, because entry-level positions in advertising are competitive (Bureau of Labor Statistics, 2008). Despite the competitive nature of entry-level positions, there is plenty of room for growth. Employment in advertising is expected to remain steady through 2016 (Bureau of Labor Statistics, 2008). Finally, careers in advertising offer comfortable salaries. In 2007, the average starting salary for advertising positions was $33,831 (Bureau of Labor Statistics, 2008).

REAL ESTATE

How does psychology relate to a career in real estate? Believe it or not, psychological principles underlie much of the work. Real estate agents bring buyers and sellers together and act as intermediaries in the sale of land and residential and commercial properties. They generate lists of available properties, learn as much as possible about them, market them through open houses and advertisements, show them to clients, and assist clients in obtaining financing and drawing up contracts to purchase properties. Real estate agents earn a commission on each property that is sold.

Sales techniques, persuasion, and attitude formation and change are important social psychological principles used daily by real estate agents in their marketing, advertising, and client activities. An effective real estate agent can "read" clients to determine which homes are an appropriate fit. Persuasive techniques are used in describing the home and its benefits (for example, the home is "cozy," rather than "cramped and tiny," or "lively," instead of "next to a late-night pub").

Real estate agents must understand the neighborhoods and surrounding communities in which they sell properties. They must be both interpersonally skilled and competent at number crunching, because they must be able to assess which neighborhoods best fit clients' needs and budgets. Real estate agents spend much of their time obtaining listings (agreements from property owners to sell their properties through a particular real estate agency). When a property is sold, both the agents who sold the property and obtained the listing receive a commission.

An advantage to a career in real estate is the flexibility. Much of the administrative work can be completed out of a home office. However, a great deal of time will be spent showing properties to clients. Real estate agents often work long hours, often more than 40 hours per week (Bureau of Labor Statistics, 2008). In addition to long hours, real estate agents must be available to meet clients on evenings and weekends. As agents gain experience, they may earn higher commission rates as well as become more efficient, and thus can handle more business. With experience, some agents are promoted to supervisory positions or open their own businesses. The primary disadvantage to a career in real estate is the reliance on commission income. Income is irregular and there are often months without income, especially for beginning agents (Evans, 1998). Real estate agents earned a median salary of $39,760 in 2006 (Bureau of Labor Statistics, 2008). Employment of real estate brokers and sales agents is expected to grow about the same as all occupations through 2016 (Bureau of Labor Statistics, 2008).

If you are considering a career in real estate, recognize that all real estate agents must be licensed. Each state has different requirements, but all include a written test with questions on basic real estate transactions and laws about the sale of property.

Many states require 30 to 90 hours of classroom instruction. Licenses must be renewed every 1 or 2 years (without an exam) and continuing education is often required because zoning restrictions and laws change (Bureau of Labor, 2008). For more information about obtaining a real estate license, contact the Association of Real Estate License Law Officials (http://www.arello.org/). Classes in real estate, finance, business administration, economics, or law will provide a helpful background for a career in real estate.

RETAIL

Approximately 15 percent of all workers in the United States are employed by retail establishments (Wetfeet.com, 2005b). Retail sales personnel sell goods, provide customer service, and help buyers make informed purchases. They must understand consumer behavior, sales techniques, and their products, because a high level of service and expertise is essential for success in retail. Many large retail stores have management training programs in which an employee learns about all aspects of the business and, after training, is placed as an assistant manager or store manager (Bureau of Labor Statistics, 2008). *Store managers* are responsible for operation and activity of a store. They manage sales staff, order and track inventory, market products, design techniques to attract customers, and promote sales and good customer relations (Wetfeet.com, 2005b). *Sales representatives* are employed directly by a manufacturer or wholesaler. Sales representatives travel often to visit clients. They develop relationships with clients, discuss the client needs, suggest how their merchandise can meet those needs, and show samples and catalogs of the products they sell (Bureau of Labor Statistics, 2008).

Retail careers are busy, people-oriented, and exciting, and provide opportunities for advancement. If you choose a career in retail, you'll meet many people from different walks of life, use your psychology skills every day, and even travel (if you become a sales representative). Retail careers usually require unusual work hours (often during evenings and weekends). Psychology majors' understanding of human behavior, motivation, and attitudes suit this career well. Strong communication skills, friendliness, decisiveness, enthusiasm, and the ability to manage stress are essential. Management careers also require leadership skills, self-direction, and interpersonal skills (for example, the ability to soothe angered customers). Prepare for a career in retail by taking additional courses in business, marketing, accounting, and communications. Retail positions are expected to grow about as rapidly as the average for all occupations through the year 2016 (Bureau of Labor Statistics, 2008). As shown in Table 11.1, retail careers offer a range of salaries, depending on the position.

PUBLIC RELATIONS SPECIALIST

Public relations specialists work to improve an organization's communication with the community, with consumer, employee, and public interest groups, and with the media. They build and maintain positive relationships with the public by informing the community and media about an organization's policies, activities, and accomplishments (Bureau of Labor Statistics, 2008). Public relations specialists write and distribute press releases to media contacts, who print or broadcast the releases.

TABLE 11.1 | SALARIES IN RETAIL (ADAPTED FROM SALARY.COM. 2008)

Title	Median salary
Assistant retail store manager	$37,001
Retail store manager	$46,178
Retail sales person	$21,724
Sales representative	$31,588

They keep organization representatives in contact with the community by arranging speaking engagements and often prepare and edit speeches for company leaders.

Public relations specialists anticipate, analyze, and interpret public opinions about organizations to influence an organization's future decisions and business practices (Public Relations Society of America, n.d.). They keep an organization's management and administrative personnel aware of the attitudes and concerns of the public and special interest groups. They give advice to management about the public ramifications of policy decisions and communications and how to build good public relations, which are critical to an organization's success (Public Relations Society of America, n.d.). Public relations also entails research on the public's attitudes and opinions, as well as evaluating the effectiveness of an organization's fundraising, marketing, community relations, and other programs. Public relations specialists are found in a variety of settings, including businesses, government, universities, hospitals, schools, and other organizations. Titles include *public relations specialist, information officer, press secretary, communications specialist, public affairs specialist*, and others.

A career in public relations offers exciting and varied work. Psychology majors are well suited to careers in public relations because of their background in survey research, interpersonal skills, writing skills, and understanding of human behavior, attitude formation, and attitude change. Some of the disadvantages of a career in public relations include long hours, irregular work schedules that are frequently interrupted, and stress (resulting from high-pressure deadlines). Sometimes public relations can be frustrating because, unlike advertising, which pays for media coverage and therefore controls the advertisement message and its distribution, public relations professionals must earn their media coverage and have little control over how the ultimate message is conveyed (Bergen, n.d.).

Entry-level positions in public relations are competitive; therefore, preparation is important. Take courses in communication, journalism, and business to enhance your marketability. Perhaps most important is hands-on experience, through internships with public relations firms, corporate departments, or nonprofit organizations (Public Relations Society of America, n.d.). Despite the competitive nature of entry-level positions, overall employment of public relations specialists is expected to increase much more rapidly than the average for all occupations through 2016 (Bureau of Labor Statistics, 2008). A final advantage of a career in public relations is the salary. In 2006, the median salary for a public relations specialist was $47,350, with half of the people employed as public relations specialists earning between $35,600 and $65,310 (Bureau of Labor Statistics, 2008).

Table 11.2	Preparation for BA–Level Careers Related to Social and Consumer Psychology

Coursework

- Accounting
- Advertising
- Business Administration
- Business Law
- Consumer Psychology/Psychology of Decision Making
- Economics
- Finance
- Industrial-Organizational Psychology
- Marketing
- Math
- Social Psychology
- Statistics
- Statistics
- Writing

Applied Experiences: Volunteer, intern, or paid part-time positions in any of the following settings

- Advertising Department or Firm
- Business Settings
- Marketing Department or Firm
- Real Estate Firm
- Retail

Research Experiences: Experiences studying and participating in research in any of the following areas*

- Consumer Behavior
- Decision Making
- Group Behavior
- Social Psychology

*Note that the content area of the research is less important than the experience itself, which enhances reasoning, quantitative, writing, and organizational skills.

OPPORTUNITIES WITH A GRADUATE DEGREE

Graduate degree holders in psychology with interests in social and consumer psychology are employed in many of the fields discussed, but at more advanced levels. They also apply their skills to solve real-world problems in a number of other fields.

MARKET RESEARCH

Market researchers are found in a variety of organizations, including public relations firms, advertising agencies, and corporations. They gather data on what people think. They conduct research on the sale of a product or service. Market researchers design methods of gathering information on products or services, as well as consumers' needs, tastes, purchasing power, and buying habits. They examine consumer reactions to products and services. Through research, they identify advertising needs, measure the effectiveness of advertising and other promotional techniques, gather data on competitors' products, services, and locations, and analyze their marketing methods and strategies (Bureau of Labor Statistics, 2008). Market researchers who work for public relations firms or in government positions often conduct opinion research to determine public attitudes on various issues, which may help political and business leaders evaluate public support for their positions or advertising policies (Bureau of Labor Statistics, 2008).

Careers in market research are fast-paced and exciting. Market researchers work on a variety of projects, and project turnover is fast. In addition to conducting research with practical implications, another advantage of a career in market research is that it is a growth field. Employment of market researchers is expected to grow more rapidly than the average for all occupations through 2016, with job opportunities being strongest for those with a masters degree or Ph.D. (Bureau of Labor Statistics, 2008). Finally, salaries in market research are very competitive. In 2006, a typical market research analyst earned a median base salary of $58,820; half of the people in this job earn between $42,190 and $84,070 (Bureau of Labor Statistics, 2008). Market research managers, on the other hand, earn an average of $88,383 (Salary.com, 2008).

PRODUCT DEVELOPMENT CONSULTANT

Psychologists use their knowledge about human development, interpersonal relations, and attitude formation and change to provide organizations with research-based information to assist them in providing goods and services that meet people's needs. Psychologists often work as consultants in product development. They examine people's reactions to particular products, as well as their needs, tastes, purchasing power, and buying habits. The resulting knowledge is used to improve the product, and develop the advertising and promotional campaigns that are used to sell the product.

Product development consultants work for companies and consulting firms, and in private practice. An important reward of a career as a consultant in product development is that you'll engage in work with practical implications and then get to see the results of your work. You will work on a variety of projects, and project turnover is fast. A regular 40-hour work week and high rates of compensation are other advantages. For example, the median salary for product development managers, who oversee the development of specific products, was $75,984 in 2008, and for product development directors, who oversee all product development activities for an organization, was $144,230 (Salary.com, 2008).

MANAGEMENT

A degree in social or consumer psychology prepares graduates for management careers in advertising, marketing, public relations, and sales. Managers in these fields coordinate the market research, marketing strategy, sales, advertising, promotion, pricing, product development, and public relations activities of large companies.

Advertising managers oversee advertising and promotional activities within a firm. If a firm contracts an advertising agency to handle promotions, then the advertising manager may serve as a liaison between the firm and the advertising agency (Bureau of Labor Statistics, 2008). Larger companies have their own advertising staff, overseen by advertising managers.

Marketing managers coordinate the work of market researchers to determine the demand for products and services offered by the firm and develop a marketing strategy (Bureau of Labor Statistics, 2008). They also develop pricing strategies that maximize profits while ensuring customer satisfaction. Marketing managers confer with advertising managers and market researchers to promote products and services and devise strategies to attract new customers.

Public relations managers supervise the work of public relations specialists and direct publicity programs. They determine the target of publicity programs and evaluate their effectiveness. In a large company, public relations managers may examine the compatibility of the advertising and public relations programs and suggest changes, when needed, to the company's top management. Public relations managers keep abreast of social, economic, and political trends, and make recommendations on how to enhance the company's visibility and positive image in light of current trends (Bureau of Labor Statistics, 2008).

Sales managers direct a company's sales program. They hire sales representatives, devise programs to train sales representatives, assign sales territories, set sales goals, and oversee the work of sales representatives (Bureau of Labor Statistics, 2008). They determine the sales potential of products, assess inventory requirements, monitor customer preferences, and communicate this information to other departments to help develop and modify or maximize products.

Like other careers, there are a variety of benefits and challenges to careers such as advertising, marketing, public relations, and sales. Long hours, including evenings and weekends, are common. For example, approximately 44 percent of advertising, marketing, and public relations managers worked more than 40 hours per week in 2002 (Bureau of Labor Statistics, 2008). Managerial careers often entail substantial travel (for example, attendance at meetings sponsored by associations or industries, meetings at national, regional, and local offices, and meetings with dealers, distributors, and clients). In addition, tight deadlines can make for stressful work.

According to the Bureau of Labor Statistics (2008), management positions in advertising, marketing, public relations, and sales are expected to remain steady through 2016; however, such positions will remain competitive. Finally, management careers pay well. In 2002, the median base salary for advertising managers was $73,060, $98,720 for marketing managers, and $91,560 for sales managers (Bureau of Labor Statistics, 2008).

If you're interested in a career as an advertising, marketing, public relations, or sales manager, take additional courses in business administration, marketing, business law, advertising, accounting, public speaking, and finance. Graduate degree holders' expertise with statistics is especially valuable. Finally, managerial careers require maturity, creativity, motivation, resistance to stress, flexibility, and the ability to communicate persuasively—all skills that are developed with graduate study in psychology.

Graduate degrees in social and consumer psychology are among the most marketable of psychology degrees. This chapter presented just a few of the opportunities for graduate degree holders in these areas. If you are interested in other alternatives to the traditional academic career as professor, consider writing and publishing careers (Chapter 13), trial consulting (Chapter 5), consulting (Chapter 9), or social policy careers (Chapter 12). With creative thinking and innovation, you'll design and achieve the career of your dreams.

SUGGESTED READINGS

Beall, A. E., & Allen, T. W. (1997). Why we buy what we buy: Consulting in consumer psychology. In R. Sternberg (Ed.), *Career paths in psychology: Where your degree can take you* (pp. 197–212). Washington, DC: American Psychological Association.

Branscombe, N. R. & Spears, R. (2001). Social psychology: Past, present, and some predictions for the future. In J. S. Halonen & S. F. Davis (Eds.), *The many faces of psychological research in the 21st century*. Retrieved July 29, 2008 at http://teachpsych.org/resources/ e-books/faces/script/Ch07.htm

Edwards, K. W. (2006). *Your successful real estate career*. New York: Amacom.

Field, S. (2001). *Career opportunities in the retail and wholesale industry*. New York: Facts on File.

Field, S., & Rubenstein, H. J. (2005). *Career opportunities in advertising and public relations*. New York: Checkmark.

Friestad, M. (2001). What is consumer psychology? *Eye on Psi Chi, 6*(1), 28–29.

Neidle, A. (2002). *How to get into advertising: A guide to careers in advertising, media, and marketing communications*. London: Cassell Academic.

Wagner, R. (2001). A hot market for social scientists in market research. *Chronicle of Higher Education*. Retrieved on June 1, 2002 at http://chronicle.com/jobs/2001/01/2001011901c.htm

Wetfeet (2008). *Careers in advertising and public relations*. Wetfeet.

WEB RESOURCES

What Is a Personality/Social Psychologist?
http://www.spsp.org/what.htm

Social Psychology
http://www.trinity.edu/~mkearl/socpsy.html

Realty Times
http://realtytimes.com

Association of Real Estate License Law Officials
http://www.arello.org/

Consumer Behavior: The Psychology of Marketing
http://www.consumerpsychologist.com/

A Guide to Public Relations Education and Training
http://www.martex.co.uk/prcareerdevelopment/index.htm

About Advertising
http://advertising.about.com/

About Retail Careers
http://retailindustry.about.com/

CHECKLIST: IS SOCIAL OR CONSUMER PSYCHOLOGY FOR YOU?

Do you:

Like shopping and spending time in stores?
Wonder what influences people's purchases?
Have an interest in attitude formation and change?
Like solving problems?
Enjoy persuading others?
Like watching the Super Bowl for the commercials?
Like "reading" people?
Find research enjoyable?
Think quickly on your feet?
Like working with numbers?

Scoring: Add up your checkmarks; the greater the score the more likely a career in social or consumer psychology is for you.

| # DEVELOPMENTAL PSYCHOLOGY

Babies, children, teenagers. That's what most people think of when they hear the phrase *developmental psychology*. Yes, developmental psychologists are interested in how vision changes over the first year of life or the ways in which the media influences children's behavior, but they are also interested in adults. Is there a midlife crisis? What is the role of social support in health and well-being in older adulthood? Developmental psychologists examine questions pertinent to our everyday lives. Historically, graduate training in developmental psychology led to academic careers; however, today more developmental psychologists are entering applied careers. In this chapter we'll explore careers for students who are interested in developmental psychology.

DEVELOPMENTAL PSYCHOLOGY

Developmental psychology is the study of how people grow, develop, and change across the lifespan. Developmental psychologists are concerned with the emotional, intellectual, and physical development of children, adolescents, and adults. Many developmental psychologists specialize with particular age groups, such as infants and young children, adolescents, young adults, or older adults. Perhaps the most rapidly growing field within developmental psychology is gerontology, or the study of the aging process from middle age through later life. Gerontologists study physical, emotional, social, and psychological changes that older adults experience as they age, how our society is changing as the population of the United States ages, and how knowledge about development can be applied to create and modify policies and programs to assist older adults and their families. Developmental psychologists conduct research on a diverse array of topics, such as the effects of divorce on adults and how they parent, how infants learn language, and influences on antisocial activity during adolescence.

A growing number of psychologists are concerned with the application of developmental science, or applied developmental psychology (part of the larger, multidisciplinary field of applied developmental science). Applied developmental psychologists conduct research on practical problems in real-world settings, such as the scope and nature of children's exposure to violence and how to promote resilience in children and adolescents reared in disenfranchised neighborhoods. Applied developmental psychologists develop and evaluate interventions that promote optimal cognitive, emotional, and social development. They disseminate knowledge about developmental processes to policymakers, businesses, industry, healthcare professionals, and parents. Applied developmental psychologists also engage in direct service delivery by constructing, administering, and interpreting assessments of developmental strengths and vulnerabilities, developing behavioral management programs for individuals and groups, and delivering psychological services in various mental health settings (Fisher & Osofsky, 1997; Kuther, 1996; Toth, Manly, & Nilsen, 2008).

OPPORTUNITIES WITH A BACHELOR'S DEGREE

Many students who earn bachelor's degrees in psychology would like to work with people and many are interested in specific age groups, such as children or older adults. Students who are interested in developmental psychology might consider jobs as gerontology aide, child life specialists, or among the many that are found in nonprofit organizations.

GERONTOLOGY AIDE

Gerontology aides are human services workers (also known as social and human services assistants) who specialize in working with older adults and provide direct and indirect services to clients. They develop programs such as health promotion, senior theater groups, and intergenerational activities for older people in senior centers, community agencies, and retirement communities. Gerontology aides also provide direct care to older adults in hospitals, clinics, and nursing homes, or through adult daycare or home care programs. They monitor and keep records on clients' progress and report to supervisors and case managers. Gerontology aides may accompany clients to group meal sites, adult daycare centers, or doctors' offices, telephone or visit clients' homes to make sure services are being received, and help some with daily living needs. Most gerontology aides work under the direction of professionals such as psychologists, nurses, counselors, or social workers, depending on the setting. Gerontology aides are found in offices, clinics, hospitals, group homes, clay programs, and clients' homes.

An important advantage to obtaining a position as a gerontology aide is the ability to help others and contribute to their welfare. Other advantages include a fairly standard 40-hour work week—but weekends and evenings may be necessary depending on the setting. Social and human services assistant positions, including gerontology aides, are projected to grow much more rapidly than the average for all occupations through 2016 (Bureau of Labor Statistics, 2008), ranking among the most rapidly growing occupations, so psychology students will have many career choices in this field. If you're interested in becoming a gerontology aide, your psychology curriculum will prepare you well. Additional courses in communication, gerontology, and social work will round out your skills.

Helping others is very rewarding, but a position as a gerontology aide can be emotionally draining. It can be difficult to work with clients you cannot help, such as clients who are dying. Human services careers are not for everyone and turnover among staff tends to be high. Finally, gerontology aides earn a relatively low salary. In 2006, the median annual earnings of social and human service assistants, such as gerontology aides, were $25,580, and 50 percent earned between $20,350 and $32,440 (Bureau of Labor Statistics, 2008).

CHILD LIFE SPECIALIST

Child life specialists help children and families adjust to a child's hospitalization. They typically are found in hospital settings and implement pediatric programs, therapies, and activities with children. Child life specialists educate and assist families in the physically and emotionally demanding process of caring for hospitalized or disabled children. They help children cope by engaging them in activities that permit children free expression and opportunities to engage in normal play that promotes social and emotional development and feelings of competence.

Helping families in crisis can be very rewarding, but it is also challenging and some child life specialists burn out. Child life specialists are found in children's hospitals across North America, but are less common in small hospitals. There are geographic restrictions on this career as hospitals that hire child life specialists tend to be located in urban areas. If you are interested in a career as a child life specialist, take courses in child and family studies, human development, and early childhood education, and obtain knowledge of common medical terms and familiarity of some of the most common serious illnesses of children.

Child life specialists must obtain certification which, in addition to a bachelor's degree, requires an internship or employment experience of at least 480 hours and completion of the certification exam offered by the Child Life Council (visit http://www.childlife.org). In 2008, a bachelor's-level child life specialist earned a median salary of $38,000; 50 percent earned between $35,000 and $43,134. A child life specialist who has earned supervision responsibilities, such as mentoring colleagues, organizing and supervising programs, and grant writing, earned a median salary of $41,196 in 2008 (50 percent earned between $36,058 and $47,382) (Child Life Council, 2008).

CAREERS IN NONPROFIT ORGANIZATIONS

The nonprofit sector offers new graduates a broad range of job opportunities. In the last 20 years, the nonprofit sector has grown at a rate surpassing both government and private business. What is a nonprofit organization? Nonprofit organizations do not operate to earn a profit; in other words, their income is not used to benefit or gain stockholders, directors, or any other persons with interests in the organization. Instead, income is funneled back into the organization to assist it in meeting its goals. There are a variety of nonprofit organizations, and most work to advance a cause or interest. For example, some nonprofits promote educational, scientific, cultural, civic, or social welfare causes. Many psychology graduates are hired by nonprofit organizations that work to improve the lives of individuals, families, and children.

Nonprofit organizations offer opportunities for both program and administrative positions. Students who are interested in applied developmental psychology often seek program positions within organizations that focus on the needs of children, youth, and families. If you seek a program position, you might assist in providing health services, counseling, crisis intervention, therapy, education, and research activities (Rowh & Suchorski, 2000). As a *program assistant*, you'll help the program director and work on analyzing issues and implementing programs. Tasks might include data entry and analysis, report writing, and office work. The typical salary range for such a position is $20,000 to $35,000 (Wetfeet.com, 2008). With several years of experience a program assistant might be eligible for a job as *program director*, which is often a mid-level management position. Duties tend to include overseeing and managing specific program, including hiring, fundraising, and administrative and management functions. The typical salary range for program directors is $45,000 to $65,000 (Wetfeet.com, 2008).

Other psychology graduates with applied developmental psychology interests are hired in direct service positions in which they work with an organization's clients by leading support groups for children, youth, and parents, conducting education and training sessions for parents, or providing education and support to families in their homes. In 2004, the typical *direct service outreach worker* earned a median salary of $25,580 (Bureau of Labor statistics, 2008). With experience a psychology graduate may be promoted to *case worker*, responsible for providing services to clients and their families, ensuring a healthy living and social environment. The median salary for case workers is $43,063 and the middle 50 percent of case workers earn between $39,746 and $46,380 (Salary.com, 2008). For more

| TABLE 12.1 | PREPARATION FOR BA–LEVEL CAREERS RELATED TO DEVELOPMENTAL PSYCHOLOGY |

Coursework

Gerontology Aide Positions
  Gerontology
  Communication
  Social Work
  Health and Wellness
  Family Studies
  Developmental Psychology or Human Development

Child Life Specialist
  Child Development
  Family Studies
  Human Development
  Early Childhood Education
  Communication
  Health and Wellness
  Child Psychopathology
  Seek Certification by The Child Life Council (Visit http://www.childlife.org)

Nonprofit Positions
  Communication
  Social Work
  Mathematics
  Writing
  Family Systems
  Child Development
  Marketing
  Accounting
  Business Administration

Applied Experiences: Volunteer, intern, or paid part-time positions in any of the following settings
  Boys and Girls Clubs
  Children's Hospitals or Pediatric Units
  Day Care
  Geriatric Facility
  Mental Retardation Facility
  Nonprofit Organizations, such as shelters, women's centers, advocacy centers
  School

Research Experiences: Experiences studying and participating in research in any of the following areas*
  Aging
  Child Development
  Child Psychopathology
  Developmental Assessment
  Developmental Psychology
  Program Development and Evaluation
  Geriatric Psychology

*Note that the content area of the research is less important than the experience itself, which enhances reasoning, quantitative, writing, and organizational skills.

information about direct service positions for baccalaureate degree holders in psychology, see Chapter 3.

Nonprofit organizations rely heavily on contributions and grants to fund their organizations. Fundraising is a critical activity and an important opportunity for psychology students. As a *fundraiser* for a nonprofit organization, you will be involved in planning and organizing programs to raise money to support the organization and its work. You will design programs and activities to encourage contributions and financial support, solicit donations from individuals, foundations, and corporations, and work to achieve and maintain positive relationships with donors. Fundraising positions also entail writing proposals for grants or donations, conducting research on prospective donors, and coordinating special fundraising events. Salaries in fundraising typically range from $30,000 to $50,000 (Wetfeet.com, 2008).

Fundraising positions require strong communication, public relations, and organizational skills in order to mobilize public support, as well as an appreciation for how people respond to solicitations and requests for help. Psychology clearly holds implications for fundraising because an understanding of interpersonal behavior, principles of persuasion, and attitude formation and change underlies successful fundraising attempts. The psychology major's people skills, problem-solving ability, understanding of social psychological principles, and critical analysis skills are very useful to a career in fundraising. Courses in marketing, accounting, communication, and business administration will broaden your skills.

An important advantage to a career in a nonprofit organization is the opportunity to help others and to improve the health and welfare of people. The work is interesting and you'll be able to influence pressing social issues. With experience, there are opportunities for advancement within an organization, taking on additional supervisory and administrative tasks, and to move from small to larger nonprofit organizations. Disadvantages to a career in the nonprofit sector include low pay relative to skills and education. In addition, most nonprofits depend on a variety of unstable funding activities including grants, public donations, and fundraising events. The financial stability of many nonprofits is uncertain, so workers are sometimes subject to layoffs. The overall lack of funding can contribute to a stressful work environment because of inadequate resources for staff development, quality equipment, and office space. Administrative positions within nonprofit organizations include public relations specialists (Chapter 11), administrative assistants (Chapter 9), computer staff (Chapter 10), and other office support workers.

Careers in childcare, gerontology services, and nonprofit organizations are just some of the opportunities available for students who are interested in developmental psychology. Also consider careers in teaching (Chapter 4), corrections (Chapter 5), and public relations (Chapter 11).

OPPORTUNITIES WITH A GRADUATE DEGREE

As with most fields, a graduate degree in developmental psychology opens up a number of career doors. The following sections explore a range of new opportunities for graduate degree holders in developmental psychology who are interested in applying their skills to solve real-world problems.

SCIENTIST-PRACTITIONER CAREERS

Applied developmental psychologists merge science with practice. They are found in medical facilities, schools, social service agencies, and private practice. Some serve as consultants who provide teachers with information about behavioral management and instructional techniques appropriate for individuals with a wide range of developmental needs, including those with developmental disabilities (Fisher & Osofsky, 1997). Others conduct developmental assessments of children who have suffered injuries or who are suspected of having a developmental delay. After diagnosing a developmental delay or learning disability, an applied developmental psychologist discusses treatment and intervention alternatives with parents, and provides teachers and parents with information about the child's condition and how to promote development. In cases of severe developmental delays, applied developmental psychologists in hospital and service settings work with a multidisciplinary team of physicians, social workers, physical therapists, and other professionals to determine the best course of treatment or intervention. As you can see, applied developmental psychologists engage in activities similar to clinical and counseling psychologists, but the applied developmental psychologist differs from other clinicians in at least two important ways: (1) applied developmental psychologists do not conduct individual therapy; and (2) applied developmental psychologists are oriented toward promoting development across the lifespan by helping individuals to develop skills to optimize their capacities.

Applied developmental psychologists design and empirically evaluate programs provided by hospitals, social service agencies, mental health clinics, and schools (Bruzzese, 2005). For example, an applied developmental psychologist might evaluate the impact of a behaviorally oriented program administered in a hospital or clinic setting, such as the effect of maternal prenatal care and education on infant health outcomes. In school settings, they might design and evaluate remedial education programs, or determine the effectiveness of mainstreaming practices. Applied developmental psychologists who work in residential care settings might evaluate the effectiveness of a program to help improve feelings of self-efficacy (or control) in older adults.

Applied developmental psychologists are also found in social services agencies and court settings, where they evaluate families who wish to provide foster parenting, determine parental fitness for regaining child custody after loss of parental rights, or participate as part of a multidisciplinary team to assist children who have suffered abuse during the subsequent investigation and court process. Applied developmental psychologists conduct evaluations of children and families during divorce and child custody cases, determine the developmental status of adolescents in criminal cases in which they might be tried as adults, and serve as expert witnesses in child abuse, custody, and trials in which the defendants are children and adolescents.

If you are interested in a career in applied developmental psychology, recognize that a masters degree will prepare you for engaging in developmental assessment activities under the supervision of a licensed psychologist. A masters degree will also prepare you for many positions in program design and evaluation. Doctoral degrees enable graduates to engage in more advanced activities, but also hold additional responsibilities, including seeking licensure.

Applied developmental psychologists who plan careers as scientist-practitioners must seek state licensure in order to offer psychological services to the public (Goldstein, Wilson, & Gerstein, 1983; Kuther, 1996). State licensure was developed to provide a measure of assurance as to the minimum competency of practitioners. Licensure provides a standard of professionalism in psychology and protects consumers from the consequences of unprofessional conduct by licensed professionals. Licensure has personal, professional, and economic implications for applied developmental psychologists. By providing statutory recognition, licensure has a legitimizing and enhancing effect on any profession. A license offers public recognition that a psychologist is competent to offer services to the public, and it is required for psychologists who wish to be reimbursed by health insurers for providing mental health services. Typically, licensure eligibility requires two years of supervised field experience, with at least one year postdoctoral, passing a written national examination and a written examination covering ethical and legal issues within a particular state, as well as an oral examination in some states. It should be noted that the requirements for licensure vary from state to state. Licensure offers scientist-practitioners additional employment and professional advancement opportunities. In 2003, licensed scientist-practitioner psychologists working in direct human services positions, regardless of experience, earned a median salary of $75,500 (Pate, Finkel, and Kohout, 2005).

Although this discussion has emphasized the applied and practice activities of applied developmental psychologists, recognize that many of these professionals conduct applied research in university, hospital, government, and private settings. For example, a researcher in a university might study risk factors for adolescent delinquency and then develop a prevention and intervention program to help at-risk adolescents. For more information about research careers in a variety of settings, see Chapter 13.

PRODUCT DEVELOPMENT AND MEDIA CONSULTANT

Psychologists use their knowledge about human development, interpersonal relations, and attitude formation and change to provide organizations with research-based information to assist them in providing goods and services that meet people's needs. Developmental psychologists offer organizations special assistance in designing and marketing developmentally appropriate toys, learning products, television programs, and more.

Psychologists often work as consultants in product development and marketing. They determine the developmental appropriateness of toys and provide insight into children's abilities and play styles. They test prototypes of toys with children and modify them based on their input. Consultants conduct focus groups with parents and children to determine their views about specific products and to get feedback on toy designs. The resulting knowledge is used to improve the product. They also conduct market research by examining children's and parents' reactions to particular toys, advertising, and promotional techniques, as well as their needs, tastes, purchasing power, and buying habits. The next time you're in a toy store and pick up a particular toy, notice the label describing the toy's age-appropriateness; that's probably the work of a developmental psychologist.

Other developmental psychologists assist companies in developing and marketing products that are appropriate for older adults. They apply developmental knowledge to improve the design of products and environments (such as a residential home). For example, a consultant might suggest modifying the design of product packaging by using contrasting colors and larger print that's easier for older adults to read. Through focus groups and research, consultants determine older adults' needs and preferences, and provide organizations with the information needed to design better products and marketing techniques.

The media offers additional marketing research opportunities for developmental psychologists. Psychologists provide developmental and educational advice to creators of children's programs. For example, they conduct and interpret research on children's attention spans that inform creative guidelines for television programs such as Sesame Street. Similar to product development, focus groups and market research forms the information base that is used to target viewers of television programs and radio shows.

Product development and marketing consultants work for companies, consulting firms, and in private practice. An important reward of a career as a consultant in product development and marketing is that you'll engage in work with practical implications and they get to see the results of your work. You'll work on a variety of projects and project turnover is fast. The research often is needed quickly as clients must make swift business decisions. A regular 40-hour per week work schedule and high rates of compensation are other advantages. In 2008, a typical market research analyst earned a median base salary of $68,574; 50 percent earn between $59,509 and $77,639 (Salary.com, 2008).

SOCIAL POLICY RESEARCH

Developmental psychologists often find satisfying careers in social policy. Social policy work typically is conducted within government positions (for example, National Institute of Mental Health, National Institute on Drug Abuse) and at think tanks or policy-oriented organizations that resemble academia. We will discuss the nature of research positions in Chapter 13; however, research careers in social policy–oriented organizations deserve special mention within this chapter because many social and developmental psychologists are interested in applying the psychological knowledge base to promote public welfare by educating legislators and lobbying for social change. If you choose a career in social policy, much of your time will be spent writing grants, conducting research, analyzing the impact of various policies, and writing, presenting, and publishing your work in various formats to ensure that your findings are accessible to the public and to policymakers.

Perhaps the best way to gain perspective on research careers in think tanks is to explore three prominent policy-oriented organizations. Remember that these are just a small sampling of the policy centers that abound.

- RAND (the acronym is a contraction of the term "research and development") is the oldest think tank, created in 1946. The mission of RAND, like other think tanks, is to apply research and analysis to improve policy and decision making.

RAND, a very large think tank, conducts policy research in a variety of areas. Projects have included creating a nationwide drug prevention program for school children, evaluating the quality of health care for older adults, and assessing the impact of Indonesia's economic crisis on its citizens. For more information about RAND, see http://www.rand.org.

- The Families and Work Institute (http://www.familiesandwork.org) is a research center that provides data about the interaction of work and family to inform decision making. Researchers at the Families and Work Institute conduct research on "work-life issues and concerns confronting workers and employers in order to inform decision-makers in government, business, communities, and families" (Families and Work Institute, n.d.). Sample projects include longitudinal studies with nationally representative samples of U.S. workers to learn about the changing nature of work, longitudinal studies of employers to understand how U.S. employers are responding to employee work-life needs, and interviews with children to understand how they make sense of their world and the implications for schools, programs, and policies.
- Manpower Demonstration Research Corporation (MDRC) is dedicated to learning what works to improve the well-being of low-income people and actively communicating findings to enhance the effectiveness of public policies and programs. Researchers at MDRC conduct evaluations of welfare reforms and other supports for the working poor as well as research on how programs affect children's development and their families' well-being. Other projects examine the effectiveness of school reform policies designed to improve academic achievement and access to college, and community approaches to increasing employment in low-income neighborhoods. For more information about MDRC, visit http://www.mdrc.org.

How do you prepare for a career in policy research? Although graduate training provides a knowledge base about research methodology, students who are interested in conducting policy-related research must learn how to formulate research questions in ways that can inform policy and must learn how to communicate findings with a wide and varied audience (Susman-Stillman et al., 1996; Weinberg & Susman-Stillman, 1999). Seek a policy-related undergraduate, predoctoral, or postdoctoral fellowship and get hands-on learning to supplement your graduate training. Researchers in think tanks and policy-oriented organizations earn salaries similar to those in academia. In 2007, doctoral degree holders with 5 to 9 years of experience earned a median salary of $76,000 in nonprofit research settings, with 50 percent earning between $66,000 and $96,000 (APA, 2008).

An interest in development across the lifespan can support a variety of careers. In addition to those discussed in this chapter, as well as Chapters 3, 4, and 5.

Suggested Readings

Acuff, D. S., & Reiher, R. H. (1999). *What kids buy and why: The psychology of marketing to kids.* New York: Free Press.

Berk. L. (2001). Trends in human development. In J. S. Halonen & S. F. Davis (Eds.), *The many faces of psychological research in the 21st century.* Retrieved June 5, 2002 at http://teachpsych.org/resources/e-books/faces/index_faces.php

Bruzzese, J.M. (2005). Medical schools and centers: The merger of developmental psychology and pediatric asthma education. In R. D. Morgan, T. L. Kuther, & C. J. Habben (Eds.), *Life after graduate school in psychology: Insider's advice from new psychologists.* New York: Psychology Press.

Burns, J. B. (2006). *Career opportunities in the nonprofit sector.* Checkmark Books.

Coffey, T. & Livingston, G. (2005). *Marketing to the new super consumer: Mom & kid.* Paramount Marketing Publishing.

Eberts, M., & Gisler, M. (2006). *Careers for kids at heart & others who adore children.* New York: McGraw-Hill.

Giacobello, J. (2001). *Choosing a career in the toy industry.* New York: Rosen.

Grabinsky, C. J. (2007). *101 careers in gerontology.* Springer.

King. R. M. (2000). *From making a profit to making a difference: How to launch your new career in nonprofits.* Planning/Communications.

Kuther, T. L. (1996). Doctoral training in applied developmental psychology: Matching graduate education and accreditation standards to student needs, career opportunity, and licensure requirements. In C. B. Fisher, J. P. Murray, & I. E. Sigel (Eds.), *Applied developmental science: Graduate training for diverse disciplines and educational settings.* (pp. 53–74). Norwood, NJ: Able.

Rowh, M., & Suchorski, J. (2000). *Opportunities in fund-raising careers.* New York: McGraw-Hill.

Susman-Stillman, A. R., Brown, J. L., Adam, E. K., Blair, C., Gaines, R., Gordon, R. A., et al. (1996). Building research and policy connections: Training and career options for developmental scientists. *Social Policy Report, 10*(4), 1–19.

Wagner, L. (2001). *Careers in fund raising.* Wiley.

WEB RESOURCES

National Child Care Association
http://www.nccanet.org/

National Association for the Education of Young Children
http://www.naeyc.org

National Network for Child Care
http://www.nncc.org

Society for Research in Child Development
http://www.srcd.org

Careers in Aging
http://www.careersinaging.com/

Careers in Gerontology
http://www.geron.org/StudentOrg/careers.htm

Toy Inventor Designer Guide
http://www.toy-tia.org/industry/publications/inventor.html

Sesame Workshop
http://www.sesameworkshop.org/

Children's Advertising Review Unit
http://www.caru.org

Society for Research on Adolescence
http://www.s-r-a.org

Families and Work Institute
http://www.familiesandwork.org

American Geriatrics Society
http://www.americangeriatrics.org

American Association of Fund-Raising Executives
http://www.afpnet.org/

Association for Gerontology in Higher Education
http://www.aghe.org

RAND
http://www.rand.org/about/

MDRC
http://www.mdrc.org/

CHECKLIST: IS DEVELOPEMENTAL PSYCHOLOGY FOR YOU?

Do you:

- ☐ Want to know how people change as they age?
- ☐ Like solving problems?
- ☐ Like learning about older adulthood?
- ☐ Have the ability to consider multiple perspectives?
- ☐ Like working with theories?
- ☐ Find infants interesting?
- ☐ Have the ability to tolerate ambiguity?
- ☐ Want to do work that helps people?
- ☐ Like children?
- ☐ Not want to be a clinician?
- ☐ Have interests in social policy?
- ☐ Think adolescents are interesting?
- ☐ Wonder how we change as we progress through adulthood?
- ☐ Enjoy conducting research?
- ☐ Find all ages interesting?
- ☐ Enjoy reading books about developmental issues (for example, What to expect the first year, What to expect during the toddler years)?

Scoring: Count the number of checkmarks; the higher the number, the more likely a career in developmental psychology is for you.

CHAPTER **13** | GRADUATE-LEVEL CAREERS IN PSYCHOLOGY

CHAPTER GUIDE

In each chapter in this book we have discussed career options for psychologists in specific disciplines, such as social, experimental, and developmental psychology. Some career options are appropriate for psychologists of all subdisciplines. In this chapter, we examine career options available to all graduate degree holders in psychology. As you know, many psychologists work as professors. However, did you know that, in addition to staffing psychology departments, psychologists are also professors in schools of business, medicine, and education? Similarly, research training in psychology prepares graduate degree holders for careers as researchers outside of academia, including the government, foundations, business, and research groups. Some psychologists seek careers in the military and engage in a variety of activities ranging from assessment and counseling to research and human factors. Others pursue publishing, journalism, and writing careers. Our goal in this chapter is to highlight these careers as a sample of the diversity a graduate degree in psychology offers; however, as you will learn throughout this book, you are by no means limited to the careers we summarize here.

THE IVORY TOWER: PSYCHOLOGISTS AS PROFESSORS

Aside from the therapist, perhaps the most familiar career path for those with graduate degrees in psychology is that of the college professor. Professors have the opportunity to share information they find fascinating with their students. Psychologists work as professors in a variety of academic departments of psychology and schools of education; however, some psychologists are professors outside of psychology departments, sometimes in places you might never have imagined. Psychologists who are trained in industrial/organizational psychology, human factors psychology, or social psychology might work in business schools and within departments of engineering. Psychologists trained in clinical or health psychology sometimes work as professors in medical schools.

Expectations and activities of professors vary by institution. There are several types of colleges and universities. For example, two-year community colleges tend to focus heavily on teaching with few requirements for engage in research. In these settings, faculty often teach five courses per semester, leaving little time to conduct research or engage in scholarly writing. Performance evaluations of faculty in community colleges are based on teaching and service to the community. Liberal arts colleges also emphasize teaching and contact with students. Faculty often teach three to four classes each semester and are expected to have scholarly contacts with students in and out of the classroom. Expectations for faculty research are that faculty incorporate students into their research programs. Faculty are expected to work closely with students on research projects, publishing jointly when appropriate. Teaching, however, is the top priority. and therefore research is viewed as pedagogy. At the other extreme of community and liberal arts colleges are research universities. Research universities are large schools with prestigious graduate programs; at these universities faculty teach only one to two courses per semester. Instead, they focus heavily on research because they are judged on their reputations as scholars, and teaching contributes less to their professional advancement (Vesilind, 2000). Many four-year universities fall somewhere between the two extremes and encourage faculty to engage in both research and teaching. As you can see, even within academia there are several career tracks for psychologist-professors.

Despite the different types of institutions, all academic careers share certain features. As you consider a career as a professor, recognize that there is more to the professorate than lecturing in front of a classroom. Before a professor steps into the classroom, a great deal of time and effort has gone into preparation. Each lecture requires background reading of chapters and journal articles in addition to the text, note taking, and preparation of overheads, activities, and discussion questions. This work is never complete, because even experienced professors must update their notes to remain current with the ever-changing field. Professors who teach three, four, or even five courses per semester may find that preparation takes all of their time, especially in the early years of a career (Roediger, 2006). A professor's teaching activities extend beyond the classroom to include grading, writing letters of recommendation for students, meeting with students to answer questions and discuss course content and professional issues, and advising students on career choices.

In addition to teaching, professorial careers entail many roles, usually including research and service to the campus and community (such as advising, committee work, or administrative work). During a typical week, professors often divide their time among multiple research tasks, including writing an article or book, conducting statistical analyses, planning research, writing grant proposals, searching the literature, reading research articles, meeting with student research assistants, advising students on their research, and preparing or giving talks at professional meetings. Professors also must spend time on service to the university and community. They participate in faculty meetings as well as some of the many committees that administer and run the university. Some faculty engage in consulting work, or serve as consultants and advisors for community agencies.

Many students seek a graduate degree in order to teach in a college or university setting. With a masters degree, it is possible to become a community college professor. However, faculty positions at community colleges have become more competitive in recent years; many are held by psychologists with doctoral degrees (Lloyd, 2000; Peters, 1992). Similarly, although masters degree holders may be hired to teach at four-year colleges on a part-time basis, they are unlikely to be hired for full-time positions. If your goal is to teach at the college level, it's in your best interest to pursue a doctoral degree that will provide you with the most opportunities for employment, mobility, and advancement as a faculty member (Lloyd, 2000; Roediger, 2006). Graduates with doctoral degrees may teach undergraduate, masters, and doctoral students in a variety of educational settings, including universities, professional schools, and medical schools.

An additional aspect of training that may not be covered in graduate school, but is necessary for success as a professor, and often for winning a faculty position in the first place, is training in pedagogy (Kuther, 2002). Pedagogy refers to the art of teaching. Successful professors master the techniques of their trade and learn how to compose lectures; lead discussions; create syllabi; enhance student learning through effective use of the blackboard, overheads, or PowerPoint presentations; and model best practices for interacting with students and handling disagreements. We hope you have experienced a professor who made the course material "come to life" and whose class you looked forward to attending. Such skill comes with work and effort; good teachers are made, not born.

If you're interested in becoming a professor, seek a graduate program that helps to prepare students for the teaching aspects of the professorate. Many graduate programs present seminars or courses in how to teach. The Preparing Future Faculty program, a program designed to prepare aspiring academics for the variety of teaching, research, and service roles entailed in the professorate, has also created a wealth of resources and a Web site available at http://www.preparing-faculty.org. Seek practical experience as a teaching assistant or adjunct professor at your university or a nearby college. You can also volunteer to teach a class or two for your primary instructors or for instructors teaching courses in your area of interest. Most important, find a mentor in graduate school who can help you with these essential aspects of training.

There are many advantages to the professorate, but perhaps the greatest advantages are academic freedom and the autonomy and flexibility of academic life. Academic freedom means that professors are intellectually free; they may conduct whatever research interests them and may "teach the truth as they see it" (Vesilind, 2000, p. 10). In other words, professors decide on the best methods to teach their courses. Texts, reading assignments, grading, and evaluation procedures are often up to the professor. Aside from class time, professors' schedules tend to be flexible. Most develop work habits that fit their lives, allowing time to pick up children from school, spend time with their families, and complete preparation and writing in the late evenings or early mornings. Another advantage is tenure, a permanent job contract, typically offered after a probationary period of six or seven years. Tenure provides complete academic freedom because it prevents professors from being fired for airing unpopular views or pursuing controversial research. Professors with documented teaching histories, excellent student evaluations, publications, campus committee work, and outreach to the community earn tenure and its associated job security. The professorate also offers intangible benefits, such as the excitement of discovery and innovation, as well as the rewards of imparting knowledge and introducing students to a life of the mind (Roediger, 2006; Vesilind, 2000).

The disadvantages of the academic life are related to the scarcity of academic positions. The academic job market is very competitive; there aren't a lot of positions available. Some applicants spend several years on the job market, working in postdoctoral research, in one-year instructor appointments, or in adjunct positions (teaching part-time, often at several colleges at once). Applicants must be prepared to seek faculty positions in a variety of geographic locations; applicants cannot limit themselves to searching in only one place. Applicants also cannot afford to limit themselves to positions in psychology departments, but must consider academic positions in other departments, medical schools, and business schools. Once a position is obtained, new professors juggle many demands. In addition to teaching loads and service responsibilities, most new faculty are expected to begin a research program, because research has increased in importance as well—even for those in "teaching" colleges (Salzinger, 1995). Faculty in research universities experience pressure to win large competitive research grants and publish in the best journals. Finally, as shown in Table 13.1, professors' salaries allow them to live comfortably, but certainly will not make them rich.

TABLE 13.1	MEAN SALARIES FOR PROFESSORS (ADAPTED FROM AMERICAN ASSOCIATION OF UNIVERSITY PROFESSORS, 2008)

Institution and Position	Average Salary
Doctoral institutions	
Professor	$118,444
Associate Professor	$80,043
Assistant Professor	$68,112
Comprehensive Institutions (masters level)	
Professor	$87,272
Associate Professor	$68,637
Assistant Professor	$57,549
Baccalaureate Institutions	
Professor	$83,560
Associate Professor	$64,277
Assistant Professor	$53,351
2-Year institutions	
Professor	$71,779
Associate Professor	$58,492
Assistant Professor	$51,183

RESEARCH IN AND OUT OF THE IVORY TOWER

A graduate degree in psychology offers many opportunities for careers in research. Research psychologists conduct basic and applied studies of human and animal behavior. They conduct their research in universities, government agencies, private organizations, and businesses and corporations. Some psychologists conduct their research in military settings, while others work in research and development departments at pharmaceutical companies and businesses. Let's take a look at the variety of settings in which psychologists conduct research.

ACADEMIA

Many psychologists work in university settings as research scientists, conducting basic and applied research. For example, a research scientist might study how neurotransmitters affect learning in rats. Another research psychologist might design a research program to examine smoking cessation. Her basic research might explore the environmental factors that help or hinder quitting smoking. She might conduct applied research as well, developing and evaluating school-based programs to prevent smoking in children. Medical schools are emerging as an important employment setting for research psychologists, who work on multidisciplinary teams addressing health problems in people of all ages. Interdisciplinary study and the merging of scientific fields such as anatomy, biochemistry, physiology, pharmacology, and microbiology are leading to more research opportunities for psychologists outside of psychology departments (Balster, 1995).

A research career in academia offers a flexible schedule and is prestigious. Research scientists gain independence and autonomy as they progress in their careers.

By writing and winning research grants, research scientists are able to fund and study problems of their choosing. With advancement, research scientists take on supervisory roles, run their own labs, and train graduate and postdoctoral students. There are also opportunities for travel and contact with the public through speaking at conferences, consulting, and writing for the popular press (Bartholomew, 2001a). A disadvantage of a research career in academia is the competition. Generally, academic positions that don't require teaching can be difficult to obtain. Applicants may need to be geographically mobile and able to relocate for available positions.

Research and professorial careers in academia entail long hours, especially in institutions that maintain the "publish or perish" mantra. Publish or perish means just that: publish many articles in prestigious journals, or lose your job! As you might imagine, psychologists in research and professorial positions can experience a great deal of stress. Publishing is a tenuous and lengthy process; therefore, professors, particularly new professors, may spend many evenings in the lab or at the computer completing or writing research results for publication. Once completed, however, the sense of accomplishment, contribution to the field, and seeing one's name in print are primary benefits of this research track.

INDUSTRY

Some psychologists conduct research in business and industry. Psychologists in business might conduct surveys of consumer opinion, for example. Others who work for pharmaceutical companies might test the effectiveness of drugs or work as statisticians, analyzing the data from a variety of research projects. Psychologists in industry design and test products for human use. For example, a psychologist might design a car's dashboard to allow drivers the ability to easily and reach the displays and knobs while viewing the road. Or a psychologist might design a computer monitor to reduce glare and eyestrain.

A career in industry is different from academia because in industry the focus is on promoting the success of the company. The goal is to create products that benefit the company, employees, and shareholders (Bartholomew, 2001b). Research takes place at a faster pace in industry than in academia because information must be gathered quickly to help create and sell products. Teams conduct the research, enabling greater productivity. In addition, psychologists in business and industry settings tend to have access to more funding than do those in academia, meaning that they tend to work with newer and more sophisticated equipment. The primary drawback of conducting research in business and industry is that your research questions are assigned based on the needs of the company, not necessarily on your interests. An important benefit of working in industry is the contact with people of diverse fields and educational backgrounds. Other benefits are the high salaries and regular work schedule; in business and industry, your weekends generally are your own.

GOVERNMENT

Although research psychologists engage in similar activities regardless of work setting, whether universities, industry, or government, the three settings differ in terms of the autonomy afforded researchers. As with researchers in industry, those employed by the government and military usually examine research questions not conceived by them (Bornstein, 2006; Herrman, 1997). Instead, researchers in government examine questions that are created by politicians and policy makers, designed to promote the security and well being of the American people. As Copper (1997) points out, "The critical aspect of working in a public-policy environment is that many people can be directly affected by decisions over a very long period of time. Therefore, the research questions and hypotheses are often more complex, sensitive, and require much broader data collection efforts and greater coordination with staff from federal branch agencies and the private sector."

An advantage of a research career in government is that you'll be exposed to many different projects. Unlike academia, where researchers spend a career focused on a particular research problem or area, research psychologists in government work on a diverse range of projects and become generalists. Most research projects initiated by the government are short in duration (about one year to complete) because the research is intended to help resolve practical problems. Also, shifts in public opinion and interest lead political leaders to eliminate some projects and initiate new ones; whether this is an advantage or disadvantage perhaps depends on your interest in the project. If you're interested in a research career in government, be prepared to engage in lots of supervisory work because contractors conduct much of the hands-on work under supervision by government researchers. This enables government researchers to work on multiple projects at once and not become overly involved in any one project. Like industry, government research involves working on a team, because the research topics that the government is interested in are applied in nature, requiring creativity and planning by an interdisciplinary team of researchers consisting of psychologists, sociologists, statisticians, computer scientists, economists, and others.

SOCIAL SERVICE AGENCIES AND NONPROFITS

Research psychologists employed at social service or nonprofit agencies conduct research to assess and improve the agency's programs and often write grants to help fund the agency. Social service and nonprofit agencies often are contracted by the government to conduct policy analyses, literature reviews, and research to improve decision making by political leaders and consumers. A psychologist at such an agency might examine the effectiveness of new drug-control interventions like mandatory minimum sanctions, residential and group home treatments for youthful offenders identified as drug users, and school-based prevention programs.

The primary benefit of working in a nonprofit or social service agency is that your time is focused on research that may lead to social change rather than teaching or academic curriculum meetings. Such agencies tend to conduct interdisciplinary research, enabling research psychologists to work with a diverse range of specialists from other fields. Though the salaries at nonprofit and social service agencies tend to be lower than in other research settings, the research often directly benefits consumers and families.

Bachelor's degree holders may obtain research assistant positions in any of these research environments discussed. Opportunities for advancement, however, come with graduate degrees. Many research positions are available to masters degree holders, especially in industry, government, and nonprofit and social service

TABLE 13.2 | MEDIAN SALARIES FOR DOCTORAL PSYCHOLOGISTS WITH 2 TO 4 YEARS OF EXPERIENCE IN RESEARCH SETTINGS (ADAPTED FROM APA, 2007; PATE, FRINCKE, & KOHOUT, 2005)

	Median Salary
University Psychology Department	$68,000
Medical School Psychiatry Department	$50,000
Medical School (not Psychiatry)	$78,500*
Private Research Organization	$85,000
Government Research Organization	$77,000
Nonprofit Organization	$76,000*
University Research Center	$59,000
Consulting/Industry	$76,500**

*Psychologists with 5–9 years experience.
**2003 data.

agencies. In academic settings, the doctoral degree offers the most flexibility, opportunities for advancement, and opportunities to serve as the primary investigator of federal grants (Lloyd, 2000). Research psychologists in academia often obtain two to three years of postdoctoral training after obtaining the doctoral degree. To be competitive for research positions within academic and nonacademic settings, hone your skills in research methods and statistics (Copper, 1997). As shown in Table 13.2, salaries for research positions vary by setting.

THE MILITARY

The military offers a range of opportunities for psychologists in all disciplines. Psychologists work in the military as enlisted military personnel and as civilian consultants. They practice and conduct research in a variety of areas, including personnel selection and classification, training, human factors, leadership and team effectiveness, as well as clinical settings (Dunivin & Ingram, 2006; Wisckoff, 1997).

PSYCHOLOGISTS IN THE MILITARY

Some military psychologists engage in personnel selection and classification. They screen, select, and place recruits, and select personnel for jobs requiring special skills such as piloting aircraft, air traffic control, and special operations personnel. They create procedures for evaluating the performance of enlisted and officer personnel, and conduct research on how to use simulators to evaluate special abilities. Psychologists in the military also train personnel. They conduct research examining the most effective techniques of training personnel in basic skills, military skills, and technical skills, as well as increasing operational readiness. They conduct research on how to design effective instructional systems, measure training performance, and best use computer-simulated scenarios and technology such as virtual reality.

Other psychologists in the military work in human factors and engineering to design the human-machine interfaces that improve the functioning of military systems and equipment. For example, how can artificial intelligence and the use of sophisticated computer systems enhance human decision making? Psychologists study how to help military personnel operate most efficiently, maintain health, enhance performance, and reduce human error under adverse circumstances, such as sleep deprivation, in extreme environmental conditions, and hazardous conditions.

Some psychologists study team effectiveness and ways to improve communication in multinational forces. Psychologists study how to promote effective leadership, as well as how to select, train, and evaluate leaders. Some psychologists might get involved in political-psychological issues such as the study of the behavior of world leaders. Others examine team processes such as structure, communication, subordinate-supervisor relations, team cohesion, the functioning of small groups, and tactical decision making.

Clinical and counseling psychologists in the military often work in counseling or mental health clinics providing mental health services and counseling to improve the lives of military personnel and their families. They focus on how to help personnel acclimate to military life, deal with stress, and cope with serious psychological reactions in the aftermath of combat. Counseling and clinical psychologists serve in a wide variety of settings, such as military hospitals, outpatient clinics, mental health centers, daycare centers, military prisons, and onboard ships.

ADVANTAGES, DISADVANTAGES, AND SALARY

Psychologists in the military often spend significant amounts of time overseas, which, depending on your inclination and family situation, may be an advantage or disadvantage. Clinical and counseling psychologists go wherever there are concentrations of troops, in peacetime and war, and to hostile environments. A uniformed psychologist can count on a change of geographical location every two to three years (Wiskoff, 1997). Thus, in spite of potential familial conflicts, military psychologists' opportunities to see the world are unmatched by nonmilitary psychology positions.

A significant limitation for practicing psychologists is the absence of the traditional confidential therapeutic relationship. Members of the military who seek or are referred for mental health services do not have the same rights and privileges to confidentiality that nonmilitary clients enjoy. Rather, higher-ranking personnel may and do request information regarding the functioning of a military client, and psychologists must become comfortable with the military process and the limits and professional dilemmas this presents. Furthermore, research psychologists will experience many of the same limitations as their colleagues in government and industry, because their research is directed by practical problems and questions rather than by their own intellectual curiosity.

A final potential limitation for psychologists in the military is the issue of enlistment. Some psychologists work as civilians in military environments; others enlist and "join the ranks." Once you have enlisted, working for the military is no longer optional; rather, you become an officer and must serve for the duration of your commitment. Psychologists in academia, business and industry, or other branches of the government have the option of leaving their jobs if they decide they no longer want to do them, but enlisted military psychologists do not have this option. Thus, it is important to consider your own level of satisfaction and comfort with the military lifestyle, because once you are sworn in as an officer, you cannot change your mind and simply go do something else. Other important benefits of military service include job security, opportunities for additional education, and an excellent benefits and retirement system. Few professional positions offer the opportunity to retire after as few as twenty years of service, and to do so with a pension. The salary scale for military psychologists is aligned with the government pay scales (Wiskoff, 1997). In 2001, government starting salary for masters-level psychologists was $33,300; starting salary for doctoral-level psychologists was $40,200 (Bureau of Labor Statistics, 2002). In addition to base pay, all military receive subsistence and housing allowances, which are not taxable, which substantially increases income.

PUBLISHING AND WRITING

Publishing and the media offer new career opportunities for students of psychology. Some psychologists pursue careers in publishing as acquisitions editors and developmental editors. Others become science writers for print, Internet, radio, and television.

BOOK PUBLISHING

Publishing generally is an apprenticeship field, so most successful editors begin in entry-level positions and work their way up. Many begin as assistants to acquisitions editors (we'll talk more about acquisitions editors in a moment) or sales representatives who ensure that every customer (for example, professor or bookstore) is informed of the publisher's book offerings. Sales representatives are often on the road, traveling to their customers, sales conferences, and professional conferences, where they market books. With time, some sales representatives gain the experience and contacts to become acquisitions editors.

An *acquisitions editor* is responsible for acquiring books for a publishing company. The job entails a variety of tasks, including reading book proposals, making decisions about the financial viability of proposals and whether to offer book contracts to authors, ensuring the quality of proposals and completed manuscripts by getting reviews from specialists in the field, interpreting reviews, approaching potential authors with book ideas, attending conferences to meet potential authors and reviewers, and discussing works-in-progress with authors. The acquisitions editor often oversees all stages of the publication process, including contract negotiation, promotional planning, manuscript delivery, and financial planning. The position is appropriate for individuals who like the messiness of problem solving in the real world and have broad interests, because acquisitions editors often oversee manuscripts in multiple sub-fields, not just the ones in which they have extensive training (Ansel, 1996).

With a graduate degree in psychology and writing experience, you might consider a position as a *developmental editor*. A developmental editor handles the day-to-day work of coordinating and editing manuscripts for large publishing projects such as psychology textbooks. The developmental editor is involved in all aspects of developing a textbook, beginning with the early stages of conceptual and structural planning before the author writes. Developmental editors often nurture authors through the writing process and coordinate the artwork, writing style, and preparation of supplements or ancillaries (large textbooks may include instructor's manuals, student study guides, test banks, Web sites, and more; Hart, 1996).

Positions in publishing offer opportunities for psychology degree holders at all levels who have interests in writing and the ability to think critically and problem solve effectively. Bachelor's degree holders usually begin in entry-level positions such as editorial assistants or sales representatives, whereas applicants with graduate degrees and editorial skill may be hired to mid-level editorial positions. More advanced positions in publishing come with extensive experience. Individuals who seek careers in publishing must be able to juggle multiple tasks, meet budgets, and cope with the pressure of deadlines.

WRITING

Scientific writing careers come in many shapes and forms. Some science writers engage in technical writing. Others work in public relations and traditional or new media venues. A *technical writer* translates large amounts of information into useful and easily digested forms for specialized readers. Technical writers create user guides, repair manuals, online help files, and reference manuals for new products, computer software, hardware, and toys (Randall, 2006). Technical writers must be able to explain complex phenomena for general readers. Other science writing positions are found in public relations or public information. Universities, medical centers, hospitals, and other institutions where research is conducted have staffs of reporters who keep track of research findings and events at the institution (Goetnick Ambrose, 2006). *Public information officers* write press releases to distribute to the media. They also contribute to institutional publications and alumni magazines, monitor news and media trends to determine which institutional staff might have something notable to contribute, and act as liaisons between journalists and the institution's staff. Some writers work in research or human services settings as grant writers, assembling the pieces of a grant proposal prepared by a group of researchers and checking for style, accuracy, formatting, grammar, and spelling.

Science writers and journalists also write as staff members and freelancers for newspapers, magazines, Internet, radio, and television. They learn about scientific findings and translate them accurately into a form that will interest the general reader. By teasing out details and anecdotes, they write to draw casual readers, listeners, or viewers into topics that they ordinarily might not care much about. Science writing requires omnivorous reading of newspapers, books, reports, journals, and Internet news groups to look for story ideas. Writers attend scientific conventions, interview scientists, and regularly check in with laboratories, factories, hospitals, universities, and government agencies for breaking news and interesting stories.

Science writing offers an opportunity to write about science without becoming immersed in the lab, focusing on one minute area of research, or being confined to the stilted and formal academic style of writing. It offers a chance to be in the real world, explore a variety of topics, interview great thinkers, share psychological findings with the rest of the world, and see your writing in print quickly

TABLE 13.3 | MEDIAN SALARIES FOR CAREERS IN WRITING AND PUBLISHING (ADAPTED FROM ABBOTT, LANGER, AND ASSOCIATES, 2006, SALARY.COM, 2008).

	Median Salary
Grants/proposal writer	$51,363
Technical writer	$65,626
Web writer	$61,882
Acquisitions editor	$70,377
Developmental editor	$50,000
Marketing specialist	$43,125
Reporter/correspondent	$26,506
Speech writer	$60,745

(Augenbraun & Vergoth, 1998; Carpenter, 2002). Individuals with broad scientific interests who love learning, are fluent writers, and like challenges, are well suited to careers in science writing. However, science writing is a highly competitive field. Writers must be able to juggle multiple stories at once, meet deadlines, and deal well with criticism (no thin skins allowed!). Freelancers must be prepared to pay for their own benefits, save for retirement, and weather ups and downs in work.

If you're interested in a science-writing career, seek opportunities to publish in nonscientific publications. Write for the university newspaper, local organizations, or any other sources to earn writing clips. Clips, or clippings of your published articles, are your ticket to a writing career. Understand that science writing is very different from the academic writing that you learned in college or graduate school. Aspiring science writers should seek training opportunities such as media fellowships, internships (often unpaid), and science journalism programs to gain excellent training, sources of networking contacts, and clips (Randall, 2006). Table 13.3 illustrates salaries for careers in writing and publishing.

A graduate degree in psychology opens doors to a variety of careers for individuals with diverse interests ranging from therapy to research, teaching to publishing, and more. Remember that the advice in this chapter is offered as a first step. Seek assistance from your advisor and the career center at your university to help you learn more so that you can choose career goals that match your interests and aspirations.

SUGGESTED READINGS

Bly, R. W. (2003). *Careers for writers and others who have a way with words.* New York: McGraw Hill. Education.

Hancock, E. (2003). *Ideas into words: Mastering the craft of science writing.* Baltimore.

Hayes, W. (2003). *So you want to be a college professor?* Lanham, MD: Scarecrow Education.

Robbins-Roth, C. (2006). *Alternative careers in science: Leaving the ivory tower* (second edition). San Diego, CA: Academic Press.

Sternberg, R. J. (2006). *Career paths in psychology: Where your degree can take you (second edition)*. Washington, D.C.: American Psychological Association.

U.S. Department of Defense. (2003). *America's top military careers: Official guide to occupations in the armed forces*. Indianapolis, IN: Jist Publishing.

Vesilind, P. A. (2000). *So you want to be a professor? A handbook for graduate students*. Thousand Oaks, CA: Sage.

Yager, F. & Yager, J. (2005). *Career opportunities in the publishing industry*. New York: Facts on File.

WEB RESOURCES

Career Path Less Traveled
http://www.apa.org/monitor/feb01/careerpath.html

Society for the Teaching of Psychology
http://teachpsych.org/

Office of Teaching Resources in Psychology
http://teachpsych.org/otrp/index.php

Preparing Future Faculty
http://www.preparing-faculty.org/

Military Career Guide Online
http://www.todaysmilitary.com/careers

About the U.S. Military
http://usmilitary.about.com/

So You Want to Be an Editor
http://www.editors.ca/join_eac/be_an_editor/so.html

A Guide to Careers in Science Writing
http://casw.org/booklet.htm

Career Development Center for Postdocs and Junior Faculty
http://nextwave.sciencemag.org/career_development

Science, Math, and Engineering Career Resources
http://www.phds.org/

So You Want to Be a Science Writer?
http://www.absw.org.uk/So_you_want_to_be_a_science_writer.htm

Advice for Beginning Science Writers
http://www.nasw.org/resource/beginning/archives/000145.htm

How Do I Become a Science Journalist?
http://www.scidev.net/en/practical-guides/how-do-i-become-a-science-journalist-.html

CHECKLIST: IS AN ADVANCED CAREER IN PSYCHOLOGY FOR YOU?

Do you:

- ☐ Want to teach college?
- ☐ Think you would enjoy a career interacting with students?
- ☐ Like to challenge others to think?

☐   Think broadly and have a unique ability to apply psychology to many different fields?
☐   Have an interest in applying psychology to a non-psychology career?
☐   Like to write?
☐   Think quickly on your feet?
☐   Enjoy giving presentations and speeches?
☐   Enjoy research?
☐   Think analytically?
☐   Want to work for an agency or the government?
☐   Want to have a career with flexible hours?
☐   Want to attend graduate school?

Scoring: The more boxes you checked, the more likely it is a graduate-level career in psychology is for you.